T0319598

CREATIVITY IN LARGE-SCALE CONTEXTS

Also by Jonathan S. Feinstein

The Nature of Creative Development (2006)

CREATIVITY IN LARGE-SCALE CONTEXTS

JONATHAN S. FEINSTEIN

STANFORD BUSINESS BOOKS
An Imprint of Stanford University Press
Stanford, California

STANFORD UNIVERSITY PRESS
Stanford, California

Special discounts for bulk quantities of Stanford Business
Books are available to corporations, professional associations,
and other organizations. For details and discount information,
contact the special sales department of Stanford University
Press by emailing sales@www.sup.org.

Printed in the United States of America on acid-free, archival-quality paper

Library of Congress Cataloging-in-Publication Data
Names: Feinstein, Jonathan S., 1960– author.
Title: Creativity in large-scale contexts : guiding creative engagement and
exploration / Jonathan S. Feinstein.
Description: Stanford, California : Stanford Business Books, an imprint of
Stanford University Press, 2023. |
Includes bibliographical references and index.
Identifiers: LCCN 2023017658 (print) | LCCN 2023017659 (ebook) |
ISBN 9781503632813 (cloth) | ISBN 9781503637153 (ebook)
Subjects: LCSH: Creative ability.
Classification: LCC BF408 .F35 2023 (print) | LCC BF408 (ebook) |
DDC 153.3/5—dc23/eng/20230624
LC record available at https://lccn.loc.gov/2023017658
LC ebook record available at https://lccn.loc.gov/2023017659

Cover design: Daniel Benneworth-Gray
Cover art: Wassily Kandinsky, *Kleine Flächen* (Small Planes), 1936. © 2023 Artists
Rights Society (ARS), New York
Typeset by Newgen in 10/15 Spectral

CONTENTS

v

IMAGES, FIGURES, AND TABLES

TABLES

INTRODUCTION

Creativity happens through our engagement with context. This context consists of our experiences, culture, knowledge, and the social and natural worlds. Navigating context, imagining new ways to use it, identifying puzzles and creative opportunities, discovering possibilities, and spanning it to create novel connections: these are the keys to successful creativity.

A key characteristic of the context in which creativity happens is that it is extremely rich and diverse, filled with a multitude of elements and almost unlimited possibilities. It is large scale. This has been true in human cultural contexts for centuries, even millennia, but is even more true today with the emergence of the Internet and access to information increasing dramatically.

The large-scale nature of context offers rich opportunities. But it also poses a great challenge: with so many options, it is simply not possible to consider them all. The range of options can be overwhelming, making it difficult to know how best to proceed. A writer facing a blank page, an artist facing a blank canvas, an engineer contemplating the design of a new product: the possibilities are nearly limitless. Even in the world of AI creativity, this issue is paramount. What makes this a great challenge is that, among the myriad possibilities, very few will lead to a highly successful creative outcome if pursued. Most will fail outright; others will lead to an outcome that is not perceived as successful by whatever standard success is measured. The question is, out of the myriad possibilities, how is it possible to discover an especially promising one that will lead to a highly successful creative outcome? This critical question, which we must address to understand the nature of the creative process in large-scale contexts, doesn't arise in small-scale contexts. In a small-scale context all creative possibilities can be explored, but in a large-scale context the huge number of elements makes this impossible.

Creativity research and popular accounts of creativity have failed to recognize that creativity happens in rich large-scale contexts and the challenge this poses; not surprisingly given this failure, they have not addressed the question of how to go about engaging in creative endeavors in large-scale contexts. Creativity is often described as something that "comes from within"—language that leaves context out entirely. When context is considered, it is typically described as if it contains only a handful of elements. This paints a false picture of context as small scale, and because the challenge of navigating through a large-scale context is missing, creativity can seem like a relatively easy, straightforward process: if the world contains just a handful of elements, all the different possibilities and combinations can be investigated, and highly creative ones will readily be identified. In the creativity literature attention is often focused on a single creative act, such as an elegant solution to a puzzle or a novel combination that produces an innovative new product. What is truly amazing, however—and is typically missing from these descriptions—is how such creative steps come to be taken among the myriad possibilities available: the remarkable process that leads to them. The failure to recognize that context is large, filled with opportunities but also posing a great challenge due to its sheer scale, limits understanding. Thus to attain a more complete understanding of creativity we must better understand how to navigate and explore large-scale contexts.

In this book I take on this challenge and address the question of how to be successful engaging in a creative endeavor in a large-scale context. The single most important part of the creative process that stands out as new in my description is *guidance*. Large-scale contexts are rich with possibilities but also for that very reason difficult to navigate and easy to get lost in. In this situation it is clear that guidance of some kind is required. Guidance not in the sense of knowing the exact creative endpoint, but in the sense of having an idea about where one should look and which kinds of opportunities and creative paths to pursue among the myriad possibilities. Trying possibilities simply at random is woefully inefficient and unlikely to lead to success in any reasonable timeframe—a basic truth despite the fact that the random combination model has been quite popular in the creativity field. The alternative is guidance. I describe two kinds of guidance and present a framework that shows how they are used jointly to guide the creative process in large-scale contexts, enabling individuals to find their way to successful creative outcomes.

What makes guidance possible is that creativity contexts, although large scale, have structure. This structure arises because the context that is relevant for creativity is the world as we perceive and understand it (including the ways we recognize we are failing to understand it). Of course it is true that we make discoveries in the world around us and create using tangible materials. But these discoveries and creations, and creative ideas in general, arise out of our engagement with the world in terms of perceptions and frames of understanding. This perception and understanding of the world—our context—is based on our experiences, what we learn, our social and cultural environment, and the natural world, yet it goes beyond this "raw material" in that it is organized by us. Our context is thus our conceptual representation and organization of the world, and this is what drives our creative choices, ideas, and activities: we imagine new possibilities and see creative opportunities based on this conceptual representation and organization. Of course a representation that is missing important elements or biased can hold back creative insight. Yet this actually shows its importance, for finding our way through a limited or incorrect understanding and representation is itself part of the creative process.

Structurally, context is organized as a network. In particular, the elements of our context do not exist in isolation but are connected to other elements that they are related to in our representation of the world. The most important feature of this network is that it has a hierarchical structure: broader, more abstract elements or concepts link downward to more specific elements, their "children." Most of our representations of the world have this hierarchy feature, with information and elements arranged in categories and subcategories. Indeed hierarchy is fundamental to the organization of knowledge, a principle that extends back at least to the ancient Greeks. But there are also additional links, so that context is not a simple hierarchy but rather has a fuller network structure. Most importantly, elements often have more than one parent, and there are lateral links among elements at the same conceptual level. Our organization of context as a network fits with how our brains are organized: brain structures and functions are organized as networks, and it makes sense that our perceptions and conceptual representations, based in the brain, also form a network.[1]

In this book I adopt a network framework to describe the context in which creativity occurs, consistent with the discussion above. In doing so I model context and its structure more explicitly than has typically been done in the past in creativity. My approach draws on mathematical network modeling and has connections with semantic networks and knowledge representation. The structure I employ for modeling purposes is relatively simple. It is holistic in modeling context as an integrated network. It is also scalable, which is useful for exploring how creative processes may change and evolve as context becomes larger and more complex.

There is a strong connection between context structure and guidance: in particular the hierarchical structure of context provides the basis for guidance. To find one's way through the thicket of possibilities in a large, rich context is challenging: How can one "see the forest for the trees" and make one's way successfully? The hierarchical network structure makes this possible. In a large-scale context conceptual vision and some degree of breadth of perspective are reqired in order to determine where to focus and to identify high-potential possibilities. Further, in viewing creativity as essentially forging new connections between elements, a widely accepted definition, more distant connections are often the most creative—thus breadth is important to span the context. Guidance based on higher-level elements in the context hierarchy provides this kind of conceptual breadth and vision, rising above and spanning context, while also penetrating down into the dense network of possibilities via downward links to more specific elements. Thus the hierarchy structure provides a natural basis for guidance.

Guidance is about using broader conceptual thinking in the creative process. My argument is not only that guidance is essential for creative work in large-scale contexts, but that in fact a great deal of creativity happens here, in the development and use of more abstract conceptual structures and processes that are themselves highly creative. The importance of this kind of higher-level conceptual thought is a topic that has been mostly neglected in the creativity field, although there are exceptions—such as Gabora's notion of a creative worldview, my discussion of creative interests in *The Nature of Creative Development*, the notion of "creative vision," and the use of templates and prompts in the emerging field of AI creativity.[2] Narrowing one's focus too soon is not a good approach in a rich context, for one is likely to get lost in details that lead nowhere. This basic point I think has not been appreciated because the richness and sheer enormity of context has not been brought into our worldview of creativity as much as it should have been. Being too broad of course is also not a good idea—it is of little use since it provides little actual guidance. Good guidance, as we shall see, has specificity, and often a good amount of creativity, as well as conceptual breadth and vision.

My purpose in this book is to show that this kind of guidance works. I will demonstrate this theoretically and also through empirical examples. Creators, by employing guidance, find their way, although admittedly frequently with many failures along their journey, ultimately producing successful creative outcomes.

I focus on several different functions guidance has in the creative process. First, it helps individuals navigate in large-scale rich contexts to identify areas rich with creative opportunities and generate seed ideas for projects. Second, it helps individuals decide which seed projects to pursue—for in large-scale rich contexts there are many options. Finally, it is also pivotal in bringing projects to a successful completion once they are underway by helping individuals identify just the right element, the "missing piece" that makes a project come together and work.

The approach I describe, grounded in empirical observation, specifically has two forms of guidance that work in tandem. The first is *guiding conceptions*, which imagine creative possibilities and opportunities. These conceptions are often highly creative. Virginia Woolf's conception of a literature that would be based on reflections described in Chapter 8 is a great example. Many important innovations start from these kinds of conceptions: Twitter, for example, started from a guiding conception rooted in Jack Dorsey's personal history. Guiding conceptions are not the same as "final" creativity, and in that sense are often not recognized for their creativity; but when we examine the creative process more closely, we find that they are the basis for exploration and imaginative thinking that leads to later creative success.

The second, *guiding principles*, defines principles that individuals desire their creative work to adhere to. Guiding principles rule out "easy" solutions. This was the case for Albert Einstein, for whom the guiding principle of relativity was an important factor motivating and guiding his long search for what became relativity theory—I discuss this in Chapter 12. It was also the case for Steve Jobs, also discussed in Chapter 12, with his aesthetic principle of simplicity in design, who was legendary for his critical eye, pushing his design teams to refine products. Guiding principles are also central for locating critical "missing pieces" that make a project come together successfully.

I believe most successful creators use both kinds of guidance, in different ways and in different stages of their creative process. In fact the two are complementary, as will be very clear in the core two-step model I present. Interestingly, the formal network model also reveals a natural complementarity shown in Chapter 13: guiding principles that lean more toward efficiency pair naturally with guiding conceptions that are associated with larger domains of possibilities, while guiding principles that are highly creative pair naturally with guiding conceptions associated with smaller domains.

Several factors support the conceptual guidance approach. First, it makes logical sense. In a rich large-scale context it is logical that guidance will be required to generate successful creativity. The guidance framework shows how this happens in steps, first with focus that narrows the range of possibilities, and then with acumen and creative reach to successfully complete projects. I demonstrate the logic of the approach with the formal modeling framework.

Second, it is empirically grounded, the approach followed by many successful creators across a wide range of fields. I have developed it based on empirical data drawn from many case studies, including Virginia Woolf, Albert Einstein, Indigenous Australian artist Clifford Possum, biochemist Hans Krebs, Twitter cofounder Jack Dorsey, Steve Jobs, and VLSI designer and transgender activist Lynn Conway, all discussed in this book, as well as many others, some of whom I discuss in brief. The specifics vary—every creative path is unique and every creative contribution has its own unique story—but conceptual guidance is integral to each case study I present, and we learn from each about how conceptual guidance can be developed and used.

Third, the approach makes intuitive sense. This not only supports its validity at face value but also makes it useful as an educational approach to help individuals develop their creativity. Although guidance approaches of the kind I describe are developed intuitively by many successful creators, for many other people understanding the approach may help them learn how to be successful in their creative enterprises. I discuss this throughout the book and also devote Chapter 18 to a discussion of how to use the approach to support individuals in their creative pursuits, drawing on my experience teaching creativity at Yale and presenting the approach in workshops and at conferences. The idea of using guidance to enhance creativity resonates with students and managers because it provides them a constructive way to think about creativity: it provides defined steps to work on to generate creativity— a point that is most clearly made in Chapter 14 where the core two-step creativity model is described and illustrated with examples.

Of course the model in this book simplifies what is inherently a complex process. The conceptual thinking involved in generating creativity can be highly fluid as ideas and complexes of thought emerge, are used and developed, and then may give way to others. Guiding conceptions and principles can be thought of as the more stable and defined part of this conceptual process. I believe and will argue that they provide core guidance, but there may be other less stable conceptual factors and influences also at work in the creative process. I discuss how the framework can be extended to model richer processes, in particular the evolution of guiding conceptions, in Chapters 15 and 16; but this is more in the manner of a sketch, and there are many open issues that hopefully will be explored in future work.

One critique of the approach I take in this book will be that it is excessively "top-down." I focus on guidance, based on broader conceptual elements and structures, and how this helps guide individuals to creative ideas, projects, and outcomes. "What about the other direction, 'bottom-up'?" is sure to be one response. The truth is that the standard view in creativity tends mainly to focus on the specifics, thus the "bottom," tending as a result also to call attention to the "bottom-up" flow. The emphasis is on brilliant creative moments, sudden random discoveries, insights, and connections—generally highly specific acts of creativity that crystalize into great creative contributions, generating revolutions in our ideas and practices, thus percolating up through the conceptual hierarchy. Unconscious processes have often been described as part of this, especially in the earlier literature—for example, by Poincaré in his discussion of the generation of random combinations in the unconscious and by Wallas in his well-known model that includes the stage of incubation followed by illumination.[3]

In reality both directions—"bottom-up" and "top-down"—are important in the larger cycle of creative development. Further, throughout the creative process there is an ongoing interplay between broader conceptual thinking and specific, more narrowly focused processing, so that movement in both directions is occurring. Specific experiences and elements trigger broader conceptual thinking, which in turn guides creative activity, in turn leading to a dive back down into specific possibilities, which can trigger another round of the creative cycle. One example of the interplay is response to failure. Failure itself normally occurs on the level of specifics, like a project whose elements don't quite work together. But even so, it is by means of conceptual guidance, in particular guiding principles, that individuals evaluate a failure, understand why it has occurred, and identify ways to revise a project, in particular new elements to try, a step that can be highly creative.

The principle that creativity involves dual conceptual processing modes is assuredly not new. Most famously, the creative process has been described as an interplay between divergent and convergent thinking. The dual processes of my model are different, spanning conceptual levels and integrated with the description of context. This larger dual process is fascinating and can, I believe, be modeled building upon the framework I present; see my discussion in Chapters 15 and 16. But for the most part this discussion is beyond the confines of this book and must be left to the future.

Overall, in relation to the larger creative cycle, with processes flowing both up and down the conceptual hierarchy, what I focus on is the part that has arguably been the most neglected. My perspective in this book will, I hope, be useful in drawing attention to the importance of these "top-down" processes and how they function in theory and practice.

Another challenging issue, which I address but not fully, is the mix between generally agreed-upon representations of context and more subjective idiosyncratic representations. At a sufficiently fine-grained level every individual in a creative field will have their own particular representation and knowledge of the world and their field, which will overlap partially but not completely with those of others. Thus, while many of the conceptual links in a context are recognized and accepted by most people in a field, other links are subjective and particular to a given person—for example, a web of interrelated memories based on individual experiences. This mix between widely recognized representations of context and more idiosyncratic reprsentations comes to the fore in empirical applications and in modeling the development of creative fields, in which different individuals working in a field contemporaneously may have different views and knowledge of the field, leading them to pursue different creative paths. I do not fully confront this topic in the formal modeling in this book, but it is evident in the case studies, especially in Chapter 17 on the development of creative fields, and can naturally fit in the conceptual framework suitably extended.

In fact this topic has greater importance, at least to me, than might at first appear. It is at the core of the vision I articulated in my first book, *The Nature of Creative Development*, which I remain committed to as an aspiration: to develop a rigorous modeling structure that has sufficient richness and scope to be able to depict each individual's rich, distinctive conceptual world yet also include all individuals in a common framework. This kind of modeling framework is missing in the social sciences. Without it we are not truly able to depict individuality and hence cannot fully explore its role in creativity and innovation and other important social and cultural processes. Individualism is also a lynchpin of a free society; hence modeling it is vital to supporting freedom. The modeling framework presented in this book can contribute toward attaining the aspiration I have set and developing models of individualism; again, much work remains.

Taken as a whole and recognizing its limitations, the framework in this book does introduce new elements into the creativity field. It will hopefully help to advance creativity modeling, maintaining roots in traditional creativity and innovation while introducing modeling techniques for large-scale contexts. I hope it will be used practically, explored empirically, and developed further theoretically.

RELATED LITERATURE: PLACING THIS BOOK IN CONTEXT

My approach in this book intersects with several different strands of literature in creativity studies and more broadly. I focus on two aspects of the creative process: the rich context and the role of guidance. Each of these is discussed in the literature, and there are some important connections; however, I do not believe these aspects have been brought together previously, certainly not in the way I do. My approach also draws upon and has connections with the biographical approach to creativity, but is quite different in terms of modeling. In this section and the next I discuss these areas of intersection to help place the book in context. I discuss more specific connections with the literature in later chapters, especially 2 (knowledge representation and context/concept modeling), 9 (guiding conceptions), 11 (guiding principles), and 16 (ways to develop the approach further). I note that the field of creativity is large, with many different approaches and subfields; it is not my purpose to provide a general review of the literature. Sawyer's book *Explaining Creativity: The Science of Human Innovation* provides an excellent review, and the recent handbook edited by Kaufman and Sternberg includes chapters that discuss a wide range of creativity topics.[4]

Context is not the dominant focus in the field of creativity, but has been recognized by some. Csikszentmihalyi pioneered the study of creativity in its system context, an approach that also has some resonance with sociological approaches such as the work of Bourdieu.[5] This approach emphasizes the interactions among the individual, the field, and the broader culture/society, including the reception of creative contributions. The breadth of this approach is especially noteworthy; however, the approach differs from mine in fundamental ways, especially in that the knowledge environment is not discussed in detail, and there is no formal model of the kind I present. In *A Cognitive Historical Approach to Creativity*, Dasgupta emphasizes that creative individuals and acts are situated within larger historical contexts; his argument and examples, linking many strands of literature together, help us understand the importance of context for creativity.[6] What I mean by context overlaps with his meaning, but I focus on describing the structure of context and how guidance is used to navigate in this structure.

Sternberg and coauthors have developed propulsion theory, which models the different ways in which creative steps forward occur in creative fields.[7] The taxonomy is useful, especially in encompassing many different kinds of creativity contributions, and it intersects with my approach in thinking about how individuals work with the elements in their fields to create something new. But there are important differences: context is kept very general, as is standard in the creativity field, so its sheer scale and richness is missing, and as a result guidance in the way I describe it doesn't have a significant role; also there is no formal model structure. There may, however, be synergies with the approach I develop in this book.

In the literature on innovation in economics, context is an important element but is described differently than the way I describe context. An important long-standing literature focuses on institutions that support creativity and their impact on economic outcomes and growth. Most notable is intellectual property protection, but other modes of support are also discussed.[8] This is quite different than my focus, although these factors could potentially be introduced into the framework I present. Knowledge as context is recognized to be important in the large literature on knowledge spillovers.[9] Geography, social connectivity, and other measures of local connection are viewed as important, which overlaps with the notion of context as network.[10] However, knowledge is generally not modeled in detail as a conceptual network the way I do and as is done in knowledge representation; rather, much of the literature is empirical and focuses on the challenge of measuring spillovers using standard data sources like patents and productivity data.[11] I note that networks as a more general mathematical structure have been introduced into economics, notably by Matthew Jackson, but these networks describe social and production linkages, not concepts.[12]

Regarding the second key focus of this book, guidance, while it has not been described the way I describe it, there are connections with literature focusing on the role of conceptual thinking in creativity. Gabora's honing theory considers the conceptual world of individuals and the interaction of individuals with their context, with creativity emerging through the generation of a global coherent state.[13] Although Gabora does not model context or the conceptual world the way I do, there is an affinity with my approach. This kind of focus on the broader conceptual world is relatively rare—most of the work in creativity has emphasized more focused processes.

The creative cognition approach emphasizes that individuals generate provisional solutions to a problem or challenge via exploration, followed by refinement to generate a solution, sometimes going through
this process multiple times until developing a satisfactory outcome.[14]
There is a sense of gaining clarity and specificity through the process,
and the approach links in some ways with the latter part of my model in
which individuals strive to find the "missing piece" to make a project
work. Ward and Kolomyts review work in this tradition, including a few
studies that show the value of abstraction in creative task definition,
which calls attention to broader conceptual thinking but in a focused
task-oriented setting.[15] Overall in this approach, as with most work on
creativity coming from the fields of psychology and cognitive science,
context is not modeled and guidance is in general not mentioned and
certainly not described the way I model it.

More generally, a number of cognitive approaches to generating creativity are discussed in the literature; these are not generally about
guidance, but do have connections with my approach. Problem solving is a long-standing, important area of research in psychology. In
relation to creativity this dates back at least to Wertheimer's original
contribution in 1945.[16] In this branch of the literature, specific tools for
generating creative solutions have been identified and shown to have
validity in various empirical and experimental settings; see for example
the interesting work of Weisberg.[17] One well-known tool is conceptual
blending, which is one route to solving problems creatively.[18] In general, the problem-solving literature focuses on the later stages of the
creative process; hence the overlap with my approach is mainly with
the second stage of the model, in which projects are brought to completion. I focus on the role of guiding principles in project completion and
not on the details of problem solution techniques, but these techniques
can be seen as complementary. The importance of guiding principles
in solving problems is recognized to be important in some areas of creativity, notably the design literature—I discuss this in Chapter 12 with
examples including Steve Jobs and Edward Tufte.

A related strand of literature focuses on metaphor as a way to think
creatively and identify creative solutions.[19] Metaphor may be seen as

one way to generate guidance; hence the insights of this literature are relevant for my approach, but the modeling is different and the focus is generally on the elements used to create the metaphor while the surrounding context ("all the roads not taken") is not modeled in detail. Gruber's notion of images of wide scope is a related conceptual tool; true to their name, such images have breadth of application and therefore can provide general guidance, and in this regard they are connected with my approach, though again the modeling approach is very different.[20]

Linked with problem solving is a smaller literature on problem finding—for example as discussed by Runco.[21] Problem finding focuses earlier in the creative process, which aligns with my approach. However, as with much of the creativity literature, the focus tends to be on more narrowly focused conceptual processes, so that finding a problem to work on is not linked to broader guidance, which is the way I model this process.

There is also a literature, spanning both the creativity field and economics, that views creativity as generated via a random search process. The economics model specifies a distribution for potential productive innovations with random draws made from the distribution.[22] In psychology the model of random search dates back to Donald Campbell's 1960 article; in this model the distribution from which draws are made is not specified in as much detail, but the idea of making random attempts is similar.[23] In these literatures, the "context" is the distribution out of which draws are made, and this has no underlying structure—it is just a population out of which elements are drawn at random. In contrast, I specify context as a network through which elements are linked to form ideas, thus adding important structure. I also include higher-level guidance, which as I have noted above is essential in large-scale contexts for which completely random search is almost sure to fail. Thus my approach can be seen as significantly enriching the random search model.

Beyond search theory there has been surprisingly little work on modeling creativity in economics, although there has been somewhat more in recent years. Weitzman models creativity as combinations, but the focus is not on the creative process itself but rather on the selection of ideas for further development.[24] I have modeled learning and the development of ideas as recombinations in the context of creative fields.[25] In recent work Rodet explores the impact of personal factors and experiences on creativity and Dutcher and Rodet explore knowledge transfer in creative domains—both papers relate to the model of context, exploration, and guidance in this book.[26] Other recent work includes Dasaratha's model of idea formation in a social network in which individuals meet to form ideas; Akcigit, Caicedo, Miguelez, Stantcheva, and Sterzi's model of innovation as a choice between individual or collaborative activity; and Giorcelli and Moser's study of the effect of copyright on creativity in the field of opera.[27] As interesting and diverse as this work is, the modeling of context and creative process is limited and there is no role for guidance.

The lack of attention to creativity in economics has always surprised me, as one of the important principles of a free society is the freedom for individuals to pursue their own creative paths and ideas, a viewpoint associated with Mill and Hayek.[28] Related to this is the notion that economic progress depends on entrepreneurs perceiving opportunities and having the freedom and capability to act on them, a view emphasized by Kirzner among others; this is a form of creativity and fits with my approach in this book.[29] It is interesting that Bloom, Jones, Van Reenen, and Webb have recently published an article presenting evidence that it may be becoming more costly to generate ideas; while my focus is different, there is a connection with the idea that the context of creativity is changing and becoming larger scale.[30] Support for creativity has always been valuable, but given that its context is changing, support may be becoming even more important, and it is my hope that the framework I present will help spur development in this neglected area.

A noteworthy emerging field is the neuroscience of creativity.[31] The neuroscience approach is surely relevant for any approach to creativity that considers rich context and representation of knowledge and experiences, providing potentially a window into these representations and how individuals use them in creative work. The 2020 edited volume by Nalbantian and Matthews illustrates this, as many chapters make links between the neuroscience of creativity and more traditional and life-course descriptions of the creative process.[32] The approach at least thus far focuses on quite short time spans and most likely will not pick up on the first stage of my model, but may map better into the second stage, project completion. See also the 2020 edited volume on creativity and the wandering mind, which has been an area of investigation in the past two decades.[33]

Another noteworthy emerging field is computational creativity—see for example recent conference volumes produced out of the International Conference on Computational Creativity conferences.[34] There are some overlaps with my approach, especially in the way templates and prompts are used to help generate creative possibilities. But what is striking is that the focus is on creativity generated out of more specific elements, what I will call the lower level of the context, and there is far less attention paid to creative intuition at the higher guidance level—I discuss this in Chapter 9.[35] There may be potential synergies of the framework in this book with computational approaches.

There is also overlap between my approach and both technology studies and the history of science. An important strand of the technology literature focuses on the process through which innovations come about based on perceived need, using what is at hand, or as a byproduct of activity.[36] These insights may be able to be brought into my model as ways individuals interact with their context. In both technology studies and especially the history of science, the discussion of fields is an area of overlap with my approach, as the field an individual works in establishes a large part of their context. Kuhn's famous work on scientific revolutions is an example of a framework in which the field is paramount; but the individual creative process is not focused on and how exactly an individual traverses a path to a revolutionary idea is not described in any detail.[37] Hull discusses field-level processes in biology, simultaneously from conceptual and social perspectives, but again the focus is not on the individual creative process.[38] Overall, much of the work on fields has focused less on the creative process in itself. However, there is much to be learned from the many outstanding contributions and valuable synergies to be developed.

THE LINK WITH BIOGRAPHY

The biographical literature on individuals engaged in creative endeavors both informs and inspires my approach. When we study an individual's creative path in detail, we see the richness both of their process and the surrounding context. Within the creativity literature Howard Gruber brought attention to this aspect of creativity, initially in his landmark study of Charles Darwin's notebooks and then in his evolving systems framework. Another inspiring early work is Lowes's description of Samuel Taylor Coleridge's creative process.[39]

Unfortunately much of the biographical literature exists quite separately from the creativity literature. Bringing the two together is a facet of this book as it was also of my earlier book *The Nature of Creative Development*. Specifically, I draw on both biographical and archival materials for the case studies. Frederic Holmes's scientific biography of Hans Krebs is remarkable, a model for assembling rich details to show how creativity unfolds. Vivien Johnson's biography of Clifford Possum provides a rich perspective on his development. Every biography fits in a network with other historical materials. In this case Possum fits within the Indigenous Australian modern art movement, which I discuss in Chapter 17, drawing on a range of works including *Papunya: A Place Made After the Story,* based on Geoffrey Bardon's notes from his time at Papunya where, at least on some accounts, this movement began. There are many other outstanding biographies that have informed my thinking across the arts, sciences, and technology; indeed, it is always a joy to find another outstanding biography and learn through the care, scholarship, and thoughtfulness of its author.

Archival materials are a very rich source of information. Virginia Woolf left us a treasure trove of materials, including not only her fiction but also her diaries, many volumes of letters, and her essays; I draw on these materials in my description of her creative path. Engineer and transgender activist Lynn Conway has posted a large collection of historical materials on her website documenting both her life path as well as her role in the development of VLSI design principles; these are the basis for my discussion of her creative journey, supplemented with materials posted by her collaborator Carver Mead. I draw on

Albert Einstein's "Autobiographical Notes," a model of clarity, as well as other articles he wrote and the extensive scholarship on his development of relativity theory. We are fortunate to have such rich materials for these individuals. But we have much less for most, and can only hope the collection and preservation of such materials, for all individuals engaged in creative endeavors no matter the scale and scope, can improve and come to match them.

As rich and informative as the biographical and archival material is, however, it does not provide a general framework for describing the creative process in a systematic, structured way. Gruber makes the imporant point that creativity comes about through many small steps, not one giant leap; but his framework is descriptive in nature, not structural. Holmes also presents a framework for creative paths in the sciences, which he calls "investigative pathways," but again his framework has limited structure.[40]

The approach in this book shows how to structure archival and biographical material and analyze it more systematically. A key step for this—a focus of this book—is developing a framework for describing the rich context in which individuals engaged in creative endeavors function. It is far too easy to focus on only a handful of contextual elements and influences, even in a very good biographical account of a creator's journey. Archival materials sometimes include more of this, but normally the individual creating these materials does not view a full description of context as the main purpose. A related key step is to recognize all the "roads not taken"—all the possibilities in the rich context that were not pursued. Even very good biographies do not generally discuss this in much depth, yet from the viewpoint of modeling and predicting the creative process, it is critical to know this. By describing context and creative paths and possibilities more systematically and more fully, we will come to a deeper, more developed understanding of creativity and the creativity inherent in every person's life journey.

PART I

CONTEXT

CHAPTER 1

THE IMPORTANCE OF CONTEXT

We create in context. Our context includes our culture, our field, and the natural world. It is extremely rich and diverse, filled with a multitude of elements and creative possibilities. It includes subjects we learn, phenomena we observe, people, events, places, the material world, ideas, and values, as well as the creative contributions made by others. Creativity emerges out of engaging with our context creatively. This can mean literally exploring the context that surrounds us with its myriad creative opportunities. Often it means creating in the inner world that we have developed through our engagement with context and our reflections and reactions to it.

KINDS OF CONTEXT
There are different kinds of contexts that are important for creativity. For many individuals engaged in a creative pursuit, their field is most central. But other contexts can also be important, including broader social and cultural factors, the natural world, and personal experiences.

Creative Fields: The plethora of creative fields cover a wide spectrum. These include the arts and sciences and other academic fields; fields of design such as interior design, game design, and fashion; creative practices such as textiles, cooking, and gardening; technology-focused fields including the engineering fields and computer science; and fields of practical activity including medicine, law, public policy, and management. The list is long and grows and evolves over time. For a given individual the field or fields they believe themselves to be a part of is subjective and may be larger or smaller: for example, a person might think of their field as "economics" or more narrowly as "development economics."

The context of a field includes different kinds of elements. Creative contributions that have been made in a field are fundamental to how we think about it, in terms of both its history and current structure. These contributions in turn are unpacked into concepts and conceptual structures, and it is these that we typically learn—for example in textbooks and classes—and that frame our understanding and mental map of a field.

The concepts and structures that frame a field include several principle kinds. The broadest, most general kind includes topics and categories that help define the overall structure of the field, as well as important definitions, assumptions, principles, frameworks, broad empirical regularities, and paradigms. Below this are medium-level concepts, including approaches, styles, genres, themes, and more specific theories, models, viewpoints, and empirical findings. Below this are a host of more specific concepts, such as specific examples and layouts. The concepts that comprise a field also include practices and protocols that define how individuals work, collaborate, and communicate. Finally, the constellation of concepts in a field at a given time also includes current anomalies, questions, and working hypotheses.

Field context includes other elements. Central to many fields are its subjects and objects of focus, which may be animate, inanimate, or mainly conceptual. In many fields equipment, tools, and materials are essential to create and thus are an important part of field practice and hence context.[1] Finally, a field is populated by the people who are active in it and the places that are important for creative practice in it.

All of these different elements are linked in conceptual structures in terms of how individuals think about them and relationships among them. For example, a certain person or group of people may be known to work at a certain place, be associated with a certain theoretical framework or empirical approach, and have produced a series of creative contributions. Thus field context has structure, the topic of the next chapter.

Fields also have history: past people and their creative contributions, places, activities, and events; past areas of focus, data, ideas, theories, and assumptions; and old equipment and protocols. This history may be more or less important depending on the field and its particular current configuration. For Virginia Woolf, for example, the history of literature was of great importance, and for Indigenous Australian artists, their cultural heritage is paramount for their art. For other individuals history has less direct importance—for example for Jack Dorsey and the invention of Twitter. The history of a field is often interconnected with its conceptual structure; for example, certain individuals and schools of thought are linked to certain bodies of knowledge or perspectives.

Fields vary in both their extent and number of elements. Field breadth can be measured in a number of ways, including conceptual range, number of active creative topics, number of recent contributions, and number of people engaged in creative activity in the field. Differences among fields in size also relate to their differing histories, both how "old" the field is as well as how fruitful and wide-ranging prior creative activity has been in generating new elements. Older fields are not necessarily more active at present, however, and thus some kinds of context may be more extensive for older fields, others for younger fields. For example, fields such as mathematics, philosophy, and visual art are generally viewed as old fields with a great deal of accumulated history. They are not, however, currently more active than new, rapidly growing fields like computer science and artificial intelligence, medical drug discovery and development, and social media. Newer fields are inevitably linked with older, more established fields. Therefore over-all size also depends on what is included in defining the field. The size of a field may influence creative trajectories of individuals in the field.

Other Contexts: There are a variety of other kinds of context that are important for creativity, depending on the field and the individual.

The natural world is important for creativity in many fields. This includes natural phenomena that we observe and that affect us, as well as the conceptual frameworks we use to describe, classify, and attempt to explain and model them. The amazing natural environment Darwin encountered while serving as naturalist on the *Beagle* exploring South America was an incredibly rich context and crucial to his creative development during these formative years. The natural world is important not only in the natural sciences but in many fields such as poetry and nature or science-based literature—think of Wordsworth's poetry and Dillard's *Pilgrim at Tinker Creek.*[2]

Social context is very important for many individuals engaged in creative endeavors. This includes collaborators, friends, mentors, teachers, and even single encounters like an inspiring speaker. Social connections provide conduits for communication through which individuals learn about the broader context and gain a sense for active areas of work. Oftentimes social connections or encounters are linked with other kinds of context elements, such as certain knowledge or skills or questions that are brought to the attention of an individual by a mentor or colleague.

Personal experiences are also an important context for creativity. Artists and writers have often been described as "transmuting" personal experience into art.[3] How an individual responds to personal experiences is an important factor in their creativity. For Virginia Woolf personal experiences, especially of family, childhood, and loss, were central features that shaped her guiding conception. As her case shows, the key here is connection: Woolf forged conceptual links between her personal experiences, especially of loss, and her literary sensibilities, in the context of the particular literary, historical moment and her knowledge of earlier literature. Thus her example, described in more detail in Chapters 3, 8, and 15, is a good example showing different kinds of context jointly shaping the creative process. Although most widely discussed in the arts, personal factors can be important for many individuals who engage in creative endeavors.

The broader historical, political, cultural, and economic context is also important for many individuals, both because of its direct relevance and because it shapes the constraints within which they work. This broader context can be important in terms of raising issues such as social problems. It is also an important grounding for values, such as principles of equality, that may serve as guiding principles for creativity. Indigenous Australian artists such as Clifford Possum view their art as rooted in their culture and its spiritual learnings. They intend through their art to help preserve the culture and its teachings. Like Virginia Woolf they create innovative artistic forms through making connections, in their case developing novel artistic styles that capture but also transcend traditional cultural forms. I discuss Possum's creative development in Chapters 3, 8, and 14, and the Indigenous Australian desert modern art movement as an example of the creative development of a field in Chapter 17.

THE INDIVIDUALITY OF CONTEXT

Each individual functions in their own context. For an individual engaged in a creative endeavor, the context that matters is whatever experiences, knowledge, and other elements enter into their creative process. For modeling creativity, and as I use the term, *context* refers primarily to this individual-specific context.

Even among individuals who enter and work creatively in a given field at around the same time, there will be significant differences in their contexts—their perceptions, experiences, interests, and knowledge—that generate differences in the way their creative paths unfold. Hans Krebs's case described in Chapter 3 illustrates this. Although his training in medicine was fairly standard for the time, his context was unique for individuals training for a scientific career in internal medicine in its combination of his particular teachers and interests, and the opportunity he had to train in a prestigious lab and learn an important new methodology. Likewise Lynn Conway's particular context in the field of engineering, working at IBM and then Xerox PARC, and her insights about her context, were specific to her.

Certain elements of a field's context are likely to be perceived and represented similarly by many individuals. In particular, standard, widely accepted knowledge in a field is likely to be represented similarly by different individuals in the field, especially those receiving education at around the same time. This means they will mainly agree on the list of standard topics, well-known accepted results and assumptions, empirical regularities, and the linkages among these elements. However, there will not be complete agreement even about these standard parts of the field context. Different schools of thought may view some contested topics differently than others do, and differ concerning what is most important, be it linkages among topics, the nature of assumptions and aims, and/or central open questions. But we can certainly attempt to describe the "standard" context structure in a field at a given time—for example based on the organization of material in widely used textbooks—even while recognizing this will never be an exact representation of any single individual's representation. Hans Krebs's case again illustrates this. Part of what he learned, especially his basic medical training, was fairly standard for students training in medicine in Germany at the time. However, even in this regard individual lecturers focused on particular topics and shared their own particular perspective—as Franz Knoop did, for example, which turned out to be profoundly influential on Krebs.

Recognizing that there is a degree of commonality, nonetheless each individual in a creative field will perceive and function in their own particular context. Individuals will differ in their encounters and exposures. Their unique experiences will color their perceptions of field context, including what they are most aware of. No one knows or is even aware of everything in their field. Individuals will differ in their interests and goals, as well as what questions draw their interest. Each individual will develop a richly articulated representation of topics and issues that draw their attention. An individual's specific context may in fact include portions of multiple fields (in terms of how these fields are conventionally defined), for the scope of each individual's creative engagement is defined in its own terms.

Just as there are commonalities and differences in field context among individuals, there are also commonalities and differences in their wider experiences and knowledge. Individuals may share similar representations of some categories—for example, dividing their life into childhood, adolescence, and adulthood, and into work and family. But the particularities of their experiences will differ, and linkages among elements may be quite different. For example, for one person their mother or father may be important in transmitting certain knowledge and history and thus be closely linked with elements in their creative context, as Virginia Woolf's father was for her, whereas for another person this may not be the case.

From the viewpoint of understanding the creative process, the quintessential activity of individuality, it is clearly important for us to be sensitive to the particularities of individual experiences and representations of context. The particularities of a person's representation, such as elements and connections in their field that they are especially attuned to, can play an important role in their creativity. At the same time, it is fascinating also to observe how individuals immersed in similar or at least related contexts, such as working in the same field, nonetheless follow different creative paths. A careful representation of context and its differences across individuals can help us untangle these different pathways to creativity and contribute to our understanding of the reasons for similarities and differences.

This is also a reason why it is valuable to both examine individual case studies in depth and explore more abstract formal modeling. Each approach illuminates aspects of patterns of creative development, and they complement one another. With respect to formal modeling of the creative process, a key issue is to allow for differences among individuals, but in a way that is sufficiently flexible and abstract to allow for effective analysis. Consider, for example, modeling the creative processes of a collection of individuals working in a common field. One approach is to draw individual contexts from correlated distributions, so individuals share some elements and subnetworks in common in their contexts, while differing in others; I discuss this further in Chapter 17. This kind of modeling can help us understand how similarities and differences in individual contexts relate to similarities and differences in creative paths and outcomes and the implications for overall field development.

THE DYNAMICS OF CONTEXT

Context evolves. This occurs for each individual and also collectively.

For an individual, their context evolves as they learn, have experiences, and encounter new elements. As an individual learns, whole new areas of context may open to them, as happened for Hans Krebs when he learned a novel set of laboratory techniques and for Clifford Possum when he became involved in a modern art movement. As an individual gains knowledge about a topic, their context enriches with the addition of new elements and linkages. We would also expect that as an individual learns and reflects, they will build additional links among elements that they may not have recognized previously, thus developing more integrated knowledge structures.

Collectively, field context evolves as new contributions are made, new data becomes available, new questions are posed, and new techniques are invented, in the field itself or in other related fields. Further, fields can be reorganized as new information and insight leads to different ways of grouping elements and topics, and new linkages among elements. Thus field structure can be highly dynamic.[4] Even more broadly, social and cultural contexts evolve due to developments in fields and many other factors.

As interesting and important as these broader dynamics are, I do not focus on them. I focus on developing a model of creative process for an individual in a given field at a given time and place, thus holding the broader context constant. And, while dynamics of individual context are present, as in the example of Virginia Woolf, they are mainly in the background. Modeling the dynamics of individual learning and evolution of an individual's context is an exciting topic that is better left to the next cycle of this work, once the basic model has been developed. I do discuss some individual context dynamics, notably for Virginia Woolf, Albert Einstein, Jack Dorsey, and Lynn Conway, to connect the model with real world creativity and illustrate richer processes of creative development.

CHAPTER 2

THE STRUCTURE OF CONTEXT

The context in which creativity happens is organized—it has structure—and this structure matters for creativity. To state this in a way that fits with the model of creativity in this book, individuals engaged in creative endeavors are embedded in contexts that are organized and that they themselves organize, and this organization plays a central role in their creative endeavors, including the guidance structures they form, their ideas, the paths they follow, and their outcomes. Organization of context in this book means primarily structured relationships among elements as in a network.

This organization of context has two sources. One source can be taken to be objective in that it is based on physical, biological, and environmental relationships, such as colocation and family relationships. However, individuals don't always agree on these relationships, so "objective" must be taken as relative.

The other source of organization is the human-based and conceptual ways in which we as humans organize our contexts. Some of this organization is foundational of human life and society. On the individual level we organize our experiences chronologically, spatially, thematically, and emotionally. Berger and Luckmann's *The Social Construction of Reality* is a well-known work in this tradition that demonstrates how all-encompassing this organization is.[1] On the societal level many systems are organized as social networks, networks that describe, define, and influence social interactions.[2]

For creativity an important part of the organization of context is based on learning and creative engagement. Learning in general is about forging connections among concepts and extending a concept network—related to the concept mapping approach in the field of education discussed below. For an individual engaged in a creative endeavor, much of their focus is on their field, a central component of their context as discussed in the previous chapter. Fields are organized conceptually. Particular assumptions and hypotheses are linked with particular theories. Theory components are linked to build larger frameworks. Empirical regularities are linked with certain approaches and data sources. Styles and techniques are interconnected, and a series of contributions made by an individual or school of thought are linked. From a different but related perspective, textbooks evidence an organized structure of a field in the way they present material.

Individuals learn and internalize a structured representation of their field, which reflects how they view it and is paramount for their creative path. Of course not everyone agrees on how a field is organized: in the modeling approach I favor, every individual has their own context with its own structure, although individuals working in the same field at around the same time likely share parts of their contexts in common.

Conceptual and more "objective" organizations of context overlap. For example, people are associated with the ideas they publish and works they create, and physical materials and apparatuses are linked with techniques and methods that use them. I might link a person with a key idea they explained to me. Note that context includes conceptual representations of physical entities like people and places. Hence many context elements have both conceptual and more objective facets; this relates to the fact that in creativity contexts many elements have multiple links, as discussed below.

For creativity the conceptual representation and organization of context is paramount, for this is the basis for much creative work and idea formation and evaluation. Thus contexts I describe and depict in this book should in most cases be viewed as attempting to describe, however imperfectly, an individual's conceptual representation of their context, a representation that is also inherently subjective.

I employ network terminology for the representation of contexts. With a network approach it is possible to describe both the elements in a particular context as well as the relationships among these elements. Both are crucial for how creativity happens. The elements are in a sense the "raw materials" for thinking and creating. The relationships are critical because creative thinking and exploration flow through these relationships, generating new creative connections that produce new ideas and discoveries. A network framework is also a mathematical framework and thus conducive to formal modeling, which is an important part of this book; I introduce the formal network model in Chapter 4.

The network framework I employ draws upon and is aligned with the field of ontology and ontology engineering. Gruber defines an ontology as defining "the concepts, relationships, and other distinctions that are relevant for modeling a domain."[3] An example of a well-known ontology is the Gene Ontology (GO) for the field of biology. The GO Consortium defines an ontology as "a formal representation of a body of knowledge within a given domain. Ontologies usually consist of a set of classes (or terms or concepts) with relations that operate between them."[4]

My approach also draws upon and has a connection with common-sense reasoning models. In this kind of modeling the emphasis is on cataloging the vast array of elements and their relationships that individuals know from life itself, not just highly specialized knowledge, which is often the focus in the development of formal ontologies. Hence there is a natural tendency toward breadth of coverage. Doug Lenat's *CYC Project* is an example: Lenat has attempted to catalog a very wide array of elements and relationships between them, in a project spanning thirty years.[5] Breadth of coverage is important for creativity since some of the most creative connections span disparate parts of a person's context. Virginia Woolf and Clifford Possum are two examples of individuals discussed in this book for whom this was the case. Thus there is an affinity with my approach in emphasizing breadth of coverage in describing a person's context—striving to describe context holistically.

More recent work building ontologies uses automated approaches that mine data sources, mainly via web crawling, to produce large-scale semantic networks. In these approaches words and phrases that co-occur in text documents are viewed as linked, and from these pairwise links the larger network is constructed. This is a burgeoning field with many applications under development, including some directly relevant to creativity such as design and patent documents.[6] The models and approach in this book naturally align and have synergies with this emerging field, for example with ChatGPT.

As compared with the field of ontology and the examples I have given, an important difference in my approach is that I focus not on describing an entire field but rather on the contexts of individuals who are engaging with the field and their culture creatively. Thus I focus more on the individuality of a person's context. The contexts I am describing are inherently subjective and will typically not contain all—or even close to all—the elements in a field, as ontologies strive for. They will, however, include other, more personal elements. This aspect of my approach, focusing on individuals' contexts, links with concept mapping, a tool for mapping a person or team's conceptual mental network originally developed by Joseph Novak and his colleagues in the field of education. The link I emphasize from context and its representation to creativity fits naturally with this approach, which emphasizes personal learning and conceptual growth.[7]

Throughout this book I employ visual representations to depict context networks. In this regard my approach has affinities with both ontology visualization and concept mapping.[8] Visualization is a good way to gain intuition about the nature of creativity contexts including case studies, and to depict the core creativity model of this book.

Finally, I note that my approach has less affinity with knowledge representation approaches that emphasize drawing logical conclusions from ontologies.[9] Creativity is not mainly about proving statements to be true, notwithstanding that in some fields such as mathematics this is an important form of creativity. Rather, creativity is about making new connections that are recognized as creative. These may turn out to be useful and to "work" in practice but are not proven in a technical sense. I focus on the processes used to find and create these new connections, and this is a different focus from much of knowledge representation. For this purpose representing context in terms of its structure and relationships is central, rather than using the structure and relationships for logical reasoning. My emphasis is more on intuitive and associative processes and less on logical reasoning.[10]

While my approach links with ontology, concept mapping, and to some extent the broader field of knowledge representation, my purpose is different than nearly all of this literature, and this makes aspects of my modeling framework and how I use it distinctive. I am describing contexts in which individuals engage in creative endeavors. Especially, I am tailoring my description to focus on how individuals navigate their contexts to create successfully.

In terms of creativity and forms of guidance that help individuals create, an essential feature of the organization of context is its fundamental hierarchical structure. Thus I start with this structural feature, discussed next. In addition, there are additional types of linkages in creativity contexts that are important for the creative process and its guidance; I describe these in the section following. Finally, I discuss the scale and scope of context.

HIERARCHY

Hierarchy is a fundamental property of the organization of knowledge.[11] Hierarchy defines a structure in which broader elements are parents to more specific elements.

Hierarchy is famously the core of the standard classification system in biology. To give a simple example, "dog" (a subspecies in the standard classification system in biology) is parent to many different dog breeds,

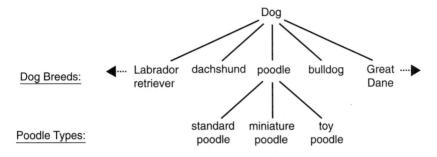

The figure shows 5 representative dog breeds; the arrows left and right indicate that there are many more not shown in the figure.

The bottom level in the figure shows poodle types. Other dog breeds also have types, such as Great Danes, not shown in the figure.

FIGURE 1. SIMPLE HIERARCHY EXAMPLE

which in turn in many cases have different types. For example, the poodle is a dog breed with three generally recognized types: standard, miniature, and toy. Figure 1 depicts this example.

This same principle of organization by hierarchy applies in many domains. Large retail stores are organized this way: departments, which in turn divide into subdepartments, and so on, for example: Clothing—women's clothing—women's casual wear. Hierarchy is an essential principle of the organization of words, which are the signifiers of concepts. This hierarchical organization is very clear in the well-known WordNet database.[12] Thus, the verb *motion* is parent to many different forms of motion, including run, walk, crawl, roll, fly, swim, and glide. Interestingly, there are striking differences in hierarchy structure across different word categories: for example, adverbs as compared with adjectives, which illustrates how context structures are diverse across different concept domains.

Hierarchy is a core principle in most large-scale ontologies. For example, the *CYC* project has hierarchy as a core feature.[13] In general, the accumulated knowledge in a field can be structured as a hierarchy, though with additional links. Consistent with this, textbooks, which define and describe standard elements in a field, are typically organized as hierarchies, divided into units, chapters, sections, and subsections. In a project conducted jointly with colleague Arthur Campbell and several students, we drew on multiple sources, including textbooks, to map the domain of microeconomics concepts taught in core doctoral microeconomic programs. In our work we developed a hierarchical structure with nearly 1,400 concepts organized into larger topics.[14] The Gene Ontology project is another example of a knowledge base in which hierarchy is a key organizing principle.[15]

To give a different example, brain systems are also modeled as organized hierarchies that process sensory inputs and structure brain functions. A prime example is the visual system, which is famous for its highly organized, hierarchical brain structure.[16] More recent work in brain mapping provides evidence that reinforces how pervasive hierarchy is in human processing of sensory input.[17]

In truth hierarchy applies very broadly, including in our organization of the world around us and our lives. We divide time with a hierarchical framework—century, decade, year, month, day, hour, minute, second. We divide space and geography using hierarchy—continent, country, state, city, neighborhood, street, dwelling, rooms. We also organize our experiences with hierarchy, using broad categories like "work," "home," "childhood," "school," and "friends," and more specific breakdowns under these.

Thus, hierarchy is truly ubiquitous in the organization of context. Consistent with this, my model has hierarchy as a central feature.

NETWORKS

As important as the principle of hierarchy is for conceptual organization, the elements of a context are not organized as simple hierarchies but generally have a rich network connectivity structure that goes beyond this.[18] These links are important for creativity especially in that they open paths ranging over a context that can facilitate new creative connections. In my formal modeling I include two types of additional links that I believe are especially important for creativity.

The first type of additional linkage is vertical and arises due to elements having multiple parents. In a strict hierarchy (sometimes called a tree) each child has a single parent. In reality many elements in a context have more than one parent, which makes the structure akin to a lattice (not typically identical to a lattice due to other features, and more akin to a semi-lattice as context networks open downward). An example is dog crossbreeds, which are formed by combining two breeds: for example, the goldendoodle is a popular crossbreed that is derived from two parent breeds, the poodle and the golden retriever. Multiple parents are actually very common and even characteristic of contexts. For example, a chemical compound or food that is made out of several component elements has each of these as parent. As another example, experiences typically have multiple links upward, including to both where and when they occur. A creative contribution has both conceptual links to "parent" concepts—where it fits in the hierarchy of concepts that comprise its field, as well as one or more links to the individual, team, or organization that produced it.

Attribute links are another kind of link that is naturally thought of as vertical in many cases. For example a standard poodle is a "large" dog whereas a toy poodle is "small." While such attributes are not parents in the same way that poodle is parent to these two types of poodle, they are naturally thought of as "upward" links in that they are links to more general concepts—"large" and "small" are general attributes. Note that attributes have their own location and local structure in the context description, so that for example "size" would be parent to both "large" and "small." Experiences and events also have attribute links that define the kind of activity involved, the social setting, and so on.[19]

A second additional type of network link in contexts is lateral links. These are links between elements at the same level in the context hierarchy. Such links can be generated in many different ways, depending on the context. Similarities among elements generate lateral links: for example, "brother" has a natural link with "sister" and, at least since John Keats's famous poem, "beauty" and "truth" are naturally linked at least for some people.[20] Analogy and metaphor generate links: for example, the attribute of being wise may be linked with "owl." Oppositions can generate links: the San Francisco Giants and Los Angeles Dodgers are baseball rivals and hence naturally linked.[21]

Lateral links are, in my view, especially salient for higher-level, broader concepts, such as the way "beauty" and "truth" are linked. The reason is that lateral links between higher-level concepts enable individuals to traverse considerable conceptual distances in their contexts—for example shifting from one broad topic to a second topic—and this is important for creative thinking since it can lead to making new connections between elements that were originally relatively far apart, such as connecting an element that is part of one topic to a second element that is part of a quite different topic. Thus I stress model structures with these types of links and do not focus on lateral links among more specific elements.

There are other kinds of linkages and structural features that have been developed to model contexts that I do not consider, in the interest of simplicity of representation and also because they seem less germane to describing the creative process. One such feature is functional relationships that describe the relationship among a set of elements in terms of some action, event, or process. For example, frame-based systems, originally proposed by Marvin Minsky, have been developed as a way to show the set of roles and actions that comprise a standard activity, event, or process.[22] Examples are what to pack for a trip, a chemical reaction, or the act of weighing something. As these examples indicate, much of the work describing functional relationships focuses on quite standardized activities and processes. Thus it does not naturally fit with my focus on creativity.

The use of templates in computational creativity is an example of a frame-based approach that does relate to creativity. Interestingly, however, the templates themselves are typically conventional in these applications, so that the kind of higher-level guidance I focus on is missing—as I have discussed already in the introduction. The kind of detailed microstructure involved with these kinds of functional models seems to me counterproductive at this stage of working to develop a formal model of creative guidance and how individuals navigate in their contexts to forge new creative connections. Thus I prefer to leave this topic to future development, building on the approach I present.[23]

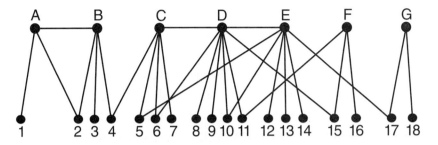

FIGURE 2. SMALL EXAMPLE CONTEXT

Figure 2 depicts a small example context that includes multiple parents and lateral links among higher-level elements. This example will be used repeatedly to illustrate model features and thus is well worth studying carefully. The example has two levels—the simplest type of network with vertical structure. It includes 7 top elements and 18 bottom elements. Each top-level element serves as "parent" to at least two bottom "children" that it is linked to vertically. Bottom elements have either one parent (10 clements) or two (8). Finally, there are three horizontal links between top elements: A and B, C and D, and D and E.

This figure is meant to be taken just as an abstract example; it is not based on a specific case study like the contexts depicted in the next chapter. It is much simpler than a real world context, which has advantages for depicting the logic of the model.

SCALE AND SCOPE

In the world of creativity contexts are generally large scale, a theme of this book. As valuable as simple descriptions and examples like Figure 2 are, they do not convey a good sense for this important point. Creative fields contain hundreds or thousands of elements, including many concepts, facts, people, places, tools, and materials, as well as the many creative contributions that have already been made in the field. Scale matters for the creative process, because in a large-scale context there are many different options. Knowing where to explore and what to try is critical. Hence guidance—my focus—comes to the fore. Indeed the failure of creativity studies generally to consider large-scale contexts is one reason guidance processes have been neglected.

The creativity contexts of individuals engaged in creative endeavors are also often wide in scope. Individuals engaged in creative endeavors often cross conventional field boundaries as they follow their own path, learn about a diverse range of topics, and bring elements from different domains together creatively. Thus scope is also important to model because it is so often central to creative exploration, idea generation, and discoveries.

The descriptions of context I provide for particular individual case studies in the next chapter are helpful in conveying a sense for the scale and scope of real creativity. To explore the importance of scale I combine case studies with computer simulations based on generating sample large-scale context networks—see Chapter 4.

CHAPTER 3

EXAMPLES OF CONTEXT

In this chapter I present examples of context for three individuals: Virginia Woolf, Clifford Possum, and Hans Krebs. Both written descriptions and visual representations are provided, and they complement one another. For each individual I describe their context around the time they formed a critical guiding conception that started them on a path to breakthrough creative contributions. This is very useful for understanding their creative path, as I believe will become clear in Parts II and III. Indeed Woolf, Possum, and Krebs are used as examples throughout the book—thus gaining familiarity with their contexts should facilitate understanding of later parts of the book.

The contexts described in this chapter fit the discussion of the organization of context in the preceding chapter. The contexts are organized hierarchically and are naturally represented as networks, in particular with many elements having multiple parents and links between higher level elements. This hierarchical network structure is especially evident in the figures. It is important to appreciate because it motivates the model development to follow.

There are two caveats worthy of mention. One is that an individual's context grows and changes over time, and while my descriptions recognize this, they cannot fully capture the rich dynamics, with the figures especially inherently static. The other is that while the descriptions in this chapter are relatively detailed and hopefully convey a sense of the richness, breadth, and depth of creativity contexts, they necessarily omit many details and focus more on some parts of a person's context than other parts, in general focusing on the parts that are in my judgment most relevant to the person's creative development. Simplifying the representation of an individual's context as I do may introduce bias into our understanding of their creative process. This problem is of course a general one: the description of any complex system and process must inevitably omit many details. I have tried both to illuminate the richness of these contexts and also to shape my discussion so as to help us best understand and appreciate these individuals' key creative steps. Put differently, my aim in these case studies is to strike a balance between depicting the richness of context, which is important for my argument, and not overwhelming the reader with details.

VIRGINIA WOOLF

Virginia Woolf is famous for her innovative modernist literary style. To appreciate her creativity and its originality, you must first understand her context. This context included especially her vast reading, encompassing literature as well as biographical materials and histories; it also included her personal experiences, people and places, and broader cultural milieu. It was out of this context, in reaction to it, building from it, transmuting it, that she developed her guiding conception that guided her literary creative development.

Woolf left us a trove of materials, including her journals, diaries, reading notebooks, letters, book reviews, stories, novels, and essays. From these we can reconstruct a picture of her context.

Figure 3 depicts Woolf's context in overview. I have kept the depiction of her context in the figure to just an outline. But even for this

IMAGE 1. VIRGINIA WOOLF, 1902. ©National Portrait Gallery, London. Photograph by George Charles Beresford.

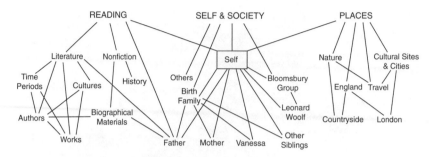

FIGURE 3. Virginia Woolf Context: Overview

very simple representation, notice the basic hierarchical structure and multiple parents (for example, "London" has 2 parents).

Note that I have not shown attributes and other kinds of abstract concepts in Figure 3. These would have many links with the kinds of context elements I focus on describing, creating a whole additional layer of structure. Woolf had strong opinions about literature; thus attributes she ascribed would be heavily interlinked with literature she read. She also had many feelings and opinions about people, so here again there would be many attribution links. Also, more abstract concepts were important and would have been part of her context. For example, as we will see in Chapter 8, the guiding conception Woolf formed included the concepts of "reflection," "infinity," and "phantoms." Of course attributions and abstract concepts are important for most people engaged in creative endeavors. Thus my comments in this paragraph should be taken to apply broadly to creativity contexts.

Virginia Woolf thought of herself as, first, a reader. Her father Leslie Stephen's library was her first source of education, she read extensively throughout her life, and she made her livelihood writing book reviews and essays.

Woolf's reading was vast and encompassing, making this part of her context voluminous. As an example, in her essay "Hours in a Library" she lists nine books a reader—who may be herself, though the person is not named—read during the January when they were twenty, including Meredith's *Rhoda Fleming*, Fielding's *Tom Jones*, Hardy's *A Laodicean*,

Dewey's *Psychology*, and *The Book of Job*. She continues: "But if we follow the reader through his months [first half of the year] it is clear that he can have done practically nothing but read. Elizabethan literature is gone through with some thoroughness; he read a great deal of Webster, Browning, Shelley, Spenser, and Congreve; Peacock he read from start to finish; and most of Jane Austen's novels two or three times over. He read the whole of Meredith, the whole of Ibsen, and a little of Bernard Shaw." This passage gives a sense of both the scope and the volume of her reading. Even if these are not literally lists of books and authors she herself read when she was twenty, we can be confident she read these authors and read at this rate during many periods of her life.[1] To give a further example, in her journal for the year 1897 when she was fifteen, her first surviving journal, Woolf describes reading incessantly, mainly books her father gave her; she describes herself as eager to "devour" books, a characterization that captures her lifelong passion for reading.[2]

Not surprisingly, Woolf read especially widely and deeply in fiction. The list of English authors she describes reading is very extensive and includes Charles Dickens, Sir Walter Scott, William Thackeray, Anthony Trollope, Thomas Hardy, and George Meredith, among many others. And she did not read just one or two works by an author: when an author wrote many books, she read many if not all of them. She also read English poetry and describes her father reading poetry out loud to the children—Tennyson, Wordsworth, Coleridge, and others.[3] While these authors are all men, Woolf had an interest from early on, which grew very important to her, in women authors and was very familiar with the works of Jane Austen, the Brontës, Elizabeth Gaskell, and George Eliot, among others. She read widely in the literature of other nations as well, including American, French, and Russian.

Woolf read widely in earlier time periods as well as those more contemporary. She loved works of the Elizabethan period, and not just Shakespeare (though of course she knew him well) but writers we do not know as well today, such as Richard Hakluyt.[4] She was steeped in classics of antiquity, especially ancient Greece, one of her greatest literary loves. She describes translating Thucydides, Aristotle's *Poetics*, and Sophocles, and we know from references in her journals and reading notebooks that she read many classical Greek and Roman authors.[5] Dante was also a favorite.

It was not just literature that Woolf read. Her journals and reading notebooks are filled with references to biographies, collected letters, and memoirs, especially of literary figures such as Carlyle and Coleridge. She also read more general history, especially English history.[6]

Beginning in 1904, Woolf published many book reviews and essays—indeed this was how she earned her living in large part. Some of the books she reviewed were popular contemporary fiction. Although she was critical of many of these books, they still formed a part of the constellation of her literary knowledge and surely impacted how she thought about her own literary creative ambitions and ideas. She was more impressed by more literary writers such as Henry James, Wharton, Conrad, and the Russian authors Tolstoy, Chekhov, and especially Dostoevsky.[7] Woolf also wrote more integrative pieces about established or deceased authors. For these she would typically review many works by the author as well as surrounding biographical material and commentary. In part this reflects the influence of her father's interest, the way he emphasized placing literary works in their social and historical context. This was her method much of the time as well: when she would review an author's work, she would typically refer to biographical material as well.

What was the overall scale of Woolf's reading? Her essay "Hours in a Library" describes a reader reading nine books in a month, which extrapolates to more than one hundred books in a year. Of course the particular month may have been one of more than average reading—perhaps that is why she singles it out. However, her description listing what was read during the first half of that year affirms a similar pace. Still it may have been a year when she read more than average; at any rate we know that there were years when she was ill and would have read less. Taking this variability into account, it is still highly likely that she had read more than 1,000 books, and quite possibly 2,000 or more, by mid-1917 when she wrote "The Mark on the Wall."[8] It is also interesting that Virginia and Leonard Woolf's library lists more than 1,800 entries for which the publication date is prior to 1918, many multivolume works that were bequeathed to Virginia by her father and thus available to her from early on. We don't know which ones she read, but she most likely at least perused many if not most.[9] And not all the books Woolf read are listed in her library, as she also borrowed many books.

The above discussion gives a sense for the great breadth and depth of Woolf's literary base. This context would naturally be organized by historical time periods, genre, nationality, and gender. Each author and work has many "parents," as discussed in Chapter 3 for contexts in general, and there would also be lateral links among certain authors and works—for example stylistic resemblances, creating a network structure. Woolf engaged actively and conceptually with her reading both for her essays and as she developed her literary theories. Thus she would have been forging links among different authors and works based on themes, styles, characters, and settings, and also linked authors with biographical materials about them. There would also be many attribution links, for she had strong opinions about literature; I have not shown these in Figure 3 or discussed them directly, but they were central in her literary criticism and creative thinking about literature.

Thus Woolf created and lived within a rich web of literary context.

As important as the world of books was for Woolf, context in relation to her literary development includes more than this: it also includes critical domains of life experiences. I discuss two here: self and society (people), and places.

People were a hugely important part of Virginia Woolf's world. In "A Sketch of the Past" Woolf wrote that until she wrote *To the Lighthouse* in her forties, "the presence of my mother obsessed me. I could hear her voice, see her, imagine what she would do or say as I went about my day's doings." She described her mother as "central" to her childhood, "living so completely in her atmosphere that one never gets far enough away from her to see her as a person."[10] Clearly, there was much to work through psychologically when her mother died when Virginia was thirteen; it was her first bout of insanity, and the loss and her response all played a central part in Woolf's literary development.

Virginia Woolf's relationship with her father was different, but equally important. In "A Sketch of the Past" she recognizes that what she has felt about him is ambivalence. Until she wrote *To the Lighthouse*, she writes, "I would find my lips moving; I would be arguing with him; raging against him; saying to myself all that I never said to him." "But," she continues, "rage alternated with love." She was her father's chosen intellectual heir and felt a natural alliance with him. After her mother died, living with him was "like being shut up in the same cage with a wild beast"—he was demanding, histrionic, and self-centered. But after he died and Virginia was asked to write a brief note about him, her journal reveals how she labored to make it worthy.[11]

Woolf's siblings were also important. She idolized her elder brother Thoby, and his death after the family trip to Greece was yet another blow that she would work through in literary form in *Jacob's Room*.[12] Her sister, Vanessa, was her close companion. Her elder half-brothers George and Gerald, very Victorian and representative of the old order to her, were important, in negative if not positive ways.[13]

Woolf was part of the "Bloomsbury Group," and this exposed her to many new ideas. The Group met regularly at least some years, and Woolf also mentions in her journals and diary late night conversations with friends, many of whom were members of the Group. While we don't know the details, we do know there were lengthy discussions about values, art and aesthetics, and the new order; these conversations, often about the emerging "modernist" age, complemented her reading. Vanessa was an artist and opened the world of visual representation to her sister. In part through Vanessa, Woolf came in contact with artists and art critics, most notably Roger Fry, whose theories influenced her. Woolf was also friends or acquainted with other authors such as E. M. Forster, and her keen critical mind evaluated their works, seeing strengths and weaknesses.[14] And then, there was Leonard Woolf. He was immersed in politics, economics, and current events, and after Virginia married him, she would have become more aware of this world. There were huge social and cultural changes occurring—World War I, the underground, changes in dress and manners and the role of women—and she would ultimately interconnect these changes with her literary conception.

Another part of Woolf's context was places, including nature and cultural sites. These were important personally and figured in her literary experimentation. It is striking that in her biography, Hermione Lee's first chapter after her introductory remarks is entitled "Houses." It begins fittingly with St. Ives, the seaside town where Woolf and her family vacationed during their summer holidays when Virginia was young. This place formed a deep and lasting memory for Virginia Woolf that she memorialized in *To the Lighthouse*. Woolf wrote many descriptions of natural scenes during her travels, and this was an important facet of her literary explorations.[15] The ancient Greeks and their arts were for Woolf an ultimate standard of beauty: "How I wish something would tear away the veil which still separates me from the Greeks," she wrote in 1905 while reading Sophocles. She visited Greece with her siblings in 1906 and was awestruck at the beauty, especially of the classical buildings and ruins; she described the Parthenon as "still radiant and young."[16] She also loved to walk as her father had, and had a lifelong interest in gardening.[17]

Woolf not only made many connections within her literary context, but there were also linkages that spanned the different realms of her context that were important. She admired ancient Greek literature and art enormously and translated works in Greek; as noted above, when she traveled to Greece she was awestruck at the classical buildings and ruins. She linked literary descriptions with visual representations, spurred most likely by her sister Vanessa, Roger Fry, and the aesthetic milieu she was a part of. She also linked works of fictions with the lives of their authors, an approach she inherited from her father.

Probably the most important large-scale interconnection in Woolf's sense of her context in the years leading up to the creative break that occurred in her mid-thirties (when she formed a guiding conception that led into her innovative modernist period) was actually a split: the sharp contrast between the old Victorian order, epitomized for her especially by her father and his friends, and the emerging new order she associated with her social circle and Bloomsbury. The old order was male dominated and constrained by rules, and had an outmoded aesthetic. The new order embraced different lifestyles and aesthetics, and was at least tending toward being more open in regard to the role of women. But up until she formed her guiding conception, she had not forged a coherent conception that would enable her to engage with this split in her creative literary endeavors—at least we have no record of such, though there were precursors.

CLIFFORD POSSUM

Clifford Possum Tjapaltjarri is one of the most highly regarded Indigenous modern artists of Australia. He is celebrated as one of the leading figures of the contemporary art movement that began at Papunya in the 1970s. In this section I outline his context around the time he began painting at Papunya, focusing on the parts most relevant for his art. My discussion of Possum's life and context draws especially on Vivien Johnson's excellent biography *Clifford Possum Tjapaltjarri* based on twenty years of engagement with Possum and his art.

Possum was a member of the Anmatyerre people of central Australia. He was born in the early 1930s at Napperby Creek and moved to Papunya in the 1960s, which is where he produced the art I discuss in this book. I divide Possum's context into four major parts: (1) places: places he lived and worked and sites that were important to him for cultural and religious reasons; (2) the Dreaming: central to Indigenous culture, the basis of the fabric of existence, stories of creation of places and ancestral beings from which all life is derived, holding meanings that inform cultural and social norms; (3) expression: his art and artistic context; and (4) society: the people and groups he knew and engaged with who influenced his development.

Figure 4 depicts Possum's context as a network. Note the clear hierarchical structure and how many elements have multiple links. The four major parts of the context are shown from left to right: Places, the Dreaming, Expression, and Society.

Despite its complexity, this figure depicts just a fraction of Possum's extensive knowledge and context. The schematic way I have arranged and labeled elements cannot be said to be the way Possum himself

IMAGE 2. CLIFFORD POSSUM TJAPALTJARRI, PAPUNYA, 1980. Gelatin silver photograph, 25.5 × 20.5 cm. Gift of J V S Megaw, Collection of Flinders University Museum of Art 5320 ©J V S Megaw.

would have viewed his context, and his own sense of context would have been fluid depending on circumstances and focus. Nonetheless the figure helps us gain a sense for the elements and interconnections, which in turn helps us understand his creative development and art.

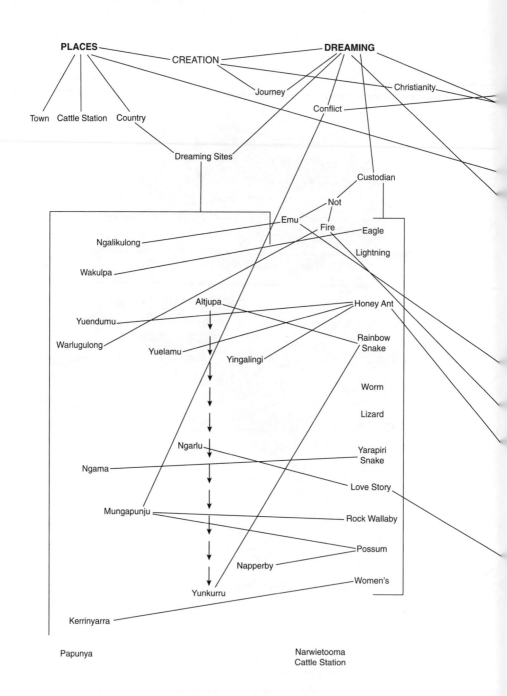

FIGURE 4. CLIFFORD POSSUM CONTEXT

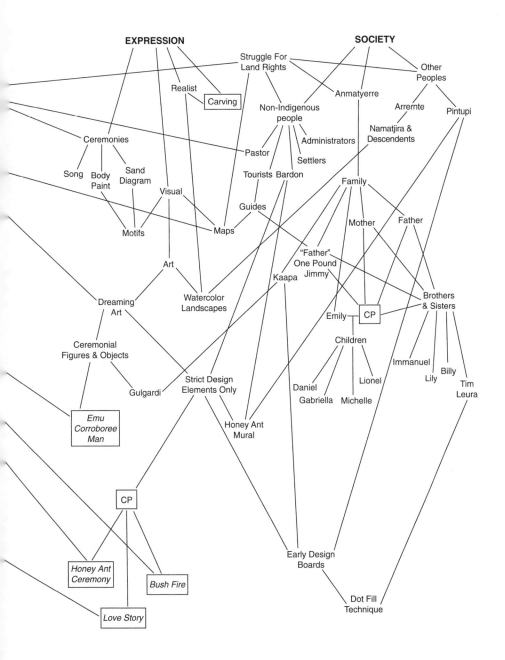

A box with CP inside signifies Clifford Possum.
A box with other wording inside signifies artwork created by Clifford Possum.

Consider first the left side of Figure 4. The *Places* category is at the far left. This is Possum's "country" where he lived most of his life and that was the traditional home of his Anmatyerre people. Places are shown in approximate geographic relation to one another, according to a Western sense of geography. While the Indigenous peoples of Australia share knowlege of the same four basic directions, their sense of geography centers on specific sites and their interrelationships; they have a mental map that is continually updating as they travel, so in this regard the figure is overly static.[18] There are two towns shown, Napperby and Papunya, and one cattle station on which Possum worked, Narwietooma. The remaining sites are his "country" (Napperby is as well) and are labeled with their traditional Anmatyerre names. The left-central part of Figure 4 shows the part of his context concerned with the *Dreaming*. Some of the Dreaming characters of which Possum had custodianship are listed, including Possum, Rainbow Snake, Eagle, and Honey Ant. Two additional Dreaming figures are also shown, Emu and Fire, which he did not have custodianship over (although there was a family connection) but used in paintings.

The Dreaming is central to the Indigenous peoples of Australia and their culture. An important cultural feature is that particular Dreaming figures are associated with particular sites through creation tales. In this way the physical world is infused with the Dreaming.[19] These connections are shown in the figure with horizontal links. For example the Honey Ant Dreaming has stories associating it with three sites shown in the figure—Yinyalingi, Yuendumu, and Yuelamu. Many Dreaming stories involve journeys, and one such journey is shown in the figure: the Rainbow Snake traveling from Altjupa to Yunkurru. Possum had more Dreaming figures than are shown, and many more site-Dreaming combinations; the figure depicts a sample, while the full set would have been an extraordinarily rich set of interconnections. His knowledge extended far beyond his own Dreamings and sites: in her biography Johnson repeatedly refers to his "encyclopedic knowledge" of the Anmatyerre culture and Dreamings.[20]

Now consider the right side of Figure 4. *Society* on the far right depicts individuals and social groups that were important for Possum.

First and foremost were his people, the Anmatyerre. Possum's biological father died when he was young, and he was raised by his mother and adoptive father Gwoya Tjungurrayi, known as "One Pound Jimmy," famous in his day in Australia for being featured on a postal stamp that sold a large number of copies. One Pound Jimmy served as a guide to Western visitors to the area, a link shown in the figure. In turn this provides a link to Western-style maps that Possum would have been aware of, for maps were constructed to aid these visitors; this is relevant for the guiding conception he formed.[21] Possum was raised with several "brothers" (not necessarily biologically related but raised together), including Billy Stockman and Tim Leura, who played an important role in his painting along with his cousin Kaapa.[22] Clifford Possum married his wife Emily in the 1960s, and they had four children, all of whom had been born by the time Possum entered into the creative phase discussed in this book.

A second branch under *Society* links to additional Indigenous peoples of the central desert region. It lists two of several that could be shown, Arrernte and Pintupi. A third branch lists non-Indigenous people with whom Possum interacted. This branch includes a node for the pastor who introduced Possum to Christianity when he was a child staying in the town of Hermannsburg. It also includes nodes for settlers and administrators—Possum was a cattle hand much of his life and interacted with the cattle ranchers, and he came into contact with administrators in the towns, including Papunya and Alice Springs. It also includes a node for travelers, who would have included the tourists to whom Possum sold his carvings and paintings, and a node for Geoffrey Bardon, the art teacher who played an important role in the emergence of the Papunya painting movement.

To the left of *Society* is the struggle for land rights. At the time Clifford Possum grew up, non-Indigenous white Australia focused on assimilating the Indigenous peoples, who had little voice of their own and essentially no legal rights to the lands they had inhabited for generations. This included a policy of bringing Indigenous people living in the bush into reserves, where they lived in crowded, often squalid conditions.[23] Clifford Possum and his family had this experience, and Possum himself was born in the bush but ultimately lived mainly in towns.[24] Beginning in the mid-twentieth century, the Indigenous populations engaged in a struggle for greater self-determination and preservation of their culture.[25] This struggle has had many dimensions, including political, economic, social, and cultural. One of the most important has been Indigenous peoples seeking to reclaim rights to their traditional lands. Land is paramount for traditional culture of the Indigenous peoples of Australia, at the very heart of cultural identity and the Dreaming, as shown by the links of specific Dreamings with specific sites.[26] Beginning around the time Possum moved to Papunya, the struggle to regain rights to land gained force. And it culminated, at least at that time, in legislation and lawsuits that have enabled Indigenous peoples to reclaim some of their land, including the landmark Aboriginal Land Rights (Northern Territory) Act of 1976.[27] While Possum was not a central figure in this struggle politically, he was well aware of it, and it was important to him. Further, its inherently spatial, land-focused orientation relates naturally to visual art, and this connection was not lost on him.[28] The struggle for land rights has involved much conflict between Indigenous and non-Indigenous peoples, and this is indicated in Figure 4 as something Possum would have been well aware of.

Also on the right side of Figure 4 is *Expression*, which depicts Possum's artistic context and work. The left branch links to ceremonies, traditional forms of ritual expression linked to the Dreaming that incorporate song, body paint, and sand diagrams. The abstract motifs of the traditional body paint and sand diagrams were an important basis for the modern art movement, and that connection is shown in the figure, via a link down to visual motifs.[29] On the right side of the Expression section is a node for carving; the box around the node indicates, here and throughout this part of the figure, that this refers to Possum's own artistic creation. Possum began carving in his youth and was highly accomplished at it. He earned significant income from selling carvings to tourists for many years. His carvings were highly realistic renderings of animals, notably lizards and snakes, hence the link to realist forms of expression; according to Johnson they were realistic to the point of being unsettling.[30]

The center branch under *Expression* links to visual forms of expression. This node in turn has three branches. The right-hand branch links to maps, which were important in the struggle for land rights and also as guides for travelers to the central Australian region, a link that in turn extends to Possum's adoptive father One Pound Jimmy as noted above. The left-hand branch links to visual motifs, which as noted above are linked with ceremonial forms of expression, in particular body paint and sand diagrams. The central branch links to art, specifically painting. This node in turn has two branches. The one on the right links to watercolors. This was an important art form for Possum because Albert Namatjira, the most famous Indigenous artist in Australia of the preceding generation, painted watercolor landscapes. Possum met Namatjira when he was a young man beginning to achieve recognition for his artistic talents as a carver. According to several sources Namatjira asked Possum if he wanted to study under him, but Possum declined:

> See—Namatjira asked me, "You want learn watercolour painting, carry on my work?" But I said, "No No. I do it my way. Carving—start from carving."[31]

Here Possum ruled out certain directions he could have gone artistically, which is a key part of finding focus in a large-scale context.

The left-hand branch under art in the figure opens downward to represent the artistic context at Papunya in which Possum participated. The art movement began around 1971 and was catalyzed by Geoffrey Bardon, an art teacher who encouraged the Indigenous people he met to paint. The first node down is Dreaming art, because from the beginning the paintings centered on depicting Dreamings, indicated also by the link up to the *Dreaming* top category. In turn, Dreaming art divides into two branches, reflecting an important sequence and shift in style that occurred as the art movement developed. The node on the left, ceremonial figures and objects, refers to early paintings done at Papunya that showed figures in ritual dress surrounded by ceremonial objects. According to Possum, he and Kaapa and Tim Leura were engaged in painting prior to the movement Bardon catalyzed, and continued to paint in their own independent style led by Kaapa.[32] The most famous of these early paintings is Kaapa's *Gulgardi*, linked in the figure. Possum also began in this style, even when he began painting with Bardon's group in early 1972: his first painting in affiliation with Bardon was *Emu Corroboree Man*, linked in the figure. This painting depicts an Emu Dreaming ceremony and thus is linked to the Emu Dreaming on the left side of Figure 4—interestingly, a Dreaming of which Possum was not custodian but rather that "belonged" to Kaapa, who surely knew and gave permission for Possum to paint it.

Although early paintings figured ceremonial figures and objects, the movement shifted to representing the Dreaming more abstractly. Bardon emphasized repeatedly to the painters that they should eschew Western-style representation, such as human figures, and instead paint solely with the traditional design motifs. The node labeled "strict design elements only" represents this principle and has links both to Bardon and to the motifs node above. Under Bardon's influence, and perhaps reflecting as well their own cultural sensibilities, the Indigenous painters embraced this approach.[33] The most famous early work in this style was the *Honey Ant Mural* painted on the side of the school house in June 1971, executed by Pintupi painters, as shown by the link to them in the figure, with encouragement from Bardon.[34] After this, a series of early design boards were executed as shown in the figure; they are called boards because they were done on spare sheets of wood, cartons, whatever was handy. A key innovation was the development of the dot fill technique—this is shown with its own node—that became a hallmark of the Papunya painting school. While many individuals were involved in this innovation, Possum's brother Tim Leura developed his own subtle aesthetic dot fill technique with which Possum would have been very familiar, hence the link to him.[35] Under "strict design elements only" is a link down to *CP* or Clifford Possum, and under this link are shown three important early paintings Possum executed after *Emu Corroboree Man*, embracing the abstract design style: *Honey Ant Ceremony*, which has (is believed to include) an association with Yinyalingi; his well-known *Man's Love Story* associated with Ngarlu; and several paintings of the fire at Warlugulong, represented by the node *Bush Fire*. In all cases links are shown to the Dreamings, and these in turn link to the sites. These paintings were completed just before Possum took the critical creative step of forming the powerful guiding conception, described in Chapter 8, that launched him into the next phase of his creative development.

A number of important facets of Possum's artistic context are not shown in Figure 4. He had mastered strong technical artistic skills by the time he began painting at Papunya. And as he often emphasized, a key motivation for his painting was transmitting traditional culture and its stories to younger individuals. The figure must be viewed as a simplification with much omitted. But it gives a sense of his context, including the rich linkages between the four major areas that proved so central to his artistic creativity.

HANS KREBS

Biochemist Hans Krebs made important discoveries in the field of metabolism, including the discovery of the chemical processes for the synthesis of urea and the Krebs cycle of carbohydrate metabolism. We have considerable information about his career and scientific path, including his training, mainly due to Frederic Holmes's masterful biography *Hans Krebs: The Formation of a Scientific Life*. For my analysis I have also drawn on Krebs's own statements and a number of other texts.[36] His case is a valuable illustrative example of my model of the creative process.

Here I depict Krebs's knowledge context around the time he was completing his apprenticeship training and establishing his own independent lab. As for Clifford Possum I depict his context as a network with many vertical hierarchy links and some lateral links. I focus on two main parts of Krebs's context: scientific and medical knowledge and information, and laboratory methods. Other parts of his context, including people and general knowledge and beliefs, were important, but I include them mainly in terms of how they directly impacted his scientific development. The broader social context, especially World War I and German politics and culture, including the hyperinflation and the great political turbulence, including the rise of the Nazis, were

IMAGE 3. HANS KREBS, 1924. Reprinted by Permission from *Hans Krebs: The Formation of a Scientific Life, 1900-1933*, Oxford University Press.

also important and impactful on Krebs, but less directly relevant to his scientific development during this time; thus, while recognizing that they were surely relevant, I omit them from my discussion.[37]

Figure 5 depicts Krebs's context. This figure is *not* intended to show all of the details of his context. It includes those details that are most salient in terms of what he learned in greatest depth, what impacted him the most, and what he spent the most time on.

The left side of the figure depicts *Concepts*, especially field knowledge. It includes medicine on the left, chemistry in the center (described in the greatest detail), as well as a branch for broader knowledge on the far left, and branches for biology and physics.[38]

Krebs chose medicine as his profession. His college coursework revolved around preparation for this career with classes in many aspects of medicine, including genetics, botany, and psychiatry. In most of these areas Krebs had just a single course and did not focus on the subject, while in others, notably anatomy and physiology, he went into considerable depth.[39] Krebs chose internal medicine as an area of specialization, and thus this is a central branch in the figure. Krebs's father was a doctor, and Krebs was following in his footsteps in choosing medicine.

One topic that Krebs found very interesting was intermediary metabolism, the study of the reactions that occurred in an organism through which it broke down inputs extracting energy and nutrients. This topic is shown in the lower left side of the figure under physiological chemistry (also linked to the medical field of physiology), metabolic processes, and carbohydrate chemistry. His first exposure to intermediary metabolism was a course in college from Franz Knoop, a pioneer in the field who had discovered the fatty acid β-oxidation reaction.[40] Knoop was inspiring: "The true goal of biochemistry," he wrote, "is to reduce the chemical transformations to an unbroken series of equations that will permit an overview of all phases of synthesis and decomposition, of the binding of energy and its release."[41] Knoop's viewpoint stood in contrast to the traditional focus on just the inputs an organism took in and the outputs it produced, with little attention to the intermediate steps through which it converted inputs to energy, nutrients, and waste

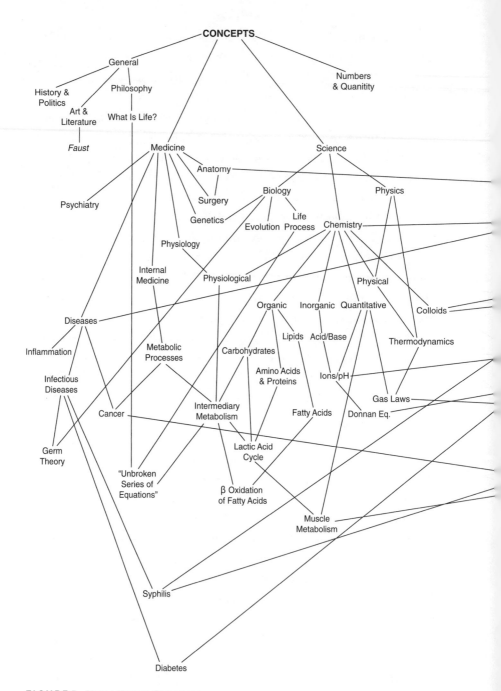

FIGURE 5. HANS KREBS CONTEXT

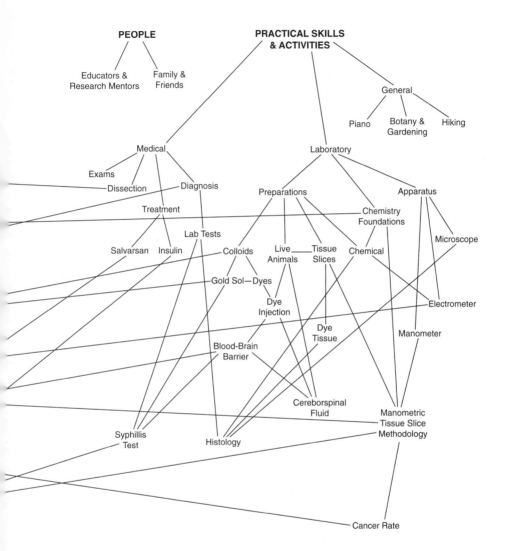

products. The figure shows a link from Knoop's quote—visionary in its goal for intermediary metabolism—to a topic under general concepts, "what is life," which Krebs viewed as important in grounding medicine and medical-biochemical research. Krebs tended to believe that life could be explained by physical-chemical processes but also recognized that this was a personal view and not fully decidable.[42]

As part of his later medical training, Krebs had a course in internal medicine that included lectures on metabolic processes, including metabolic diseases, which further stimulated his interest. He learned about insulin, recently discovered, and its power to help diabetics. He also learned from his friend Bruno Mendel about Otto Warburg's important ongoing research in cancer metabolism, and from Mendel and a second friend about the important work that had been done on muscle metabolism and the lactic acid cycle in muscle tissue.[43] These elements of his knowledge base are shown in the figure.

Around the time he was completing his education, Krebs had the clear sense, as he stated it later to his biographer Holmes, "that chemistry was fundamental to the further development of medicine," and that he would like to pursue research "based somehow on physiological chemistry."[44] The course with Knoop and his excitement about intermediary metabolism was surely part of this, and it led him to take more courses in chemistry. This is a good illustration of how excitement about a topic can shape a person's path and influence how their knowledge context develops. The left side of Figure 5 depicts the main areas of chemistry Krebs learned: inorganic, organic, physical, and quantitative. It also shows physiological chemistry, which has links up to both chemistry and physiology and down to intermediary metabolism.

Certain specific topics that Krebs learned about in detail are also shown in the figure. One of his research projects in college focused on the dispersion of dyes related to tissue staining, a topic grounded in colloid chemistry, which focuses on the suspension of particles in solution. Colloid chemistry was a burgeoning field of investigation, and Krebs followed up this project by taking a course in colloid chemistry and reading independently. During his clinical training Krebs engaged in additional directed research that also centered on colloid chemistry as well as physical chemistry. The first part of this research focused on examining the properties of gold sols, which had fairly recently been identified as a means to diagnose syphilis based on their color reaction in cerebrospinal fluid. In the second part of the research Krebs studied the passage of substances from the blood into the cerebrospinal fluid—crossing the blood-brain barrier. He realized as he reviewed the literature that this problem was not well understood. A paper he read that had just been published suggested use of the Donnan equilibrium equation to explore this question, and this spurred him to explore this approach.[45]

The right side of Figure 5 shows the other main part of Krebs's context, his *Practical Skills and Activities*. This part divides into three branches: medical, laboratory, and a branch on the far right for general activities and hobbies.[46] There is also an abbreviated segment for people, which could of course be greatly expanded.

The medical branch is divided into 4 parts: dissection, exams, diagnosis, and treatment. Although Krebs had training in all of these (for example many courses in dissection), he received the most in-depth training in the area of diagnosis, specifically laboratory and chemical-based diagnosis. The figure shows links from this node to the diseases node on the left side of the figure. Under treatment there are two branches, insulin for treating diabetes and salvarsan for treating syphilis.

The laboratory part of the right side of Figure 5 divides into three parts: apparatus, chemistry foundations, and preparations. Listed under these are more specialized areas of expertise that Krebs acquired either through courses or research experience. For example, preparations branches into four kinds: colloids, which he gained experience preparing in his research project on gold sols; live animals, which he worked with in the project exploring which compounds cross the blood-brain barrier, injecting dyes and then drawing cerebrospinal fluid; tissue slices, which he learned how to prepare and fix; and general chemical preparations. Chemical preparations also have a parent link to chemistry foundations and should be thought of as including many different reagents and conditions with which he gained familiarity. These details are omitted for parsimony.[47]

Krebs's most important laboratory training occurred with Otto Warburg, whose lab he entered as a research assistant after completing his medical training.[48] Warburg pioneered the development of manometric techniques that allowed quantitative measurement of the rate at which reactions proceeded. The method required the preparation of tissue slices, in which intact cells continued to have metabolic activity. Given the setup, Warburg's methods allowed measurement of the rate of respiration in living cells by measuring the rate of consumption of oxygen as well as the rate of production of carbon dioxide, also a key indicator of metabolic activity, and other gases. Warburg had developed a set of mathematical calculations to translate the manometric readings into measures of rates of consumption or production of individual gases. Krebs mastered the manometric techniques during his first several months in Warburg's lab. The figure links manometric tissue slice methodology with manometer, tissue slices, chemistry foundations, and gas laws; a link is also shown to muscle metabolism as an application.[49]

Warburg had discovered that tumors had a higher rate of metabolic activity. This is why under the manometric tissue slice methodology I include a link to cancer rates, which links to cancer the disease on the left side of the figure. During his time in the lab, Krebs worked on projects under Warburg's guidance, including a project investigating the rate of metabolism in human cancer tissue.[50]

Note that there a considerable number of links in Figure 5 between the left and right sides of the figure. Thus dissection is part of practical medical training but links to anatomy on the *Concepts* side of the figure. Likewise, there is a link between chemistry on the *Concepts* side and chemistry foundations on the right, and between the manometric tissue slice methodology and gas laws because these laws were central to the calculations of manometric rates of reaction. As noted above, there is a link crossing the figure from measuring cancer cell rates of metabolism using the manometric tissue slice methodology to cancer the disease, which reflects Warburg's main focus in his lab, measuring rates of metabolism in cancer cells. These cross-linkages can be important for an individual forming guiding conceptions and seeking creative opportunities.

COMPARISONS

Comparisons of the contexts of Woolf, Possum, and Krebs reveal both similarities and differences. All three contexts have the feature that there are a few large topic areas, each of which has many elements. This fits with the hierarchical nature of context. In addition, as noted in the discussions of Possum and Krebs, many bottom elements have multiple parents and there are links between top elements. Beyond these similarities there are some differences. If we compare Krebs's context to Possum's—the two depicted in most detail—the nature of the structure and complexity is different. Krebs's has considerable vertical depth in a number of parts but relatively fewer horizontal linkages. Possum's in contrast has many horizontal links, creating a highly integrated structure. Some of the difference may reflect the representation I have chosen, but I believe there is a real difference. In part this reflects their different creative domains, science and art, but also in part their different cultural contexts.

More broadly in terms of how context develops, the stories of these three individuals show us that context is often built up from roles and exposure to new learning and cultural movements. For Krebs, being exposed to new frontiers in biology and chemistry as a student and then working as a lab technician in an innovative lab were critical for his development. For Possum, the art movement at Papunya was central in spurring his own artistic development. For Woolf, her reading was more self-directed but linked to her father and her family background; in addition she wrote many reviews, and the books she read for these reviews as well as writing the reviews clearly informed her developing ideas about literature.

The stories also show that context can be wide ranging. In particular, Woolf and Possum share in common that technical learning in their field was important for their development, but so were broader social concerns. For Woolf, beyond her very extensive reading, the split between the old Victorian order (represented for her personally by her father) and the new worldview of her Bloomsbury circle was a key cultural factor, while for Possum the issue of the struggle for

Indigenous land rights and preservation of the traditional way of life were important broader cultural and political factors. From the perspective of managing creativity, if we consider applying the framework to think about the context of someone currently engaged in a creative endeavor, given that what is important only becomes clear after the fact, so to speak, it is wise to cast a wide net, recognizing that factors that do not appear directly relevant may turn out to be critical.

Describing context is important and requires gathering and organizing a great deal of information. I have presented three examples to illustrate how context can be modeled as a network. Many additional individuals will appear in this book: Albert Einstein, Steve Jobs, engineer and transgender activist Lynn Conway, Twitter cofounder Jack Dorsey, and others. Each had or has a rich context like the ones described. Their contexts will not always be described or will be described just in brief in order to keep this work to a manageable length. That should not take away from the important lesson that to understand an individual's creative path and contribution, we must understand their context.

CHAPTER 4

MODELING CONTEXT

In this chapter I introduce the formal model of context, focusing mainly on the simulation branch of the analysis. I describe the methodology I use to generate simulated contexts and then present statistics about the contexts generated using this methodology. These contexts are analyzed in subsequent chapters to explore implications of the model. The analytic model together with the simulation analysis should be thought of as offering complementary information and insights to the case studies. When these different approaches converge in their implications, this offers good support for the overall framework; when they diverge, this shows areas for further development.

Following the discussion of the structure of context and the case study examples in the preceding chapters, the simulated contexts are networks. These networks have a hierarchical form and include lateral links that add additional connectivity.

LEVELS AND LINK STRUCTURE

The analytic modeling and simulations focus on contexts that consist of two levels. The top level contains broader elements, the bottom level more specific, narrower elements. For example, *dog* is more general, *poodle* a specific breed of dog. Real-world contexts generally have more than two levels. This is true for dogs, as there are often multiple types associated with specific breeds, as shown in Figure 1 for poodles. It is also true for the empirical cases in this book: Hans Krebs's context as depicted in Figure 5 has 7 levels, and the right-hand side of Possum's context depicted in Figure 4 has 6.

Notwithstanding that empirical cases are more complex, two levels are sufficient to develop the main theoretical approach, and the parsimony of this representation makes it simpler to describe, model, and simulate. The key distinction between the levels is that bottom-level elements do not have any children, whereas top-level elements can and generally do. I discuss extending the model to more levels in Chapter 16.[1]

The simplest type of context is a hierarchy or tree. For this case, the two-level context has two key parameters that determine its size. The first is the number of top elements, and the second is the number of bottom elements—children—associated with each top element parent. The simplest case of this type of structure is one in which the number of children is the same for each parent. More generally parents differ in their number of children; this is the main case I focus on, and it fits better with empirical data.

Creativity contexts have two types of additional links. First, bottom elements may have additional links to top elements, that is, additional parents. The example given earlier was the goldendoodle, a crossbreed linked to both the poodle and the golden retriever as parent breeds. An example in Hans Krebs's context is gold sols, which are both colloids and solutions that can be used for diagnosing syphilis. These examples are cases in which the second parent link is also a topic, so that the bottom element is a subtopic of each parent. Alternatively additional parents may be attributes. These attributes also reside on the top level because they are general, and they link to bottom elements that have them as attributes or are associated with them. For example, a poodle may be friendly or old, and a particular medicine may be widely viewed as effective. It is possible to label these different types of vertical links—topic or attribute—to make the distinction clear. This labeling approach is used in some parts of the knowledge representation literature, but I do not use labels in order to keep the modeling as simple as possible and focus on other issues.[2]

The second type of additional link is lateral: elements on a level may have links with each other. These lateral links capture a variety of kinds of connection, such as conceptual affinity or opposition, topic links, and personal, historical, and cultural links. In Krebs's context, for example, there is a lateral link between colloids as a field of study in chemistry and colloids as laboratory preparations. In the broader culture, values or attributes may be linked because their roles in the history or culture are viewed as connected, the way, for example, beauty and truth are linked in the minds of some people, and some people view freedom and creativity as linked. Such lateral links enable an individual, through associative conceptual thinking, to travel considerable lateral distances in the network.

I confine my models to lateral links between top elements. Lateral links between bottom elements may also be important in some contexts, especially for detailed search and experimentation on projects—such as shifting from one shade of a color to a second adjacent shade while working on a painting, or substituting one element for a second related one in designing a product.[3] However, my focus is primarily on conceptual guidance, for which top lateral links are especially salient.

In general, the number of links any particular element has varies. For an empirical case study this can be specified directly. For example, in Hans Krebs's context the number of parent links that elements have varies a great deal; further, some higher-level elements have many lateral links, others none or few. For abstract mathematical modeling I employ stochastic approaches to generate links. The key parameters specify (i) the average number of additional parent links each bottom element has and (ii) the average number of additional lateral links each top element has.[4]

Figure 2 (p. 39) is a small-scale example of the kind of network used in this book. There are 7 top-level "parent" elements and 18 bottom-level "children." Note that many of the children have multiple parents, and there are lateral links between top elements. The networks I generate via computational simulation, described below, have similar structure but are far larger in scale.

I use abstract mathematical modeling to explore how the features of contexts in which individuals engage in creativity influence their creative process. One question is which types of approaches are "good" ones in given kinds of contexts. For example, which forms of guidance work best in given kinds of contexts, and how does what works best vary with context features? Other questions have to do with outcomes and creative paths. For example, are some highly desirable creative outcomes harder to reach than others, and how does this relate to their location in the network and the guidance strategies individuals use?[5]

GENERATING CONTEXTS

I generate several different types of network contexts via computational simulation. I describe how this is done in this section and the next; details of the construction are presented in the notes. In later chapters I present analysis of how creative guidance functions in these simulated contexts.

The two key features of the generated contexts are scale and structure. Real creativity contexts are large scale, containing hundreds, thousands, or even more elements. This makes modeling and analysis challenging, but also potentially highly illuminating. Analysis of these large-scale contexts sheds light on how best to go about being creative in larger-scale contexts and also provides insights into the nature of creativity in these kinds of contexts.

I specify scale in terms of two parameters: the first is the number of top elements, and the second is the total number of bottom elements, defined as a multiple of the number of top elements. For computer modeling I consider two network sizes.

The simplest type of network is a hierarchy in which each bottom element has just one parent. Although I do not believe most contexts have this form, it is useful for building intuition about guidance. An especially simple hierarchy is one in which each top element has the same number of children. More general hierarchies are stochastic, which means that top elements can differ in the number of children they have. For simulations I begin from this stochastic hierarchy, then add links.

To generate a stochastic hierarchy I use the following protocol: for each bottom element, select one top element at random and connect the bottom element to it. This ensures that every bottom element has a link to a top element and is not isolated, while for top elements the number of links is stochastic.[6] I use these simple hierarchy networks to show the logic of the model and for some simple illustrative calculations.

For computer modeling I use richer network structures, building on the stochastic hierarchy in two ways. One, I specify models in which bottom elements can have multiple parents. This type of structure resembles a lattice in some respects, and I refer to it as the lattice model; it can also be described as a bipartite graph. Two, I specify full network models—my focus for the simulations—in which, in addition to the lattice structure, some top elements are linked.

I specify three kinds of network models. The first is a random network model. For this case, beginning from a stochastic hierarchy, I generate additional top-bottom ("parent-child") links: for each parent-child pair not already linked, I draw a random value that determines whether they are connected; the probability of a link is the same for all pairs, and the draws across pairs are independent.[7] Likewise, I generate lateral links between top elements with the probability of each link identical and the draws independent.

The two additional types of network models modify the random network model. One focuses on the degree distribution for top elements. A large body of work has shown that many real-world networks have the property that a relatively small proportion of nodes have high degree, meaning they are central in the network with many links to other nodes, whereas most nodes have relatively low degree.[8] A well-known example is the Internet: a few websites have very high traffic compared with most websites. Another example is the pattern of citation data of both academic and patent citations.[9] Interestingly, the representation of the brain as a network also exhibits this phenomenon, with nodes either individual neurons or brain regions, although at least some of the evidence suggests it may be less pronounced than other applications.

Given that the contexts I describe can be thought of as the mental representations individuals develop based on their experiences and learning, thus instantiated in the brain, this provides at least some support for the view that creativity contexts as networks also may exhibit this feature.[10]

The most commonly used model to describe these kinds of networks has been a power law model (described in the next section and the notes and references).[11] I follow the literature and use this model to generate a set of simulated networks in which some top nodes have high degree. I note that some recent statistical analyses find that many networks in which a few nodes have relatively high degree do not exactly match the power law model; nevertheless, it is a reasonable approximation and appropriate for my purpose, which is not to fit exact empirical data but rather to explore the creativity framework I present and its implications in general.[12]

It is also important to note that the examples that have been described fitting the power law model are not specifically creativity contexts; hence it is not immediately apparent whether a power law is applicable for the kinds of context networks studied in this book. While recognizing that we simply do not know enough about the nature of creativity contexts at the moment to be able to characterize the degree distribution in detail, this kind of distribution is likely to be important for creativity. It makes sense that certain higher-level elements in a field may be very central in the network and influence the creative work of many individuals. These elements may be well-known assumptions, principles, or paradigms that inform thinking and work in the field widely. These elements are likely to have more links to bottom elements because they are part of many creative projects and also more links to other top elements because they inform higher-level understanding in the field. The networks I generate allow for this linkage pattern. Some bottom elements may also have a high degree beyond what is predicted by the random network model—for example a given component that is widely used; however, this seems less directly pertinent to creativity guidance, and I do not incorporate this into the networks.

To the extent it does fit creativity contexts, the power law model has a number of interesting features for the pursuit of creativity. First, projects that are composed of elements that are linked to parents of low degree may be inherently "harder to find" because they are more isolated in the context. This doesn't necessarily mean they are inherently more valuable, but it does mean they are more of a rare contribution and therefore may be quite unique. Hence it is of interest to explore what kinds of guidance are best for finding them. Second, upper-level elements with many links may be powerful forces for guidance since they can generate many creative possibilities and paths to explore. However, they also may tend to lead to more typical kinds of projects that are more likely to also be discovered by others. An interesting question I explore is the relationship between guiding conceptions that have high degree and thus can spawn many potential projects and how rare those projects are. Finally, degree is also important for calculations of shortest paths, with high-degree elements typically having shorter paths to other elements; this is important for the way I describe the function of guiding principles.

The other network structure I model is clustering, the tendency for elements in a network to be organized into clusters. In cluster networks elements within a cluster are highly interconnected to each other and have fewer connections to other network elements outside the cluster. Clustering has been identified as an important feature of many networks, including many social and biological networks.[13] Although clustering is mainly associated with these network applications, clustering makes a great deal sense for conceptual networks, since concepts are naturally grouped (for example by topic) and concepts in the same group (for example subtopics under a given topic) are more likely to link with other concepts in the group. Hans Krebs's context clearly shows this kind of clustering (for example within the domain of laboratory preparations). Utilizing this principle of concept groupings, I form clusters in my context networks based on top elements.

Clustering is likely to be important for modeling creativity especially because in a network with a high degree of clustering, elements in different clusters may be quite far apart. Given that making connections between elements that are distant from one another can be highly creative, it is clear that there may be many opportunities for creativity in highly clustered networks. Thus to the extent that creativity contexts are organized in this kind of cluster structure, this can provide opportunities for creativity and also may impact creative strategies.

GENERATED CONTEXTS

I generate a set of networks for each of the three models outlined above—random, power law, and cluster. All networks have two levels. The number of top elements is denoted N. I generate networks for two different scales: small scale, $N = 100$ and large scale, $N = 1,000$. The large scale is reasonably large and thus helps demonstrate the creativity model at larger scale; however, it is still undoubtedly smaller than many real-world creativity contexts. I define the total number of bottom elements as a multiple m of the number of top elements: the number of bottom elements is mN. I fix m at 3 for both scales, thus maintaining the same ratio of bottom to top elements as scale increases. There are thus 300 bottom elements for the small-scale networks and 3,000 bottom elements for the large-scale networks. Table 1 summarizes this basic information about the different types of network contexts.

Taking into account the three types of networks and two scales, there are 6 different types of contexts in total. For each I generate 10 networks using simulation following the protocols described below. I assume independence across draws for all simulations, but note that probabilities of links between elements vary in both the power law and cluster models. Independence is a strong assumption, and it would certainly be useful to explore implications of relaxing this assumption.

TABLE 1. SIMULATED NETWORK CONTEXTS

	Small Scale	**Large Scale**
N: Number of Top Elements	100	1,000
m: Ratio of Bottom to Top Elements	3	3
$m x N$: Number of Bottom Elements	300	3,000
	Random	Random
Types of Networks:	Cluster	Cluster
	Power Law	Power Law

For all the networks I start from the stochastic hierarchy model introduced in the previous section: for each bottom element I select one of the top elements at random and link the bottom element with it.

In order to generate a random network context, I proceed in two additional steps. First, for each bottom element I consider each top element that it has not been linked with in the initial hierarchy and make a random draw to determine whether the two are linked. I set the probability of a link in this random draw such that each bottom element has on average one additional parent link.[14] Pair outcomes (realizations) are assumed to be independent of one another, and a child cannot link again to the parent it linked to in the generation of the initial stochastic hierarchy. This model exhibits variability in the number of links different elements have. For top elements, the variability is due to variation in link formation in both the initial stochastic hierarchy generation as well as this step generating additional random parent-child links; for bottom elements there is variation in degree due to the additional parent-child links generated in this step.

Step 2 for random networks generates additional top horizontal links. I generate links in both directions for convenience, so that element i can link to j but if it does not, then when j's links are being created there is a second opportunity for the $i - j$ link to be created. I choose the link probability such that for a large network, on average each top element has approximately one horizontal link.[15] Independence is assumed: the probability of any given horizontal link is independent of all other horizontal links and also independent of all vertical links. Note that there is random variation in the number of horizontal links that different top elements possess.

To generate power law networks, I specify an approximate power law degree distribution for top elements. I use a weighting function to specify degree: each top element is assigned a weight, which specifies its relative likelihood of being selected for a link. The smallest weight is 1, and top elements that have weight 1 will on average have the fewest links, while elements with larger weights will on average have more links. I note that in the exact power law model, the likelihood of an element having degree k is proportional to $k^{-\gamma}$ with γ around 2 in many applications; I approximate this formula in defining the number of elements of each weight.[16]

Consider the smaller-scale networks with $N = 100$. I set the highest value of k to be 20. Such an element will have, based on the power law model, a frequency of occurrence of just a fraction of a percent (for $\gamma = 2$, the frequency is $\frac{1}{400}$). Thus for $N = 100$ there will most likely be at most one top element having this high a weight, and I assign the weight of 20 to a single top element. For the next highest degrees I choose the value 10 as representative weight and assign two elements this weight. Proceeding by proportionality, elements of weight 7 should be twice as frequent; thus I assign 4 top elements this weight. I continue in this way, with the final 40 elements assigned a weight of 1.[17]

I use the weights to generate links with the sum of the weights as normalization factor. Thus the probability a top element is chosen as target for a specific link is equal to its weight divided by the sum of the weights. The protocol ensures that the overall density of links is similar to that of the random network, meaning that each bottom element on average has 2 links and top elements overall average 6 links, while generating a network in which a few top elements have many links. For the initial stochastic hierarchy, each bottom element is assigned a top element at random, and top elements with higher weights are more likely to be chosen.[18] Likewise, in generating additional vertical links, the top elements of higher weight are more likely to be chosen, and the protocol used is such that on average each bottom element forms one additional link.[19] Finally, additional horizontal links are generated, again following a protocol such that each top element has on average one horizontal link, and top elements with higher weights have on average more links while elements with lower weights have fewer.[20]

I follow a similar procedure for $N = 1,000$. I assign one top element a weight of 60 (so that its relative frequency of $1/1,225$ is close to one in a thousand), 2 elements a weight of 50, and continue in this way, with 200 elements assigned a weight of 2 and 500 a weight of 1.[21] The network generation process then follows the same protocol described above for $N = 100$.

Last, I generate networks for the clustering model as follows.[22] First I divide the top elements into clusters. I set the number of clusters to 10 and allocate top elements evenly among clusters. This means that for the scale $N = 100$ there are 10 top elements in each cluster, and for the larger scale $N = 1,000$ there are 100. I then generate an initial stochastic hierarchy with one parent assigned at random to each bottom element, following the approach described above for random networks. The bottom element then inherits the cluster of its parent. Then I combine the random network model with clustering. I introduce the parameter q that governs cluster intensity and set it to 0.7.[23] I then generate random links to top elements such that on average each bottom element has one additional parent link, and the probability this link is to a parent in the same cluster is q.[24] For top horizontal links, similarly I define a link probability for pairs of top elements in the same cluster and a different smaller link probability for pairs in different clusters, such that the overall probability of a top element having a horizontal link is 1 and the probability this link is inside the cluster is q.

I generate 10 realizations of each of the 6 types of simulated networks. For each type, the 10 realizations are generated using the same set of parameters and following the same protocol; thus differences among them are entirely due to differences in the random outcomes of the link draws.

DESCRIPTIVE STATISTICS

Figures 6 and 7 present descriptive statistics for the simulated networks. Figure 6 depicts degree distributions. As discussed above, the degree of an element is its number of links, and the degree distribution for a network shows, for each degree value, the fraction of elements having that degree. I compute degree distributions separately for top and bottom elements because top elements have significantly more links.

Panel A shows the degree distributions for top and bottom elements for the small-scale networks. For each type of network—random, cluster, and power law—I compute the degree distribution for each of the

Panel A: Small Scale (100 Top Elements, 300 Bottom Elements)

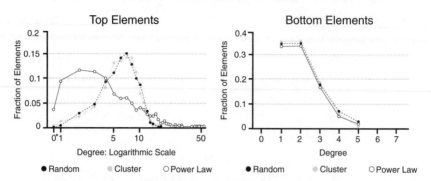

Note that the Power Law distribution extends far to the right for the top elements because in each network there are a few top elements with high degree. The values for the 3 network types are very similar for the bottom elements, and as a result the circles representing the values overlay one another.

*The logarithmic scale begins at 1; 0 with its corresponding values is placed separately to the left.

Panel B: Large Scale (1,000 Top Elements, 3,000 Bottom Elements)

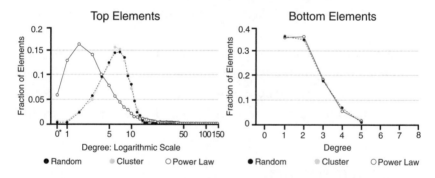

Note that the Power Law distribution extends far to the right for the top elements because in each network there are a few top elements with high degree. The values for the 3 network types are very similar for the bottom elements, and as a result the circles representing the values overlay one another.

*The logarithmic scale begins at 1; 0 with its corresponding values is placed separately to the left.

FIGURE 6. SIMULATED NETWORK CONTEXTS: DEGREE DISTRIBUTIONS: AVERAGE VALUES OVER THE 10 SIMULATED NETWORKS FOR EACH NETWORK TYPE

Panel A: Small Scale (100 Top Elements, 300 Bottom Elements)

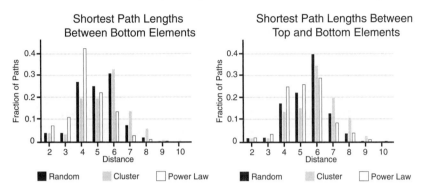

Panel B: Large Scale (1,000 Top Elements, 3,000 Bottom Elements)

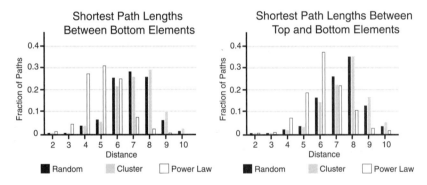

FIGURE 7. SIMULATED NETWORK CONTEXTS: SHORTEST PATH LENGTH DISTRIBUTIONS: AVERAGE VALUES OVER THE 10 SIMULATED NETWORKS FOR EACH NETWORK TYPE

10 simulated networks, then average these values. The most striking feature of these graphs is that for the power law model, the top element degree distribution is spread out compared with the distributions for the random and cluster models. In particular the power law model has, as expected and by design, a long right-hand tail that shows a few top elements having high degree: for these networks the average maximum degree is 47, and the average second highest degree is 27. This pattern likely fits many real-world creativity contexts as discussed in the previous section. For bottom elements the degree distributions are very

similar across all three types of networks and are relatively compact. But there is still variation among bottom elements, and this is important for the creativity model—elements with only one link have just one parent and thus will be reachable by fewer paths compared with elements with multiple parents.

Panel B shows the same distributions for the large-scale networks. Qualitatively the distributions are similar, with the key difference that the power law large-scale model has an even longer right-hand tail. The average maximum degree over the 10 simulated power law networks is 132, most of which are to bottom elements; thus the highest-degree top elements connect with over 4 percent of bottom elements. The average second highest degree is 110, also very large.

Figure 7 depicts shortest path distributions. A path between two elements is a path following links from one element to the other, usually passing through several intermediate elements. I compute shortest paths between pairs of bottom elements and separately between top and bottom elements. As for the degree distribution calculation, I compute the shortest path distributions for each of the 10 networks of each type, then average these values.[25] Note that there is considerable variation in the shortest path lengths; a fair fraction of elements are further than four steps apart, some as much as seven or more. This is important for creativity. We tend to believe that linking two elements that are further apart in a context, meaning the shortest path between them in the pre-existing network is longer, is more creative than linking two elements that have a shorter path. Finding ways to generate these longer path connections is important and is a part of the creativity model I present in Parts II and III. Paths are on average longer by about one step in the large-scale networks compared to the small-scale. This shows the value of modeling at the larger scale, as it makes it possible to explore how the creative process may be affected by longer path lengths. Paths are somewhat shorter for the power law model, which is not surprising because paths can pass through highly connected hub top elements. Paths are slightly longer for the cluster model than for the random model, also important for creativity.

Panel A: Degree Distributions

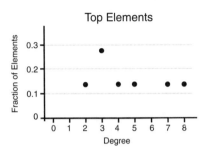

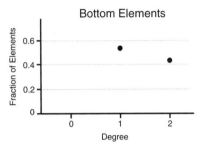

Panel B: Shortest Path Length Distributions

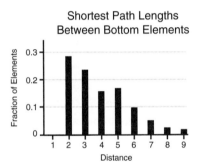

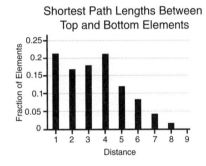

FIGURE 8. SMALL EXAMPLE CONTEXT: DEGREE AND SHORTEST PATH LENGTH DISTRIBUTIONS

As a comparison with these simulated networks, Figure 8 shows comparable statistics for the small-scale network introduced in Figure 2. In this small network all bottom elements have degree either 1 or 2, thus somewhat below the simulated network values, and top elements have a range of degree values between 2 and 8, also below the ranges for the simulated networks. Shortest path lengths are also shorter on average than for the simulated networks but do exhibit a range of values, especially between top and bottom elements, for which the distribution varies over the range 1 to 8. The relative sparseness of this example is why the path lengths are not overly short, and this makes this example helpful for illustrating the creativity model I present. It also reinforces the fact that in order for a network this small to exhibit a reasonable shortest path length distribution requires degree values and hence connectivity levels to be small relative to real-world contexts. This shows the value in working with simulated larger-scale networks in which it is possible to have both larger degree values together with more realistic shortest path lengths.

It is natural to wonder about the properties of the Clifford Possum and Hans Krebs contexts and how they compare with the simulated networks. A direct comparison doesn't make sense because Figures 4 and 5 show schematics of the Possum and Krebs contexts, intentionally simplified and omitting elements and some links. One result of this simplification is that the degrees of elements are lower than they would be if all elements were included. For example, in the Hans Krebs context, the node for inorganic chemistry has just one child, acid/base reactions. This is clearly far lower than it would have been: Krebs learned a great deal of inorganic chemistry, and his actual context representation would surely include many links to specific inorganic chemistry topics. Likewise for Clifford Possum I include not only just a subset of his Dreamings but also for each Dreaming a subset of its associated sites. Even with the simplifications there are hub elements in these context representations: for example in Possum's context the node for custodian is shown associated with 11 Dreamings. Shortest paths for the networks depicted in these figures are also not very valid, since not only are many elements omitted, so also are some links.

The fact that the empirical contexts are simpler, schematic representations reinforces the value of computer modeling. The computer simulations enable exploration of the creativity model in larger scale, focusing on general patterns and implications over many different networks rather than on the details of a given network. It is best to take the simulation results as complementary to the empirical case studies, and to recognize that there are important differences in the nature of the insights these two approaches provide.

Overall, the simulated network distributions demonstrate that there is considerable range in shortest paths and that specifics vary for both degree and shortest path distributions across different types of networks. In particular, degree distributions are quite different for the power law model as compared with the other two models, and paths are on average longer for the larger-scale contexts and for the cluster models. This variation is important since creativity contexts can vary a great deal across fields, time, and locales. Recognizing that good or "optimal" creative processes depend on context, this reinforces the importance of incorporating context in models of creativity and exploring the relationships among context, creative process, and outcomes.

CHAPTER 5

IDEAS AND PROJECTS

Context is not only the environment in which individuals create; it also provides the essential materials out of which ideas and creative projects are constructed. The model of context I have presented provides a natural way to model how this occurs. I define ideas and projects in this framework in this chapter; in turn this leads into Parts II and III that follow, in which I describe how the creative process unfolds.

DEFINITION OF CREATIVITY: IDEAS

A standard definition of creativity is connecting two elements that have not previously been connected or related.[1] This definition in fact covers a wide range of forms of creativity, more than might be realized at first glance. For example, connecting a novel solution with a problem fits this definition, as does applying a theory or statistical framework in a novel application, creating a melody that links notes in a novel way, and blending design elements that have not previously been connected. Sometimes these creative connections make creative contributions as is, but often they form the creative seed of a project that is developed based on them, adding further elements that fit with and build out the core idea.

There is a natural fit between this definition and the model of context I have introduced: a novel idea is a connection between two elements in the context network that are not directly connected at present. Indeed, we can go further, following Mednick's idea of remote associates and state that ideas that are the most novel forge connections between elements that are more distant in the existing network, meaning the path connecting them is relatively long and, especially, not extremely short, since this would imply they are already fairly closely related.[2]

It is worth noting that this description, while grounded in the external world of context, also fits with creativity as a mental operation. Since John Locke it has been recognized that our mental representations are built up from our experiences, including what we learn.[3] Put in terms of my framework, we internalize elements from our context. We then manipulate these elements, which can include many operations, including categorizations and generalizations, doubts and questions, analytical thought and, importantly, creative and imaginative thinking—forming new connections and combinations and imagining new scenarios and possibilities. Thus context elements are the basis for ideas, whether directly or more usually via internalization and mental manipulation.[4]

THE MODEL: IDEAS AND PROJECTS

The model I present describes a two-step creative process that builds on this definition of creativity. In the first step an idea is generated (or in an alternative interpretation, discovered) by connecting two context elements; this creates a seed for a project. In the second step a further creative link is made, adding a new element to the seed so that it grows from a seed project into a full-fledged project. Thus projects grow from seed ideas, which makes sense for creativity. The third element that is added in step two can be thought of as an element that completes the original seed idea, that makes the project "work" by adding a crucial missing ingredient. Three elements is a small number, and the three-element project is best thought of as not containing everything the project will eventually include but rather representing the core project design that specifies key creative features—see below for more discussion of this.

This two-step model is the simplest one that captures the elements and features of the creative process I wish to highlight. This will become clear as the argument and description unfold in the following chapters. Later in the book I discuss how it can be extended in a variety of ways, but the simple model provides key insights.

I impose two restrictions in the model. First, seed ideas and projects are composed entirely out of bottom elements. I focus on bottom-level elements because these have the sharpness and specificity that is inherent to creative projects and outcomes. Think of a painting or an invention: each is composed of specific elements, like specific colors and shapes or specific design elements like circuit components. In some fields like philosophy, top-level elements may form part of creative projects and outcomes. Or, as a different pattern, seed ideas might include top elements and then morph into projects that are composed entirely or mainly out of bottom elements. I do not pursue these alternative possibilities in order to keep the argument streamlined. Further, by focusing on projects defined by bottom elements, I am able to distinguish clearly between guiding structures, formed out of top elements, and seeds and projects, which is useful for exposition.

Second, I impose the restriction that project elements do not share any common parents. Sharing common parents would make two elements close in the existing context, which would make connecting them seemingly not very creative. There may be exceptions, but it is a reasonable restriction to impose in order to focus on genuinely novel new connections that are more likely to lead to a highly creative outcome. This second restriction also ensures that the elements of a project are conceptually distinct—that is, they do not fall under the same broader topic or conceptual heading.[5]

As stated above, the model is best interpreted as focusing on core project designs. A three-element project is best interpreted this way, as a core project design that is used as the template for building out the final completed project. This could be literally a formal design document, a preliminary engineering or design sketch, a recipe, a marketing campaign strategy, or notes outlining a dance performance or the basic plot of a novel. The final design will contain more elements and the final project even more, and there is creativity along each step of development. Thus, a painting may be created with dozens or hundreds of brushstrokes and details; and a mathematical proof or complex large-scale circuit may also contain hundreds of elements that fit together in subtle, intricate ways. But the core design contains a great deal of creativity in and of itself and is a worthy focus. Indeed in many cases the gist of what is most creative about a final project centers on a few key elements that embody the central idea of the project. Note also that the core design is more than just the seed idea, for it marks a crucial step toward practical development with the third element that is added. Of course there are often many additional steps and modifications in developing the core project design into the final creative outcome. I do not model this phase of the process in very much detail in order to keep the model as streamlined as possible, but it arises in the empirical case studies.[6] I will call three-element core project designs "projects" to simplify wording, while acknowledging that a completed project will contain many more elements that build this design out.

It is also true that there are ideas that do not become project seeds that are nonetheless still important—for example, critiques of existing work and anomalies, that may spark subsequent creativity in the field. It would be interesting to add these into the model, but I do not pursue that line of development as it would detract from the main points I wish to emphasize. The model I present has a streamlined logic: it describes and models a direct line of creative development, from seed idea to completed project. As I will show, it has the flexibility to describe different pathways through which this process unfolds and delivers implications about "optimal" or good ways to go about pursuing creativity especially in large-scale contexts.

It is natural to ask where completed projects fit in the context. A project can be conceptualized as a newly added element, with links to the set of elements it is composed out of. Also, it may have links to upper-level concepts such as attributes or themes that it is viewed as possessing or informs. For a field that has maturity, an individual entering the field will learn about many completed projects, such as scientific projects, techniques, and theoretical results. Thus completed projects form an important part of the learning process. However, much of what individuals learn from projects results from unpacking them, learning constituent elements, and learning indirectly about the attributes and other higher-level concepts associated with them. Thus in my discussion I don't focus on projects as context elements but rather presuppose that for creating new projects, individuals are working directly with constituent elements and higher-level concepts. In Chapter 16 I discuss context elements that are sets of elements as one way to model previous contributions.

To summarize, I focus on a two-step model of creativity: an individual or team starts from a seed idea and then adds a critical additional element to develop their seed into a core project design.

EXAMPLES

Figure 9 depicts the small-scale network example first shown in Figure 2. In the figure an example project is shown, consisting of the three bottom elements 1, 7, and 16.

Although this is a very small example context, nonetheless there are a considerable number of three-element projects: 295 total.[7] This reinforces the point that there are many creative possibilities: if the number

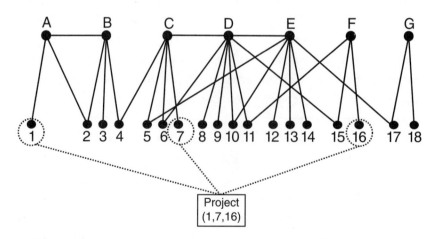

FIGURE 9. SMALL EXAMPLE CONTEXT: PROJECT EXAMPLE

of possible projects is this large even in such a tiny context, it will surely be very large in larger, more realistic contexts.

Another way to consider the generation of projects, in line with the model to follow, is as paths from two-element seed ideas to three-element projects. This context has 110 valid seed project ideas—pairs of bottom elements that do not share a common parent. Different seeds can spawn different numbers of full projects: the maximum number in this context is 14, spawned by seeds (1, 18) and (1, 3).

Note that each valid project can be reached from 3 distinct seeds, each seed consisting of two of its elements. For the example project in the figure, (1, 7, 16), seeds (1, 7), (1, 16), and (7, 16) can each serve as the seed from which the full project is developed. Thus there are three distinct creative paths to every project.

THE LARGE NUMBER OF PROJECTS AND PROJECT SEEDS IN LARGER-SCALE CONTEXTS

There are a huge number of potential projects in large-scale contexts. Tables 2 and 3 present statistics about the number of valid project seeds and projects in the simulated contexts to demonstrate this point.

Table 2 shows the number of valid seed pairs, showing average values and ranges over the 10 realizations for each type of network. There

TABLE 2. SIMULATED NETWORK CONTEXTS: NUMBER OF VALID SEED PAIRS: AVERAGE VALUES AND RANGES

	Type of Network	Average Value* Over 10 Simulated Networks	Range** [Min – Max]
Small Scale	Random	43,059	[42,834 – 43,200]
	Cluster	43,111	[42,980 – 43,268]
	Power Law	41,639	[41,283 – 41,988]
Large Scale	Random	4.48 million	[4.48 – 4.48]
	Cluster	4.48 million	[4.48 – 4.48]
	Power Law	4.44 million	[4.43 – 4.44]

* The average value is the average of the number of valid seed pairs over each of the 10 simulated networks.
** The range shows the smallest and largest number of valid seed pairs over the 10 networks.

TABLE 3. SIMULATED NETWORK CONTEXTS: NUMBER OF VALID PROJECTS: AVERAGE VALUES AND RANGES

	Type of Network	Average Value* Over 10 Simulated Networks	Range** [Min – Max]
Small Scale	Random	3.94 million	[3.88 – 3.98]
	Cluster	3.96 million	[3.92 – 4.0]
	Power Law	3.58 million	[3.50 – 3.67]
Large Scale	Random	4.44 billion	[4.44 – 4.44]
	Cluster	4.44 billion	[4.44 – 4.44]
	Power Law	4.31 billion	[4.30 – 4.32]

* The average value is the average of the number of valid projects over each of the 10 simulated networks of that type.
** The range shows the smallest and largest number of valid projects over the 10 networks.

are over 40,000 seed pairs in the smaller contexts and over 4 million in the larger contexts. These are large numbers especially for the larger contexts.

Table 3 shows the number of valid projects, again showing average values and ranges. In the smaller-scale models there are nearly 4 million valid three-element projects, and in the larger-scale contexts over 4 billion! These are very large numbers, and arise in contexts that although having reasonable scale are still undoubtedly smaller than many real-world creativity contexts. Many of these potential projects may not be sensible or have any creative appeal. But even if just a small percentage do, there will still be a very large number of possibilities.

The magnitudes of the numbers in Tables 2 and 3 demonstrate two facts about creativity in large-scale contexts. First, it is more efficient to search for a promising seed pair and then develop it into a successful project than to search directly over projects, because there are simply too many potential projects. Second, even when searching over seeds, it is crucial to use guidance to identify promising pools of seed pairs to explore, given the large numbers of seeds, in many circumstances far too many to search over at random, especially given that in many cases it will require time and resources to detemine whether a seed has potential. Thus, setting creativity in its natural large-scale, rich network context highlights the enormous number of creative possibilities, which makes clear the need for guidance.

PART II

GUIDANCE

CHAPTER 6

THE CHALLENGE OF CREATIVITY

In a context rich with elements and possibilities, there are a vast number of potential novel creative projects that can be attempted. The examples in the last section of the preceding chapter demonstrate this: contexts with 100 top elements and 300 bottom elements, certainly not as big as many real-world contexts, contain close to 4 million potential projects, while contexts with 1,000 top elements and 3,000 bottom elements contain more than 4 billion!

In such rich contexts the problem is not that there are too few options to explore, although sometimes a person stuck creatively might think so. The problem is that there are so many. A writer facing a blank page, an artist facing a blank canvas, an engineer contemplating the design of a new product–the possibilities are nearly limitless. In a world with so many possibilities, it is critical to develop approaches and strategies for navigating successfully.

The reality is that most projects, if attempted, will not be success-ful. Many projects, if attempted, will fail outright. And many others, although they may generate viable outcomes, will generate outcomes that turn out not to be very successful.

What is successful is inherently subjective, and I prefer to think about "success" in terms of an individual viewing their creative outcome as successful based on whatever criteria they use to make that assessment–see below for more. Nonetheless anyone engaging over any extended period of time in a creative endeavor, with a sense of personal development and aspirations, will view many if not most of their attempts as not very successful or at least as not as successful as they believe is possible for them to achieve. In terms of more conventional views of success, it is a well-established empirical regularity that in many fields only a small percentage of projects lead to highly successful outcomes: the distribution of creative outcomes has a "long right-hand tail" as established, for example, in patent and invention and citation data, so that a handful of contributions generate very high values while the vast majority generate relatively low values.

Regardless of exactly how success is defined, the big challenge facing individuals engaged in creative activities is to develop a core project design that has a chance of leading to significant success—among the myriad possibilities that do not.

GUIDANCE

Given the multitude of options, an individual or team engaged in a creative endeavor needs an approach that will enable them to navigate their context effectively in order to identify and develop potentially high-value creative projects. What is a good approach? My answer in this book is: guidance.

The key to effective navigation through guidance lies in the structure of the contexts in which creativity happens. As described in Part I, these contexts have network structures in which hierarchy is a fundamental organizing factor. This hierarchy organization opens up strategies for effective guidance, because higher-level, broader, more abstract conceptual elements can be used to imagine, identify, and delimit promising topics, approaches, and criteria of evaluation. This focuses attention on particular regions of the context and defines pathways into the vast and dense network of lower-level elements used to create projects. Without knowing exactly which specific lower-level elements to combine, this kind of conceptual strategy focuses, from a higher-level vantage point, on promising pathways and pools to explore, while also setting criteria to identify truly outstanding possibilities. It is efficient without being too narrow, imaginative without trying to fill in all the details at once, while also helping to home in on the very best creative projects. Thus my argument is that the key to creativity in large-scale,rich creativity contexts is guidance based, at least to a considerable extent, on higher-level concepts.

Guidance is far better than the alternative. In large-scale creativity contexts there are such a vast number of possible new combinations of elements that it is not possible to try them all or even close to all of them; trying them simply at random is unlikely to lead to success. Finding one's way through the thicket of pathways and possibilities to a successful outcome without guidance is highly unlikely—it is more likely one will get lost in the tangle of details without finding a great project. Higher-level guidance enables a more organized, conceptually based search, which is more likely to be successful. In the following chapters I will present an argument to support this statement and show with a model general conditions under which it is true.

Several factors support the conceptual guidance approach. First, it makes logical sense, as a systematic, structured way to winnow down options. My formal model demonstrates this and shows that this kind of guidance can dramatically increase the likelihood of ultimately generating a highly successful creative outcome in creativity contexts structured as networks, the more so the larger the network.

Second, it is empirically grounded, the approach followed by many successful creators across a wide range of fields. The examples I provide illustrate this. They range from scientists such as Hans Krebs and Albert Einstein to engineers such as Lynn Conway, writers such as Virginia Woolf, artists such as Clifford Possum, and entrepreneurs such as Twitter cofounder Jack Dorsey. Of course the specifics vary—every creative contribution has its own unique story—but conceptual guidance is integral to each case study, and we learn from each about how conceptual guidance can be developed and used.

Third, the approach makes intuitive sense. This supports its validity on face value and also makes it useful as an educational approach to help individuals develop their creativity, an issue I discuss in Chapter 18.

TWO KINDS OF GUIDANCE

There are two kinds of conceptual guidance. One kind is constructive, imagining creative possibilities. This includes identifying and defining themes, topics, and approaches to pursue, setting goals, and formulating questions to attempt to answer. I call a guidance structure that provides this kind of guidance a *guiding conception*. Guiding conceptions are at the heart of this book. I believe they have not been well described in the creativity literature previously, and they both are used by many successful creators and have a logic that can be described and modeled.

The second kind of guidance operates later in the process and helps both to constrain creativity, ruling out errant paths and ideas, and to identify the missing pieces to complete creative projects. I call a guidance structure that provide this kind of guidance a *guiding principle*. Guiding principles are more widely recognized but not integrated within an overall framework of creativity such as I present.

One of the noteworthy features of creativity that I focus on is the way these two forms of guidance are complementary and work best when they work together. In my experience highly successful individuals engaged in creative endeavors utilize both; but also many individuals could learn to use them in tandem more effectively. In fact certain kinds of pairings are especially effective, a result I show in Chapter 13.

These two forms of guidance, working together, break the creative process down into two steps. The first step is identifying, imagining, and defining a promising creative direction or topic to explore; exploration based on this guidance spawns seed projects. Guiding conceptions provide the critical guidance for this first step. The second step is to identify a promising seed and then develop it into a full, high-value project; this involves finding just the right combination of elements building from the seed. Guiding principles are the critical factor in this second step.

Proceeding in two steps this way makes a great deal of sense. Focusing extremely narrowly too soon is unlikely to succeed, because it is very difficult to know where to focus at the level of details without having a larger sense of where creative potential lies. This is especially true in large-scale, rich contexts teeming with possibilities. Guiding conceptions, functioning on a broader level, do just this: they define promising pools and avenues to explore, without having all the details filled in. Exploring these pools and avenues generates potential seed ideas for projects. Next one uses guiding principles in two ways: to rule out false prospects—seed projects that are flawed because they don't fit with principles one wants one's creative work to adhere to—and to discover just the right additional elements to add to a promising seed to develop it into a full-fledged project with high potential. This two-step process of exploration and refinement is an efficient process that, if things work out well, can lead to a high-value creative outcome. This isn't necessarily the only route to producing a high-value creative outcome, but it has a powerful logic, as I will show, and it is used by successful creators.

In the following chapters I describe these two kinds of conceptual guidance, show the logic of how they function in network contexts, and provide examples of real-world creators using them. As I will show, they fit naturally in the formal model of context introduced in Part I and produce an intuitive and logical formal model of the creative process.

DYNAMICS AND THE ROLE OF BOTTOM-UP PROCESSES

The guidance processes I focus on have the flavor of "top-down" processes. Broader conceptions guide exploration and search to discover more specific elements that can form the basis for creative projects. It is natural to wonder about other parts of the creative process I am not focusing on, especially the role of bottom-up processes. The creative process is dynamic, and there are important influences running in both top-down and bottom-up directions. There are in particular two kinds of bottom-up processes we might imagine can be important for creativity: specific elements and experiences spark creativity directly, without much guidance; and specific elements and experiences trigger the development of higher-level conceptions that in turn guide creative exploration.

The first of these—specific elements and experiences sparking creativity without any prior guidance—I am convinced is rare. This kind of process fits the random search model that has been popular in the creativity field, as discussed in the Introduction. Random search has been an attractive model mainly because of the failure to recognize the large-scale, rich nature of creative contexts. Random search may work in a small context with few options. In a large-scale context, however, random search without any guidance is extremely unlikely to uncover a highly productive creative combination. There are simply too many possibilities, most of which fail. I demonstrate this formally in Chapter 10. Pasteur's famous dictum, "Chance favors the prepared mind," reminds us that without a prepared mind, serendipitous opportunities, even if they occur, won't be recognized for what they are. When we observe a process that looks like random search leading to a successful outcome, we should dig deeper into the mental set of the individual engaged in the search. Invariably when we do we will discover that this individual did have prior higher-level thinking that led them to the creative outcome. Sometimes individuals describe a discovery they have made as arising by chance: Virginia Woolf did so in regard to her discovery of a literary form that opened up to her a way forward in developing her guiding conception creatively, as I discuss in Chapter 15. In fact, however, in her case, as in most, there was guidance behind the scenes: she was not exploring at random in the vast domain of literary styles, but in a directed way. Hitting upon the specific form she did, at the time she did, was to a degree a chance event, but it happened within a guided search process she had been engaged in for over two years.[1]

The second pattern, a specific element or experience sparking higher-level thinking, fits with the framework I present and indeed adds an additional important pathway to it. For example, an individual may hit upon a puzzle or encounter a surprising phenomenon, and this may spark a desire to explore ways to explain the puzzle or phenomenon, which in turn leads them to form a guiding conception.

Albert Einstein's creative development fits this pattern. A paradox he hit upon according to his own account at the age of sixteen revealed to him a conceptual puzzle that he wrestled with over the ensuing decade. Over time he seems to have expanded the scope of his thinking about the paradox and the issues it raised, a hallmark of bringing higher-level conceptual guidance to bear. Sometimes several fragmentary experiences coalesce into a guiding conception. Virginia Woolf's formation of her guiding conception of reflections fits this pattern in some respects.

During the creative process there is thus a dynamic interplay between bottom-up and top-down processes. The former spark higher-level thinking, and this higher-level thinking in turn guides creative exploration, which in turn leads to new experiences and discoveries that can generate creativity and also spur further higher-level thinking. For example, a common pattern is for an individual's guiding conception to evolve over time in response to what they have learned, their project experiences, and changes in their context. The full recursive dynamic is beyond the scope of the main focus of this book. I discuss it in Part III both with examples of richer creative journeys and in terms of how the model can be extended to incorporate it. However, my focus is on a relatively simple two-step model centering on guidance and its role in helping individuals develop seed ideas and projects, one part of the overall dynamic.

MEASURING SUCCESS

Given that I will focus on how individuals develop high-value creative projects that can lead to successful creative outcomes, it is appropriate to pause from the main line of argument here to note the many issues that surround the concept of "success" in creative endeavors.

Notwithstanding that there are accepted objective measures of success in certain fields, such as the market value associated with an invention, it must be recognized that what is meant by success in a creative activity is inherently subjective, and further that there are different kinds of success.

For some individuals in some circumstances, simply producing an outcome, like a completed painting, is a successful outcome. But for most individuals who move beyond the novice level in a creative field, a successful outcome means more than this.

There are three distinct kinds of criteria for evaluating success in creative endeavors. One is intrinsic: valuing engaging in the creative process for its own sake, separate from specific outcomes. The second is success based on personal values: for example, appreciating a painting in terms of a personal standard of beauty or liking the taste of a creative new food preparation. The third is extrinsically grounded success: producing creative outcomes that are highly valued in the creative field or broader society. This includes, for example, producing an invention that generates a high market return or a painting that sells for a high price or is widely praised by critics.

Individuals engaged in creative careers evaluate their creative outcomes in terms of their larger creative aspirations. Does a particular project outcome fulfill or increase the prospects of fulfilling their aspirations? These aspirations can be more internal, such as producing a worthy creative work, or more externally focused, such as achieving career success, earning compensation for their creative products, and influencing evolving tastes.

In this book I do not focus on comparing and contrasting different standards of evaluation of creative outcomes, as interesting and important as this is. Rather I assume certain outcomes have high value for individuals attempting to produce creative outcomes and focus on how these individuals can reach these outcomes. The framework allows for either objective or subjective assessments. Thus, individuals may share similar assessments of the relative values of different outcomes, or may differ in their assessments. The valuation assessments are taken as specified and are not probed as to their basis. Keeping valuation simple helps streamline the analysis and focus the argument on the main topic of the book, which is about the mechanics of how to go about creative engagement in large-scale contexts.

This doesn't mean the issue of how success is measured and the impact of different measures of success on creative fields isn't important, just that it is not a central concern of mine in this book. My focus is on the creative process, and I provide insights about the process that hold across the many different ways of valuing creative outcomes. Thus the approach should be valuable in many different creative settings and for individuals and organizations that approach creativity from a variety of different value orientations.

CHAPTER 7

GUIDING CONCEPTIONS INTRODUCED

Guiding conceptions imagine creative possibilities and opportunities. They imagine them abstractly, not in full detail, but with sufficient structure to guide creative exploration and spur creative thinking. A guiding conception provides a kind of mental scaffolding that defines creative avenues to explore and helps spawn creative ideas that may turn into creative projects.

Guiding conceptions are mental constructs. In particular, they are not simple singleton elements, but include multiple elements linked together to form a larger conception. Many of these elements have a degree of breadth and abstraction, and thus reside in higher levels of contexts. A guiding conception might for example focus on writing stories centering on surprising talents of dogs. This conception would guide exploration and ideation of stories. It would not fill in all the details but rather have a degree of breadth. Thus it would not specify exactly what the talent is, how it is used, or in most cases the specific dog: it leaves room for creativity in how it is developed. Likewise, a guiding conception might focus on a certain photographic approach and general subject matter but would not specify all the details down to a specific photograph, leaving these details to further creative development. Guiding conceptions are a level above detailed specificity, and that is what gives them imaginative breadth and creative generativity. Hans Krebs's guiding conception of applying the laboratory techniques he had learned in the Warburg lab to an area in which they had not previously been applied, intermediary metabolism, is a great example of this presented in the next chapter; it did not specify a specific experiment to conduct but rather envisioned a research program. His conception and the other examples I give should clarify guiding conceptions, and the formal model in Chapter 10 provides additional clarity and detail.

Building on this sense of breadth, in terms of describing guiding conceptions and their role in creativity, it is both helpful and important to distinguish them from more specific ideas as well as creative projects and outcomes. A result, an outcome, an idea that can be directly executed and presented—these are specific, delimited, even concrete; they are sufficiently defined to translate directly into a creative product or outcome, even if they can perhaps be interpreted, extended, or modified. Examples are a painting, a story, a photograph, a solution to a problem, a smartphone. In contrast, a guiding conception has a sense of openness. It is not generally meant to be presented as a contribution itself; indeed, it is often quite private to the individual who forms it and is meant to be developed further–it provides space and opportunity for further creative development. Guiding conceptions provide a vision, imagine a creative path or domain to explore; they do not define a finished product or "solution." When an artist or a writer forms a guiding conception, for example, it is not equivalent to a specific work of art they will produce but rather a broader template that helps them ultimately produce original creative works. This can also breed frustration as the artist or writer would prefer to jump directly to a project to work on and complete. The example of Virginia Woolf's conception presented in the next chapter is a great illustration both of a guiding conception and also of this frustration. It is important to recognize the great creativity that can be unleashed by pursuing a guiding conception even if this is not fully apparent when it is first formed.

The distinction between guiding conceptions on the one hand and results, outcomes, projects, and ideas on the other carries through in the modeling framework I present. Ideas, projects, and outcomes are composed mainly out of elements that reside in the lower levels of context hierarchies, elements that have high specificity. In contrast, guiding conceptions are composed out of more abstract, conceptually broader elements that reside in the upper levels of context hiearchies.

The distinction between a guiding conception and more specific elements is not always as clear as I have presented it, of course. A problem is an example of a conceptual construct that can fall in either category, depending on how broadly it is posed in relation to its context. Ideas also can fall in either category—a guiding conception after all is an idea, as we shall see; however, many ideas are highly specific and would not serve well as guiding conceptions. Even if the distinction is sometimes blurry, it is a useful one and helps structure a theoretical understanding of the creative process. As I present the model, guiding conceptions are developed first and are generative of creative ideas and projects that individuals develop into creative outcomes; thus guiding conceptions are precursors to later creativity. As noted in the preceding chapter, sometimes there is an earlier step, in the reverse flow direction, in which an observation or idea sparks a guiding conception that in turn guides the creative process. But the basic sequence of a guiding conception being formed prior to a seed idea and project is something I have observed over and over in my empirical studies of creativity, including the examples I present in this book that illustrate it. While this does not prove there is a causal link, it makes it seem likely and worthy of developing a theoretical model that can help us understand the logic of such a link.

Guiding conceptions have several functions. First and foremost, they define creative pools to explore and spawn ideas. In doing this they focus creative activity. From the myriad possibilities–far too many to consider—a guiding conception narrows an individual's attention down to a more manageable scope. Individuals focus on opportunities and ideas that align with or are in some way related to their guiding conception—still a relatively rich set and certainly broader than a specific project, but narrow enough that they can think through the possibilities and make good choices about which to pursue further. The flip side of this, which is just as important, is that individuals will often not pursue ideas and projects that do not fit with their guiding conception, recognizing that these ideas and projects do not align with their larger vision and thus are unlikely to lead to outcomes that will be fulfilling and successful for them.

Being too rigid can be bad for creativity; however, focus is essential, and if rigidity is a problem, it points to the individual's guiding conception being too limiting or flawed in its vision, in which case it needs to be reformulated. Indeed it is not unusual for individuals to refine an initial guiding conception and for this to be critical in attaining success. Virginia Woolf is an example of someone whose pattern of development fits this case. This process of refining a guiding conception is part of the larger activity of reflecting upon one's creative activity, including failures, to understand how to improve and possibly shift direction or approach. Guiding conceptions often play an important role in this kind of reflection. This is a second key function they have. Sometimes they facilitate changes in other aspects of an individual's approach; other times they become the focus of this reflective process, as an individual examines their guiding conception and sees how to revise it or develop it further, as Virginia Woolf did.

Finally, guiding conceptions are valuable for communicating with others. This kind of communication of broader vision and aims can be crucial for gaining support, including resources. It can also help individuals connect with potential collaborators who share overlapping or complementary guiding conceptions—combining two guiding conceptions that share a zone of overlap but are also different can be a wonderful pathway to creativity.

Forming a productive guiding conception is itself a skill and requires appreciating and adopting a certain mindset toward creative engagement. To form a well-developed guiding conception means to imagine without feeling the need to fill in all the specifics of what one will ultimately create, thus not being overly constrained by what is immediately feasible—letting go of that constraint. This kind of imaginative thinking comes naturally to some, but I believe can be learned by anyone–something we work on in my creativity class at Yale. Being willing to engage in this kind of imaginative thinking and follow where it leads requires tolerating the uncertainty of not prespecifying and assuming to know precisely how one's creative path will unfold. This can be challenging for people who either are relative novices in creativity or have been trained in a different approach, for example a focus on more concrete problem solving. I believe most individuals can improve their ability to tolerate this uncertainty through experience, education, and support. Consciously focusing on forming a guiding conception and understanding its uses can help with this process.

The fact that forming a productive guiding conception is important for creativity does not mean that it is not also important to be able to execute creative projects successfully. Project execution has several important facets including working with real materials and other people, solving concrete problems that arise, and paying attention to and incorporating myriad details; guiding principles are critical for this, as I describe later. There is a natural complementarity: skill at project activities is most valuable when projects are developed under the guidance of guiding conceptions that are formed with good intuition and hold creative potential. Creativity flowers when each of these different parts of the overall creative process—forming abstract conceptions and executing project work—is mastered and they fit together.

CHAPTER 8

EXAMPLES OF GUIDING CONCEPTIONS

In this chapter I present examples of guiding conceptions for the three individuals whose contexts I have already discussed—Hans Krebs, Clifford Possum, and Virginia Woolf—and one further individual, Jack Dorsey. All were able to develop their guiding conception successfully, as I describe in later chapters.

HANS KREBS

Hans Krebs formed a guiding conception while working in Otto Warburg's lab. His guiding conception links two distinct topics of his context, topics that had not previously been linked.

Recall that Warburg had developed manometric tissue slice techniques that enabled the quantitative measurement of rates of metabolic activity in intact cells. Warburg used these techniques to compare metabolic rates between cancerous and normal cells under varying conditions. Krebs worked on two projects that Warburg assigned him during his first year and a half, mastering the techniques; however, they were not projects that specifically aligned with his own interests.

Krebs stated later to his biographer Holmes that while he was working on these projects, it occurred to him that the methodology Warburg had developed "might be applicable to many processes beyond those with which Warburg was presently concerned." Around the time he completed the second project, seventeen months after joining the lab, he extended his thinking about how the methodology might be applied and formed his guiding conception. In particular, he recognized that it might be possible *to apply the manometric tissue slice methodology as the basis for experimental investigations in the field of intermediary metabolism.*

The emerging field of intermediary metabolism had sparked Krebs's interest, especially the vision of the field that he had, as he put it later, "absorbed" from his professor Franz Knoop in college. Krebs recognized that the ability to measure rates of metabolic activity in cells would be of great value for the investigation of intermediary metabolism, since a key feature of these processes is the production and subsequent utilization of intermediaries along metabolic pathways. Krebs told his biographer Holmes that at the time "he thought he would like to explore such possibilities" and that such investigations might potentially have "general significance" and lead to important discoveries.[1]

Referring to Figure 5 (pp. 62–63), we see that Krebs's guiding conception links the topic of intermediary metabolism, shown on the center-left of the diagram, with the manometric tissue slice methodology shown on the right. Both topics are midlevel concepts in the context; thus they are not overly specific, although not as broad as the field of chemistry, for example. Note also that linking these two elements links two regions of the context that are quite far apart in the figure and not directly linked. Thus his guiding conception was quite creative in the link it proposed. There are a few related links, notably between cancer as a disease on the left and cancer rate measurement as an application of the manometric tissue slice methodology on the right, and between muscle metabolism on the left, a subtopic of intermediary metabolism, and the manometric tissue slice methodology on the right. The first of these is outside the scope of Krebs's conception, and the second is more specific and interestingly not a topic to which he was particularly drawn.[2] It is noteworthy that, at least looking back, Krebs emphasized that at the time he formed his conception while working in Warburg's lab, he "did not pick out a particular process to study, or develop a detailed plan of action." He had "not fixed his attention on any concrete set of problems within the field [of intermediary metabolism] when it [his conception] occurred to him," at least in part because he simply did not know enough at the time to do so. Thus his guiding conception had breadth, as I have emphasized in my discussion introducing guiding conceptions in the preceding chapter.

Krebs was not able to pursue his guiding conception immediately. He told Holmes that one day he went to Warburg and told him that, "in his opinion the tissue slice [manometric] method 'is a useful tool for studying intermediary metabolism,' and that he would like to study [such] metabolic processes with the techniques that Warburg had developed." He said that he had been rebuffed by Warburg, who stated that "such experiments would be of no interest to him" and "there was no room" in his lab for this work. But as Krebs described it to Holmes, "the vista that had opened up to him seemed compelling," and "he clung to the idea that when he was in an independent position he would do something about it." Which is exactly what happened when two years later he left the Warburg lab and set up his own lab.

CLIFFORD POSSUM

Clifford Possum developed his guiding conception in the context of the Papunya art movement. Geoffrey Bardon began teaching art to school children at Papunya in 1971. The Indigenous adult men of the community became interested, and he supplied them art materials and they began painting. An important early artwork was the *Honey Ant Mural* painted on a wall of the school building during July and early August of 1971, which made a public statement about the Indigenous presence at Papunya.[3] A group of painters formed around Bardon, and he strongly encouraged their art. From the beginning they painted Dreaming stories, developing a rich, original artistic language.

Possum was not initially part of the Bardon group. His brother Tim Leura joined Bardon in February 1972, and a few months later brought Clifford Possum along, telling Bardon, "This is my brother, Clifford. I can't beat him."[4] Possum's first painting with Bardon, *Emu Corroboree Man* (1972), already evidences a great deal of technical mastery—recall he had been a carver for many years. Like many of the paintings done in the early days at Papunya, it depicts ceremonial figures and objects. Bardon viewed these images as influenced by Western-style iconography, and strongly encouraged the men to be true to their own culture and paint strictly using traditional Indigenous design motifs, including circles for fires and water holes, u-shapes for people, and journey lines.[5] Following this impulse, the Indigenous painters developed an abstract visual language based on traditional design motifs but also going beyond them. For example, they developed a technique of employing small dots to depict the terrain and vegetation; this background dotting functions as a powerful unifying artistic backdrop to the scenes and stories depicted. They also used abstraction to avoid depicting "secret-sacred" elements that in the traditional culture should not be viewed by women, children, or outsiders.

Possum embraced the abstract style and over the ensuing two years completed a series of paintings, developing his technical fluency especially with the dotting technique and scene layout. As this happened he made a transition to employing an aerial perspective in his paintings. This seems to have been natural for many of the Indigenous painters, given their deep and encyclopedic grasp of the geography of their land. Possum's *Love Story* paintings of 1972 and 1973 exhibit this perspective, as do a series of paintings of the great mythological bushfire at Warlugulong he also painted in these years. It was from this aerial perspective that Possum took a key creative step to form his guiding conception.

Up to this time the Indigenous artists had focused on depicting a single Dreaming on each painting. Possum developed a different guiding conception: *to depict on a single painting multiple Dreaming stories associated with the geographic area centering around a particular site.* The Dreaming stories would be placed accurately according to the

Indigenous peoples' sense of spatial layout, but also in an aesthetically balanced way. The approach would use the aerial perspective and draw on his encyclopedic knowledge of Dreamings in his country. It would introduce greater visual complexity, opening up new artistic challenges and opportunities.

Possum's guiding conception and its shift to a geographic-centered perspective resonates with several different facets of his context shown in Figure 4 (pp. 52–53). Note on the left-hand side of the figure the links of Dreaming figures with the sites they are associated with, as well as the journey node and the one journey depicted of the Rainbow Snake. These linkages make the Dreaming, which is the religious basis and cultural heart of Possum's culture, inherently spatial and geographic. The other Indigenous painters all knew this, of course, but perhaps had tended to focus on the Dreaming side of the linkage more than the geographic. Possum's idea was to begin from a specific site and then incorporate the Dreamings around this site. His painting *Warlugulong* that I discuss in Chapter 14 is a great example: it is centered on the Warlugulong site and incorporates many Dreamings around it.

Possum's conception also links with the traditional sand diagrams used to teach the young. When asked later in an interview about the origins of his guiding conception and from whom he might have gotten the idea, Possum replied:

> Nobody. My idea. I think, I do it this way: make it flash [stand out, be outstanding]. Well, I got to do all the story [stories] now, like [the] old people do'm. ... They draw'm in the sand first—might be with a stick. [They would say to their gathered audience,] "And all this story come this way. And this [other] story go [like this]—this one come half way [line in the sand]. And this one here, he come up here and finish up here. This one from right up there and he come right back around and finish up there." Like you see'm [in] my picture.[6]

This quote is interesting in showing how Possum made a clear link between the traditional sand diagram teaching and painting: the paintings were already based on the traditional motifs, but he saw how the actual storytelling would center on a place and tell many stories.[7]

There is another different connection with his context as well: a link with Western-style maps. Like the Indigenous sand diagrams and paintings, Western-style maps also take an aerial perspective to depict the landscape. Possum was surely aware of these kinds of maps, for they were constructed for visitors to his land. He had a personal link as well through his adoptive father One Pound Jimmy, who acted as a guide to visitors. This familiarity may have made it easier for him to envision the kind of art he wished to make. Possum thus made a creative link between art and maps in forming his guiding conception. Note that in Figure 4 there is no such link—this was his innovation.

Beyond his familiarity with maps, there also may have been a political aspect to Possum's intentions with his guiding conception linked to map making. Beginning in the 1960s the Indigenous peoples' struggle to reclaim rights to their traditional lands became an important political movement. An important part of this struggle was being able to make strong claims to their lands. Maps were important as a way to assist in making these land claims. Johnson notes that following passage of the Australian Land Rights Act in 1976, there was a concerted movement to produce maps of the Indigenous peoples' territories to assist in land claims. The fact that this issue was in the air may well have spurred Possum as he formed his conception in the years leading up to 1976, for his paintings, as Johnson puts it, are like "deeds of title" and he may have believed that through their "monumental size, complexity and sheer visual impact [they] would proclaim their cultural authority." Their precision, as Johnson states, can be argued to have given them "the validity of legal documents," making them "the Western Desert graphic equivalent of European land titles."[8] In addition, his brother Tim Leura with whom he collaborated artistically in these years served on the Aboriginal Arts Board in 1974 and may have come into direct contact with political discussions of land reclamation.[9] Later when Possum had the first solo exhibition by an Indigenous Australian artist in London in 1988, a reviewer described the paintings as "topographical depictions, establishing Aboriginal land rights."[10]

Thus Possum brought several distinct elements together in forming his guiding conception. In this sense his creativity in developing his guiding conception was integrative of multiple nodes, whereas Krebs linked two disparate parts of his context. Like Krebs's guiding conception, Possum's has breadth greater than an individual creative project. It is truly a template for what he would create. And create he did— see Chapter 14 for his process of creation of the first in the series of masterpieces that emanated from his conception.

VIRGINIA WOOLF

In 1917 at the age of thirty-five, while working on her second novel, *Night and Day*, Virginia Woolf took a break from the novel and "all in a flash," as she later told a friend, wrote her first short story in many years, "The Mark on the Wall." In this story she sets forth a guiding conception for what literature can and should be in the future, a conception that was implicitly a guide for her own literary development. Linked to her guiding conception, she also sets forth a guiding principle. I discuss both here as it is natural to do so, but note that I discuss guiding principles extensively in Chapters 11–13.

"The Mark on the Wall" opens with the narrator contemplating a mark on the wall opposite her. After contemplating the mark, the mystery of life in general, and the afterlife, where there will be no distinct things, "nothing but spaces of light and dark," the story shifts: "The tree outside the window taps very gently on the pane.... I want to think quietly, calmly, spaciously, never to be interrupted ... to slip easily from one thing to another, without any sense of hostility, or obstacle. I want to sink deeper and deeper, away from the surface, with its hard separate facts."[11] Shakespeare comes to her mind, his brilliance and creativity; then her thoughts flow on and land on herself.

"All the time" in social interactions, the narrator says, "I'm dressing up the figure of myself in my own mind," arranging social interactions so that they are "indirectly reflecting credit upon myself." If "the looking-glass smashes" and we no longer experience these reflections supporting our self-image, we are left in a "world not to be lived in."[12] The narrator then presents a striking conception of life centering on these "reflections" and their importance for literature:

> As we face each other in omnibuses and underground railways we are looking into the mirror; that accounts for the vagueness, the gleam of glassiness, in our eyes. And the novelists in future will realise more and more the importance of these reflections, for of course there is not one reflection but an almost infinite number; those are the depths they will explore, those the phantoms they will pursue, leaving the description of reality more and more out of their stories, taking a knowledge of it for granted, as the Greeks did and Shakespeare perhaps—but these generalisations are very worthless.[13]

This passage presents a guiding conception for a new form of literature. The core element is reflections, meaning here the gaze and opinions of others and how they affect us. We should not be fooled by the impersonal reference to "novelists in future." Woolf is drawn to this conception for herself, and in the ensuing years she would embrace it and seek to develop it in her own creative writing. Note also in this regard the final comment in this passage that "these generalisations are very worthless." Her frustration reveals that she does have a personal desire to find a way to develop this conception in literary form, and is frustrated by the fact that the conception is abstract and she is not sure how to go about this.

Yes, this guiding conception is indeed abstract in the way it refers to reflections in general, not referring to a specific setting or type of reflection; indeed it is philosophical in tone.[14] Contrary to Woolf's frustration at the time, however, I think this abstractness is a strength: it is the nature of guiding conceptions and what enables them to be effective for creative search. The conception does not provide a detailed blueprint for exactly what story to write, but it defines a realm of exploration that would ultimately bear her great fruit. It is also noteworthy that her conception is very creative in that it imagines an aspect of life previously neglected in literature as the basis for a new form of literature. Her guiding conception is an exemplar of what guiding conceptions can be, both in terms of creativity and providing guidance.

The passage states that reflections are "the depths" novelists "will explore," "the phantoms they will pursue." It is certainly striking, and I am sure no accident, that the term *reflection*—which we associate with the surface of things, like a mirror—is here paired with the opposite concept, *depth*. The opposition calls out that these reflections are important, serious, deep. I think in fact there are two levels of meaning in Woolf's statement. One is that the reflections help manifest the underlying self that is otherwise hidden from view. The Oxford English Dictionary gives a definition of "reflection" that is relevant for this interpretation: "A thing that is a consequence of or arises from something else," as in, "a healthy skin is a reflection of good health." Similarly, others' views of us reflect the state or nature of our inner self. The second meaning is that these reflections are not trivial or simple, but a deep concern for the future novel. This view is reinforced by calling the reflections "phantoms."[15] In using the word *phantom* here, Woolf seems to be alluding to the challenges that novelists will face in attempting successfully to capture and depict these reflections in all their depth of significance.

The passage also states that there is "not one reflection but an almost infinite number." This adds to the abstractness and also to our sense that this is a sweeping, ambitious conception. It also links her conception with her interest in biographies and lives, which I have discussed earlier in describing her context: the self is revealed by the "almost infinite number" of reflections it encounters and produces, and the novelist will need to depict these to manifest a human life.[16]

After the powerful conception of reflections, the passage goes on to state that novelists of the future will leave "the description of reality more and more out of their stories, taking a knowledge of it for granted, as the Greeks did and Shakespeare perhaps." This clause is also important and in fact turned out to be just as important for Woolf's literary development. The challenge she sets is to rely as much as possible on reflections to depict human life and not standard elements of description that hold a work together, what she later called "scaffolding" and compared to "brick." She also links this approach to perhaps the two highest stars in her literary firmament: the ancient Greeks, with their sparse dramas, and Shakespeare, with his economy of language, abstraction of character, and minimal description. She thus charts a return to their style, hoping perhaps to return to their level of literary brilliance but through a different path.

There is yet another layer of significance in this clause—lying behind it is a powerful connection to her own context, albeit one of opposition: the desire to negate the conventional Victorian novel. Woolf had grown up immersed in the Victorian world, a point that is well made by Hermione Lee in her detailed biography. Her father, steeped in a commitment to rigid rules and "objective" reality, exemplified this culture to her. I think it is fair to say she found this culture stifling despite whatever attachments she had to it. Her desire to negate this worldview was surely linked with her father in her mind, with whom she had a deep but conflicted bond.

The opposition to the Victorian worldview is present from the very first passage of the story, when the narrator notices a mark on the wall but does not want to get up and look closely to see what it is. This is a way of showing her desire not to become immersed in the world of objective facts. Then she imagines the afterlife as a place exactly without distinct objects, all just light and dark and blurry images. Shortly after, she states that she wants "to sink deeper and deeper, away from the surface, with its hard separate facts." Commenting later in the story on the word "generalisations," she states: "The military sound of the word is enough. It recalls leading articles, cabinet ministers—a whole class of things indeed which as a child one thought the thing itself, the standard thing, the real thing, from which one could not depart save at the risk of nameless damnation." The narrator goes on to say about Sundays, perhaps the epitome of the rigid way of life in which Woolf had grown up: "There was a rule for everything." Then she states her belief, in opposition to this Victorian mindset, that there is no objective knowledge: "No, no, nothing is proved, nothing is known."[17]

Toward the end of the story a lyrical image is depicted: "Yes, one could imagine a very pleasant world. A quiet spacious world, with the flowers so red and blue in the open fields. A world without professors or specialists or house-keepers with the profiles of policemen, a world which one could slice with one's thoughts as a fish slices the water with his fin, grazing the stems of the water-lilies, hanging suspended over nests of white sea eggs....[ellipses in original] How peaceful it is down here, rooted in the centre of the world and gazing up through the grey waters, with their sudden gleams of light, and their reflections."[18] This is an image of the self, suspended far below the surface, illuminated by reflections, set free from the conventional world epitomized by specialists, professors, and "house-keepers with the profiles of policemen." Thus the tension between the old rule-bound order and the freedom to escape from this to a world far away from objective facts, centering on reflections, runs through the entire story.

From the point of view of the framework in this book, the desire to negate the rule-bound Victorian world is better viewed not as part of Woolf's guiding conception of reflections, but rather as a guiding principle that sets forth a principle for what to eliminate. The narrator's statement that modern novelists will leave "the description of reality more and more out of their stories" reveals this—this is a statement about what to eliminate: the heavy, reality-based description so characteristic of literature of the nineteenth century. In modeling Woolf's creative process, it is valuable to separate this desire to leave reality out from the guiding conception of reflections; they function differently, as I will discuss, and by keeping them separate we can more clearly understand the logic of her creative process and literary development.

Woolf's guiding conception and guiding principle link important parts of her context on an abstract level and are an example of the creativity that is possible using this approach. Figure 10 provides a schematic of this. I have just described her powerful negative connection with the Victorian world—the old order, the world of her father. In some ways this guiding principle sets up the guiding conception, for Woolf was seeking a literary approach that would move away from this kind of representation.

The next element, which is at the core of her guiding conception, is the idea of reflections of the self. Reflections can be viewed as opposite

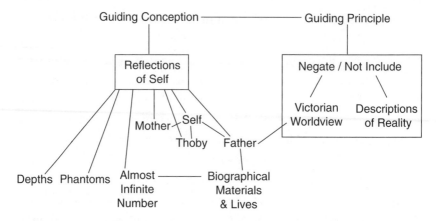

FIGURE 10. VIRGINIA WOOLF'S GUIDING CONCEPTION AND GUIDING PRINCIPLE

to reality itself—the material world that produces the reflections—and thus negate the old order. But I believe there is also a more personal resonance. Woolf lost her mother at the age of thirteen, and both her father and elder brother Thoby in the ensuing years. She thus lost these critical sources of personal reflection, reflections that show us ourselves and help us gain maturity and perspective on who we are. The importance of parental figures and others in providing reflections is emphasized by many psychologists, such as by Kohut in his work on self psychology.[19] Having lost these reflections so young seems to have made Woolf acutely aware of their importance in building and maintaining the self, which is exactly one of the themes in "The Mark on the Wall"—a view strongly supported both by her many comments about the importance of her mother and father to her and by the subject matter of her novels. Bouts of madness, which she had experienced by 1917, may also have heightened her sense of being cut off from ordinary human interaction at times, thus again heightening her awareness of its importance. Balancing these factors, Woolf also had much experience of reflections, for she was a highly social creature who engaged in many long conversations with friends as a young adult. All of these factors are relevant for understanding the powerful resonance her conception would have had for her.

Woolf adds additional descriptive elements to the core idea of reflections, which enrich her guiding conception. She describes the reflections as "phantoms," a term that fits in opposition to the hard-edged reality of the Victorian world. Yet these phantoms also have "depths" to be explored. Her conception also includes the idea that there are an "almost infinite number" of reflections. As noted above, this shows how her conception can depict a human life in full, which links with her longstanding interest in biography and lives—this link is shown in Figure 10.

Woolf's guiding conception very much fits the way I describe guiding conceptions. It imagines a literary realm to explore: different scenarios in which reflections of selves can arise such as overheard conversations, gossip, parties, letters, strung together in an "almost infinite" series; scenarios that will cast light on personalities, all the while leaving "the description of reality more and more out" of the account. Woolf would engage in just such exploration in the ensuing two and a half years in a series of stories, until she made a creative breakthrough that enabled her to refine her guiding conception.

"The Mark on the Wall" marks a crucial juncture in Virginia Woolf's creative development. Looking back on her development prior to this point, it is interesting to note scattered passages that in some respects anticipate the guiding conception she formed. It's not surprising that there were earlier, more fragmentary ideas that foreshadow the more coherent conception she formed in this story, somewhat like Gabora's notion of "honing" that eventually achieves coherence.[20]

The notion of mirrors of the self arises in Virginia's short story "Phyllis and Rosamond" of 1906, which is about two young women who attend a party in Bloomsbury. A hostess of the party, Sylvia, engages Phyllis in conversation; Phyllis tells Sylvia, "Yours is such a wonderful life; it is so strange to us." The narrator remarks, "Sylvia who wrote and had a literary delight in seeing herself reflected in strange looking-glasses, and of holding up her own mirror to the lives of others, settled herself to the task [of conversing with Phyllis] with gusto."

The conversation affects Phyllis's sense of self, and afterward the narrator comments, "In penetrating to her real self Phyllis had let in some chill gust of air to that closely guarded place; what did she really want, she asked herself?"[21] The language of the mirror and the self marks a clear link with "The Mark on the Wall." Nonetheless, these comments are just an aside in the story.

More interesting are connections with material in Woolf's journals during her trips to Greece and Italy in 1906 and 1908. In her 1906 journal she describes her fascination reading Prosper Mérimée's *Lettres à une inconnue*.[22] Only Mérimée's letters to his friend, an unknown woman, are presented, not her letters to him; Virginia comments that this creates a "puzzle"—"you do not hear her voice once." "To read the letters intelligently," she writes, "you must construct a reply; they demand it as imperiously as certain notes struck on the piano demand, & seem to imply their harmonies." Woolf remarks at how fascinating it is to try "to draw forth her notes from his" and speculates about their relationship. This guessing game of reconstruction may have helped her recognize how vital characters' replies to one another are as reflections in social interactions, and perhaps sparked some appreciation of the possibilities they held for literature.

In 1908 traveling in Italy, Woolf's creativity was stimulated by a fresco she saw by the Renaissance artist Perugino. "He saw things grouped," she writes. "Each part has a dependence upon the others; they compose one idea in his mind.... & express some view of beauty in his brain." She contrasts this with a creative aspiration for herself: "As for writing—I want to express beauty too—but beauty (symmetry?) of life & the world, in action." "I attain a different kind of beauty, achieve a symmetry by means of infinite discords, showing all the traces of the mind[']s passage through the world; & achieve in the end, some kind of whole made of shivering fragments."[23] Her vision for herself here in some ways foreshadows her later conception. She recognizes the idea of a whole composed out of disjoint fragments. She states that she will focus on the "mind[']s passage through the world," which indicates that even at this time she recognized that she wanted to illuminate the inner human world and not focus on the "objective" surface of reality.

However, despite how inspired this passage is, it is a significant conceptual distance from her later conception. She shifts in the latter from "discords" and "fragments" to the more defined, though still abstract, language of "reflections." And her aim shifts from depicting the mind's passage through the world, which is more strictly mental, to the self, which can include the life of the mind but also our emotional tenor, which for Woolf was complex and linked to mirroring, having lost her mother at a young age. Nonetheless, this passage is brilliant and supports the view that developing a guiding conception can take time and happen in stages.

JACK DORSEY

The origins of Twitter, founded in 2006, lie in a guiding conception Jack Dorsey formed much earlier. For those who do not know the story and imagine that Twitter emerged in a straightforward, simple manner in the world of technology, it is a great example illustrating how a distinctive guiding conception, held in mind yet not able to be realized successfully for a number of years, can ultimately bear fruit. In telling this story here and in Chapter 14, I note that the biographical information about Dorsey is limited and details may emerge later that significantly alter the story.[24]

Dorsey grew up in St. Louis. He was fascinated by the city life around him, especially the constant movement around the city—in his words, "what's going on in them right now."[25] He borrowed his father's CB radio, added a police scanner, and listened in. As he described, emergency units would report where they were, where they were going, and why. "So, for an ambulance in St. Louis: 'I'm at Fifth and Broadway, I'm going to St. John's Mercy, patient in cardiac arrest.' "[26] Dorsey learned to program and wrote a program to visualize the movements of these vehicles. Later, he got a job with a dispatch company in New York and wrote code for them. Then he and his supervisor moved to San Francisco and started another company.[27]

As Dorsey describes it, a key step in his development was recognizing that he wanted to incorporate people into his visualization of city life: "It's [the visualization program] missing the public. It's missing normal people."[28] He tried this a few different ways, but in his recollection an important attempt occurred around 2000–2001 with Instant Messenger (IM). IM itself was bound to a computer and thus wasn't mobile or real-time enough for Dorsey. He wanted people to be able to communicate where they were and what they were up to in real time to their friends. He explored a personal blogging platform called LiveJournal, also at that time computer based: "And it was cystallizing the thought: What if you have LiveJournal, but you just make it more live.... It all happens in real time, and you can update it from anywhere."[29]

Summarizing his interest and development, we can paraphrase Dorsey's guiding conception (this is my wording, not to be attributed to him): *A way to enable people to provide dispatches to (mainly) friends about their current status, in real time and mobile.* Although Dorsey had not been able to find a way to develop this guiding conception successfully through 2001, it came to the fore a few years later when he recognized a way to realize it, leading to the founding of Twitter.

Dorsey's context was rich and multifaceted, like the other creative people we have discussed. A diagram depicting his context would include many elements, including: St. Louis and his experience growing up in this city; his mother and father, each of whom had a role in his engagement with the city; the fact that he had a speech impediment and learned to be a good listener; his programming experiences and expertise; and his minimalist aesthetic.[30] Just as for Woolf and the others, he developed an original guiding conception based upon his context that made a new creative connection and pointed the way forward to creative possibilities. His example, added to the other three, helps make the point that this is a general pattern of creativity, not confined to any one field but rather broadly applicable.

ON THE ROAD TO CREATIVITY

The four examples in this chapter illustrate both the breadth and the creativity of guiding conceptions. Because guiding conceptions are not the same as "final" creativity, their creativity and originality is often not recognized. When we examine the creative process more closely, however, we see that the originality of a person's guiding conception often appears to be a vital basis for creative flowering that happens later, sometimes years later. This is true for each of the individuals discussed in this chapter, as will become clear when I present the creativity that flowed from their guiding conceptions in Chapters 14 and 15.

Nonetheless it is important to recognize that a guiding conception is not the same as final creativity: it does not have the same sense of a breakthrough achieved. Rather, guiding conceptions set us up to be creative. The reader may be frustrated to see the guiding conceptions of Hans Krebs, Clifford Possum, Virginia Woolf, and Jack Dorsey but not have the creative breakthroughs for which they are known also be presented. I must ask the reader to be patient: an important feature of creativity, as it happens in the real world and as I present it in this book, is that it happens in stages through an unfolding process. Guiding conceptions come first—the actual creative breakthroughs and final products come later.

CHAPTER 9

GUIDING CONCEPTIONS IN GREATER DEPTH

In this chapter I introduce the model of guiding conceptions used for formal analysis, then discuss characteristics of guiding conceptions and processes through which they are formed. In the last section I discuss related ideas in the literature and how guiding conceptions differ.

SIMPLE GUIDING CONCEPTIONS AND MODELING

A guiding conception is composed out of concepts that a person links imaginatively to form their overall conception. Most of these elements have a degree of breadth or abstraction; hence in terms of contexts modeled as networks with hierarchical structure, the framework introduced in Part I, they reside in the upper levels of contexts.

For the formal model in this book, I focus on the case in which a context has a two-level hierarchical structure and a guiding conception consists of two top-level elements. This is the simplest case that maintains the key structural feature that a guiding conception is composed by linking higher-level elements. In most cases these two elements are not directly linked; thus connecting them forges a novel creative

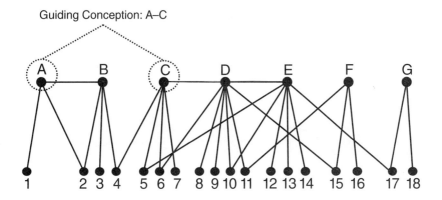

Seed Pool for Guiding Conception A–C: (1,4), (1,5),(1,6), (1,7), (2,5), (2,6), (2,7)

FIGURE 11. SMALL EXAMPLE CONTEXT: GUIDING CONCEPTION EXAMPLE

connection, albeit one that is strictly conceptual and imagined and must be developed further to yield an actual creative result.[1] A guiding conception might, for example, imagine combining two styles that have not previously been related to create a new fashion line, with the details of how this is done remaining to be worked out. Or it might envision applying a method (one element) to a topic (second element) to which the method has not previously been applied, as in the example of Hans Krebs.

As an illustration of this kind of guiding conception, consider the small example context originally introduced in Figure 2. Figure 11 depicts this context and highlights one guiding conception, consisting of the pair of top elements *A–C*.

Real-world guiding conceptions are in many cases more complex than this and consist of more than just two elements. More generally a guiding conception is a conceptual structure, a set of interlinked elements; certainly this set can consist of more than two elements, and the conception may itself have structure, as in the case where one element is particularly central. However, notwithstanding the potentially greater complexity of real-world guiding conceptions, the core of a guiding conception is in many cases just a few elements, so the assumption of two is not so far off. The model can be extended to guiding conceptions composed out of more than two elements (see Chapter 16); however, this

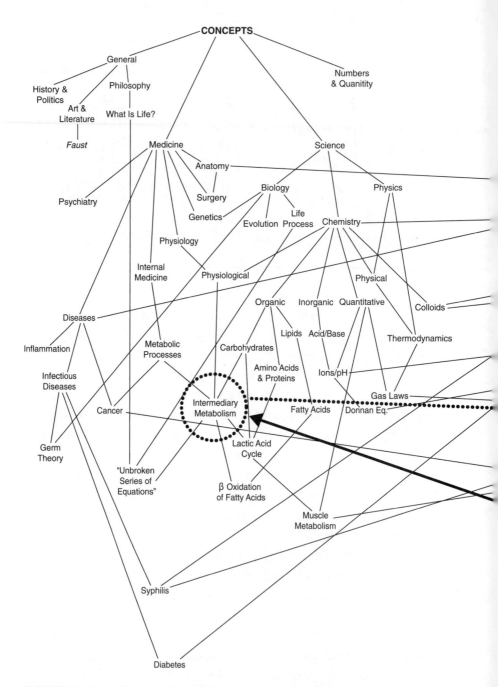

FIGURE 12. Hans Krebs's Guiding Conception in His Context

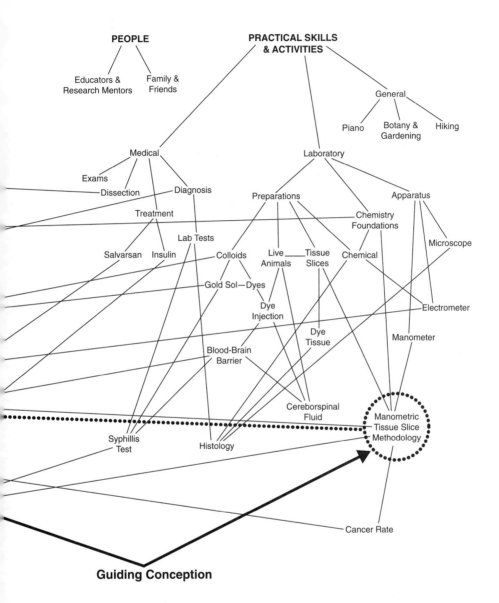

PEOPLE

Educators & Research Mentors

Family & Friends

PRACTICAL SKILLS & ACTIVITIES

General

Piano

Botany & Gardening

Hiking

Medical

Laboratory

Exams

Dissection

Diagnosis

Preparations

Apparatus

Treatment

Chemistry Foundations

Microscope

Lab Tests

Salvarsan

Insulin

Colloids

Live Animals

Tissue Slices

Chemical

Gold Sol—Dyes

Dye Injection

Electrometer

Dye Tissue

Manometer

Blood-Brain Barrier

Cereborspinal Fluid

Manometric Tissue Slice Methodology

Syphillis Test

Histology

Cancer Rate

Guiding Conception

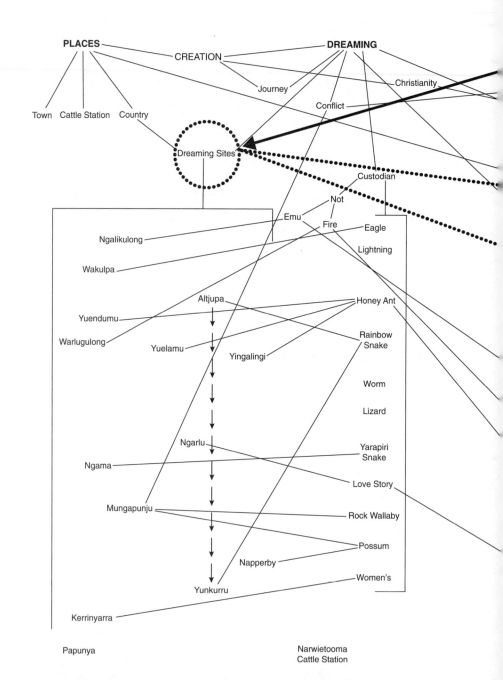

FIGURE 13. CLIFFORD POSSUM'S GUIDING CONCEPTION IN HIS CONTEXT

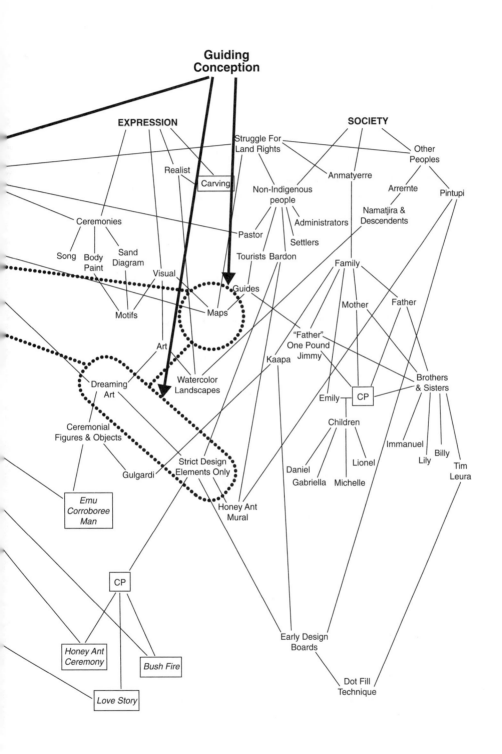

comes at the expense of greater complexity. Further, many insights can be gained from the simple two-element case.

For real-world evidence that confirms the basic structure of guiding conceptions consider the examples of the previous chapter. Figure 12 reproduces Hans Krebs's context with his guiding conception delineated. In his guiding conception Krebs linked two elements, "intermediary metabolism" shown on the left side with "manometric tissue slice methodology" shown on the right. In the figure these two elements are circled and connected. Note that they are three steps apart in the original context and quite separated, highlighting the creativity of this link. Figure 13 reproduces Clifford Possum's context with his guiding conception delineated. The elements at the core of his guiding conception are circled and connected in the figure: the Dreaming art node, also including "strict design elements only" as this was the artistic style he would employ; Dreaming sites—this is an important shift, as up to this time the artists linked the art with individual Dreamings, not directly to Dreaming sites; and maps, a node shown on the right in the figure, but not previously linked with the art. The creativity is clear in the new links created by his conception.

Next consider Virginia Woolf and Jack Dorsey. I have not depicted these two individuals' contexts in detail, but again their guiding conceptions link a few core elements. Referring to Figure 10 (p. 120), Woolf's guiding conception has a central element "reflections of self," which is actually a composite of two elements, "reflections" and "self." This central element links with "depths" and "phantoms" as well as with an "almost infinite number," which is itself a composite of elements. Additional links shown, to her mother and father and her allied guiding principle, I do not view as part of her guiding conception but rather supporting elements. Finally Jack Dorsey's guiding conception as I have paraphrased it can also be defined in terms of a few key elements: communication, mobile and in real time, about current conditions, to friends.

Guiding conceptions focus creative attention and generate seed ideas that may be able to be developed into creative projects. I focus on the following simple structure that defines how seeds are generated. Each guiding conception element is linked to its "children" on the bottom level. Potential seeds are generated by combining pairs of child elements, where one child comes from each "parent" guiding conception element. This defines a seed pool consisting of all these pairwise combinations of children of the two guiding conception parent elements.

I assume this seed pool is explored in a random sequence. If the guiding conception is based on sound intuition, then at least one seed in the pool should have high potential to be developed into a successful project. I assume the individual who has formed the guiding conception and is exploring it is able to recognize such high-potential seeds when they try them. If no high-potential seeds are discovered after trying all seeds in the pool, then the pool is exhausted and a new guiding conception must be formed in order to generate a new pool to search. It is also possible that the individual may form a new conception before exhausting the pool, due to some new insight or experience, and shift to the new pool associated with their new conception.[2]

Refer again to Figure 11. Element A has two children, 1 and 2, and element C has four children, 4, 5, 6, and 7. The seed pool consists of pairs of these elements formed by linking a child of one guiding conception element with a child of the other. Recall that a pair is valid only if it satisfies the condition that its two members do not share a common parent. This rules out one of the eight potental seeds, pair (2, 4), since these two elements share a common parent B. Therefore there are seven valid seed pairs in the seed pool defined by this guiding conception, listed in the figure.

In mathematical terms, a seed pool is a set that contains sets of elements, since a seed is itself a set of elements—in the simple model, pairs of bottom elements. Pairing the children of the two guiding conception elements to form seeds is an especially simple and easy case to model. This simple form is useful for exposition and formal modeling, and I focus on it. However, the essential argument does not depend on this specific structure. The essential point is that guiding conceptions define seed pools and that these seed pools are relatively small compared with the number of potential seeds in the context as a whole, which, as we have seen in Table 2, can be enormous.[3]

While I focus on the simple model in which guiding conceptions consist of two elements and seeds consist of pairs of children, it is useful to consider how the model can be extended to model guiding conceptions that define other types of seed pools. There are three generalizations in particular that I discuss here; they are relevant for the examples in this book and likely to be important for many empirical applications. One is guiding conceptions with more vertical layers. This only makes sense for contexts with more than two levels, but real contexts typically have more levels as discussed earlier—this is true of both the Hans Krebs and Clifford Possum contexts. For example, a guiding conception might include a high-level element and then refine this with additional elements one or more levels down in the context hierarchy that have a degree of breadth but also greater specificity; this is the case for Clifford Possum's conception that refines "Dreaming art" by linking it downward with the particular Papunya style of "strict design elements only."

A second generalization is pools of lower-level elements linked to a guiding conception being qualified by one or more additional guiding conception elements that filter these pools, ruling out certain seeds and leaving a smaller pool to explore. As an example, an individual may desire to focus on linking two topics, but may wish to restrict to seeds that also possess a particular attribute. Thus an artist or photographer may be interested in a certain kind of image but restrict their focus in terms of the color range or light intensity they wish to explore. This refines the pool of seeds to be explored, which clearly can make search more targeted and thus more efficient. I discuss modeling this kind of guiding conception in Chapter 16, including results of simulations exploring how these kinds of guiding conceptions act to restrict seed pools.

The third and most challenging generalization is guiding conceptions whose elements act jointly to define seeds. Rather than a seed consisting of children each of which is linked with a single guiding element, more generally a guiding conception can act as a unit to define seeds. For example, if a guiding conception involves "striped diagonal patterns" then seeds in its pool will consist of sets of elements that conform to this pattern, such as alternating white and black stripes on diagonals. It is clear in this case that we cannot identify one seed element with one guiding conception element and another with a different guiding conception element because the attribute "striped" applies holistically to a seed. This argument applies far more broadly than this simple visual example. Many guiding conceptions describe overall patterns or themes that a seed as a whole fits. Extending the model to this case adds conceptual range and will help increase empirical applicability. I believe the main arguments I make should continue to hold under this kind of generalization, but it will be important to determine the conditions under which this is the case.

Beyond issues of generality, it is important to recognize that conceptual thinking is fluid, and this extends to creative thinking. Douglas Hofstadter for example has emphasized fluid thinking as an important attribute of creative thinking in *Fluid Concepts and Creative Analogies*.[4] Guiding conceptions can be thought of as a part of the conceptual creative process that is more stable. Even so, an individual's mental representation of their guiding conception may be subject to instability and an individual may focus on different aspects of their conception and different connections it has with other elements at different timepoints. Further, as noted above, guiding conceptions evolve and individuals oftentimes replace one conception with a second, more developed related conception; this occurred for Virginia Woolf, for example. Guiding conceptions may also have additional roles. For example, they may help guide individuals as they build their context, and they may help bring elements more clearly into consciousness. I discuss a number of these issues in more detail in Chapter 16.

Finally, guiding conceptions do not work alone. Rather, it is best to think of them as working in tandem with other factors. I focus in particlar on how they work in tandem with guiding principles. This is one of the themes of this book and the core of the two-step creativity model I present. A host of other more fluid conceptual processes may also enter into the creative process. For example, conversations and chance encounters may spur someone to rethink their guiding conception. Also, practical issues like resources as well as organizational factors can be important for how someone forms and frames their guiding conception and how they go about exploring it. A further issue is collaborative creativity in regard to guiding conceptions—guiding conceptions formed collectively in teams and thus influenced by interpersonal factors including group dynamics. The framework presented in this book should not be taken as standing alone; rather, it provides a structure that can be combined with many other factors to help us understand and model the creative process better.

FORMS OF GUIDING CONCEPTIONS

Guiding conceptions have some characteristic features: they are abstract, broader than specific projects or finalized ideas, and there is a sense of openness about them—they imagine avenues and pools to explore creatively. However, they also vary in their structure and form. I describe three forms here that are especially common.

One common form of guiding conception is imagining connecting or combining distinct areas, themes, or approaches that have not previously been connected. This feature fits with the general definition of creativity, and indeed guiding conceptions can be very creative. But here the connection envisioned is at a higher, more abstract level and is not a final creative product but rather must be realized via more specific elements. An example is applying an approach or technique that has been developed in one field or area to a new area to which it has never previously been applied. Hans Krebs's guiding conception had this form: he envisioned applying a laboratory methodology to a novel area. Another example would be combining two styles that have previously been seen as disconnected, like two disparate fashion styles.

A second common form of guiding conception is envisioning an aspiration or aim. Indeed this may well be the first thought that comes to mind when the term *guiding conception* is mentioned. Sometimes the aspiration or aim is quite tangibly defined: landing a man on the moon was a guiding conception for the American space program in the 1960s. It is important to note that even in this case the guiding conception, although visionary, did not include details for the steps required to achieve the aspiration. It took more than eight years following President Kennedy's speech in which he articulated this vision until it was realized, during which time there were many steps taken to develop the technology and protocols needed to achieve this goal.[5] A guiding conception is not a detailed blueprint but a vision that may be far off and may never be achieved in the form in which it is imagined. However, it does provide guidance and focus as well as motivation. Elon Musk's stated goal of establishing a human colony on Mars is another guiding aspiration for humans in space.[6] The realization of this is undoubtedly further off than realizing Kennedy's aspiration was when he gave his speech, and it remains to be seen how far humans can move toward realizing it in the decades ahead; even so, it can provide guidance for a targeted space program.

In some cases a guiding conception aim or aspiration is quite abstract. For example, Virginia Woolf's conception of a literary form based on reflections was aspirational as well as abstract. Indeed her initial reaction was frustration that it consisted of, in her words, "generalisations" that were potentially too abstract to prove useful. Nonetheless it did provide a vision to work toward, even if initially she was unclear about this and did not fully recognize how important it would turn out to be for her literary development.

A third form of guiding conception centers on finding an answer to a question or puzzle. To be most helpful for guidance, the guiding conception will not only identify the question but also imagine possible avenues to explore to answer, solve, or resolve it. Albert Einstein's path of development fits this general form. At the age of sixteen, according to his later account, he hit upon a paradox involving Maxwell's equations and traveling behind a light beam. He was unable to resolve the paradox at first. Later, with greater knowledge and experience, he seems to have recognized the need to explore more widely including in the realm of philosophy, which led him on an intellectual voyage that brought him ultimately to David Hume's *Treatise of Human Nature*, which was, again on his own account, critical for his resolution of the paradox with the development of the special theory of relativity.[7] Thus he widened his initial paradox into a broader guiding conception, and this proved valuable and possibly critical in resolving the paradox. I discuss his development after this, developing the general theory of relativity, specifically his key guiding principle, in Chapter 12.

An additional, important issue related to the form of guiding conceptions is that in some cases there is a negativity orientation associated with a guiding conception. I write "associated with" because when a negativity orientation is present, it is often better thought of as a guiding principle. Negativity here means opposing something, which could be an established tradition, line of inquiry, style, or particular assumption or value, and striving to create something different. This kind of negative thinking can help a person sharpen their thinking: knowing what they oppose and desire to challenge or change can help them define more clearly what they want to create and achieve. Virginia Woolf wished to develop a literary form that would cut against traditional Victorian literature and culture by "leaving the description of reality more and more out," and this was arguably just as important in helping her achieve a new literary form as her positive conception of reflections. Thus she had a positively oriented guiding conception linked with a negative guiding principle. A positive guiding conception linked with a negative guiding principle can be a powerful combination for creative guidance and is an approach utilized by many individuals who achieve successful creative outcomes.

THE FORMATION OF GUIDING CONCEPTIONS

Given how important guiding conceptions are for guiding the creative process, it is natural to wonder how they are developed. Understanding this not only can help us better understand the creative process but also can be valuable for mentoring individuals and helping them form a guiding conception of their own. I do not specify a model of how guiding conceptions come to be developed in this book; this is an issue to be explored as part of modeling the rich dynamics of creative development. However, this process of development is part of many of the examples in this book, and from them we can learn something about it. I have identified a number of common patterns and outline three here.

Perhaps most evidently, individuals form guiding conceptions based on thinking about their experiences and what they have learned. The case of Hans Krebs illustrates this. Working in the Warburg lab and recognizing the power of the laboratory techniques he was learning, he connected them with a topic that had fascinated him since college, intermediary metabolism. Notice that one of the two prongs of his conception was based on recent learning and experience. I believe it is not uncommon for an individual to form a guiding conception by linking a current experience or recent learning with prior experiences and learning.

A second way in which guiding conceptions are formed is through the coalescing of disparate experiences and elements into a coherent whole. The case of Virginia Woolf illustrates this pattern. During the decade prior to her formulation of her guiding conception in "The Mark on the Wall," she made comments on several occasions that involved concepts and elements that figured in her later conception. Notably she described reflection of the self and the sense of a hidden self revealed only partially via reflection, and also her desire to depict a whole life as a series of fragments, later to be viewed as a series of reflections. In addition she was wrestling with the deaths of her parents and brother Thoby over these years and the loss of the mirroring they had provided. Her guiding conception links these different, more fragmentary descriptions and her personal feelings of loss into a powerful vision for literature.

Another form of this kind of coalescence is recognizing a larger pattern among a series of observations. Charles Darwin made many observations as naturalist on the *Beagle* during its voyage circumnavigating South America. Ultimately on the long voyage home he recognized, fitting these observations together, that they provided support for what he at the time called the theory of "transmutation" of species. This broader conception became his guide, and he embarked on a quest to develop a coherent model to explain his observations.[8]

It is noteworthy that this second pattern illustrated by Woolf and Darwin is one in which lower-level, more specific elements have an important role, being drawn together into a more abstract, higher-level conception. This is an example of bottom-up processes having an important role in the creative process. As I have discussed in earlier chapters, there are important dynamic flows in both bottom-up and top-down directions over the course of the creative process. Although I focus mainly on top-down processes, the framework should be able to be extended to incorporate bottom-up processes.

Finally, a third way in which guiding conceptions form is through recognizing a gap or opportunity or an anomaly in a field. If one perceives a gap, one can form a guiding conception to explore how to fill the gap. In economics the role of the entrepreneur is sometimes taken to be to recognize such gaps and the opportunities they afford; this perspective was emphasized by Israel Kirzner in *Perception, Opportunity, and Profit.*[9] Clifford Possum recognized a gap in the art being made at Papunya in that it focused on depicting just a single Dreaming, and this was surely an important factor leading him to formulate his guiding conception of depicting many Dreamings in a single painting. The paradox Einstein hit upon at the age of sixteen was an anomaly; he may or may not have realized just how profound it was initially, but as the years went by and he could not solve it, he came to appreciate its depth and challenge.

The idea that anomalies spark guiding conceptions fits with Kuhn's idea of anomalies playing a pivotal role in scientific revolutions.[10] However, Kuhn does not explicitly discuss how individuals recognize and respond to anomalies or through which creative processes they create new paradigms. The model I present provides a way to pursue developing such an account.

STANDARD CREATIVITY PERSPECTIVES IGNORE GUIDING CONCEPTIONS

Guiding conceptions do not appear in the creativity literature, although there are related concepts in creativity and allied fields. However, none of these is the same and none centers on guidance the way I describe the function of guiding conceptions. Indeed guidance generally is absent from the field of creativity. This absence has left a gap. It has limited the ability to model and understand how creativity arises, especially in large-scale, more complex contexts; and it has limited focus on related issues such as how individuals organize their experiences and both organize and direct their learning and creative exploration.

Two examples of related concepts are Howard Gruber's notion of images of wide scope and Liane Gabora's honing principle.[11] Gruber's images of wide scope are broad and can generate multiple insights, but they are less abstract than guiding conceptions, at least as he describes them. I view them as tools for generating creativity but not designed for guidance in the same way as a guiding conception. Gabora's honing principle is broad in that it is rooted in an emerging worldview, can help organize experiences and perceptions, and can generate creativity. However, her model does not include guidance as I describe it. Instead it offers a fascinating but different viewpoint on the creative process, describing attaining a global mental state of coherence and the way this process is linked to expressing creativity.

The use of higher-level concepts to structure thinking relates to the idea of frames and frame-based reasoning in computer science introduced by Marvin Minsky, also related to the idea of scripts and cognitive schemata in psychology.[12] Frames and scripts have most commonly been used to model fairly noncreative, routine activities like going to a restaurant for a meal. In contrast I emphasize the creativity and distinctiveness of individuals' guiding conceptions—these conceptions are themselves creative, which in turn leads to creative projects and outcomes.

In the computational creativity field, frames have evolved into templates. For example, a narrative template specifies a structure—such as a plot structure having key elements like a protagonist and action sequences—and this blank structure is then filled in with specifics. This is done by searching over combinations, mostly at random, in an effort to find a combination that is highly creative. In their review of computational generative poetry techniques Carolyn Lamb, Daniel Brown, and Charles Clarke discuss templates as one of the principal approaches for computationally generating poetry.[13] Related approaches combine elements from two domains or categories to search for valuable novel combinations.[14] These kinds of "top-down" approaches bear a resemblance to my approach in that a higher-level structure is used to restrict the search process to combining elements from specified sets.[15] However, there is a significant difference in that in these computational models, the templates or category pairs are not linked to creative intuition but rather are quite standardized and not themselves very creative. Thus in the computational template world, the generation of creativity is focused at the bottom level of "filling in the blanks." In reality I believe there is much creativity at the higher level—that guiding conceptions are far from standard but rather encapsulate creative intuition and are often highly creative and distinctive. I believe that the approach in this book could be brought to the computational template approach with potentially fruitful results.

It is important to recognize that guidance is antithetical to the widespread view of creativity as generated through a random search process. This view has been put forward by many over the years, notably Donald Campbell and more recently Dean Simonton.[16] In this view the creative exploratory process is not directed but consists of randomly trying new combinations until a successful combination is hit upon. As I emphasize throughout this book, this is a woefully inefficient approach: trying out a creative connection or combination is time consuming and often costly in other ways as well, and if there are many possibilities, it will not be possible to try more than a small fraction.[17] See the next chapter for a demonstration and discussion.

In addition to how inefficient this random approach is, this view of the creative process gives surprisingly little credit to the intuition and thoughtfulness with which individuals go about directing their creative endeavors. In my experience studying, interviewing, and examining the creative process of many individuals across many fields, there is a great deal of guidance in the creative process. Yes, creativity does strike unexpectedly—if we knew exactly which combination would work, of course we would start with that one and there would be little to the process. The fact that someone does not know exactly which creative combination will succeed, however, does not mean their process as a whole is unguided. Individuals and teams engaged in creative endeavors are very thoughtful about where and what they search. They do not know exactly which combination to try, but they develop intuition about which kinds of combinations to try and where to explore creatively. This guidance enables them to search far more efficiently through the myriad of possibilities. The fallacy of models based on random search is that they jump from the truth that creativity is unexpected to the false conclusion that therefore the creative process must be random.

Standard economic models of creativity also focus on random search, in this case by drawing values from a distribution.[18] This approach largely eschews modeling the actual creative process. Further, the distribution of outcomes from which draws are made is given in a prespecified, largely ad-hoc manner, although it may depend on parameters and thus have some empirical flexibility. Weitzman's model of combinatoric search does generate the distribution from an underlying combinatoric process; however, it does not have any sense of guidance.[19]

Problem finding is another branch of the creativity literature related to guidance. This literature is surprisingly small: in a survey of the literature, Ahmed Abdulla and Bonnie Cramond identify just 199 papers published over the period 1960–2015.[20] Guidance is scarcely mentioned in the small literature that does exist. In many discussions problem finding or the related concept of problem formulation are framed as bringing clarity to an ambiguous, ill-defined situation. This is important but a narrower frame than a guiding conception provides. Guiding conceptions are more open and initiate creative exploration rather than responding to ambiguity—think for example of Virginia Woolf's conception of reflections—although ambiguity might be a factor in someone's development of a guiding conception.[21]

A guiding conception can spawn a problem. But I think a more interesting and relevant link is that formulating a problem can resemble forming a guiding conception, even if it isn't often framed this way. The connection is most evident and valid when the problem is sufficiently broadly stated initially that there are many possible routes to explore. Also, sometimes a set of problems fit together and identify a larger issue to be resolved. Einstein certainly expanded the scope for exploring his paradox, linking it with the problem of induction and then expanding his focus to read in the field of philosophy. Notwithstanding this connection, however, in most discussions of problem finding in the creativity literature, the focus is narrow, the problem viewed as quite specifically defined, and the notion that it functions like a higher-level conception that opens up into many different pathways to explore is largely absent and certainly not the focus. Thus the guiding conception model in this book can enrich the problem-finding literature.

Further, the approach in this book can link problem finding with a formal model and especially models of context, viewed in this book as networks. This is important as the search for problems surely happens in large-scale, rich contexts, and thus the modeling approach is highly relevant.

Probably the concept that is closest to the idea of a guiding conception is "creative vision." This concept is not used very much in the academic literature but is central to many popular discussions of creativity. In fact, creative vision is used in two different ways and neither is the same as a guiding conception, although there are connections.

Most commonly creative vision is used to describe a vision for a creative project. Many artists and designers describe creative vision in these terms, such as this quote attributed to Michelangelo about the creation of his *David*: "I created a vision of David in my mind and simply carved away everything that was not David."[22] As a more current example, on the MasterClass website there is an interesting post about creative vision that fits with this framing: "Jodie Foster's 5 Tips for Realizing Your Creative Vision in Film." Foster's tips are couched in terms of realizing one's creative vision for a specific film through effective communication, the aim being to "bring your creative vision to life."[23] Similar usage is prevalent in photography. Ansel Adams emphasized the importance of what he called "visualization" over technical skill. "Over the years," he writes in *Examples: The Making of 40 Phtographs*, "I became increasingly aware of the importance of visualization. The ability to anticipate—to see in the mind's eye so to speak—the final print while viewing the subject."[24] Part one of David Noton's *Waiting for the Light* is titled "Vision" and centers on the expertise required to be able to visualize what a photo will look like. Being able to "see the potential in a location, envisaging how a scene could look, appreciating the nuances of light, motion, colour, perspective and composition, is what photography is all about."[25] In terms of the model in this book, this kind of creative vision is narrower than a guiding conception; it is about envisioning how a project will turn out. A guiding conception will be formed earlier, helping to generate visions for multiple potential projects.

The second way "creative vision" is used, also prevalent in the arts, refers to a creative person's overarching vision for the art they aspire to create. Used this way the phrase is closer to the concept of a guiding conception but seems to have a longer time duration, used in a way that implies that a person develops a creative vision that serves them over their entire career. For example, in an article for the New York Institute of Photography titled "Finding Your Creative Vision," Anthony Luke writes: "I think one of the most important and difficult stages of one's creative life is finding one's creative vision. A lucky few seem to come out of the gate with a unique and wonderful style, or artistic vision. For most of us, however, it takes years, even decades, to really find that inner creative voice."[26] Renée Phillips has an article titled "Expressing Your Unique Creative Vision as an Artist" on her website for artists, again the sense being one of developing a lifelong artistic vision.[27] A guiding conception can include these kinds of overarching stylistic elements but is more limited in temporal scope, focused on the creative projects directly ahead. Virginia Woolf's conception of reflections, as broad and deep as it is, did not define her creative vision over her entire literary career but rather provided a template for her work over the next several years, after which time her conception evolved.

Each of these two definitions of creative vision could presumably be worked out in the formal modeling framework I present, which would be an interesting exercise. I don't believe either would be coincident with the way I define guiding conceptions. The first would target a more specific domain for a project and probably be more meaningful in models with larger projects, for which project creative vision helps fill in all the missing pieces; this fits with my model but would be an extension of it. The latter definition seems quite broad and probably would fit better in a model with more than two levels of context, so that such an overarching style could be formed at very high levels while guiding conceptions would sit slightly lower down in the context hierarchy; this would be an interesting extension and might well fit naturally.

A related concept is the idea of a vision statement of an organization. In his post titled "The 101 Most Inspiring Vision Statement Examples For 2022!" Tom Wright writes: "A vision statement is an aspirational statement made by an organization that articulates what they would like to achieve. Furthermore, the vision guides the direction of the organization's efforts."[28] The use for guidance does resonate with the concept of a guiding conception. Most such vision statements are very broad, however. To give an example, Pfizer provides a statement of "Our Purpose" on their website: "We're in relentless pursuit of breakthroughs that change patients' lives. We innovate every day to make the world a healthier place. It was Charles Pfizer's vision at the beginning and it holds true today."[29] The wording of this statment is definitely broader than a guiding conception, and would seem to limit effective guidance. As a second example, on their website home page IBM states, "We discover, design and develop advanced information technology, and translate that into value for our clients through consulting services."[30] This provides some guidance in the focus on advanced information technology, but still seems very broad, certainly far broader than the kinds of guiding conceptions presented in case studies in this book. Thus organization vision statements, although they could potentially fit with the concept of a guiding conception, in reality are broader, and as a result are not likely to be very effective in guiding creative exploration.

We can speculate as to why guidance has been largely overlooked in the field of creativity. I think one reason is that guidance structures represent an intermediate creative step, illuminators of creative paths, rather than ultimate creative ideas and outcomes. The final outcome, and the final step that leads to it, gets the most attention and can be dazzling—but the entire process and creative path is important. Hopefully my argument and model in this book will help to correct this failing and help us move toward better descriptions and models of the overall creative process.

CHAPTER 10

THE MODEL OF GUIDING CONCEPTIONS AND THE BENEFITS OF GUIDED SEARCH

In this chapter I describe how guiding conceptions function in the formal model to guide creative search. The main result is that guiding conceptions based on valid intuition are a very efficient way to discover a promising seed project. To this end I compare search based on a guiding conception, which involves searching just over the pool of possibilities associated with the guiding conception, what I call its *seed pool*, to random search over the entire context. Random search over all or much of a person's context is often explicitly or implicitly the way creative search is modeled, as discussed in the preceding chapter. I show that guiding conceptions based on correct intuition provide a large gain in efficiency compared to this kind of unfocused, random search. I both quantify and bound this gain, using a mixture of analytic and simulation results. The results show that scale is a critical factor: the benefit of using a guiding conception compared with random search increases dramatically with the scale of creative contexts.

The analysis also highlights two additional points. One, for any context of even moderate scale there are a large number of guiding conceptions. The implication is that there is a lot of intuition involved in forming a highly productive guiding conception. Two, there is considerable variability in the size of seed pools associated with different guiding conceptions; hence some guiding conceptions require more search than others.

In the last section of the chapter I turn to a second question: How many guiding conceptions cover a given project? As I define this term, a guiding conception covers a project when one of the seeds in its seed pool is composed of two of the three project elements, so that starting from this seed, it is possible to develop the full project by identifying the third element. Based on the simulations there is substantial variation across projects in terms of how many guiding conceptions cover them. In particular I show that some projects are unusual in the sense that only a few guiding conceptions cover them. These projects may or may not have more creative potential than others, but they will be less likely to be discovered by many individuals and thus will make a distinctive contribution. In turn this raises the interesting question of whether the guiding conceptions that cover these rare projects themselves have smaller seed pools, so that they are highly focused. I explore this issue and show that while it does not hold for the most standard networks, it does hold for some network contexts.

I focus in this chapter on the formal model in which there are two layers of elements. Each bottom element has a vertical link to at least one top element and may have additional vertical links to other top elements. There may also be horizontal links between top elements; however, this feature turns out not to be important for the analysis in this chapter, so I do not discuss it.

Guiding conceptions are assumed to be composed of two top elements; this follows the discussion in the preceding chapter. Although this is simpler than many real-world guiding conceptions, there is much insight to be gained from this simple model.[1] A guiding conception has associated with it a set of *seed projects*, or as I will more simply call them, *seeds*. A seed consists of a pair of bottom-level elements. The aim is to create or discover a seed with high creative potential.

I focus on the simple model introduced in the previous chapter—the seeds associated with a guiding conception pair children of the respective guiding conception elements. Thus each seed consists of two elements, with one element being a child of one of the guiding conception elements and the other a child of the other guiding conception element. For a pair of bottom elements to be a valid seed pair, the two elements cannot share a common parent; hence not all pairs of children will be valid seeds. I call the set of valid seeds associated with a guiding conception its *seed pool*.[2]

This model that defines seeds as pairs of children is especially tractable and clear and helps elucidate the main point about guidance. But it is not essential for the overall framework. The essential point is that guiding conception seed pools, although they may contain a considerable number of valid seeds, contain far fewer than are in the context as a whole. Further, when a guiding conception is based on valid intuition—this is critical for it to be useful for creativity generation—there will be at least one seed in its pool with high creative potential. One can certainly imagine conceptually richer ways of generating seeds from guiding conceptions; this will be important for developing the model further, which I discuss in Chapter 16.

The results in this chapter are based on the two-step model of the creative process: step 1 is searching to discover or create a high-potential-value seed, and step 2 is developing the seed into a successful project by adding the crucial third element. The focus in this chapter is on the first step. I model this as trying out or testing seeds sequentially until one identifies a seed that has potential to be developed into a high-value creative project.

There are other possible search protocols and models of the creative process one could consider, but I believe they are less intuitive and do not match empirical observations of creative search. Given that in the base model a project consists of three bottom elements, one alternative is to search directly over triplets of bottom elements. This would imply that a complete project is created in one step. This is not generally the way the creative process works, and it is easy to see why from the point of view of search efficiency: there are a lot fewer pairs than triples. For example, in the large-scale simulated contexts there are around 4.4 million pairs but 4.4 billion projects! In this kind of context, if it is possible to recognize the creative potential of a seed pair when one tries it, then it is clearly more efficient to search over seed pairs first because there are far fewer of these, and then develop a promising seed into a full project. This is literally starting from a creative kernel—a seed— and then developing it; my observations convince me this is very much the way the creative process works most of the time.

A different approach would be to search for individual bottom elements that have high potential and, once one identifies such an element, search for two additional elements to develop it into a full project. The difficulty with this approach is that the essence of creativity is creating new creative connections, and this requires fitting two elements together. Focusing on single elements runs counter to this: it will be hard to determine the creative potential of a single isolated element. Having said that, I think sometimes individuals do identify individual elements, and the model can be extended to develop this approach. However, searching for a high-value seed pair fits better with the idea of creativity as making new connections, the seed being the incipient idea from which the project is developed.[3]

The remainder of the chapter is divided into three main subparts: A, seed pool sizes; B, the main result concerning the benefits of guided search; and C, guiding conception project coverage distributions. I begin first with a short discussion of the number of guiding conceptions.

THE NUMBER OF GUIDING CONCEPTIONS

Before moving to part A, it is useful to consider the number of guiding conceptions in a context. A guiding conception as defined above and in the preceding chapter is composed out of a pair of top elements. In the small-scale example context there are 7 top elements. Each pair of top elements can be used to form a guiding conception. Using standard combinatoric notation, there are $\binom{7}{2} = \frac{7 \times 6}{2} = 21$ distinct guiding conceptions in this context. More generally in a network with N top elements there are $\binom{N}{2} = \frac{N(N-1)}{2}$ distinct pairs of top elements, and hence this many potential guiding conceptions.[4] One immediate conclusion is that in even a reasonably sized context there will be many potential guiding conceptions. For example, if $N = 100$, there are $4,950$ possible guiding conceptions, and if $N = 1,000$, there are $499,500$ possible guiding conceptions. These are large numbers, and real contexts may well be even larger. This shows that there is plenty of scope for originality and diversity in forming guiding conceptions, meaning that different individuals will naturally tend to form different guiding conceptions and hence follow different creative paths.

A. SEED POOL SIZES

The size of a seed pool is the number of valid seed pairs it contains. A larger pool is likely to require more exploration to hit upon a high-value seed. For example, if there is a single high-value seed pair in the pool—what I call a "golden seed" in the argument to follow—and pairs in the pool are investigated in a random order, then the larger the pool, the greater the expected number of seeds that will need to be investigated to find this golden seed. Thus pool size is a critical factor governing the amount of search associated with a guiding conception.

My purpose here and in part B is to show the validity of the following statement: In a large-scale network context, seed pools associated with guiding conceptions are small relative to the total number of valid seeds in the network. This statement is important because it is the reason why guidance is so valuable in large-scale contexts. It is the main result of this chapter and central to the thesis of this book.

Without guidance, the entire set of valid seeds in a context must be searched over to try to find a high-value seed. When guiding conception pool sizes are small relative to the total number of seeds, search guided by a guiding conception will be very focused and will generally involve investigating a far smaller number of seeds than will need to be investigated without guidance, that is, under random search. I show this explicitly for the case in which guiding conceptions are constituted out of two top elements and seeds consist of pairs of their children, but it will hold more generally for guiding conceptions that focus search. A key factor for the result is that in a large-scale network there are a very large number of valid seeds in the network as a whole, making random search over the entire network extremely inefficient; I show this in part B using a bounding argument that holds under weak assumptions. Contrasted with the large number of valid seeds in an entire network, a seed pool, even one of relatively large size, will still be small.

Now consider the base model in which guiding conceptions consist of pairs of top elements and the seed pool associated with a guiding conception consists of pairs of children, one from each guiding conception parent. The size of a guiding conception's seed pool depends on two factors. One is the number of children each member of the guiding conception has. Seeds are formed by pairing children of one with children of the other. Hence if one guiding conception element has X children and the other has Y, the number of potential seeds is XY. The second factor is how many of these pairs of children share a common parent. When a child of the first guiding conception element shares a parent with a child of the second, the pair formed by these two children is not a valid seed; this reduces pool size below XY. In this section I provide some calculations of the estimated size of valid seed pools and at the end present statistics on seed pool sizes for the simulated networks.

The calculation of seed pool sizes is especially simple for hierarchies because each child has only a single parent. As a result the second factor above does not apply; hence every seed formed by matching children of two top elements is valid. In a symmetric hierarchy in which each top element has m children, it follows that each guiding conception seed pool is of size m^2. This is quite a small pool as long as the number of children is not too large. For example, if $m = 3$ as in the simulated networks (note: the simulated networks are not hierarchies!), each guiding conception has a seed pool size equal to 9. This is very small; even if intensive investigation is required, it should be possible to investigate such a small number of pairs to find one that has high potential value.

In a random hierarchy in which each bottom element is assigned a top element at random, the sizes of seed pools associated with different guiding conceptions will be different because different top elements have different numbers of children. Further, the size depends on the number of children of each guiding conception element, since these two numbers are multiplied together, and as a result can vary considerably. The size of the seed pool associated with a guiding conception that pairs a top element having 12 children with a top element having 2 is 24, whereas the seed pool size for a guiding conception that pairs a top element with 12 children with a top element that also has 12 children is 144, far higher. In hierarchies for which there are a few hub elements, as in the power law model, seed pool sizes will vary the most. Guiding conceptions that pair two nonhub top elements will have small seed pools, guiding conceptions that pair a hub with a nonhub top element will have relatively modest-sized seed pools, and the few guiding conceptions that pair two hub elements will have large pools.

Now consider seed pool sizes in more general networks in which bottom elements have more than one parent. The calculation of seed pool sizes is more complex for these kinds of networks due to the second factor described above, shared parents.

For more general networks the maximum number of valid seeds for a seed pool, ignoring this issue of shared parents, is simply the multiplication of the number of children of the respective guiding conception elements, which I called XY above. It is important to note that in lattice-type networks in which bottom elements have more than one parent, top elements in turn on average have more children, and this tends to increase the maximum seed pool size. Consider for example a network in which each bottom element has two parents and all top elements have the same number of children. In this case each top element will have twice as many children as in the corresponding hierarchy. It follows that maximum seed pool size is four times the pool size for the corresponding hierarchy. To see the logic, let m refer to the ratio of bottom to top elements and set it at 3 as in the simulated networks. Then for a hierarchy each top element has 3 children, and the seed pool size for a guiding conception is 9 just as above. In contrast, in a network with the same ratio $m = 3$ of bottom to top elements but in which each bottom element has two parents, maximum seed pool size (ignoring shared parents and assuming all top elements have the same number of children) is 36 (6 times 6) because each top element has twice as many children.

This simple calculation is useful, but it ignores two issues. One, for a more careful calculation, maximum seed pool size must be reduced by the number of seeds that share a common parent. This will occur whenever either a bottom element has both guiding conception elements as parents or there is a seed for which the two seed elements share a third top element as a common parent. It turns out that in the kinds of sparse networks that characterize many creativity contexts, the frequency of these two cases is relatively rare and the result above holds true to a good approximation. Two, the reasoning is more complex for stochastic networks in which bottom elements are assigned to top elements stochastically. The reasoning above calculating 36 can be thought of as similar to an expected seed pool size calculation for random networks—but details and the argument differ. See the note to this sentence which also references the online Appendix for more details.[5]

It is important to note that the calculation of expected seed pool sizes is not necessarily the most useful statistic for studying the role of guiding conceptions in the creative process, because in reality seed pool sizes vary considerably over the guiding conceptions in a network. For power law degree models in particular, the size of seed pools varies a great deal—hub elements tend to have large pools. Even in random networks there is a good deal of variation in seed pool sizes across guiding conceptions, as the simulated network statistics presented below show.

SEED POOL SIZE DISTRIBUTIONS

The comment at the end of the last paragraph leads naturally into the third part of the discussion of seed pool sizes, presentation and discussion of statistics on seed pool sizes for the simulated networks introduced in Chapter 4.

To compute the seed pool size distribution for a given network, I divide its guiding conceptions into three bins based on their seed pool sizes: small, medium, and large. I determine cut-off values for these bins so that 25 percent of the guiding conceptions are in the small bin, 50 percent are in the medium bin, and 25 percent are in the large bin.[6] This provides standardization to compare statistics across networks and helps illuminate the high degree of variation in seed pool sizes.

Figure 14 presents these seed pool size bin values for each of the six kinds of simulated networks: random, cluster, and power law, smaller scale ($N = 100$) and larger scale ($N = 1,000$).

Consider first the small-scale networks. The top left graph shows the distribution for the small-scale random networks. Recall there are 10 simulated networks for each kind. The graph horizontal axis has marks for small pool size (S), medium pool size (M), and large pool size (L). Above each mark a thick black line shows the overall average seed pool size for the guiding conceptions in this bin; this overall average is the average of the 10 individual network averages for this bin, which are shown around this black line as thin gray marks. The average pool size in the small bin is 13.3; in the medium bin 31.5; and in the large bin 62.2. Thus there is considerable range over bins, with the average seed pool size over guiding conceptions ranked in the largest quartile in their network being more than four times larger than the average over guiding conceptions ranked in the smallest quartile. There is also some variation in the individual network averages in each of these bins: the lowest average seed pool size in the small bin is under 10, and the greatest average seed pool size in the large bin is nearly 70. For the small-scale cluster networks the values are similar to the random networks. But for the power law networks there is much greater range. The average pool size for guiding conceptions in the small bin is just 3. This tiny value reflects the fact that many top elements in these networks have just a single child. In contrast, the average pool size for guiding conceptions in the large bin is 92.

In the large-scale contexts the average values for the random and cluster networks are similar to the small-scale network averages, reflecting the fact that degree distributions for top elements are comparable, although the variation in the individual network averages in each bin is smaller. For the power law networks the range is greater than at

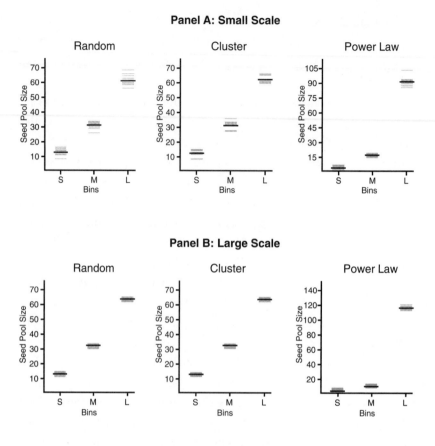

Panel A: Small Scale

Random Cluster Power Law

Panel B: Large Scale

Random Cluster Power Law

For each simulated network guiding conceptions are divided into 3 bins based on their seed pool sizes: S = small, 25% of guiding conceptions with smallest pools; M = medium, 50% of guiding conceptions with middle-sized pools; and L = large, 25% of guiding conceptions with largest pools. The average pool size in each bin is computed. Each graph shows the overall average pool size over the 10 simulated networks of that type for each bin, as well as the individual network average values.

FIGURE 14. GUIDING CONCEPTION SEED POOL SIZES: AVERAGE VALUES FOR EACH TYPE OF NETWORK AND INDIVIDUAL NETWORK AVERAGE VALUES BY SEED POOL SIZE BINS

the smaller scale: for guiding conceptions in the small bin, average seed pool size is just over 2, for the middle bin 11, and for the large bin 118, reflecting the fact that there are a handful of hub elements with many children.

The important takeaway from Figure 14 is that there is considerable variation in seed pool sizes across guiding conceptions in a network. This variability in seed pool size is linked to the variability in degree values of top elements, presented previously in Figure 6. Numerically it is greater because guiding conceptions are composed out of two top elements, so pool size is based on pairs of top elements, and this increases variability. Also pool size is somewhat reduced, as discussed above, due to ruling out as seeds pairs of bottom elements that share a common parent.

The high degree of variation in seed pool size is important for thinking about creativity and differences in creative styles across individuals who are pursuing different guiding conceptions. Guiding conceptions that have small pools are highly focused, and their pool of potential seeds can be investigated quite thoroughly. In contrast, for guiding conceptions that have large pools, the style of exploration will be less exhaustive, so that there will be uncertainty regarding whether a given high-value seed is actually discovered. In forming a guiding conception an individual or team may or may not have a sense for the size of the seed pool associated with their conception. From the viewpoint of managing the creative process, it may be useful to raise this issue as it may influence how the individual or team goes about exploring their seed pool.

B. MAIN RESULT: THE BENEFITS OF GUIDED SEARCH

In a large-scale creativity context there are a vast number of potential seeds that might be explored. The statistics in Table 2 for the simulated networks show that in the large-scale simulated networks, the number is over 4 million! Even in the smaller-scale networks there are over 40,000. These numbers are much larger than the seed pool sizes computed in the previous section. This shows how enormously beneficial guidance based on a guiding conception can be. However, the simulated networks are just examples. There is a benefit in quantifying the benefit of guided versus unguided search over seeds more generally.

The main point of this chapter is that *in large-scale contexts, guiding conceptions based on valid intuition are highly efficient for discovering high-potential project seeds, as compared with unguided search, that is, random search over the network.* In this section, the central one of this chapter, I show that this holds true with a bounding argument for large-scale networks under fairly general conditions.

This may seem like an obvious result. But despite the fact that it may seem obvious that search guided by sound intuition is superior to random search, it is nonetheless the case that much of the discussion of creativity assumes, explicitly or implicitly, random search with little or no guidance. The results in this section show that this kind of unguided random search is a very inefficient approach in a large-scale network. Other parts of the book show through empirical examples that it is also false for describing the creative process of at least some and I believe many individuals who engage successfully in creative endeavors.

It is crucial for the result that the guiding conception that an individual uses for guidance has valid intuition, meaning specifically that there are seeds in its pool that can be turned into successful high-value projects. Without valid intuition it will not lead to a high-value seed. This calls our attention to the importance of forming a guiding conception that embodies valid intuition. It also shows that there is risk in a strategy of searching based on a guiding conception, in that the conception may be based on faulty intuition. However, the results below also show that intuition does not have to be infallible—even if an individual pursues a number of guiding conceptions that do not reflect sound intuition, as long as they hit upon a guiding conception that is based on sound intuition in a reasonable number of attempts, the expected search is still low compared with random search.

One might argue that someone might develop intuition directly over seed pairs rather than developing intuition at the higher level of a guiding conception. An important crux of my argument is that it is far more difficult and I believe rare in practice for individuals to do this, for two reasons. One, there are many more bottom-level seed pairs than top-level guiding conceptions in most large-scale contexts. For example, in the large-scale simulated contexts there are close to 4.5 million seeds as compared with just under 0.5 million guiding conceptions, a ratio of nearly 10 to 1. Note also that in these simulated contexts the number of children per parent element is relatively low at three—in contexts in which this ratio is larger, the ratio of seeds to guiding conceptions will also be larger. The fact that there are so many potential seeds makes it a complex, potentially confusing, and possibly insurmountable challenge to develop an intuitive sense for exactly which seed will yield a high-value outcome. Two, based on many case studies I have explored, intuition for identifying promising search pools operates more naturally at higher conceptual levels in many circumstances. Indeed it is hard to see how one would go about choosing bottom seed pairs to try without using some degree of reasoning, based on higher-level elements, to guide one's choice. Hence inevitably higher-level concepts are used, and the guiding conception framework is a useful way to describe how this process works and how it can work efficiently.

I discuss two topics first that lay the groundwork for the main argument to follow. One is developing seeds into full projects. The other is to restrict analysis to situations in which there is one very-high-value project—the "golden project"—with the focus on discovering this project. The remainder of the section after these two topics is divided into six subsections. The first four describe different approaches to calibrating the benefits of guided search. The second-to-last provides the general bounding argument, and the last considers real world application.

DEVELOPING SEEDS INTO FULL PROJECTS

To analyze how guiding conceptions help individuals reach high-value projects and how an approach based on guiding conceptions compares to a simple random search protocol, we must incorporate into the analysis the process through which seeds are developed into full projects.

Recall from Chapter 5 that a project as defined in the model consists of three bottom elements that do not share any common parents. This structure introduces one important technical feature into the model: there are three pathways to a given project, each starting from one of the three seed pairs that can be expanded into the project.

The logic of this is shown in Figure 9 (p. 90), a project in the small example context. The project in the figure consists of elements 1, 7, and 16. There are three seeds that can be developed into this project: $(1, 7)$, $(1, 16)$, and $(7, 16)$. There are therefore three distinct pathways to this project. This means that there are at least three different guiding conceptions that can be the starting point from which this project is reached. For example, pair $(1, 7)$, a seed under guiding conception $A - C$, can serve as a seed from which to add third element 16 to complete the project.

It follows that in general for any context, there are at least three guiding conceptions and possibly more that can lead to a given project, since every pair of bottom elements that can form a valid seed is covered by at least one guiding conception. Note that three is the smallest number of guiding conceptions that can lead to a project; most seeds will be covered by more, because many bottom elements have multiple parents in a general network context.

The implication is that there are different paths to a project. These paths are in no way equivalent from the point of view of creativity. Some may be more feasible and more intuitive than others. Thus it may be easier, simpler, or more feasible to create the full project along one of the paths compared with the others. As one example of the difference, the distance to the third element will in general be different for each starting seed, which impacts the search to find this critical third element—see Chapter 13 for a full discussion. If the model is extended to larger projects, there will typically be even more paths to any given project. Thus this is a general feature of the modeling framework.

THE GOLDEN PROJECT AND GOLDEN SEEDS

The interpretation of the results given below is cleanest under the restriction that in a given context at a given time there is a single high-value project, which I call the "golden project." In accordance with the model, the golden project consists of three elements. Following the logic of the preceding section, there are then three "golden seed pairs" that can be developed into this project. The aim is to discover one of these three golden seed pairs that can then be developed (hopefully) into the golden project.

This example of a single golden project can be thought of as a field in which a key discovery or theoretical insight will generate uniquely high value—either directly, like the cure for a disease, or indirectly, by unlocking new pathways for further creative development. While this is useful for the exposition and interpretation, it is restrictive in that creativity is inherently diverse in most contexts. In Chapter 17 I discuss the creative development of fields in which there are potentially many valuable projects that can be created. As I discuss there, this more general case is especially important for exploring diversity of outcomes in a field with a cohort of individuals each striving to produce a valuable creative outcome. The final section of this chapter discusses the full set of projects in a context; this leads to other questions and insights.

The assumption that there is a single golden project makes the objective of creative exploration of seed pairs especially straightforward: discover one of the three golden seeds that can be transformed into the golden project, and do so as quickly as possible. There may be differences over the three paths in terms of ultimately forging the full three-element project, so this rule may be overly simple; this relates to the second step of the creative process, finding the crucial third element to complete a seed. Here I leave this issue aside. Hence any creative search strategy over seeds can be evaluated in terms of: (i) whether it will discover one of the "golden" seeds, and (ii) if so, how quickly it can be expected to discover the first such seed in its domain. Point (i) aligns with the previous discussion of seed pools: a given strategy can discover a particular seed if that seed is in its search pool. Point (ii) requires modeling search within a pool, and I turn to this next.

SEARCH WITHIN A POOL

The simplest model of search within a seed pool is random search. It turns out this is not the optimal search protocol to follow—see the next section—but it is still useful as a general guide. The key assumption, which applies both to random search and the optimal protocol I describe, is that an individual considering the seeds in a pool does not know which seed is the golden seed. With respect to guidance this fits with the perspective throughout this book: individuals build intuition for which region to explore creatively at a higher conceptual level, without knowing precise details.

For random search, the search protocol is to first pick a seed pair in the pool at random and determine if it is the golden seed. If it is, the search ends successfully; if it is not, cross it off and pick another seed pair, making sure never to resample a pair one has already tried that has failed.[7] This protocol assumes individuals can correctly determine if a given seed pair, once it is tried, is in fact a "golden" seed pair that can be developed into the golden project. How this determination is made will depend on the field and circumstances. It could be as simple as imagining the pair and what it can become, a kind of thought experiment, or it might be far more elaborate, such as building a prototype seed project and evaluating its potential.[8]

Given the search protocol, the golden seed in a pool might be discovered first, second, even last. A natural measure of the amount of search that is likely to be required is the expected number of trials it will take to discover the golden seed. A well-known result in discrete mathematics tells us that if there are M elements in a pool, here M seeds, the expected number of trials to discover any given element under random search is $\frac{M+1}{2}$ or approximately one-half the size of the pool.[9] Thus the expected amount of search required to find the golden seed if there is one such seed in a pool is approximately one-half the size of the pool. For example, if there are 100 seeds and 1 is golden, the result says that the expected number of trials to find it is approximately 50.[10]

COMPARING SEARCH BASED ON A GUIDING CONCEPTION TO SEARCH OVER THE ENTIRE NETWORK

For search based on a guiding conception, the expected amount of search is approximately one-half the size of the seed pool, as discussed above. We have seen that in the base model, in which seeds are composed of pairs of children of guiding conception elements, the seed pools of guiding conceptions range in value from very small, just a handful of seeds, to modest size such as 30, 60, or perhaps somewhat over 100—but even in the large-scale simulated networks not much larger than this.

For search over the entire network, the argument to show that search will generally be far larger than this is more involved. I first discuss the simple case of hierarchies; then I introduce as a key feature of the problem the distinction between seeds and projects; then I develop a more general bounding argument.

EXAMPLE RESULT FOR HIERARCHIES

Consider again a regular hierarchy in which there are N top-level elements, each top element has m children, and each bottom element has just this one parent. Assume that there is a single golden project, and hence 3 golden seeds. There are three guiding conceptions with valid intuition—each has a golden seed in its seed pool. We know from results in part A that the seed pool associated with each guiding conception has m^2 elements. Hence for each guiding conception with valid intuition, the expected search required to find its golden seed is approximately $m^2/2$.

Now consider random search over the entire network. Random search requires searching over all valid pairs of bottom elements, since one does not have any intuitive sense for where the golden seed pairs reside. How many such valid seed pairs are there? Each pair of top elements can spawn valid seed pairs, and each such pair has m^2 seeds in its pool. Further, there is no duplication over pools in a hierarchy—each seed is covered by just a single top element pair. Recalling that there are $\frac{N(N-1)}{2}$ top element pairs, it follows that there are $\frac{N(N-1)}{2} m^2$ seeds. This is a far larger pool than the pool associated with a guiding conception. Indeed it is larger by the factor $\frac{N(N-1)}{2}$.

A key conclusion from this simple calculation is that the relative benefit of search based on a guiding conception with valid intuition compared to random search increases with scale, at a rate that is approximately proportional to the number of top elements in the network squared. Hence as scale increases, developing a guiding conception with valid intuition becomes ever more valuable. This is hugely important because nearly all discussions of creativity assume, usually implicitly, a small context, and do not come to grips with the fact that the contexts in which real creativity happens are actually large.

In fact this very simple argument overstates the case somewhat. There are 3 golden seeds, and random search will be successful and stop when the first of these is discovered. If we think of all the seeds placed in a random order, the correct calculation is the expected amount of search to find the first of the 3 golden seeds in this randomly ordered list. Given that the 3 golden seeds are randomly placed in the overall sequence, the one that is discovered first will be found on average more quickly than halfway through. For a list of M items it can be shown that the expected number of search trials to find the first out of three designated items is approximately $\frac{M}{4}$ for large M; see the online Appendix for details. This is half as large as the simpler calculation of $\frac{M}{2}$, and we must take this into account in comparing random search with guided search. However, it is still much larger than for search based on a valid guiding conception, and the ratio of the two still increases approximately proportionally to the number of top elements squared. To give an example, if $N = 100$ and $m = 3$, the expected number of trials for random search is over $11,000$ whereas for a valid guiding conception it is just 5!

As scale increases and in particular the number of top elements increases, there are more potential guiding conceptions; thus identifying and forming a guiding conception with valid intuition may become more difficult. In this regard it is important to recognize that one does not have to hit upon a guiding conception with valid intuition immediately for this still to be a far better creative approach than random search. As long as one hits on a guiding conception with valid intuition reasonably quickly, the benefits are still large. After all, in the example above the search pool associated with each guiding conception is 9, and one could search many such pools before hitting on a golden seed and still end up searching over far fewer than 11,000 seeds.

SEEDS VERSUS PROJECTS AND THE SEARCH PROTOCOL

The calculation above misses an important feature: search is over pairs of bottom elements—seeds—while projects consist of triplets. The correct calculation of search values must work under the assumption that when a seed is considered, if it is found not to be able to be developed into the golden project, this rules out all of the projects based upon it (all projects for which its elements are two of the three project elements). As search progresses some seeds will have more active projects (projects not yet ruled out) associated with them than other seeds; and optimal search proceeds by selecting at each step one of the seeds that has the most active projects. The note to this sentence provides an example that illustrates the logic of this analysis for a hierarchy and then gives the reasoning showing why it is true generally.[11]

The main takeaway is that when searching over seeds, random search is not optimal. Rather it is better to search seeds associated with the most active projects first. Further, following this optimal sequence protocol impacts the calculation of the expected amount of search.

In general, because different seeds are associated with different numbers of projects, the calculation of expected search is complex in general networks. Rather than try to calculate expected search values directly, I focus on a different measure: the number of seeds that need to be searched such that *one-half of the total number of valid projects has been considered*. When the optimal search sequence is followed, this number is a lower bound on the expected search required to find a golden seed; the note to this sentence gives the argument demonstrating this.[12] This is therefore a very useful measure for considering search over the entire network because it establishes a lower bound on expected search. In particular, when it is large this supports the argument that search over the entire network is very inefficient.

Now consider again briefly guiding conception search. In a regular hierarchy every seed is associated with the same number of projects; therefore, searching seeds in a random order is optimal, and the computation of expected search as one-half the number of seeds is valid. For general networks, however, the calculation is different, and the value of one-half the number of seeds is an upper bound on the expected amount of search to find a golden seed in a guiding conception seed pool (optimal search will always do at least as well as random search). Since my argument is that guiding conception search is very efficient, one-half the number of seeds is therefore a useful number as a benchmark: actual expected search associated with a guiding conception will be no larger than this value and typically smaller.

THE MORE GENERAL BOUNDING ARGUMENT

Now consider search over seeds in a more general network structure not based on a guiding conception. I continue to assume that there are two levels. The main additional issue is that bottom elements, since they can have multiple parents, are more likely to share a common parent, which makes the number of valid seeds and projects smaller than for a hierarchy.[13]

Given this structure, assuming there is a single "golden" project, what is the number of seeds that must be evaluated such that one-half of all projects have been considered? As noted in the previous section, this number is a lower bound on the expected amount of search. This works with my bounding argument: I compute a lower bound on the number of seeds that must be evaluated such that one-half of all projects have been considered, and it follows that this lower bound is also a lower bound for expected search.

Exact computation of the number of seeds that must be evaluated such that one-half of all projects have been considered would require determining the optimal sequence of seeds and then seeing at what point in this sequence one-half of all projects have been considered. Determining this optimal sequence is challenging for general networks, especially because once a seed is tried and found not to be golden, that impacts the list of active projects since all projects it participates in are ruled out.

Rather than doing this computation directly, I compute a lower bound on the number of seeds that must be tried in order for it to be possible that one-half of all valid projects have been considered. The bound ensures that if the number of seeds tried is below the bound, then it is certain that fewer than one-half of all valid projects will have been considered regardless of network details, which in turn means that expected search is also greater than the bound. I show that this lower bound is large for the kinds of large-scale sparse network creativity contexts discussed in this book. I note that the bound I compute is fairly coarse, meaning that the actual expected value can be well above this lower bound. Table 4 presented below makes this point by comparing the bound to values for the simulated networks. But although coarse, the bound is nonetheless large.

I develop the lower bound in two parts. First I outline the key parameters and assumptions. Second I sketch the computation of the lower bound. Details of the computation are presented in the Appendix at the end of the book. Throughout the argument is constructed so as to make the lower bound as small as possible, for the point is to show that even when this is done, it is still large.

I consider networks in which there are two layers, top and bottom elements, as used in the formal modeling throughout the book, and allow bottom elements to have multiple parents. I do not consider lateral links between top elements because these play no role in the argument (they can be present without altering the argument). There are no lateral links between bottom elements, as throughout the book.[14] Assume there are N top elements, which for these bounding calculations is assumed to be large, and mN bottom elements where m is a positive integer.

A key issue that must be addressed is the possibility that some top elements have a very high degree, that is, are hub elements, so that the top element degree distribution follows a power law similar to the power law simulated networks. This is important to take into account in the argument and is also likely to be important in practice. The reason it is important for the argument is that the children of such a hub element cannot form valid seed pairs with each other, which reduces the number of valid pairs. To give an example that demonstrates how big an impact this can have, in the extreme case in which there is one top element that *all* bottom elements are linked with, there are no valid seeds or projects. I rule this out but do allow for more limited hubs, which reduces the lower bound estimates. In general there may be a number of hubs; in particular let there be l hubs where l is fixed and small relative to N. In fact the bound is reduced the most when there is just one very large hub, so I focus on this case as it subsumes the case of multiple hubs—see below.

Assume that each bottom element has at most h parents.[15] It is simplest to think of h as a fixed number; but it is possible for it to grow slowly with overall network scale N (this is discussed in the Appendix). For example, for the simulated networks h is 8; in calculations I do later, I set $h = 10$, thus slightly above this value.

Next assume that each top element other than the hubs has at most k children. Again, it is simplest to think of k as fixed, but it is possible for it to grow slowly with network scale N. For the simulated random and cluster networks, for which there are no top elements of very high degree, k is approximately 20. For the power law networks one must first define the set of hub elements, and then k is the maximum degree among the remaining elements. Taking into account these statistics and allowing for some elements to be hubs, I set k at 20 in the calculations done later.

Figure 15 presents a diagram that visualizes the network with its bottom elements laid out along a line segment that extends from 1 to mN. Bottom elements are divided into two groups: those that have at least

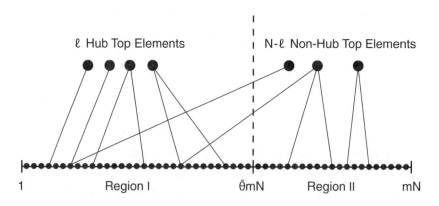

There are ℓ hub elements. The lowest bound occurs when $\ell = 1$.
Each bottom element in Region I links to at least one hub element and may link to non-hub elements. Elements in Region II do not link to hub elements. A few example links are shown.

FIGURE 15. VISUALIZATION OF NETWORK FOR LOWER BOUND CALCULATION OF NUMBER OF VALID SEEDS AND PROJECTS

one link to a hub element, included in region I, and the remaining bottom elements, included in region II. The key assumption is that region II exists, that is, the hubs do not link to all bottom elements. In particular define $\bar{\theta}$ to be the fraction of bottom elements in region I. In specifying such a fraction I ignore integer issues, appropriate for a large-scale context; to maintain the lower bound integrity, if the initial calculation of $\bar{\theta}mN$ is not an integer, reset it to the least integer above this computed value. The statement that region II exists is equivalent to requiring that $\bar{\theta}$ is bounded below 1; as an example we might assume it is bounded by 0.9.

Given this structure, holding all other aspects of the network fixed, the minimum lower bound occurs when all elements in region I are assumed to have a common hub parent, for in this case there are no valid seed pairs for which both members of the pair are in region I—whereas if there are multiple hubs, some of these pairs are likely to be valid. Hence I make the calculation under this assumption—see the footnote to this sentence for more.[16]

This division of bottom elements into two regions structures the argument. I compute a lower bound on the number of valid seeds by computing and adding two values: (i) the smallest number of valid seeds that combine an element from region I with an element from region II, and (ii) the smallest number of valid seeds that combine a pair of elements both in region II. Note that pairs of elements both in region I are not valid given the single large hub assumption. Given computation of these bounds, I then use them to compute a bound on the smallest number of valid projects. Again I compute and add two values: (i) the smallest number of valid projects for which two elements come from region II and one from region I, and (ii) the smallest number of valid projects for which all three elements come from region II. All other triples, for which either two or three members come from region I, are not valid. See the Appendix for details.

This division into regions is useful because the calculation of the number of valid partners a bottom element has is different depending on its region. An element in region II has at most h parents, and each of its parents has at most $k-1$ other children. In contrast an element in region I has one parent, the hub, that has many children, while its other at most $h - 1$ parents each has at most $k - 1$ other children. The restriction on the maximum number of parents and their children for region II elements means that of the total number $mN - 1$, or approximately mN, of bottom elements that might be a valid partner for a region II element, at most $h(k - 1)$ are ruled out because they share a parent with the given element, leaving $mN - h(k - 1)$ that can be paired with it. As long as h and k are fixed, this quantity $mN - h(k - 1)$ will be large for large N, and this is why the number of valid seeds bound is quite high. Even if h and k grow, but sufficiently slowly with N, this number will be large for large N.

The final step in the argument computes the minimum number of seeds that must be investigated in order to cover one-half of the computed lower bound number of valid projects. To do this I assume that each seed that is tried covers the maximum number of projects that can be associated with a seed, which is $mN - 2$ or approximately mN.[17] This ensures that this computation delivers a lower bound on the number of seeds that must be explored to cover one-half the lower bound number of projects.

Table 4 summarizes calculations of these bounds for a pair of networks: the first is very similar to the large-scale simulated random networks; the second is similar to the large-scale power networks but has a substantially larger hub. In particular I set $N = 1,000$ and $m = 3$ for these calculations to make the comparison with the simulated networks as close as possible. Row 1 shows values for a random network so that there are no high-degree top elements, with $k = 20$ and $h = 10$; this means all bottom elements reside in region II. As is shown the lower bound on the number of valid seeds is just over 4.2 million, quite close to the actual computed average value for the simulated random networks. The lower bound on the number of valid projects is a little bit over 3.6 billion, whereas the computed average value for the simulated networks is over 4.4 billion. Critically, the last column shows the lower bound on the number of seeds that must be tried in order to cover one-half of the lower bound number of projects. This value is $600,000$! This is much, much larger than the kinds of expected search values for guiding conception seed pool search I have computed throughout

TABLE 4. LOWER BOUNDS ON NUMBER OF VALID SEEDS AND PROJECTS: COMPARISON WITH SIMULATED NETWORK CONTEXTS

Parameters				Seed Pairs		Projects		
N	m	h	k	Percentage of Bottom Elements Linked to HUB	Lower Bound	Average* for Comparable Simulated Networks	Lower Bound	Average* for Comparable Simulated Networks	Number of Seeds Needed to Cover 1/2 of Projects
1,000	3	10	20	0	4.22 million	4.48 million	3.68 billion	4.44 billion	610,000
1,000	3	10	20	0.7	2.04 million	- - - - -	2.1 billion	- - - - -	350,000

* Average value over the 10 large-scale random simulated network contexts.

this chapter, which are on the order of a few dozen for these kinds of networks.

Row 2 shows computations for a network with a single very-high-degree top element, the kind of network for which the bounds will be the smallest: $\bar{\theta} = 0.7$. The bound on the number of valid seeds is just over 2 million, which is considerably smaller than for the row 1 calculation and the simulated networks, but still large. Likewise, the bound on the number of valid projects is just over 2 billion, smaller than for row 1 but still large. Finally, the minimum number of seeds that must be tried to cover one-half the lower bound number of projects is approximately $350,000$, which is again smaller but still very large compared to search over a guiding conception seed pool.

Thus the bounding argument demonstrates that under quite general conditions, guidance has huge benefits for finding a high-value seed in large-scale networks.

COMPARISON WITH SEED POOLS AND SEARCH IN THE REAL WORLD

It is a useful exercise to consider how the model and results presented above relate to real-world creative processes. I believe that the main result that guiding conceptions focus search into relatively small seed pools compared with the number of potential seeds in a large-scale context holds as a quite general truth in the world of creativity. However, a fuller empirical demonstration requires more empirical study. It will also be helpful to generalize the model in terms of how guiding conceptions are defined and how they generate seeds.

Consider as an example of the application of the model Hans Krebs at the time he set up his independent lab. His aim was to initiate research applying the manometric tissue slice methodology in the field of intermediary metabolism. There were certainly a set of projects he could have chosen to pursue fitting this guiding conception. We can think of a "seed project" for Krebs as a specific biochemical process he might choose to study together with suitable experimental conditions for exploring it. From this a full project would be developed and completed by identifying the mechanisms at work in this process. Krebs, when asked about this by his interviewer Holmes, stated that there were "many pebbles on the beach," that is, projects he could have chosen to pursue in the purview of his guiding conception, of which he chose one, the synthesis of urea. "Many" here seems to mean perhaps a few dozen, taking into account the state of the field and his own knowledge at the time. In contrast, if we consider the number of research avenues and projects he could have pursued in his overall context, it would be far larger. He could have chosen to pursue a project linked with Warburg's focus on comparing metabolic rates between cancerous and noncancerous tissue. There also would have been many alternatives in the area of dyes for staining, in which he had done previous work, and many diseases, including syphilis that he had studied previously, and potential treatments for those diseases. At the time he took up the synthesis of urea, he also had been studying a number of other metabolic processes and could have developed a project from one of these.[18] What seems clear is that his guiding conception focused his pool of potential projects down to a far smaller size than the overall context. Further in his case the quantitative values discussed above—a few dozen or at most one to two hundred potential seeds in the seed pool associated with a guiding conception—seem to be a reasonable empirical fit.

Evaluating seeds for Virginia Woolf is a challenging task, but we can learn from that challenge. For her a seed project would presumably be an idea for a story. In the two and one-half years after she formulated her guiding conception, up to the time she had the insight that enabled her to reformulate her conception, she wrote a series of five stories that are extant. We can take these, in the language of this book, as projects. Thus the number of projects she pursued to completion was quite small. Of course the pool of ideas that would have occurred to her but that she chose not to pursue was surely larger than this. It is worth noting that she does not generally mention potential story ideas during these years, for example in her diary, and thus there is no direct evidence suggesting a vastly larger pool size at least in terms of seed ideas that she took seriously enough to reflect upon as potential stories.[19] Certainly many ideas may have occurred to her more fleetingly, and the question becomes to what extent these would have been genuine seed ideas for stories.

While we cannot definitively answer the question of how many fleeting ideas occurred to Woolf, the model set forth in this book could be used in a constructive way to explore this issue. Once a context is specified and a guiding conception defined, seeds can be generated. Woolf's context was very rich and her guiding conception was more conceptually complex than the simple two-element guiding conceptions I focus on in this chapter. However, the style of analysis I have employed in this chapter could be brought to bear. The key for this kind of analysis is to specify which combinations of lower-level elements could be generated as seeds of her guiding conception. I have done this quite simply, with seeds of a guiding conception defined as pairs of children of the guiding conception elements. For the kind of conceptually rich guiding conception that Woolf formed, a more complex process is at work, but it should be possible to explore seed generation with suitable definitions. In general this kind of endeavor could lead to richer computer-assisted modeling and might help map out a variety of creative processes and also help individuals and organizations develop their guiding conceptions creatively.[20]

Just considering seeds, however, does not do justice to the extent of Woolf's experimentation by a long shot. In these crucial transition years after forming her conception in "The Mark on the Wall," she was developing as a writer in several ways. She was gaining conceptual understanding of what a new literary form could be, as for example she discusses in her essay "Modern Novels" written in 1919.[21] Concurrently she was experimenting and developing her literary style and skill at character sketches in her diary. Her character sketches in particular are "reflections" of people she met and interacted with, highly creative in the way she uses metaphor and analogy to characterize and sometimes caricature them. Thus Woolf was operating both at a high conceptual level, as in her essays, and also at more specific levels generating seeds—not only project seeds but also seeds that were fragments of stylistic innovation she could later draw upon. Her process was thus more complex than the model in this chapter, but it is also possible to see a way forward from the model here to a model better describing her process—see Chapters 15 and 16 for more discussion.

We must recognize that we have far too little information about how individuals generate project seed ideas. Too often in creativity the focus is on the end product. Even stepping back to consider how a given end product was created does not get to the question of the other potential project ideas someone considered. The discussion in this chapter highlights how valuable it would be to gather more empirical evidence about the seed pools creative individuals explore and seeds they consider developing further. The framework in this book should help structure that empirical-data-gathering process, and in turn more data will surely lead to further model development.[22]

C. PROJECT COVERAGE DISTRIBUTIONS

In this section I present statistics describing guiding conception project coverage for the simulated network contexts. Recall that in the model with three-element projects, every valid project is covered by at least three guiding conceptions. This is because there are three seeds associated with the project, and each seed is covered by at least one guiding conception. In networks whose bottom elements have multiple parents, most seeds are covered by more than one guiding conception.[23] It follows that most projects are covered by more than three guiding conceptions, and in general different projects are covered by different numbers of guiding conceptions. Thus for a given network context we can ask, what is the distribution of coverage values over projects?

The fact that different projects are covered by different numbers of guiding conceptions is important for modeling creativity. Each guiding conception that covers a project defines a particular creative path to that project. More guiding conceptions means more paths; hence a project covered by more guiding conceptions is more likely, other things equal, to be discovered—and more likely to be discovered by multiple individuals or teams.[24]

Figure 16 presents statistics on guiding conception project coverage for the simulated networks. Consider the top left figure, which shows the distribution for the small-scale random networks. The horizontal axis is divided into bins. The furthest left bin is for projects covered by just three guiding conceptions, the minimum number. The black

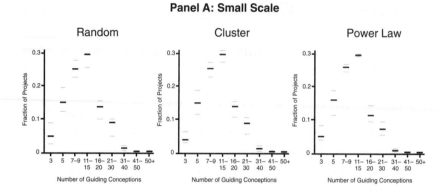

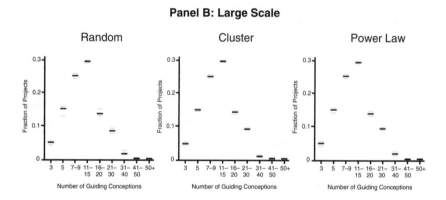

Each graph shows the average values over the 10 simulated networks as black bars and the maximum and minimum values over the 10 networks as gray lines.

FIGURE 16. THE NUMBER OF GUIDING CONCEPTIONS THAT COVER A PROJECT: PROJECT DISTRIBUTIONS

vertical bar for that bin is at approximate height 0.05, indicating that on average over all 10 simulated networks of this kind, approximately 5 percent of projects fall into this minimum coverage bin; the shading around it shows the range of values over the 10 networks and shows substantial variation, indicating that such low-coverage projects are more common in some network contexts than others. The projects in this first bin are especially rare in the sense that very few guiding conceptions lead to them. Such a project may or may not actually yield high value if created, but if any project in this category does have high value, it is made especially valuable by the fact that not many guiding conceptions lead to it: an individual who forms one of the 3 guiding conceptions that does lead to the project has the potential to produce a rare, high-value contribution. Keep in mind also that in general the number of potential guiding conceptions is itself large, so the three that lead to this rare project are themselves very specific within a landscape of numerous possibilities.

The next bin to the right in this figure is for projects covered by 5 guiding conceptions—still quite rare; the value here indicates that approximately 15 percent of projects fall in this category. The next bin to the right is for projects covered by 7–9 guiding conceptions— approximately 25 percent of projects fall in this category. Following this are bins for 11–15 guiding conceptions, and so on, with the last category consisting of projects covered by 50 or more guiding conceptions. Note as shown in the figure that there are some numerical values for which coverage is not possible; for example, given the model it is not possible for 4 guiding conceptions to cover a project.[25]

The remaining figures show the distributions for the remaining kinds of networks. It is noteworthy that in all these figures there is a small percentage of projects covered by just 3 guiding conceptions. Thus projects of low coverage exist in all these networks, but in relatively low numbers.

ARE RARE PROJECTS COVERED BY HIGHLY FOCUSED GUIDING CONCEPTIONS?

The fact that some projects are covered by a small number of guiding conceptions raises another question: Are these guiding conceptions themselves unusual, and in particular are they associated on average with smaller seed pools, so that rare projects are covered by guiding conceptions that are themselves highly focused? If this is the case, then these kinds of guiding conceptions, which presumably involve less centrally located elements, cover fewer seeds but seeds that are more unusual in that they may be able to be developed into relatively difficult-to-reach projects. Knowing whether this is the case for a given context can inform best strategies for developing guiding conceptions and thus can be important for managing the creative process.

The earlier statistics presented in Figure 14 show that there is considerable varation in seed pool sizes across guiding conceptions. Here we are going one step further to ask whether this variation is itself correlated with the variation across projects in the number of guiding conceptions that cover them. It turns out, based on analysis I have done, that for the simulated networks there is not a significant correlation. However, models of this kind can exhibit such correlation, in particular models with top hub elements—see the footnote to this sentence for an example.[26]

A more general question is whether the correlation envisioned between focused guiding conceptions and rare projects holds especially strongly in certain kinds of network contexts. The answer is yes, specifically networks for which there is preferential attachment based on degree between top and bottom elements. Here is an example of the kind of structure that delivers this result. There are N top elements and mN bottom elements as for all the simulated networks; also the two-step process described in Chapter 4 is used to generate links. Top elements are divided into two groups, high connectivity and low connectivity. Likewise bottom elements are also divided into two groups, high connectivity and low connectivity. This last structure is new: in all the simulated networks thus far, bottom elements all have the same expected connectivity degree. Low-connectivity bottom elements make just a single connection (to their first parent in step 1) while high-connectivity bottom elements have on average 2 additional connections to top elements beyond their first. Further, crucially, high-connectivity bottom elements are more likely to connect to high-connectivity top elements, and low-connectivity bottom elements are more likely to connect to low-connectivity top elements. This is a context in which bottom elements that are more isolated are linked with less central top elements, and more connected bottom elements are linked with central top elements.

Table 5 displays statistics for networks simulated based on this model, separately for small-scale and large-scale simulated contexts.

TABLE 5. MODEL WITH POSITIVE ASSORTATIVE VERTICAL CONNECTIONS: GUIDING CONCEPTIONS WITH SMALL SEED POOLS DISPROPORTIONATELY COVER PROJECTS THAT ARE COVERED BY FEW GUIDING CONCEPTIONS: SIMULATED RANDOM NETWORKS: AVERAGE VALUES*

		Low	Medium	High	Total
Panel A: Small Scale					
		Project Bins Based on Number of Guiding Conceptions that Cover			
		Low	Medium	High	Total
Guiding Conception	Small	0.327	0.419	0.254	1
Bins Based on	Medium	0.183	0.431	0.386	1
Seed Pools	Large	0.071	0.347	0.582	1
Panel B: Large Scale					
		Project Bins Based on Number of Guiding Conceptions that Cover			
		Low	Medium	High	Total
Guiding Conception	Small	0.255	0.441	0.304	1
Bins Based on	Medium	0.156	0.433	0.411	1
Seed Pools	Large	0.051	0.326	0.623	1

The numbers in each row divide the total projects covered by guiding conceptions in that seed pool bin based on project coverage level; the values are presented as fractions of the total and sum to 1. Values are averages of the simulated network values for that row.

The probability a low connectivity bottom element connects to a high connectivity top element is 0.3. The probability a high connectivity bottom element connects to a high connectivity top element is 0.9. Number of high connectivity bottom elements is 1/2 of number of bottom elements. The number of high connectivity top elements is 30 for the small scale, 300 for the large scale. Weights are set for step 2 for high connectivity bottom elements such that the expected number of links is 2.

*At each scale 3 simulations were undertaken; the numbers in the table are average values over these 3 simulated realizations.

Each table has three rows that divide guiding conceptions into bins based on their seed pool size, divided into the smallest 25 percent, the middle 50 percent, and the largest 25 percent, as in the earlier discussion of seed pools. Each table also has three columns that divide projects into bins based on the number of guiding conceptions that cover them: Low, Medium, and High, such that 25 percent are in the Low category, 50 percent in the Medium, and 25 percent in the High. Note that each row sums to 1 so that each cell in a row shows the relative proportion of projects in that project coverage bin compared to all projects covered by guiding conceptions in that seed pool size bin.

Consider the top table, which presents results for the small-scale contexts. The numbers in the table show that for guiding conceptions with small seed pools, nearly one-third of the projects they cover have low guiding conception coverage (the top left cell), whereas for guiding conceptions with medium seed pools, just 18 percent of covered projects fall in this bin, and for guiding conceptions with large seed pools, just 7 percent fall in this bin. The pattern is similar for the large-scale networks. Thus in these contexts rare projects do tend systematically to be covered by guiding conceptions with small seed pools.

Thus this final section identifies another dimension to consider in evaluating creativity contexts: the nature of the linkage patterns between higher- and lower-level elements. Certainly different creativity contexts are likely to have different connectivity patterns, and the example given here indicates that this is important to consider in thinking about creative strategies.

CHAPTER 11

GUIDING PRINCIPLES INTRODUCED

Guiding principles provide a second kind of guidance in the creative process. They function differently than guiding conceptions and work in tandem with them. In this chapter I describe them, the next chapter provides examples, and the following chapter brings them into the formal model.

Guiding principles are principles that individuals strive to adhere to in their creative work and to have their work embody. Guiding principles provide standards that individuals aim for and against which they measure their creative work. They are generally broad and apply widely. For example, a design principle of simplicity has broad applicability and may be employed by a creative design team on many projects. Many guiding principles represent ideals: principles of justice, or of aesthetic harmony and unity, for example, are frequently framed as ideals. We cannot attain such ideals, but they provide guidance, setting lofty standards.[1] Some guiding principles are about the way a person works, an approach or style; Hans Krebs is an example of someone who had this kind of guiding principle—see the next chapter.

In the creative process guiding principles operate through both negative and positive channels. I discuss both kinds of channels here, and the examples illustrate both kinds. Guiding principles may vary in terms of whether they provide stronger negative or positive guidance, an issue I discuss further in Chapter 13.

The main negative channel through which guiding principles operate is in setting standards to evaluate ideas and projects. Does an artwork meet a standard of beauty? Does a scientific experiment meet standards of experimental design? Put simply, a project or idea will either be accepted as meeting the standard or coming close enough to be acceptable, or will be viewed as failing to meet the standard and thus be rejected in its current form.

Guiding principles may differ in how efficiently they evaluate projects and ideas. Some principles, like a rigorous design standard of "correct" proportions, may be able to be applied directly and quickly. Others, such as a principle of justice, may require careful consideration of many factors. In the formal model I link the importance of the degree of efficiency of a guiding principle with the guiding conception with which it is paired, arguing that the importance of efficiency varies depending on the nature of the seed pool being explored, the broader context, and the project being developed.

A guiding principle, even one shared by many people working in a field, may be inherently quite subjective, especially in terms of how it is applied to evaluate ideas and projects; as it is said, "Beauty is in the eye of the beholder."[2] Steve Jobs had a strong commitment to the guiding principle of simplicity.[3] He employed it highly efficiently, and also very strictly and in his own terms: he was famous for rejecting project designs that others might not have rejected in the same situation. Practically, it follows that team members working together on a creative project may differ in the way they apply a guiding principle, making it important to discuss their differences of interpretation.[4]

A key positive channel through which guiding principles operate is in guiding the search to improve or complete a project or idea. When an idea or project is judged not to be acceptable according to the standard a guiding principle sets, there is a choice to be made. Either the idea or project is abandoned and a fresh start is made, or the perceived failing triggers a search to revise and improve it. When the decision is made to try to revise and improve the idea or project, the guiding principle again comes to the fore and helps guide this process.

Guiding principles provide several different forms of guidance. First, a guiding principle can help identify which parts of an idea or project— for example which design elements or assumptions—are the main cause of failure to meet the guiding principle standard. This focuses the search in terms of which elements need to be replaced. Second, a guiding principle helps guide the search for replacements. The guidance provided by a guiding principle in this search has several facets. More narrowly, keeping the guiding principle in mind can help identify specific candidate replacement elements to try, elements that the individual envisions will bring the project or idea into conformance with the guiding principle. More broadly, the guiding principle may suggest search avenues to explore—for example, a class of potential solutions to try to resolve an engineering problem, or a range of colors that may help a painting achieve coherence it is lacking. As a style or approach, a guiding principle can guide how a person goes about searching for key elements: very quickly so as to scan many possibilities; slowly and carefully, perhaps emphasizing feedback from others; or scanning recent developments in the field. I note that all of the forms of guidance I have mentioned are likely to be especially important in rich, large-scale contexts, in which there are many possibilities. Thus, as with guiding conceptions, the importance of guiding principles comes to the fore in rich large-scale contexts, the kinds of contexts in which creative engagement typically occurs.

The cycle of evaluating and then revising a project or idea can be a powerful iterative dynamic that continues until either an acceptable project or idea is created or the decision is made to abandon this line of development. This iterative process pushes individuals and teams: their guiding principles rule out "easy" solutions and drive them to keep searching and experimenting, trying out new possibilities; the result ultimately achieved through this process often turns out to be far more creative and successful than their initial design would have produced.

Indeed this dynamic is a central, crucial part of the creative process for many individuals and teams. Steve Jobs was known for constantly saying no to design options that were presented to him because they did not fit his high standards of simple, efficient, elegant design. In turn, his rejections forced his teams to continue improving their designs so they would be more fully aligned with these guiding principles.[5] This search to meet an exacting principle was also critical for Albert Einstein. For him, the guiding principle of relativity was crucial in ruling out easy solutions to a paradox he had hit upon, driving him to continue searching, leading him ultimately, after what he described as "ten years of groping," to his theory of special relativity, and again providing guidance over the ensuing decade as he extended his framework to develop the theory of general relativity.

In the formal model, I simplify from this discussion of project revision and focus on project completion. Specifically, the model focuses on how guiding principles help individuals develop an incipient project seed into a more complete project design by adding the crucial "third element," as described in Chapter 5 and in more detail in Chapter 13. Despite some differences, however, this focus on project completion is broadly similar to project revision in that it also involves a search for a new element to bring to an existing, not-yet-completed project. Thus many of the insights gained from analyzing this model of project completion should carry through to the case of project revision.

One important final point about guiding principles and their role in project completion or revision is that there is likely to be considerable variation across guiding principles in how much creativity and insight they bring to the search for new and improved project elements. Some guiding principles may spark a great deal of creativity and insight, identifying elements far off in the context to bring to a project to make it work, thus making highly creative linkages. Others may be more narrow in focus and largely aid the identification of more close-in elements. Thus a standard of beauty, employed subjectively and intuitively, may trigger a link to a novel element that somehow, surprisingly, completes a project so it "works" aesthetically. In contrast, a narrow standard of efficiency of operation may be suited primarily to helping identify more narrowly delineated replacements or additions that improve a project, but without so much creativity being brought to bear. In Chapter 13 I model the creative reach of a guiding principle in terms of distances to third project elements.

In conclusion of this overview I note that guiding principles also are important in many cases in the generation of initial project ideas. In this role they generally are part of or linked with guiding conceptions, as discussed already for Virginia Woolf. As with their later role in project evaluation, completion, and revision, guiding principles act through both positive and negative channels in this earlier phase of the creative process.

On the positive side, a guiding principle can call an individual's attention to an idea or project possibility or help spark an idea by being on a person's mind while they are thinking, observing, experimenting, or simply living. For example, Rawls's guiding principle of justice, based on the idea of using the "original position"—in which individuals do not know what their later standing in society will be—as a mental construct with which to discuss and evaluate choices in terms of justice and fairness, has sparked approaches for both environmental and health policy.[6]

On the negative side, individuals employ their guiding principles to avoid searching and trying project ideas they believe will violate their principles, which focuses their creativity. In the years after writing "The Mark on the Wall," Virginia Woolf focused her literary experimentation in short stories on literary forms that would fit her guiding principle of "leaving descriptions of reality out" of the account.

Somewhere between positive and negative, guiding principles help individuals focus their search. Ad Reinhardt was committed to making art consistent with abstract minimalist principles of great strictness. This led him to focus on exploring black (just black) in great depth, which in turn led him to original artistic compositions incorporating different shades of black.[7]

GUIDING PRINCIPLES VERSUS GUIDING CONCEPTIONS

Guiding principles are different in several important respects from guiding conceptions. A guiding principle does not necessarily envision creative possibilities and thus is not necessarily actively imaginative in the same way a guiding conception is. When a guiding principle is employed to envision possibilities, it is most commonly linked with a guiding conception, the way Woolf used her literary principle of "leaving descriptions of reality out" by linking it with her guiding conception of reflections.

Whereas guiding conceptions are quite individualistic and often highly creative, guiding principles are more likely to be more widely accepted by a larger community in a field. Some community members may champion a particular guiding principle more than others do, and be stricter about striving for their work to adhere to and reflect it, as Einstein was so strictly committed to the principle of relativity. Further, as discussed above, the application of guiding principles can be quite subjective and thus individualized. Nonetheless, most guiding principles are at least recognized by a larger community, as the principle of relativity was in the field of physics, and thus are more adopted than created by individuals, quite different than guiding conceptions.[8]

Finally, guiding principles tend to have quite broad scope of application. A principle of justice may have relevance for many ethical and policy projects and evaluations. Likewise a design principle has relevance for a very wide range of design projects.

Guiding conceptions and guiding principles complement each other and work very well in tandem. Many, I would say most, successful creators I have studied use both kinds of guidance, in different ways and in different stages of their creative process. Albert Einstein's adherence to the principle of relativity was the great foundation of his development of relativity theory, but he allied it with an evolving guiding conception that, at each stage, helped orient him as to what he wanted to achieve. Virginia Woolf is a great example of how the two work together: her guiding conception of reflections was interwoven with her guiding principle of working against the Victorian worldview and leaving descriptions of reality out of her stories. Jack Dorsey's guiding conception of developing a way to enable people to provide real-time, mobile status dispatches to friends dovetailed with his minimalist aesthetic design principle. In many cases guiding conceptions are central in generating initial project ideas, while guiding principles are especially important later in the creative process, guiding idea and project evaluation and revision, as discussed above. For example, this is a common sequence for designers and artists, such as Clifford Possum. This sequence is captured in the formal model set forth in more detail in Chapter 14.

THE LITERATURE AND GUIDING PRINCIPLES

Although the creativity literature has not in general focused on guidance, in the wider literature guiding principles and analogous ideas arise. The area in which I have found the greatest similarity of usage is the field of design, in which design principles—which function as guiding principles—are part of the language of design. While there are some differences from my approach, there are also similarities. (See my discussion and examples in the next chapter.)

Heuristics, important in psychology and widely used in computer science, also relate to guiding principles as I define them.[9] Heuristics provide rules for how to proceed. For example, a heuristic of symmetry might identify a flaw in a proposed composition and might also suggest some avenues to pursue to try to revise the composition so that it fits the symmetry heuristic. Heuristics are used differently in psychology and in computer science, in each case with key characteristics that distinguish guiding principles from them.

In psychology heuristics generally refer to simple rules to guide decision making and behavior; the emphasis is on speed, limited processing, and standard application. This kind of heuristic works well in standard situations but can deliver poor results in unusual situations. I view guiding principles as more deeply defined and applied, not necessarily oriented toward speed, and definitely able to be applied effectively in unusual, first-time situations, which occur frequently in creative applications. Albert Einstein's principle of relativity is a good example—it was not a heuristic in the psychology sense but something deeply rooted, essential, and far-reaching.

In computer science heuristics are rules that a program can follow in making choices. As such the rules tend to be rigid in that they must be defined with sufficient detail and completeness that a computer can know when and how to apply them. In addition, as with the usage in psychology, they tend to simplify so as to avoid the program having to work through very complex calculations. A guiding principle might never be defined as completely or rigidly as a computer heuristic, yet a human will be able to apply it effectively. Further, as a principle it is meant to bring intuition to bear with considerable breadth and depth, so simplifying is not the main purpose. Lynn Conway's principle of fluid communication and integration across design levels discussed in the next chapter, for example, was the product of her experiences and had a depth and flexibility in how it might be applied depending on the organization, the product, and the broader situation. Likewise an aesthetic principle like harmony is subjective and used by an artist or designer in ways that are context and project dependent—it is richly rather than rigidly defined and is about subtlety of application, not simplification. This is not to say guiding principles cannot be developed in some fashion as heuristics in a computational creativity program; however, this would require some modification from existing usage, emphasizing their subtlety and originality in application. Indeed, as with my model and approach as a whole, I hope my discussion and examples of guiding principles will prompt efforts to bring them into the computational creativity domain.

Guiding principles also arise in the study of creative problem solving. The use of rules, heuristics, or higher-level principles to guide the search for a solution to a challenging problem is widely discussed in this literature, including by Donald Schön in his classic work *The Reflective Practitioner* and by Robert Weisberg.[10] An example is using the principle of symmetry to solve a problem. This fits with the general definition of guiding principles and how they are used. An important difference, however, is that in this book I focus on how guiding principles are used to complete and improve projects, which may or may not involve problem solving as customarily defined. Thus guiding principles are important for problem solving but also for a number of other creative processes.

A key distinctive feature of my approach compared with the way guiding principles are used in the design and problem-solving literatures is that I link guiding principles with guiding conceptions in a model of the creative process, showing how guiding conceptions and guiding principles work in sequence and in tandem. The problem-solving literature tends to focus just on the end stage, which has the unfortunate consequence of foreshortening the creative process, so that it appears simpler and to involve fewer steps than is true in reality: both Schön's and Weisberg's descriptions, although they are valuable and provide insights, are examples of this tendency. What is left out are the more abstract, broader, less defined stages of the process. It is in these stages, often earlier in the process, that guiding conceptions come to the fore, helping individuals identify conceptual avenues and pools on which to focus their attention. The framework in this book includes both these earlier stages as well as the later stages of project completion and thus provides a more complete picture of the creative process. It also shows that to attain a successful outcome, it is likely to be desirable to pair certain kinds of guiding conceptions with certain kinds of guiding principles, a connection that as far as I know is new to the literature.

In the broader culture, references to guiding principles in terms of creativity oftentimes refer to principles for how to go about being creative; that is, they are rules for process. For example, a principle might be to brainstorm many ideas quickly. Or for a team, that everyone has a voice—listen to everyone fairly and avoid letting power relationships influence the process. These are important and practically useful principles, but different from guiding principles the way I define them.

One other link that is useful to note is to Gerald Holton's notion of "themes" as essential backdrops to the scientific process and scientific explanation. Holton defines a thematic position or methodology as "a guiding theme in the pursuit of scientific work" and gives as an example the preference to express scientific theories in terms of maximizing or minimizing functions.[11] He lists as further examples of themes several principles that Newton lays down for scientific inquiry and theory building in Book III of his *Principia*. One principle (Holton's paraphrasing) is "Nature is essentially simple," meaning our explanations should be as simple as possible. A second is "As far as possible, similar effects must be assigned to the same cause," which Holton calls the principle of uniformity of nature.[12] Thus Holton's themes are arguably guiding principles for how to construct scientific theories.

CHAPTER 12

EXAMPLES OF GUIDING PRINCIPLES

Guiding principles are central to creativity across the entire spectrum of creative fields. In this chapter I provide examples of guiding principles and their use in the arts, sciences, technology, and design.

CLIFFORD POSSUM: AESTHETIC PRINCIPLES

In Chapter 8 I described Clifford Possum Tjapaltjarri's guiding conception for his art: to depict on a single painting multiple Dreaming stories associated with the geographic area centering on a particular site. This conception was paramount in his creative process. However, it also raised further issues in terms of how multiple Dreamings would be positioned and might interact within a given painting.

As Possum's biographer Vivien Johnson makes clear, Possum did not adhere to a single point of perspective in his paintings. Rather, he presented different Dreamings from different directional perspectives in a single painting. This provided great flexibility in how Dreamings were positioned. It also raises the question of how Possum made choices about perspective and positioning.

Interestingly, based on the evidence and documentation of the most important of these paintings, Possum employed a guiding principle of aesthetic balance to guide his choices about positioning. Johnson refers to this as his "sense of balance" and states that he drew on this principle in making decisions about Dreaming placements and directionality in his compositions. Thus his paintings were created through combining his guiding conception with his aesthetic guiding principle of aesthetic balance.[1]

The role of balance is clear in Possum's five great "maps of the country" paintings. A notable example is *Warlugulong* of 1976, the first painting in the series and widely regarded as a masterpiece. (See https://www.artgallery.nsw.gov.au/collection/works/321.1981/ to view the painting online.) The detailed notes on this painting made at the time discuss the issue of balance repeatedly. Discussing the placement of the bushfire that is the central motif in the painting and the paths followed by the mythological characters around this motif, the notes state that in the creation of the painting, "The bushfire was centrally placed to give artistic balance, [and] certain of the mythological routes were slightly altered to maintain this balance."[2]

Further, an element was added to the painting for which Possum and his brother Tim Leura who collaborated with him on the painting did not have cultural authority, so that normally Possum would have been reticent to depict it: the track of an Emu ancestral being. In discussing this addition the commentators state:

> Interestingly enough, this is the one element of the painting over which the two Tjapaltjarri artist brothers have no direct authority. However, perceiving a need for some further mythological element to give even greater balance to the canvas, they asked permission of two Tjampitjinpa subsection brothers to depict part of a mythological trail over which they had ownership rights. The Tjampitjinpa men agreed, and so a further travelling route was added.[3]

Clifford Possum's use of his guiding principle aligns well with the formal model I present in the next two chapters. He began from his guiding conception, then drew upon his guiding principle to add elements to his composition in order to achieve aesthetic balance and create a more pleasing and successful final outcome.

HANS KREBS

Krebs's most important guiding principle was his approach to work, which emphasized trying many alternatives, often in parallel, and switching rapidly from one avenue of inquiry to another. Thus his case is an example of a guiding principle as an approach to creative work.

Krebs remarked, "When I had an idea and thought it worthwhile exploring whether it would lead anywhere [I would do so—pursue the lead]. I tried out a lot of things." "I always had the habit of trying out many things and exploring just whether there was a possibility." He said that in general he was an optimist: "I was confident that something would turn up if you try long enough, and do different kinds of experiments, not just doing the same [over and over]."[4]

Holmes writes that Krebs's research approach "lent itself to short-term switches." "New ideas for experiments often occurred to him, and when they did he liked to try them out as soon as possible." Consistent with this, Krebs said he "would make a decision every day" about what to do next. Thus he was adaptable and opportunistic on the day-to-day level and able to explore a multiplicity of possibilities. In terms of the creativity model in this book, much of this experimentation was at the level of trying to identify the critical additional element or elements to turn a seed into a successful project.

Krebs's guiding approach fit naturally with his specific skill with the tissue slice manometric methodology. With these methods, honed to great expertise, he could conduct multiple experiments a day, thus explore dozens of possibilities. His approach also was well suited to pursuing his guiding conception, which was based on applying these methods to study intermediary metabolism.[5] Other scientists might have used these methods as well of course, even to study intermediary metabolism (though Krebs was a pioneer in this regard), but without the same guiding principle of trying many alternatives, they would quite likely never have made discoveries of the magnitude that he made.

Thus Hans Krebs is an example of someone for whom the combination of a particular guiding conception with a complementary guiding principle was critical to achieving success. The description in Chapter 14 of his first highly successful project, the synthesis of urea, illustrates this. Interestingly, while we don't know for certain when his guiding principle crystallized, it appears based on his later remarks that he did not consciously begin to articulate it to himself until after he left Warburg's lab and set out on his own as an independent researcher. If that is true then his guiding conception formed first, followed by the guiding principle a few years later. This shows that the two do not need to form at the same time, and often indeed one will form before the other; but once both are in place, the stage is set for outstanding creative activity.

DESIGN PRINCIPLES

Design principles are paramount in the world of design, an integral part of the language of design. In essence design principles are guiding principles tailored to the field of design. The Interaction Design Foundation defines design principles as "widely applicable laws, guidelines ... and design considerations which designers apply with discretion." They list four general principles: hierarchy, proximity, contrast, and balance.[6] Their definition fits with the way I have defined guiding principles, and the specific principles also fit—for example note that "balance" is listed, Clifford Possum's guiding principle.

There are different kinds of design principles with different functions. Aesthetic design principles include balance as well as unity and harmony. These kinds of principles apply to a project as a whole and can guide project development and revisions. Thus they fit with the way I describe guiding principles and their roles in the creative process. Beyond aesthetic considerations, design principles also include behavioral rules to increase functionality and improve user experience. Indeed as design has shifted from a focus on physical objects and architecture to user interfaces and online platforms, the list of principles has expanded to include additional principles—for example, principles to facilitate positive and productive human-computer interaction.

These kinds of principles also fit with the way I describe guiding principles and their roles—for example, helping to identify a critical element to make an innovative human-computer interactive tool function successfully.

There are also many specific design principles that apply more narrowly. For example, the Interaction Design Foundation gives as a rule setting a fixed size ratio of 3:1 between headers and body text. This is an example of a fixed rule as compared with broader, more flexible guidelines they give, such as the principle of making content easy to read.[7] Such very narrow design principles do not fit my usage as well.

Design is a diverse field, and there are many different design principles favored by different individuals and groups. The book *Universal Principles of Design* describes one hundred design principles of varying kinds, some narrower, some broader. The sheer fact that this book has been written, with this title and structure, shows how important design principles are in the world of design.[8]

In his classic text *The Visual Display of Quantitative Information*, Edward Tufte sets forth principles for data presentation, which in the way he discusses it is a branch of design.[9] He organizes the text around principles illustrated through examples. Some principles he espouses are broad. For example, his opening chapter "Graphical Excellence" lists a set of guidelines for data presentation, including

- *induce the viewer to think about the substance rather than about methodology*

and

- *make large datasets coherent.*[10]

Others are far more specific to the point that they do not align as well with guiding principles as I describe them. For example, the chapter titled "Graphical Integrity" closes with what he calls "six principles" to be followed, including

- *The representation of numbers, as physically measured on the surface of the graphic itself, should be directly proportional to the numerical quantities represented.*[11]

A rule like this can certainly make a project better, but it is not likely to be integral to the more creative aspects of developing a project.

Guiding principles are very important in the world of technology design. As discussed in the preceding chapter, Steve Jobs honed an aesthetic of simplicity that served as a guiding principle, helping him guide Apple teams in their design of a series of outstanding products. Walter Isaacson remarks in his interesting article on Jobs, "How Steve Jobs' Love of Simplicity Fueled a Design Revolution," that Jobs fused an aesthetic of simplicity with a sense of playfulness, which was a second guiding principle.[12] Jack Dorsey is committed to minimalist design principles, and one can see the impact of this in Twitter and other projects in which he has participated.[13]

The fact that different individuals list and adhere to different design principles is consistent with the view I have expressed in the preceding chapter, which is that although guiding principles tend to be in wide circulation in a field, different individuals will adopt different principles. Further, individuals may apply the same principle differently—Steve Jobs applied the principle of simplicity strictly and rejected designs that others might have accepted.

LYNN CONWAY AND VLSI DESIGN

Lynn Conway, codeveloper of the Very Large-Scale Integrated (VLSI) circuit design paradigm, developed a pair of guiding principles that were central to her pioneering work on VLSI. Conway developed these principles during her years working at IBM on the ACS (Advanced Computing Systems) supercomputer project in the 1960s. She formulated her principles in response to gaps she perceived in the design process.

One important issue Conway encountered was barriers to communication due to idiosyncracies in terminology and the lack of an agreed-upon language for logic design. She described these and how confusing they can be, and called as her first principle for a unified language, in a memo she wrote in 1967.[14]

A second related issue was the informality and lack of more deliberate thinking about the design process, especially the importance of

IMAGE 4. LYNN CONWAY AT XEROX PARC, 1983. Photo by Margaret Moulton for the *Palo Alto Weekly*.

integration across multiple design levels. In her 1968 memo "The Computer Design Process: A Proposed Plan for ACS," Conway wrote, "The careful planning of the design process itself is as necessary for success of the project as is the careful planning of the computer design." She then articulated her second principle: "The design process should be planned as one integrated system." If this is done, "A common termi-nology would then develop for all the many design phases, simulation and design automation programs, design languages, etc., and better un-derstanding and communication would develop across design group boundaries."[15] Thus her second principle facilitates the first and vice versa: standardized and shared communication systems will facilitate communication and integration across design levels.

What are the design levels Conway referred to? She described four: system architecture, the design of the system as a whole in terms of its highest level of function (what it will be designed to do); logic design and engineering; physical layout design; and details of wiring and circuit board construction. These levels, albeit modified, were basic also for VLSI design.[16]

Conway elaborated on the importance of integration across design levels in an article she wrote later, looking back on her experience on ACS. The "lesson" she learned, she wrote, "deeply affected my later work in VLSI, when creating innovative methods for working across multiple levels in digital-design."[17] She wrote that at the time at IBM her perception was that a "chasm had developed between the various specialist subgroups working on computer architecture, logic design, [and] circuit design. "

> As a result, most computer architects lacked knowledge about the details of the machine's logic design ... and thus could not envision how to reach down into and more fully exploit that circuitry. Neither could many top logic designers grasp the arcane architectural tradeoffs being made at the level above.[18]

She came away committed to the idea that more effective design required the ability to "innovate across all those compartments of knowledge."[19]

Conway also related this compartmentalization to the first issue, a confusing plethora of notations for logic. Noting that designers used different "conventions and notations for writing logic equations," she stated:

> It is no wonder that walls had built up between ACS architecture and logic design. An architect would have to invest a lot of time in learning a number of different logic design shorthands in order to follow that work…. This also explained why I never saw architects sketching logic diagrams. Instead, architects would toss block diagrams and state machine descriptions over the wall to the logic designers, and wait for a response.[20]

Thus she formed dual linked guiding principles: simple, standardized notation; and fluid communication and integration across design levels, especially system level and logic design.

At the time she was working on ACS, Conway went through a gender transition. In the aftermath she was fired by IBM. She describes this time as "terrifying" as she kept her change private and restarted her career. But after working her way back up the job ladder, in 1973 she began working at the Xerox PARC center.[21]

In 1976 PARC joined forces with Carver Mead and his team at Caltech to work on developing methods for improved design of large-scale integrated circuits in MOS (metal-oxide semiconductor) technology. See Chapter 15 for her creative burst during this project; the design revolution in VLSI it engendered is discussed in Chapter 17.

ALBERT EINSTEIN: THE PRINCIPLE OF RELATIVITY

There is no more powerful illustration of a guiding principle and its use in creativity than Albert Einstein and the principle of relativity. According to his statement in his "Autobiographical Notes," Einstein hit upon a paradox at the age of sixteen:

> If I pursue a beam of light with the velocity c [that is, travel just behind the beam at the same velocity] I should observe such a beam of light as a spatially oscillatory electromagnetic field at rest [since he will be moving at the same speed as the beam it will, according to classical physics, not appear to be moving from his perspective]. However, there seems to be no such thing, whether on the basis of experience or according to Maxwell's equations.[22]

Einstein continues, "From the very beginning it appeared to me intuitively clear that, judged from the standpoint of such an observer, everything would have to happen according to the same laws as for an observer who, relative to the earth, was at rest.[23] This statement indicates that he grasped the importance of the relativity principle from the start of his work on the paradox. But despite his recognizing its importance, the principle of relativity was not as central in his overall thinking about physics at the time. For at the same time he came up with the paradox, he still believed in the existence of the "ether" filling space; this is based on a memo he wrote at the time referring to experiments he was interested in that would measure the "deformation of the ether" due to an electromagnetic field.[24] The ether was conceptualized as a substance that was fixed in one particular frame of reference, which thus was viewed as primary or absolute.

As the years went on Einstein's views evolved. Einstein gave up his belief in the ether, adopting the view that electromagnetic radiation passes through empty space.[25] Further, he came to focus on a second problem relatd to the paradox, the problem of induction. In a later paper (1919/20) summarizing parts of his theory, Einstein discussed the importance of this problem for his invention of special relativity. He stated that the "following idea"—the inherent contradiction in the way this problem was conceptualized—"played a leading role for me when I established the theory of special relativity":

> According to Faraday, during the movement of a magnet relative to an electric circuit, an electric current is induced in the latter. It is irrelevant whether the magnet or the conductor is moved; what counts only is the relative motion. But according to the [then current] Maxwell-Lorentz theory, the theoretical interpretation of the phenomena is very different for the two cases.
>
> If the magnet is moved, there exists in space a magnetic field variable with time, which, according to Maxwell, forms ... a physically real electric field; this electric field then puts the [charges in the conductor] ... into motion [establishes a current].

However, no electric field arises if the magnet is at rest and the circuit is moved; instead, the current in the conductor is created because the electricities moving with it due to the ... movement relative to the magnetic field suffer [experience] an electromotive force....

The idea that these two cases should essentially be different was unbearable to me. According to my conviction, the difference between the two could only lie in the choice of the point of view, but not in a real difference <in the reality of nature>. As seen from the magnet, there was certainly *no* electric field; whereas seen from the circuit there certainly was an electric field.[26]

Einstein's use of the word "unbearable" stands out for its strengh of conviction, showing us that he became committed to the principle of relativity. As Arthur Miller documents, the induction problem was an active area of research focus in the early 1900s. Many different models were proposed, and many of these were inconsistent with the postulate that phenomena must be described the same way in different frames, so that the chosen frame did not impact the nature of the physical process described.[27] Thus this problem highlighted that the principle of relativity was not fully integrated into contemporary thought in physics at the time and also that it brought a great deal of power to bear in ruling out proposed solutions—one of the hallmark uses of a guiding principle.

Ultimately, according to his later statement, it was apparently through resolving the paradox that Einstein invented special relativity theory. As he described it, he was speaking with his close friend Michele Besso, discussing this "difficult problem":

Then suddenly I understood where the key to this problem lay. Next day I came back to him again and said to him, without even saying hello, "Thank you. I've completely solved the problem." An analysis of the concept of time was my solution. Time cannot be absolutely defined, and there is an inseparable relation between time and signal velocity.[28]

Thus he developed the conception of time being measured differently in different frames in relative motion.[29]

At this point Einstein pushed on. Having invented special relativity, he wanted to generalize it. He convinced himself that the theory could be extended to deal with other kinds of motion, but found that it could not accommodate gravity. At this juncture again the principle of relativity came to the fore, and Einstein had what he later described as "the happiest thought of my life":

> The breakthrough came suddenly one day [in 1907]. I was sitting on a chair in my patent office in Bern. Suddenly a thought struck me: If a man falls freely, he would not feel his weight. I was taken aback. This simple thought experiment made a deep impression on me. This led me to the theory of gravity. I continued my thought: A falling man is accelerated. Then what he feels and judges is happening in the accelerated frame of reference. I decided to extend the theory of relativity to the reference frame with acceleration. I felt that in doing so I could solve the problem of gravity at the same time.[30]

There is an equivalence between a uniform gravitational field and acceleration—each imposes a like force. Thus these two situations can be essentially equated, as shown by Einstein's thought picture of a person with a physics lab in a sealed elevator: seeing an effect of force, such as a ball thrown from one side to the other curving downward, no experiment can distinguish whether this effect is due to the elevator being in a gravitational field or being subject to uniform acceleration in open space. Thus the principle of relativity suitably interpreted also covers this pairing, expanding its range of application.

It is noteworthy that the principle of relativity played a critical role in the two creative breakthroughs Einstein discussed. Guiding principles can be central to creativity generation as a project progresses, and Einstein's development is a brilliant case showing this.

Even armed with this equivalence principle, Einstein's path to the general theory of relativity was a long and hard one; historian of science John Norton describes it as "tortured." After a number of years of failed attempts, according to Norton, Einstein realized that he had actually made a mistake in first trying to work out the theory for a limited set of examples and coordinate systems: "He needed a theory that would work in as many coordinate systems as possible. Ideally it would work in all coordinate systems. That is, it would be 'generally covariant.'" This statement is interesting in showing that again the principle of relativity became paramount, helping guide Einstein's search and creative process.[31] This renewed search succeeded, and general relativity theory as it has come down to us was created.

Einstein viewed the principle of relativity as the core of his theory. In his book *Relativity: The Special and the General Theory*, for which the first edition was written just a short time after he published his general theory, Einstein discusses the principle of relativity repeatedly: it is the centerpiece of the book.[32] This book was written after his development of the theory and cannot be taken to reflect his thinking earlier. But it does show a deep commitment to the principle of relativity as the way to illuminate the laws of nature.

Einstein begins with a restricted definition appropriate to the world of special relativity, then steadily expands the generality and range of application of the principle to encompass acceleration and gravity. In the first part of the book, on special relativity, Einstein frames the principle as follows. There is a railway car in uniform motion relative to a train embankment. Thus motion is relative—either can be taken as the frame of reference at rest. But there is more to the principle:

> If we formulate the general laws of nature as they are obtained from experience, by making use of
>
> (a) the embankment as reference-body,
>
> (b) the railway carriage as reference-body,
>
> then these general laws of nature ... have exactly the same form in both cases.[33]

In the later part of the book on the general theory, he makes a more general statement: The general laws of nature are formulated in the same way for all Gaussian coordinate systems, in particular those of arbitrary curvature (but with local continuity). He goes on to state why the principle is so important: "The great power possessed by the general principle of relativity lies in the comprehensive limitation which is imposed on the laws of nature in consequence."[34] We see here how the principle would rule out many proposed theories, a classic use of a guiding principle to restrict possibilities.

Einstein was not the only physicist working with the idea of relativity in the years during which he developed his theory. Notably Henri Poincaré used the phrase "principle of relativity" in these years and used it to study similar physical problems. However, Poincaré does not seem to have had the same thoroughgoing commitment to it. He continued to believe in the ether and hence a privileged state of absolute rest and a "true" time. He also combined the principle of relativity with other physical assumptions in ways that did not lead down the path Einstein followed.[35] Einstein's commitment to the principle and the way he applied it were distinctive to him. Two individuals may both espouse the same guiding principle (or similar principles) but differ in the way they use it in their creative work.

I close by noting that Einstein's commitment to and use of the principle of relativity fits the model I present in this book: guiding principles are central in the ongoing development and pursuit of a creative project.

GUIDING PRINCIPLES ALLIED WITH GUIDING CONCEPTIONS

As discussed in the preceding chapter, guiding principles are often allied with guiding conceptions. A guiding principle can function as a complement to a guiding conception, adding structure and limits. Either can form first, but the greatest creativity utilizes both working in tandem.

Virginia Woolf formed a guiding principle that linked to her guiding conception: the principle of "leaving descriptions of reality" out of stories, to negate the Victorian world with its hard, androcentric objectivity, in which "there was a rule for everything." She developed this principle as a product of both her upbringing in the Victorian era and her relationship with her father (and other male relatives and acquaintances of his); it also aligned with similar principles of her friends in the Bloomsbury circle. In the stories she wrote after "The Mark on the Wall," this principle played an important role; she strove to adhere to it against many of the literary conventions she had learned and the Victorian literature she was so steeped in. As I describe in Chapter 15, after two and a half years of experimenting she did hit upon a style that incorporated both her guiding conception and this guiding principle. Thus the two worked in tandem in helping her create her modernist literary style.

In summary, guiding principles are ubiquitous in the world of creativity. The examples I have given convey a sense of this, and many more could be given across many different fields. A whole book could be written just about guiding principles and their role in creativity. However, rather than pursue that line I will move forward with the larger argument of this book.

CHAPTER 13

MODELING GUIDING PRINCIPLES AND HOW THEY FUNCTION IN TANDEM WITH GUIDING CONCEPTIONS

In this chapter I incorporate guiding principles into the formal modeling framework. I focus on the role they have helping individuals evaluate and complete seed projects. Recall that seed projects are pairs of bottom elements that define seed ideas, the embryos out of which full projects are developed. I focus on the model outlined in Chapter 5 for which, once a high-potential seed is identified, it must be completed by adding one additional element to produce a full project design. An example is finding the crucial missing piece to complete a design or solve a problem. A high degree of specificity is required to find just the right element and guidance is invaluable. The model can be extended to adding more elements—something I address in Chapter 16, but I keep it simple for the main argument of this book.

Guiding principles thus work in tandem with guiding conceptions. Guiding conceptions are used to generate seeds, and guiding principles are used to evaluate seeds and develop high-potential seeds into full project designs. Of course there are other creative pathways for which guiding principles are also important. For example, they play a crucial role in project revision, guiding the search for replacement elements. This and other pathways can be integrated into the formal model as natural extensions of the simple version I discuss.

I model guiding principles differently than guiding conceptions. One might expect that, since both provide guidance, they might be modeled similarly. However, they are actually quite different and provide different kinds of guidance. Further, for my purposes in developing a framework that encompasses both, it is especially important to clarify their differences so they are seen as clearly distinct. This also helps clarify how they work together and why individuals need to develop both forms of guidance to have the greatest chance of success in creative endeavors.

Specifically, I model guiding principles in terms of two key attributes. One is efficiency in evaluating seeds to determine if they can be successfully developed into high-value creative contributions. The other is creativity, the capability to help an individual discover the "missing piece" that can successfully complete a seed project, turning it into a successful full project. At the end of the chapter I present a result from the simulations that demonstrates an interesting interrelationship between these attributes and guiding conception seed pool size.

DEFINITION

A guiding principle, like a guiding conception, is defined in terms of higher-level abstract elements. The examples in the preceding chapter illustrate this: the principle of relativity, aesthetic balance, fluid communication, and integration across design levels—all are abstract principles.

Given that guiding principles are abstract, one might imagine modeling them directly as higher-level elements in the context, the way I model guiding conceptions. However, I adopt a different approach for guiding principles. Guiding conceptions guide idea and seed project generation through links they have to other more specific elements, in the model I focus on, their children. For this reason defining guiding conceptions in terms of their location in the context and their connections is central for modeling their function.

Guiding principles, however, function differently. They do not necessarily or even typically act directly through children or other links. Rather, they act more holistically and generally, in a manner less tied to their local network context. Consider for example an artist evaluating the aesthetic harmony or balance of a composition. They use their guiding principle to evaluate the composition as a whole, not individual elements, and their guiding principle is typically not linked directly to any of these individual elements. Further, a principle such as harmony or balance will apply to many compositions, and thus its application transcends its local network of linkages. In some cases a guiding principle may be linked to particular exemplars, as in a work of art an artist views as especially harmonious; it also may have important links to related higher-level concepts. Overall, however, while conceptually a guiding principle must reside somewhere in context, its actual location is secondary for its function, at least as I model it. For these reasons I do not explicitly locate guiding principles in the context but rather view them separately.[1]

Essentially I model guiding principles as functions that act on seeds and projects, which are their inputs, and generate outputs that contribute to moving the creative process forward. I merely sketch this approach and do not fill in all modeling details; far more could be written and developed than what I present. Viewing guiding principles as functions, their location in the context as elements with links is secondary, as noted above, and I do not consider their location explicitly in the model. As I have discussed in the preceding chapters, sometimes guiding principles are linked with guiding conceptions; I do not model this kind of direct link between the two forms of guidance as an explicit network connection, but I do focus on how the two work in tandem.

In my experience most individuals and teams engaged in a particular creative endeavor have only one or a few guiding principles.

For simplicity I focus on the case in which each individual or team has just one, recognizing that this is an oversimplification in many cases. For Albert Einstein, for example, the principle of relativity stands out as a fundamental guiding principle; but he also expressed the principle of making a theory as simple as possible. His model of Brownian motion is an exemplar of such theory construction, with its famous fluctuation-dissipation result.[2] Regarding this second principle, although it seems that Einstein did not utter the famous quotation often attributed to him that "everything should be made as simple as possible, but no simpler," he did reportedly say something with a somewhat similar meaning: "It can scarcely be denied that the supreme goal of all theory is to make the irreducible basic elements as simple and as few as possible without having to surrender the adequate representation of a single datum of experience."[3] Extending the model to more guiding principles is quite direct, with the guiding principles acting either in sequence or in tandem. Such an extension would be very useful in some cases, such as for modeling the creative process of Lynn Conway, who had a pair of linked guiding principles.

INPUTS

Guiding principles are functions, which means they act on inputs to generate outputs. The input for a guiding principle is a seed or project, thus a set of elements. For the formal model in this book, with a two-level context these sets include exclusively bottom elements, but more generally such sets could contain a mixture of elements from different levels of a context. I focus on describing how guiding principles act on seeds, following the model outlined in Chapter 5.

As functions acting on sets of elements, guiding principles stand outside standard network models. In standard models the focus is on nodes and links between nodes.[4] A guiding principle operates globally, not through local network links, as discussed above. Indeed as the examples in the preceding chapter illustrate, guiding principles have wide scope. A principle like aesthetic balance will have something to say about a very wide range of art and design compositions. Thus guiding principles don't fit the standard models that focus on network location as the primary factor in modeling network processes and outcomes. Hence in this regard the model I develop in this book is not reducible to standard network models, although it draws on them in important ways.[5]

A second related point is that although guiding principles have wide scope, they do not apply to all conceivable seeds and projects. The aesthetic principle of harmony, for example, would most likely not be applied to a chemical reaction; it is not inconceivable that it could be, but that would not be typical. Thus the input domain of a guiding principle cannot in general be assumed to cover every conceivable seed and project that might be developed in a given context. This statement is perhaps better expressed in a manner that emphasizes the inherent subjectivity in the way guiding principles are applied. Consider an individual who adheres to a particular guiding principle. For a seed or project he encounters to lie in the domain of his guiding principle means that, based on the way the individual conceives of his guiding principle and the particular seed or project, he is able to apply the guiding principle to the seed or project in a meaningful and informative way.[6] If that is not the case, it means that from the individual's point of view, his guiding principle has "nothing to say" about the given seed or project. Exactly which seeds and projects will lie in the domain of an individual's guiding principle is not typically explicitly defined ahead of time but rather is implicit, for in a large-scale context there are far too many potential seeds and projects for them all to be enumerated.

Regarding range of application of guiding principles, the model affords a natural assumption that enables this issue to be addressed quite simply. Focusing on guiding principles working in tandem with guiding conceptions, I assume that whichever seeds are discovered or created by an individual pursuing her guiding conception lie in the domain of her guiding principle. For example Clifford Possum had the guiding principle of aesthetic balance, and it makes sense that he evaluated the paintings he worked on that emanated from his guiding conception of making "maps of the country" with multiple Dreamings in terms of this criterion. The guiding principle will apply to many other seeds and projects as well, of course, but an individual will not encounter these while pursuing their guiding conception.[7] Specifying the domain of a guiding principle based on the guiding conception it is linked with greatly simplifies the analysis because we do not need to specify the domain for a guiding principle explicitly but rather simply impose the rule that it includes all seeds that can be generated by the guiding conception.

Figure 11 (p. 127) shows an example of a guiding conception and its seed pool in the small context example. The guiding conception highlighted consists of top elements A and C. There are 7 valid seeds associated with this guiding conception; each is shown in the figure with an arc between its constituent pair. In terms of evaluating seeds and projects, when an individual or team pursuing this guiding conception has an associated guiding principle to help guide them, their guiding principle will have as its input domain, at a minimum, these 7 seeds as well as the potential three-element projects they may be developed into.

Now that the input domain for a guiding principle is specified, let us turn to how the guiding principle is used: its outputs.

OUTPUT I: EVALUATION AND EFFICIENCY

The model focuses on the ways in which guiding principles as functions act on seeds. Guiding principles may act similarly on full projects, but modeling this, especially iterative project revision, increases the complexity of the model, and I do not pursue it for the main model development of this book.

There are two ways in which a guiding principle acts on a seed. First, the guiding principle helps an individual or team evaluate the seed and determine whether it has potential to be developed into a successful full project. Second, if it does have potential to be developed successfully, the guiding principle provides guidance helping to identify the critical additional third element that will make the project work. I discuss the first process in this section and the second in the next.

Evaluation is straightforward, at least in theory. Given that the guiding principle is allied with the guiding conception used to generate seeds, the guiding principle will be able to evaluate every such seed, for each seed lies in the guiding principle's domain, as discussed above. For example consider an artist whose guiding principle is aesthetic balance, as was the case for Clifford Possum. Each seed is an incipient artistic composition: a painting partially developed, a sketch, or even just an imagined composition. This seed is evaluated as to whether it is considered possible to develop the painting in such a way as to achieve aesthetic balance, which will contribute to the final painting being successful. Assume for simplicity that the evaluation returns a simple yes or no answer; a more mixed answer might call for further investigation of the seed.

No means this seed project is evaluated as not able to be developed in a manner that will attain conformity with the guiding principle. It is too deeply flawed, in a way the individual or team judges cannot be rectified; in their judgement there is no additional element that will enable it to conform with the principle. In this case it is dropped and a new seed is investigated. If there are no further seeds in this guiding conception seed pool to be evaluated, then the guiding conception must be modified or abandoned.

Yes means the individual or team assesses that this seed can be developed successfully and barring other factors will pursue its further development. Thus for example Possum might judge that an incipient painting can be developed to achieve aesthetic balance.

This same yes/no evaluation can also apply to full projects, but with some differences in the way the process plays out. If a project is evaluated as a *no*, it may be dropped, but the same seed may be used to explore development into a different project. Alternatively, attempts may be made to revise the project—this is an important part of the creative process, but I do not focus on it as noted above. If a project is evaluated as a *yes*, it may be viewed as complete or may be developed further—in which case the guiding principle may well be applied again at a later stage.

Guiding principle evaluation of seeds and projects may be holistic, capturing issues of the seed or project in its entirety. Alternatively, it may be more targeted, with the guiding principle identifying a particular element as especially weak or unsuited to the overall design.[8]

Finally note that I am considering only cases in which the evaluations made using guiding principles are correct and recognized to be correct. Thus if an individual or team believes a seed can be developed successfully, it means there is an additional element, somewhere in the context, that will enable a successful project to be produced. Conversely, if they believe the seed will fail as a project, then there is no such additional element and the seed cannot be developed into a successful project. Of course none of us is infallible, even highly experienced creators, and this is a simplification of a complex process of judgment. The simple assumption can certainly be relaxed, and in the more general case the likelihood of success guides the decision about whether to pursue developing a given seed project.

Refer again to Figure 11 in which the seven seeds associated with the guiding conception consisting of elements A and C are highlighted. Employing their guiding principle, the individual will be able to ascertain, for each seed, whether it has potential to be developed into a successful project. Let us suppose for purposes of illustration that one of these seven seeds, seed $(1, 7)$, is evaluated as able to be developed successfully, while each of the other six if evaluated will be viewed as unable to be developed successfully. Note that the model assumes these seven seeds are sampled in a random order, so that exactly when in the sequence of trials seed $(1, 7)$ will be encountered is random.

EFFICIENCY:
The formal model focuses on contexts in which there is just one "golden" project, as introduced in Chapter 10. As also explained in that chapter, each guiding conception from which this golden project can be developed has in its seed pool one of the golden seeds that can be developed into the golden project. Given that seed pools can contain many seeds—anywhere from a few to more than a 100, as shown in Figure 14 for the simulated contexts—it follows that an individual or team following the guidance of a guiding conception that covers a golden seed are still likely to experience a string of nos as they evaluate a series of seeds that do not have potential before finally hitting upon the one seed in their guiding conception pool that does have potential.

In turn, this raises an important issue of *efficiency*: How efficient will an individual or team be in using their guiding principle to rapidly evaluate seed projects? This evaluation may involve both evaluating the seed itself, in terms of its creative potential, and evaluating projects it may be able to be developed into, which may be done more as a thought experiment or through prototyping. The more rapidly seeds and projects can be evaluated, the more likely the individual or team is to find the golden seed in a timely manner. If their evaluation process is too slow, they may run out of resources or time, lose motivation, or may be scooped as others find their way to the golden project more quickly, possibly through different routes, that is, different guiding conceptions and seeds. Thus efficiency of evaluation is important.

Importantly, guiding principles may differ in their level of efficiency of use, as discussed in Chapter 11. Some principles, such as a rigorous design standard of proportionality, may be able to be applied directly and quickly. Others, such as harmony or a principle of justice, may require careful consideration of many factors. Further, individuals may differ in their efficiency of application of a guiding principle due to differences in experience and subjective interpretation of the principle.

Hans Krebs is an example of someone for whom high efficiency was a key attribute of his guiding principle approach of trying many things. I describe how good he was at this in the next chapter, in which I discuss the project he pursued after setting up his own independent lab, the synthesis of urea. His efficiency in evaluating alternatives was crucial in enabling him to be successful on this project, for it enabled him to explore a wide range of alternatives.

Efficiency will be especially important, other things equal, when the seed pool of the associated guiding conception is large or there are many possible ways to develop seeds into full projects. Related to the latter case, a different way to state it is that efficiency will be important when there is a lot of work involved in getting a project "just right," so that there are likely to be many iterations revising a project until it meets the strict standards set. Albert Einstein had a strict interpretation of relativity, and this led him to reject many proposed solutions as he worked out his theory. In this situation if a guiding principle is not employed efficiently, an individual or team may never make it through the necessary cycles to produce a successful final product.

Related to these points and especially the issue of getting a project just right is the issue of the accuracy of guiding principle evaluation. Higher accuracy is associated with higher efficiency. A guiding principle that is applied with high accuracy—and hence is reliable in determining which seeds can be successful and whether a project truly meets a strict standard—is inherently more efficient than a guiding principle applied with low accuracy, which may lead to many false leads being pursued and a successful path not being discovered as quickly. I do not consider accuracy in the model of this book in any direct way, in the interest of keeping the model relatively simple, but it is clearly important and clear that certain individuals, such as Einstein and Jobs, are very precise in the way they apply their guiding principles and that this is key for their success.[9]

OUTPUT II: THE THIRD ELEMENT AND CREATIVITY

When a seed is evaluated as having potential to be developed into a successful project, the creative process moves to the next phase: the search to identify the critical third element. I assume for formal modeling purposes that there is just one element that can fulfill this role; hence this is a very targeted search. Importantly this third element can be located anywhere in the context, near or far. Allowing for this captures the idea that this additional element may be a highly creative link, which is more likely to be the case if it is far away in the context, or may be less creative and more routine, meaning it is more likely relatively close. In terms of the formal model, the third element can be any element in the bottom level of the context that does not share a parent with either of the seed elements.

Figure 18 in the next section presents distributions of distances to third elements for the simulated networks. As shown in that figure, the range is quite large, indicating that this part of the creative process has a good deal of variability.

There are two natural ways the model can be extended that are worthy of mention; both are important for empirical application. First, there may be a number of candidate third elements that can be added to the seed and yield a successful final outcome—for example, the way a design can be completed in a variety of ways. Second, in most applications more than one element is added, even if we confine the analysis to core design elements. Both extensions fit naturally within the overall framework, and I discuss them in Chapter 16.

Now consider a specific seed and assume that there is—somewhere in the context—a critical third element that can develop it into a successful project. As I model it, and as I believe is true in reality in many cases, the guiding principle an individual or team adheres to is the key to finding this critical third element. For Albert Einstein there is little doubt that his strict adherence to the principle of relativity was the key to his development of both special and general relativity. In each case his guiding principle provided the guidance that enabled him to take the critical step needed to move from a challenging puzzle and incipient direction provided by his guiding conception to a proposed theory. Likewise for Steve Jobs, his strict adherence to design principles of simplicity and playful elegance were critical for him and his team as they worked to develop incipient designs into full working products. Likewise also for Clifford Possum, once he had a partially completed painting, according to his biographer Vivien Johnson and observers at the time, his guiding principle of aesthetic balance was central in helping him choose elements to add to the painting to produce an aesthetically balanced final composition. Note that the guiding conception an individual or team pursues, although essential in generating the initial seed, is not necessarily as much use in identifying the third element, given that this element does not lie in the pool of elements covered by the guiding conception and may in fact be quite far away from it. Thus the two forms of guidance have different roles; in reality their roles may be more overlapping than this, but maintaining a distinction is useful in clarifying our understanding of the different roles and how they fit together.

To keep the model parsimonious I assume that the guiding principle used to identify the third element is the same one that is used to evaluate seeds. As noted above, a principle like aesthetic balance clearly will perform both functions. Indeed aesthetic balance is the only guiding principle Clifford Possum's biographer has identified as a principle of artistic composition he adhered to. Thus in Possum's case this assumption fits with what we know about his creative process. To give a second example, a guiding principle of justice clearly would be used both to evaluate incipient policies in terms of how just they might turn out to be when fully developed, and also would be used to help identify additional elements to help make a policy more just. Thus assuming the same guiding principle is used for both actions makes sense and also fits with the documented creative process of at least some creators. However, it seems likely that in many cases different guiding principles will be employed for these different functions. The model can accommodate this: the assumption that the same guiding principle is used both for evaluation and to help find a critical element to complete a project is not essential.[10]

Given that the third element can reside anywhere in the context, there are an enormous number of possibilities for what it may be, especially in a large context. I do not think we have enough information at present to model in detail how a guiding principle directs attention to just the right element in this situation, which is a question for the psychology and neuroscience of creativity. But it is clear that it happens, the way Clifford Possum discovered elements to create balance in his paintings and the way Albert Einstein recognized how to generalize relativity theory to include gravity. In the case of Einstein, he said he was sitting in his office; we do not know for sure what triggered his insight—lore has it that he saw a man on a ladder outside his office window, and this image triggered the thought of what it would be like to be in free fall in the Earth's gravitational field. Without knowing for sure, what we can say is that his guiding principle linked up with a separate image or conception—which may have been based on reflection or an actual image he saw—to generate the key insight. For Clifford Possum, there is no evidence of experiences triggering his insights; they seem more to have been internally generated based on his looking at his painting, seeing where balance was lacking and then thinking of an additional element that could rectify the situation. Just from these two examples it is clear there are different pathways through which guiding principles help discover additional project elements.

Consider now a network context, a seed, and a third element that can expand the seed into a successful project. From the network perspective, the key characteristic of the third element is how far away it is. In creativity it is generally believed that links that are further away will require more insight and creativity to think of and discover.[11] Thus it is natural to use distance to parameterize the needed degree of creativity for this important step of project development. In networks the distance between two elements is measured as the length of the shortest path between them. Thus it will require more creativity to connect two elements for which the shortest path connecting them is relatively long than to connect two elements for which the shortest path connecting them is relatively short.

How far away is the third element? Logically, by "distance" we mean its distance away from the individual's current mindset, for this is the chasm that must be bridged to find it. To operationalize such a measure, we must define the individual's mindset in a way that enables this distance to be calculated. This is challenging: it is clear that a person's mindset might include many things of which we would have no knowledge that might influence this distance calculation.

The approach I follow is to consider a minimum set of elements the individual should have in their mindset and define the distance to the third element as the shortest distance to this set, that is, the distance to the member of this set that is closest to the third element. For an individual engaged in a creative endeavor who has reached the point of having developed a potentially viable seed, their current mindset certainly includes their guiding conception and the seed they have hit upon and would like to develop further. Thus at a minimum their mindset would include their seed and their guiding conception. Their mindset also includes their guiding principle, but as I model it the guiding principle does not have a fixed location in context and thus is best thought of as operating independently, not linked to the calculation of distances.

Given that in the model guiding conceptions are composed of a pair of top elements and seeds are composed of a pair of bottom elements, there are four elements in this minimal set. Any one of these four elements might be the starting point for a path leading to the critical third element. It is clear that a seed element may trigger a path since the aim is to find a third element that fits well with the seed. Guiding conception elements may also guide attention to the third element. After all, the guiding conception specifies the overall vision for developing the project, and thus, if the project is missing something, this overall vision can help identify what it is. For Einstein, his conception in the years after he invented special relativity was to expand the framework to a broader class of reference frames, specifically incorporating gravity. It makes sense that it was this conceptual link that helped him think and recognize the importance of what the experience would be for a man in free fall in the Earth's gravitational field. Following the logic I have outlined, I compute the shortest path from each of the four elements to the critical third element needed to complete the project. I then define the distance to the third element as the minimum distance over these four paths.

This specification is parsimonious and internally consistent with the overall model and provides a natural way to close the model. However, it is also limited by the restriction that the mindset includes only the seed and guiding conception elements. More elements could be incorporated into the model. For example, elements might be introduced into a person's mindset through feedback from a mentor, a discussion about the project with colleagues, or even chance encounters. Any such elements could be added into the framework as additional elements for which path lengths are computed. It follows that this is a part of the creative process where these kinds of activities—mentoring, discussions, chance encounters—can have a constructive role. For example an experienced mentor, hearing the seed project described, might be able to suggest some candidate ideas to consider, even if they do not know the exact element that will work; to the extent any of these candidates is closer to the third element than the seed and guiding conception elements, this will shorten the distance to the third element.[12]

As described above, guiding principles evaluate seeds and projects as a whole. Evaluating the shortest distance over both seed and guiding conception elements fits with this to the degree that it encompasses all elements. However, it does not incorporate the possibility that the seed and/or guiding conception complex acting as a unit might illuminate a path to the third element that is distinct from all of the paths that emanate from the four components separately. To model this requires an extension to something like a hypergraph approach—see Chapter 16 for further discussion.

An important general point that my discussion highlights, which is valuable for understanding this phase of the creative process, is that guiding principles function both holistically, acting on sets, and also more narrowly, focusing on single elements. Thus a guiding principle may be holistic in evaluating seeds or projects but may also focus attention more narrowly in helping to identify the specific critical element to add to a seed to expand it into a successful project. Clifford Possum would have evaluated aesthetic balance in a composition he was working on as a whole; but if he identified an imbalance, he would then use his guiding principle to help identify an element that he could add to the composition to create balance.

DISTANCE CALCULATIONS AND DISTRIBUTIONS

In this section I use the small example context to show how the distance to the third element is computed, then present a figure showing third project element distance distributions for the simulated networks.

Consider again the small example context. Figure 17 builds on Figure 11. It focuses on the seed $(1, 7)$ and adds a third element. For this seed, there are 12 bottom elements that do not share parents in common with either seed element and thus might be the third element that can successfully complete the project: $3, 8, 9, 10, 11, 12, 13, 14, 15, 16, 17, 18$. Note that most of these lie to the right-hand side of the context, relatively distant from the seed elements. Now suppose following Figure 9 that, as an example, the third element that can successfully complete this seed to forge a successful full project is element 16. The shortest path from element 16 to each of the project elements 1 and 7 and guiding conception elements A and C is computed, and the minimum of these four values is defined to be the distance to this third element.

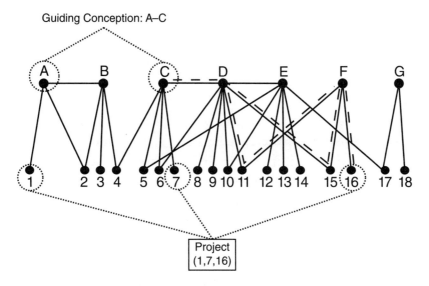

The third element is 16. Shortest distances to guiding conception and other project elements:

16–C: 4
16–7: 5
16–A: 7
16–1: 8

There are two paths of length 4 from 16 to C, shown in the figure as dashed lines.

FIGURE 17. SMALL EXAMPLE CONTEXT: DISTANCE TO THIRD ELEMENT EXAMPLE

These distances are:

$$16\text{–}C : \quad 4$$

$$16\text{-}7 : \quad 5$$

$$16\text{–}A : \quad 7$$

$$16\text{-}1 : \quad 8$$

Thus the minimum distance is a path of length 4 to guiding conception element C (the two paths of this length are shown in the figure). It is interesting to note that there is considerable variation in these four shortest path lengths—highlighting the fact that there are different creative paths to finding the third element and they are not all equivalent in terms of distance.

Now consider distributions of distances to third elements in the simulated networks. Figure 18 shows these distributions by network type. Recall there are 10 simulated networks of each type. For a given network, first the set of valid guiding conceptions is identified, as discussed in Chapter 10. Each guiding conception defines a seed pool as also discussed in that chapter, and each seed in the pool can be developed into a set of valid projects by adding valid third elements (elements that do not share any parents in common with the seed elements). For each seed in the pool, the distance to each valid third element is computed, and these numbers are combined over all such third elements and then over all seeds in the pool and finally over all guiding conception pools in the network to generate the distance distribution for that network.[13] Finally, for each type of network these 10 distance distributions are averaged to generate the distribution shown.

The results show that distances to third elements vary considerably, ranging from 2 to 9. There are also considerable differences in the distributions over the six kinds of networks. Distances are shortest for the power law degree networks, which is not surprising as paths can go through hubs that have a very large number of connections to bottom elements. Distances are longest for the cluster networks, indicating that the challenge of finding third elements will be especially important for these kinds of contexts. Distances are shorter in the smaller-scale contexts and longer in the larger-scale contexts. This is also not surprising and indicates that the challenge of finding just the right third element will be greater as scale grows. For all networks, but especially the random and cluster types, there is a significant right-hand tail, indicating that some third elements are quite far away from the seed and guiding conception elements with which they are associated. This leads naturally to the next topic: the creativity needed to identify third elements, especially third elements that are far away in the context.

Panel A: Small Scale

Average Values over the 10 Simulated Networks for Each Network Type

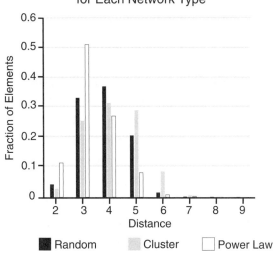

Panel B: Large Scale

Average Values over the 10 Simulated Networks for Each Network Type

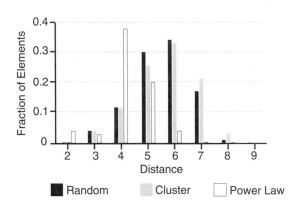

FIGURE 18. DISTANCES TO THIRD PROJECT ELEMENTS: DISTRIBUTIONS

CREATIVITY:

As stated above, it is generally thought that forging a meaningful new connection between elements that are far apart in their context is a highly creative act. This is because more distant connections lie outside standard thinking paths, which are typically short; more creative thinking is involved in making distant connections than in making closer connections. Following this logic, creativity will be important for discovering third elements that are far away from the seed and guiding conception elements with which they are associated.

Given that guiding principles are central in discovering third elements, this in turn implies that the creativity of a guiding principle, in particular in terms of how it can be and is used to expand seeds into projects, will be important for creative success, especially for projects involving distant third elements. The importance of creativity and employing a guiding principle creatively for discovering the critical element to make a project come together successfully fits with many empirical cases. Albert Einstein employed his guiding principle of relativity with enormous creativity. Likewise Steve Jobs used his guiding principle of simplicity in design to make highly creative distant links to help resolve aesthetic design challenges, as when he made a creative link with a Cuisinart he saw at Macy's to spur the development of the original Macintosh design.[14]

Creativity is thus a second important attribute of guiding principles. Just as some guiding principles will be more efficient than others, so too it is natural that some guiding principles are better than others at helping individuals discover highly creative links to distant third elements. In general, a broad principle such as a design principle of harmony or simplicity will likely be able to be used more creatively than a narrow principle such as the rule to set a fixed size ratio of 3:1 between headers and body text. Creativity also depends on how a guiding principle is employed by the individual who is seeking to discover the key additional project element—a design principle of simplicity can be expected to be used in more creative ways by some designers than by others—Steve Jobs was remarkably creative in his application of this principle.

Whereas the use of guiding principles for evaluation, and the need to be accurate and efficient in this task, would seem likely to be widely appreciated, the need for creativity might be less evident. It is thus important to stress the creativity of guiding principles when mentoring individuals engaged in creative endeavors.

PAIRING GUIDING CONCEPTIONS AND GUIDING PRINCIPLES: A COMPLEMENTARITY RESULT

Guiding conceptions and guiding principles work together and in sequence to generate creative outcomes. In that sense they are inter-dependent. This raises the question of whether there are certain kinds of guiding conceptions that work best when paired with certain kinds of guiding principles. As it turns out, based on the simulations, the answer is yes in regard to the creativity guidance framework I have presented.

Specifically, the simulations reveal a natural pairing in terms of the key attributes of guiding conceptions and guiding principles. One of the key attributes of guiding conceptions is their seed pool size. Key attributes of guiding principles are efficiency and creativity.

Intuitively, it makes sense that efficiency of evaluation will be more important when being used in conjunction with larger seed pools. More seeds will need to be evaluated, and while it is not definite that this will also mean more projects to consider, it would seem likely in most cases. Thus guiding principle efficiency is especially important when a guiding principle is paired with a guiding conception that has a large seed pool.

The more surprising result is the opposite pairing. It turns out, at least in the simulated network contexts, that smaller seed pools are as-sociated with longer distances to third project elements. As a result, creativity of a guiding principle is especially important when the guid-ing principle is paired with a guiding conception that has a small seed pool.

Figure 19 shows this pattern of interrelationship for the simulated networks, separately for each of the six network types. For this figure the guiding conceptions in a network are divided into three bins based on the size of their seed pools just as in Figure 14: small, the 25 percent of guiding conceptions with the smallest seed pools; medium, the 50 percent of guiding conceptions with middle-sized seed pools; and large, the 25 percent of guiding conceptions with the largest seed pools. Then distances to third projects are computed over all valid projects that can be produced from each seed in each guiding conception seed pool in the bin.

For each type of network the figure shows the cumulative distribution function (CDF) over these third element distances for each of the three guiding conception bins. What stands out is that in every case the small bin CDF rises more slowly (that is, is below) the medium bin CDF, which in turn is below the large bin CDF. In the language of mathematics this is a first-order stochastic dominance result. The interpretation is that at each distance, the fraction of projects for which the third element distance is equal to or greater than this distance is largest for the small seed pool guiding conceptions, in between for the middle seed pool guiding conceptions, and smallest for the large seed pool guiding conceptions.[15] This is a strong result showing a link between distances to third elements and seed pool size. The result is consistent across the networks; in fact, it holds in all 60 simulated network contexts. This is at least suggestive of an analytic stochastic dominance result, but I have not attempted to prove such a result.

The results in Figure 19 indicate that there is a robust complementarity: distances to third elements to complete projects tend to be larger for guiding conceptions with smaller seed pools. Linking distance with creativity, it follows that the creativity of a guiding principle is brought to the fore when it is paired with a guiding conception with a small seed pool.

Thus there is a double complementarity. Guiding conceptions with large seed pools will benefit from being paired with guiding principles having high efficiency of evaluation. Guiding conceptions with small seed pools will benefit from being paired with guiding principles having high creativity for discovering critical additional project elements. This is not only interesting conceptually but also clearly has implications for managing and mentoring creativity. A manager or mentor should consider the likely seed pool of the guiding conception an individual or

Panel A: Small Scale

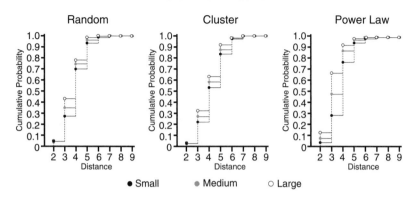

Panel B: Large Scale

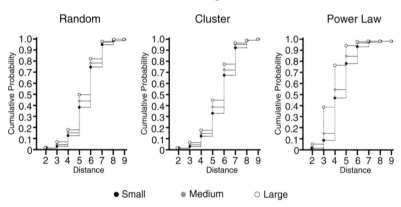

Each graph shows 3 cumulative distribution functions, corresponding to the division of guiding conceptions by seed pool sizes. Small = 25% of guiding conceptions with smallest seed pools; Medium = 50% of guiding conceptions with middle-sized pools; and Large = 25% of guiding conceptions with largest pools. Values for the graphs are computed as follows. For each type of network, bins are formed for each individual network and for each bin the CDF is computed. On the graph, for each bin the value of the CDF displayed at each distance is the average of the 10 network CDF values for that bin for that distance.

FIGURE 19. THE RELATIONSHIP BETWEEN GUIDING CONCEPTION SEED POOL SIZE AND DISTANCE TO THIRD PROJECT ELEMENTS: AVERAGE CUMULATIVE DISTRIBUTION FUNCTIONS BY SEED POOL SIZE BINS FOR EACH TYPE OF NET-WORK

team is working with and stress the relevant attribute for the guiding principles they are employing in tandem with their guiding conception.

This result holds for the main model in this book in which seed pools are defined as children of guiding conception elements. It is natural to wonder whether it holds more generally. The difference between guiding conceptions with large seed pools and guiding conceptions with small seed pools in the main model is that in the former case, the guiding conception elements have more children.[16] Thus we can conjecture that the difference in distances to third elements is due to the fact that for guiding conceptions with small seed pools, there are fewer pathways to a third element that pass through another child of one of the guiding conception elements—that is, a child that is not one of the seed elements—and therefore less likelihood of a shortest path of this kind. In networks with preferential attachment or other kinds of nonindependence, it is possible that this will no longer hold true, in which case the result might not hold.

Another interesting question relates to the way seed pools are defined. As I have noted in previous chapters and discuss in more detail in Chapter 16, guiding conceptions can be defined in conceptually richer ways, as sets that in turn generate seeds that are themselves sets linked functionally (not necessarily as children) to the guiding conception. It requires further analysis to determine under what conditions the complementarity result continues to hold for this kind of model.

PART III

CREATION

CHAPTER 14

A CORE MODEL OF CREATIVITY

In Parts I and II, I described the rich network context of creativity and introduced two key forms of guidance, guiding conceptions and guiding principles. In Part III, I show how these guidance processes work together to generate creativity, defining a core model of creativity. I then build on this model to discuss creative journeys, modeling richer creative processes, the development of creative fields, and best practices for supporting creativity.

Creativity does not just happen out of the blue, although sometimes it seems that way. Rather, we follow paths that lead us to creative breakthroughs. This is true of the greatest creators and the most humble. It is important not only because of its general truth but also because it provides a perspective for identifying factors that are critical to these paths and thus to generating creativity. It is also a way to help individuals understand creativity, realize it is within their power, and give them guidance and support in their creative endeavors.

The creativity model I focus on fits with this perspective, as a key building block of creative paths. In fact, a good way to understand the logic of creative paths is to think about them as constructed out of building blocks. These building blocks link to one another, not in a fixed way, but in diverse patterns, generating the rich diversity of creative paths we see. The model I describe is an especially important building block.

In this chapter I first describe this model. Then to illustrate how the model maps onto real-world creativity, I present and discuss creative projects of Clifford Possum, Hans Krebs, and Jack Dorsey. I then briefly discuss collaborative creativity, giving the example of Uber. In the final section, I discuss how richer creative paths are built up out of building blocks.

TWO-STEP: THE CORE CREATIVE GUIDANCE MODEL

There are two key steps to develop a creative project, which I have described in the preceding chapters. The first step is exploration to discover a high-potential project seed. A seed is a creative combination of elements; it may hold creative potential, but must be developed to realize this potential. In the base model a seed is composed of two elements; in reality, seeds can be composed of more elements but—excepting very large projects—would not be expected to be composed of many elements, given that they are seeds and not fully developed projects. A guiding conception provides the essential guidance for this step: it envisions the pool of possibilities to explore—where to look in the rich large-scale context.

The second step is to identify a seed with high potential and then develop it into a full project, or more precisely, a core project design, which can then be fashioned into a completed project. Guiding principles provide the essential guidance for this step. They help sort through possible seeds, reject those that don't have sufficient potential, and identify a seed with potentially high value. Second, they help identify additional elements, the critical "missing pieces," that develop the seed into a successful project.

This is the simplest version of this core two-step creative process. Later in this chapter, and in the following chapter when more complex real-world cases are presented, a few different forms of this process will be described. But this simple model captures the gist of it.

In the base model that I have used for formal analysis and simulations, the context network has two levels and projects are composed out of three elements: two define the seed, and the third element completes the project. Guiding conceptions are composed out of higher-level elements, and in the base model they consist of two elements that jointly define the creative pool to explore. Guiding principles have two key attributes: efficiency, to sort through possible seed pairs efficiently, and creativity, to identify the third element, somewhere out in the network, possibly quite far away, that develops the seed into a successful full project.

Figure 20 illustrates the base two-step model for the small example context. This figure depicts the model elements and creative process for an individual, call them "Z." Z has formed the guiding conception composed of top elements A and C, and we assume also has a guiding principle. There are seven seeds that lie in the search pool covered by this guiding conception, formed from pairs of children of A and C, indicated in the figure, similar to Figure 11. Assuming valid intuition lies behind Z's guiding conception, one of these seven seeds will be able to be developed into a successful project, but Z does not know which one. Not knowing which will work, Z tries each in turn at random. Assume (again, this is just an illustrative example), that seed pair $(1, 7)$ is the one seed in the pool that has high potential. Assuming Z's guiding principle does what it should, Z will reject the other seeds and recognize that this seed has potential. The more efficient Z is in using their guiding principle, the more rapidly this seed will be discovered.

Now, Z's task is to discover the missing third element that will create a successful project. The third element can be anywhere in the context; the only constraint is that it cannot share a common parent with either of the seed elements. Z's guiding principle guides the search for this third element. The further away the third element is, the more creativity is required to identify it, hence the increased importance of their guiding principle's creativity, or, put slightly differently, Z's ability to employ it creatively. Of course, this is a small context, so distance is less of a factor. But in larger contexts the distance to third elements is quite variable, something evident in the results presented for the

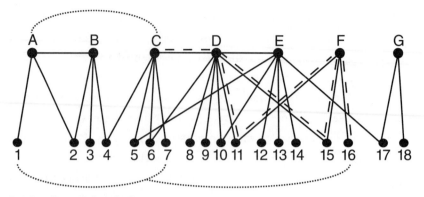

Guiding Conception: A–C
Seed Pool: (1,4), (1,5), (1,6), (1,7), (2,5), (2,6), (2,7)
High Potential Seed: (1,7)
Third Element: 16
⟶ Golden Project: (1,7,16)
Minimum Distance from 16 to {A,C,1,7} is 4, to element C; there are two paths
of this length, shown in the figure as dashed lines.

FIGURE 20. SMALL EXAMPLE CONTEXT: EXAMPLE OF THE CORE CREATIVE GUIDANCE MODEL

simulated networks in Figure 18 in the previous chapter, and thus creativity to identify distant third elements can be critical to developing a high-potential "golden" project.

Let us suppose (again for illustrative purposes) that element 16 is the required third element to form a successful three-element project as in Figures 9 and 17. As outlined in the preceding chapter, calculate the distance from this element to each of the seed elements and each guiding conception element; these distances are listed in Figure 17. The shortest distance is to guiding conception element C and is a distance of 4. Thus, this is the shortest path from Z's original mindset to the third element and hence is a reasonable measure of how far away it is and how much creativity is required to identify it. With sufficient creativity and skill in using their guiding principle, Z will discover that element 16 is the third element, forming the full project—or perhaps better thought of as the core project design—(1, 7, 16). Z can pursue this project, and if it is truly golden, it will deliver a high-value outcome.

Notice how the two forms of guidance work together: first Z's guiding conception to focus the search for a valuable seed, and second Z's guiding principle to help reject seeds that will not work and identify the seed that has creative potential, and then to help scan the entire context to identify the critical third element that makes the project come together as a whole.

The two-step guidance process can be identified empirically in the creative processes of many individuals who create and make valuable contributions, across most creative fields. Next, I present examples of creativity that illustrate this process at work: Hans Krebs's discovery of the biochemical process for the synthesis of urea, Clifford Possum's creation of his masterpiece *Warlugulong*, and Jack Dorsey and the development of Twitter.

HANS KREBS

Hans Krebs's creative process illustrates the core two-step model. I focus here on his discovery of the biochemical process through which urea is synthesized in the body, his first well-known research contribution.

As discussed in Chapter 8 Krebs formed a guiding conception during his time working in Otto Warburg's lab: to apply the tissue slice manometric methodology to the study of intermediary metabolism. Warburg did not allow him to pursue this topic while he was working in the lab. However, Krebs left the Warburg lab after four years and set up his own independent lab. Now at last he was free to pursue his guiding conception, and this is exactly what he did, using funds provided by grants and mentors to purchase the equipment necessary for the manometric methodology.

Krebs's guiding principle, which was an approach to his work emphasizing trying many alternatives, often in parallel and ranging widely, was just as critical to his success as his guiding conception: they worked in tandem as they typically do. The main reason his guiding principle was so important is that, even within his chosen focus, there were a vast array of options: in the area of intermediary metabolism there was not a fully developed theory to guide experiments, and there were many possible metabolic pathways and potential intermediaries that might be explored experimentally. As discussed in Chapter 13, guiding principles have an important role in evaluating projects and helping to complete projects, and in certain contexts the *efficiency* of a guiding principle comes to the fore. This was the case for Krebs. His approach with its emphasis on efficient and wide-ranging exploration enabled him to navigate the rich network of experimental possibilities and, without being too sure where success would lie, to explore widely, efficiently, and deeply when needed.

Initially, while busy with clinical responsibilities and establishing his lab, Krebs still found time to pursue four different projects. Although he had been directed to study one of these projects by Warburg, the other three were his own ideas. Each of these projects was in the area of intermediary metabolism and fit with his guiding conception. They represent his first attempt to pursue his guiding conception, and while none was hugely successful, they were important in helping him establish his independence as a researcher—they were in a sense trial runs.[1]

Krebs's first independent position was temporary, but less than a year after leaving Warburg's lab he found a more permanent position better suited to research. Now, more settled, he was ready to take on a more ambitious project. The project he chose to pursue was the study of the synthesis of urea. Urea is the output of the metabolic pathways through which proteins containing nitrogen are broken down. Studying how it is synthesized in the body fit with Krebs's guiding conception: if he could determine the steps leading to its synthesis, he would have uncovered some of the final steps in the "unbroken chain of reactions" through which food is metabolized.

Why this particular project? There are several reasons why this project appealed to Krebs. Perhaps most importantly, although the synthesis of urea had been a topic of study for more than sixty years, at the time Krebs took it up in 1931, it was poorly understood. A review published in 1929 in a handbook that Krebs purchased stated that the topic had been studied with many different methods that generated "contradictory results" and that much of the difficulty lay in the use of inadequate experimental procedures.[2] Hence this was very much an open topic and one to which he could bring more sophisticated experimental techniques to bear—the manometric tissue slice methodology—and thus hope to obtain more definitive results. Further, a recent article he was familiar with argued that the synthesis of urea only occurred in intact cells in which the cell structures could support the integrative metabolic activity. The tissue slice method specifically worked with intact cells and thus was ideally suited to study this kind of process, whereas most approaches at the time used ground-up cells so that, although the chemicals in the cell could be tested, the cell structure itself was lost. In addition urea was known to be synthesized at a relatively high rate so that quantitative measurement was feasible, again a good fit with the manometric technique at which Krebs was so skilled. Techniques had also already been developed to measure the production of urea, although in a less sophisticated manner than Krebs might have thought he could develop using his manometric equipment. We can think of these reasons as fitting with guiding principles he would have held, including wanting the project he chose to fit with the experimental skills he had developed, specifically the manometric tissue slice method, and to provide an opportunity to make a contribution to the field. These are quite standard principles we would expect many researchers to use in selecting seed projects to pursue.

Although we can look back with hindsight and identify several reasons why the urea project would have appealed to Krebs, it is important to recognize that this hindsight may overstate the case. Interestingly, when biographer Holmes showed Krebs these reasons "explaining" why he chose to study urea, Krebs wrote a note in the margin of Holmes's notes that there were "many pebbles on the beach," that is, many potential projects, and he simply chose this one as a "suitable system" to study.[3] This is consistent with the view that his guiding conception had a rich seed pool of potential projects, any one of which might have turned out to lead to success. Regardless of how strong his reasons were, Krebs's choice turned out to be a good one. It is also of note that Krebs had already pursued several less successful projects, and this may have helped him make a good choice this time.

As Krebs began to pursue the urea synthesis project, his guiding principle of trying many possibilities came to the fore. He described his approach to the project in this way:

> It was just, without any too specific ideas, that we tested the effect of all sorts of substances. That was part of the general philosophy—just to investigate systematically which substances influence the rate either as inhibitors or activators.[4]

We can think of this process as seeking additional "third" elements that would help focus the project more precisely, fitting the second step of the two-step model.

Reviewing the urea project in an article he wrote much later, Krebs stated that he had several questions in mind at the start. Any of these might have triggered the discovery of an additional factor producing greater focus, but all required testing many alternatives.[5] Ammonia was thought to be a key intermediary in the synthesis of urea so that amino acids (the building blocks of proteins) would first be broken down into ammonia and byproducts, and the ammonia would, in turn, be incorporated into urea. His first question was whether ammonia is always an intermediary or whether some amino acids were converted directly into urea.[6] Another question was how the rates of formation of urea varied over the different amino acids. He also posed the question of whether there were other intermediaries.

Following his guiding principle approach of trying many things, Krebs plunged into his project. We are fortunate to have the careful documentation of his biographer Holmes, based on Krebs's lab notebooks, that details what he did on the day-to-day level, showing his energy and frequent shifts. I will describe some of the details, but not all, and suffice to say he truly did "try many things" searching for that first (there would be a second) elusive missing piece of the puzzle.

Krebs's first experiments explored the effect of adding the amino acids alanine and phenylalanine to liver tissue slice preparation. Next he added sugar into the preparation, as well as ammonium chloride, a source of ammonia. He found that sugar inhibited the formation of urea from alanine, but not from ammonium chloride. Metabolism is broken into two phases: anaerobic, meaning oxygen is not present, and aerobic, meaning oxygen is present. Krebs's result recalled to his mind an earlier result by Warburg, who had shown that sugar inhibits the anaerobic phase of metabolism of proteins. Thus the results were consistent with the idea that the first stage of an amino acid breaking down into an ammonia byproduct was anaerobic and could be blocked by sugar.

Krebs explored the effect of ammonium chloride on urea production under various chemical conditions and deduced that this reaction was aerobic in nature. Next, he tested four different tissues—liver, spleen, kidney, and diaphragm—and found significant urea production only in the liver tissue. He then returned to exploring the effect of sugar on urea production, but after a few more experiments dropped this line of inquiry. He and his assistant continued to run experiments, checking how different experimental conditions, such as pH and solution composition, affected urea production, trying the amino acid glycine, and exploring the degree to which the effect of ammonia on urea production attenuated over time.[7] We can think of this in part as refining his project focus. His guiding conception directed using the manometric tissue slice approach, but many details needed to be worked out, such as which types of tissue to use and appropriate experimental conditions. Working these details out defined the precise "seed" of his project. Thus identifying a viable seed for him was really a two-step process: first, settle on the synthesis of urea as the topic; then determine the details—kind of tissue and experimental conditions—for how best to go about studying this phenomenon.

Krebs and his assistant continued to test many substances and different conditions, in line with his guiding principle of "trying many things." They branched out to test whether the nucleotide thymine could directly produce urea (the pyrimidines contain nitrogen and it was thought might directly yield urea). Initial results were promising and a bevy of additional experiments were run; ultimately the effect did not seem robust, and Krebs abandoned this line of inquiry. Next Krebs had his assistant check the basic conditions of the setup, including tissue slice thickness, pH, and anaerobic versus aerobic conditions, checking how these various factors impacted urea production. This was important as a way to standardize conditions so that if a novel effect was present, it would be clear enough to detect.[8] Again, we can think of this as refining his seed to get to an appropriate experimental setup.

At this point, several months into the project, no dramatic effect had been discovered: Krebs had the seed, but had not discovered the critical third element. Krebs persisted, however; describing his general mind-set, he called himself an optimist, thinking that "if you persist and keep at it something might turn up."[9] This philosophy can be thought of as part of his guiding principle. Krebs was not hugely theoretical, indeed his knowledge of the biochemistry of urea synthesis was modest at this time. Thus his guiding principle guided him not to focus on a partic-ular theoretical mechanism that had been proposed, but to try many alternatives, and, when faced with failure, simply to try more.

Krebs now turned his attention to exploring the effect of different amino acids on urea synthesis.[10] The first set of amino acids he investi-gated included arginine, alanine, glycine, and phenylalanine. Of these, arginine gave a very high rate of urea production. This was not surpris-ing, because it was known that arginine directly produced urea in the presence of the enzyme arginase according to the reaction:

Arginine + Water → Urea + Ornithine

Ornithine is another amino acid. Next Krebs tested amino acids to-gether with various ammonia compounds.[11] Again many experiments were run with different compounds and different amino acids.[12]

At this juncture, Krebs made another turn: he tested ornithine itself. The results were striking and surprising: the rate of urea synthesis was extremely high in the solution containing both ornithine and ammonia. Ornithine is the output in the reaction above, not an input, making it surprising that it would play a large role in the production of urea.

At last Krebs had found a dramatic effect! We can think of ornithine as the critical third element added to the project, as the two-step model of the creative process specifies. In this case it didn't complete the project by itself, as one additional step was needed, but it was a crucial step of project development.

Looking over Krebs's pattern of work, it seems quite likely that he never would have made this discovery if not for his approach of "trying many things." Ornithine was fairly distant in the network context of chemical possibilities to try, in that it really hadn't been discussed much in the literature, so it took many experiments—and failures—before his attention was drawn to it. A scientist more wedded to an existing theoretical hypothesis or trying a more limited range of options might never have reached this point. Thus his guiding principle was critical to his discovery.

Why ornithine? Holmes put this question to Krebs. Ornithine and lysine are the two amino acids that have two amino groups, and thus Krebs might have wondered if they had a more direct pathway to urea than other amino acids that have just one such group. Krebs also knew the arginine reaction stated above and might have wondered if he could explore what happened to the ornithine produced in this reaction, a puzzle that had not yet been solved. But Krebs rejected these arguments from Holmes. He reiterated his guiding philosophy: "I took ornithine because really it was there [he had access to it]." "I tested, I think, all of the amino acids I could get.... I think it was really just a blind, or unprejudiced collection of facts."[13]

In the following months Krebs worked to understand the ornithine effect. He tested other substances with a similar chemical composition but found no effect comparable to that for ornithine. The evidence showed that the ornithine effect was real and that it was specific to ornithine—no other compound had the same effect.[14]

Ultimately, the experimental results for ornithine led Krebs to believe that ornithine acted as a catalyst. We might say that his belief that ornithine was a catalyst reflected a second guiding principle, the general view that catalytic action is important in chemical reactions. This would be a widely held view—as many guiding principles are. Further, an influential book on enzymes as catalysts had been published by J.B.S. Haldane in 1930, which Krebs had almost certainly read, and this may have helped implant the principle actively in his mind.[15]

Believing that ornithine had a catalytic action meant that even in very small quantities it would exert its effect. Krebs tested this and found it to be largely true.[16] This confirmed his belief in the catalytic action. Now he had to determine which reaction ornithine catalyzed. Krebs focused more and more on the arginine reaction given above, since this was known to involve ornithine as an end product. It was a puzzle because arginine is an input into the reaction and ornithine is an output, and it was not clear how ornithine could act as a catalyst.

The key to solving the puzzle was the realization that there is a cycle: Just as arginine gives rise to ornithine, in turn, ornithine gives rise to arginine:

$$\text{ornithine} + 2 \text{ ammonia molecules} + \text{carbon dioxide} \rightarrow \text{arginine}$$
$$+ 2 \text{ water molecules}$$

Krebs said that once he recognized this conceptual possibility, he immediately realized it fit with all his data and was the likely metabolic pathway.[17] Thus he added a further, final element to his project, the explanation in terms of chemical reactions.

Overall, Krebs's process fits the model quite well. His guiding conception was key in leading him to study the synthesis of urea. His guiding principle of "trying many things" was critical in making a surprising, important discovery on this project. And a second guiding principle of catalytic action helped him resolve the resulting puzzle and find the second critical "missing piece" to complete the project successfully. One difference is that he identified two additional elements—the first an experimental finding, the ornithine effect, and the second the explanation of the role of ornithine as the catalyst in a chemical cycle. Thus the general structure of the model holds, but with two main steps rather than one to move from seed to full project and outcome. This is in no way surprising, as the model is meant to describe the simplest possible creative process, and real-world creative processes will elaborate upon this structure.

CLIFFORD POSSUM

Recall Clifford Possum's guiding conception from Chapter 8: depict multiple Dreamings on a single canvas, centering on a geographic site. Possum executed a series of paintings in the 1970s following this guiding conception, each centered on a different site. His guiding conception was ambitious, and the paintings he produced were compelling and complex, taking the Papunya art movement to a new level.

Possum did not achieve success with his conception immediately. His first known work aligned with his conception is dated September 1973. It is not extant, but is described as including nine different Dreamings around Mt. Allan Station.[18] It was painted on a board, which may have been more challenging for Possum with the detail he wished to include. Even so it was described at the time as a "map" of the area that was, in the words of the commentator of the time, "probably accurate, although there was some difficulty in placing English names on it."[19] Around this time canvas was introduced to the artists to replace the boards they had been painting on, which would have made it easier to paint the kind of large-scale works rich in detail that Possum was after. Possum may have shared his idea with his brothers Billy Stockman and Tim Leura, for in the spring of 1974, possibly at a time when Possum was not at Papunya but rather at Narwietooma serving as a cattle hand, they executed a large painting *Life at Yuwa* that has a connection with Possum's conception. This painting is not extant, but based on annotations for it, it showed an aerial view of the area around Yuwa, a mountain near Napperby, and tracks of movement of an ancestral extended family that lived there. It did not show multiple Dreamings the way Possum would do, but its aerial perspective and inclusion of multiple tracks around a center can be seen as a precursor of Possum's map paintings.[20]

Possum's first "map of the country" painting is *Warlugulong*, painted in 1976. (See https://www.artgallery.nsw.gov.au/collection/works/321. 1981/ to view the painting online.) Possum did not actually choose the site of this painting. A BBC film crew arrived to film the making of a painting. The Papunya art advisors asked Possum to be the featured artist and he agreed, and they assigned him the Warlugulong mythologic fire as the painting's main subject, a topic he and Tim Leura had both painted several times in the preceding years. Tim Leura collaborated and the two brothers completed the painting in twenty hours.[21]

Although his directions may have been to paint the Warlugulong bush fire, Possum went far beyond this in the full composition as he pursued his guiding conception. In the myth of the Warlugulong fire, an old man, Blue-Tongue Lizard Man, started a fire in which his two sons perished, punishing them for killing and eating a sacred kangaroo. In the painting the bonfire is at the center and the footprints of the two sons are shown as they flee the fire to the south, which is toward the top of the painting as Possum oriented it. But this is just a starting point. Many additional Dreaming stories are shown, showing the tracks of the Dreaming characters and in some cases sites where important events are said to have occurred in the vicinity of Warlugulong. In fact the detailed notes on the canvas list twenty additional motifs, demonstrating the incredible detail that is packed into the painting.[22] Several of these additional Dreamings are linked to sites and Dreamings shown in Figure 4, which depicts Possum's context, including the Eagle Dreaming at Wakulpa, where the Eagle kills a Euro (related to the kangaroo), the Yarapiri Snake, whose tracks of his journey north are shown in the painting, and the great fight between the Rock Wallaby Men and the Possum Men at Yakuti near Mungapunju. The painting was described at the time by one of the Papunya art advisors as "the most complex [painting] ever created by any of the Papunya Tula artists." Thus Possum, following his guiding conception, was able to break into new artistic territory.

It is useful to compare Possum's creative process for *Warlugulong* with the model. Seeds for him would have been sites that he believed had a sufficient number of Dreamings centering around the site to be good choices to center a composition. Also, he would want the Dreamings not all to be concentrated in one direction but spread out over several directions around the central site in order to fit with his guiding principle of aesthetic balance. Warlugulong as a site fit these criteria, and thus it makes sense that he was willing to follow the suggestion of making this site the center. For Possum, if the central site was the seed, then the seed would grow into a full project by adding multiple Dreamings around it. Clearly this would involve adding not just a single third element but many more elements, as in fact he did for *Warlugulong*.

As noted in discussing Hans Krebs's process investigating the synthesis of urea, it is not surprising that real-world processes are more complex, as the model is meant to be the simplest possible representation. Nonetheless, Possum's process fits the model of using a guiding conception to identify a promising seed and then growing the seed, taking into account the greater number of elements he added in growing his seed into a full project.

While Possum's guiding conception was the source of the rich complexity of *Warlugulong*, his guiding principle of aesthetic balance also played a key role in his creative process and the final product. One might think Possum simply painted each Dreaming on the painting in its fixed position relative to the main Warlugulong site. In fact, however, he employed a shifting perspective, so that different Dreamings are oriented differently in relation to Warlugulong. This kind of shifting, rotating perspective is consistent with the way the Indigenous peoples of central Australia navigate. Directionally fluid, they can orient from any particular site in many different directions, leading to other sites, all infused with Dreaming signification.

Johnson offers a detailed discussion of how Possum used shifting perspective systematically as he executed the painting. Traditionally the Indigenous peoples living in central Australia executed sand diagrams on the ground, and could walk around them to view them from different orientations. Possum, in her opinion, did this while painting *Warlugulong* by rotating the canvas. He seems to have started with the "top" of the painting pointing south from the main site, but he rotated the painting once so that the Yarapiri Snake, traveling south to north, could be shown traveling horizontally (in the way the painting is conventionally viewed) on the top part of the canvas rather than vertically on a side. He then rotated it again so that now the top of the painting was north of *Warlugulong*.[23] Possum, Johnson writes,

> is drawing up the map [painting] in stages, taking his bearings from different sides of the canvas. The sites and journey lines relating to each narrative strand [each Dreaming story] are correctly positioned in space with respect to one another [so that for example, the Rock Wallaby and

Possum Men trails are correctly positioned with respect to one another]
and also to at least one other strand, so that two or more Dreamings tie in
with each new directional re-alignment.[24]

This use of shifting perspective granted Possum considerable flexibility in how the various Dreaming stories were laid out on the canvas.
In turn this enabled him to employ his guiding principle to determine
placements that in his view provided the greatest aesthetic balance. We
don't know all the details of his thought process, not in the same detail
as we have in the record of the sequence of experiments Hans Krebs
carried out. But we can see his guiding principle clearly in the end
result: the Dreamings are remarkably balanced around the center fire
site, with trails and key sites in all four quadrants. Indeed as described
in Chapter 12, Possum was so committed to the principle of balance
that he took the step of approaching two members of the Tjampitjinpa
section, asking them for permission to depict part of a mythological
trail of an Emu ancestral being over which they had custodianship, believing he needed to add this to his painting to give it a stronger sense of
aesthetic balance. In this case, his guiding principle helped him identify a key missing element that he was able to add to complete the
painting.

Overall, Possum's creative process, like Krebs's, fits the model quite
well. His guiding conception was ambitious, and it seems to have taken
him a few years before he pursued it with the complexity and richness it
required, working from a seed—centering on Warlugulong—that gave
him the potential to add multiple Dreamings. When Possum did this,
he moved artistically beyond the paintings previously done by him and
others at Papunya. As discussed above, his process of growing the seed
involved more steps than the model describes, but still fits the overall
pattern. Possum's guiding principle came to the fore as he worked on
the painting, employing shifting perspective, even asking permission to
include a Dreaming that was not his, in order to achieve the aesthetic
balance he sought.

Possum executed a series of four more "maps of the country" in the
next three years. All involve multiple Dreamings and all reflect the

principle of aesthetic balance.[25] Thus all flowed from the same core guiding conception and guiding principle, although each is also unique.

JACK DORSEY AND TWITTER

Jack Dorsey formed a guiding conception around the year 2000 that I have paraphrased as *A way to enable people to provide dispatches to (mainly) friends about their current status, in real time and mobile.* Around this same time Dorsey attempted to implement his conception using a primitive mobile email device called the RIM 850. The idea was to send status updates to his friend group. His idea failed to catch on because his friends didn't have the device, so the real-time aspect was lost.[26] However, the seed he had tried, a device for mobile real-time status messaging, was promising even though this project incarnation failed.

A few years later in 2005, after a stint at home and then moving back to San Francisco and finding limited employment success, Dorsey began working at Odeo, a San Francisco start-up focused on enabling users to create and share podcasts. Apple announced its own podcast venture through iTunes, and Odeo's future seemed bleak. The company had its employees engage in hackathons to try and find a new direction.

By 2006, early smartphones had been developed with text messaging capabilities, in particular SMS or Short Message Service.[27] Dorsey recognized the perfect fit with his guiding conception: "I fell in love with the technology," he is quoted as saying. "It was rough around the edges, cheap, and it was on every single device out there."[28]

I have not discussed Dorsey's guiding principle, but here is where it came to the fore. Dorsey is described as a "minimalist." "Constraint inspires creativity" is attributed to him as his creed in a *New Yorker* article about him by D. T. Max. His aesthetics are stark, according to Max, focused on "getting something down to its essence, the economy of words," extreme simplicity of design and function.[29] His guiding principle is this minimalist aesthetic applied to creative projects as well as in his daily life.

SMS fit with Dorsey's guiding principle. It was designed to send short texts and was "no frills" in being inexpensive and widely available. We can recognize here the critical "missing piece" that develops a promising guiding conception, but one for which an earlier seed attempt didn't work, into a successful project by modifying the earlier seed. In Dorsey's case this missing piece was a complementary technology that fit beautifully with his guiding conception. He had to be patient as it was several years after his earlier attempt with the RIM 850 before this key element came along with widespread adoption. This is a lesson: there is a role for patience in the creative process, and serendipity, in waiting for just the right missing piece to bring a guiding conception and seed to life. But there is also a role for a guiding principle to recognize the key missing piece when it turns up.

Dorsey suggested using SMS to send status updates, and his group decided to propose it to the company leaders. The SMS technology also led to a natural constraint on length, which also aligns with Dorsey's guiding principle: single messages are limited to 160 characters. The company decided to limit the size of any given post to fit this constraint, in Dorsey's words "to minimize the hassle" of sending and receiving messages—a view again aligned with his guiding principle.[30] Hence after reserving 20 characters for user identification, 140 characters were left for the message, and this became the allowed length. The name Twitter was thought of a bit later, Dorsey issued the first tweet in July 2006, and the platform grew from there.

COLLABORATIVE CREATIVITY AND MULTIPLE PATHS: RIDESHARE

It is possible that the two distinct steps of the creativity model may be contributed by different individuals, even different teams or organizations. One individual or team may form a guiding conception that leads to a seed project. But this seed may be difficult for them to develop, and it may require a fresh perspective and guiding principle from another person or team to identify how to move forward successfully to develop the seed. In the world of business innovation we often see this, a multistep development of an idea into a successful line of business. This topic fits also with Chapter 17 in which I discuss the creative development of fields. There can also be multiple paths to the same outcome, as discussed in Chapter 10.

An example illustrating both collaborative creativity and multiple paths is the development of rideshare. There were multiple individuals and organizations that had a role, and the innovation developed in steps.[31]

One starting point is Garrett Camp, cofounder of Uber. Camp was living in San Francisco and found himself frequently frustrated trying to get a cab. He started ordering multiple cabs and taking the first that showed up. This did not endear him to the cab companies and they blacklisted him, which made getting a cab even more challenging. He wanted to find a better way to get around the town. We can take this as his guiding conception: he wanted to address this issue to find a way to make city transit easier.

One day Camp had a realization: he could use his iPhone to bypass the central dispatcher and simply contact a cab or limo driver directly. Further, he could then also track the driver's car's movement on his phone to see when it would be arriving.[32] This was his initial seed idea for what—after further creative development—became Uber.

Travis Kalanick improved upon Camp's idea with an insight rooted in a guiding principle. At UCLA Kalanick was involved with the start-up Scour, which enabled people to share music over the Internet. When that company was outcompeted by Napster, he quickly launched a new venture named Red Swoosh with a cofounder. Red Swoosh enabled file sharing by drawing on files on personal computers; hence the files were never centralized but just used on an opportunistic basis. For each of these ventures the core idea exploits the notion of resource sharing.[33] We can deduce from this Kalanick's guiding principle: enabling idle resources, typically decentralized, to be shared and thus employed more productively.

Teaming up with Camp, Kalanick helped move the effort forward by leveraging his guiding principle with a key insight: "Rather than buying a fleet of vehicles, which Camp was envisioning, Kalanick told him that he didn't need to buy cars—just give the app to drivers and let them be free agents" servicing clients on their own time schedule.[34] This was an important step. However, Kalanick and Camp were still focusing on commercially licensed drivers offering rides in limousines and town cars, not ordinary people with ordinary cars.

The emergence of rideshare as we know it today involved two other companies, which prompted Uber to take this further step. Entrepreneur Sunil Paul "saw what Uber was doing" and "realized there was a much larger market opportunity in what he called 'peer-to-peer ride-sharing.'"[35] This was the idea of linking ordinary people who had a vehicle and time to drive with those needing a ride. He launched Sidecar, which became very popular in San Francisco initially, although it eventually went out of business.[36]

Meanwhile, Logan Green and John Zimmer, who had been running a carpooling venture called Zimride, also entered the field by launching Lyft. Green stated that the company had a hackathon to "figure out what does Zimride look like on mobile."[37] We can take this as a guiding conception, and we can think of the hackathon as a forum for generating seed project ideas based on it, which led to the idea for Lyft.

Rideshare is a case in which there were two different routes to the same project outcome. Uber and Lyft had different guiding conceptions, one coming out of an individual's frustration and desire for a more certain ride, which initially focused on providing high-end limo rides, the other based on the idea of extending carpooling to make it a more mobile, immediately available service.

In fact Uber's path to rideshare involved more steps. Initially Uber resisted the rideshare concept and in fact pressed San Francisco city officials to bar Sidecar and Lyft from operating. But they soon shifted focus from commercial drivers to ordinary people and embraced the rideshare model.[38] This shift had multiple causes, including the recognition of how successful the rideshare business model would be. Kalanick's guiding principle surely also had a role, as he would have recognized this as another example of sharing enabling utilization of idle resources.

Thus the story of modern ridesharing shows how different individuals and organizations can contribute to the development of an innovation. Guiding conceptions and principles are central for the development of these innovations but distributed among different individuals and organizations.

BUILDING BLOCKS OF CREATIVE PATHS

I believe the two-step creative process is central to the creative process of many individuals engaged in creative endeavors. However, real-world creative paths and processes are complex and involve many additional elements and steps. The model I have described can and must be extended in order to describe creativity more fully; the next few chapters address this important challenge and at least point the way toward how this can be done.

One way to describe longer creative paths is in terms of building block modules that link together. The core two-step process is one important module, and it is instructive to explore how it fits with other modules.

One common pattern of creativity we observe for longer creative paths is for an individual to pursue a series of projects under the guidance of a stable guiding conception. For example, a painter may paint a series of paintings, all under the guidance of the same basic guiding conception—Clifford Possum's series of "maps of the country" paintings are an example. Stability is a matter of degree, since every creative project, indeed every experience, can subtly alter one's guiding conception. Nonetheless, from the viewpoint of understanding and describing creative paths, it is useful to make a distinction between times of stability, when a person's guiding conception is relatively stable, and times of change, when their guiding conception changes.

Indeed the key way the model must be extended is to incorporate the changes that occur along creative paths. One important change is forming a new guiding conception, in many cases evolved from an earlier guiding conception; this is a focus in the examples in the next chapter. Another related kind of change is forming a new guiding principle. Context also changes, and this can be central to how creativity unfolds. Context is increased through experiences and exploration. In addition, even if the elements of a context remain fixed, new connections may form and others may weaken over time, and these changes can also affect the creative process.

There are of course many other important factors that arise along creative journeys. Not all of these are directly about creativity, but all can affect the creative path. Examples include changes in employment, transitions from school to work, moving, changes in health status and personal life, and important public events. All of these transitions can be associated with shifts in creative engagement. They can and do spark creative responses, such as the formation of a new or evolved guiding conception. Hans Krebs's journey, so carefully documented by Frederic Holmes, is an example. In addition to the more internal processes in his creative development, other factors were also significant. These included his medical training, securing the position in Warburg's lab, transitioning to his own laboratory with funding to purchase the equipment needed to pursue research using the manometric techniques he had been trained in, and later, as the Nazis rose to power in Germany, moving to England. Likewise Virginia Woolf's creative journey was a rich combination of social, cultural, and personal elements with her own creative responses and engagement. Context must be described in sufficient detail and range in order to capture these different factors and their roles in creative journeys—another reason why modeling context is so important for modeling creativity.

Ultimately creative journeys involve many different processes, including the core model described in this book, changes in context and guiding conceptions and principles, and broader life experiences and transitions.

CHAPTER 15

CREATIVE JOURNEYS

Creative paths are often long and winding. Most individuals do not know when they begin a creative endeavor where it will lead. It is through following their own particular creative journey, a journey that often extends for years, that they are able to develop their creativity and make their own unique creative contributions. Analyzing these journeys, what we might call the biography of creativity, is critical to understanding how creativity comes about.

There are many shifts and developments that take place along a creative path. There are crucial events, decisions, emotions, ideas, insights and illuminations, conceptual shifts and development, collaborations, projects and outcomes, and reflections upon the process that may in turn trigger new conceptual guidance structures leading in new directions. Context can also change over time, and its changes in turn link to new ideas and approaches and new guidance structures.

A significant long-term objective is to develop a modeling framework in which we can analyze these issues and develop more satisfactory models of the creative process in its full, rich extent. This will enable us to better understand creativity and develop implications—for example, how context and changes in context relate to creative outcomes—and develop approaches for supporting individuals along their creative journeys.

In this book I have outlined a core model that is important for how individuals navigate creatively in large-scale contexts. Extending from this core to model richer processes and longer creative journeys requires going beyond the core in various ways, and most of this lies beyond this book. But, without yet having a full model, it is useful to present examples and learn from these something about the nature of longer creative journeys. A particular focus is how guidance processes evolve and shift along longer creative paths.

In this chapter I describe the creative journeys of Virginia Woolf and Lynn Conway as two examples that illustrate the richness of creative paths. Although these examples scarcely scratch the surface in terms of depicting the diversity of real-world creative journeys, they do call attention to at least some of the creative processes that are integral to longer creative journeys.

In the following companion chapter I focus on how the model can be extended to describe richer contexts and richer creative processess, which will bring it closer to being able to describe real-world creativity and longer creative journeys.

EVOLUTION OF GUIDANCE

Of the different ways the model can be developed further to capture additional facets of real-world creativity, one of the most important is modeling guiding conceptions and principles that are richer and change over time. I discuss some of the modeling issues in the next chapter. Here I describe some typical patterns of change of these guiding structures that occur over the course of creative journeys.

Guiding conceptions in particular typically change over the course of creative journeys, especially for individuals who pursue creativity over relatively longer periods of time. Indeed this is often a key factor in enabling individuals to find their way to outstanding creative outcomes that they did not imagine when they began their journey. Virginia Woolf is an excellent example: exploring her guiding conception of reflections led to a creative breakthrough, which enabled her to recast her guiding conception into a form that she developed successfully in her great modernist novels.

Intuitively, it makes sense that guiding conceptions change. As discussed in Chapter 10, the pool of project seeds covered by a given guiding conception is limited and will ultimately be exhausted; absent a major influx of new possibilities, it will make sense to shift to a new guiding conception. Further, individuals tend naturally to develop new visions for what they want to create over time, whether due to new interactions and stimulating events, reflection on what they have done and how their field is changing, or simply the desire for change.

In most cases, in my experience, an individual's guiding conception isn't just dropped and replaced by a completely different conception. Rather, it evolves: a new conception is formed that is linked to the preceding one and builds on it. It is certainly possible for an individual to change their focus more drastically and shift to an entirely different guiding conception, but it is not as common because individuals tend to be wedded to their guiding conceptions and often have developed expertise around them, as for example Hans Krebs had developed expertise in the application of the manometric tissue slice methodology. Evolution may be triggered by a series of project failures pursuing an initial conception that causes someone to recast their conception. Or as happened for Virginia Woolf, a creative breakthrough may enable a person to develop a new, improved conception. Alternatively, evolution of a guiding conception may be triggered by new experiences or circumstances that raise new issues and possibilities; this was the case for Lynn Conway. These different pathways through which change is triggered can be tracked; gathering more data about this would help us better understand the logic and patterns of creative journeys.

Guiding principles can also change over the course of a creative journey, although this is less common. One pattern is for a guiding principle to evolve by being extended or refined. A designer, for example, might extend and refine a key design principle as they gain experience. Albert Einstein extended his principle of relativity to the case of a gravitational field, and this was, on his own account, one of the greatest creative breakthroughs of his life. But in other cases it is surprising how fixed a guiding principle can be. Lynn Conway's guiding principles seem to have remained constant in the midst of many other changes.[1] Field dynamics can also lead to changes in guiding principles. When a new principle is introduced in a person's field, they may embrace it and use it in their own creative work. For example in economics when a new concept of equilibrium has been introduced, such as rational expectations equilibrium, individuals active in branches of inquiry that can use or are impacted by the new equilibrium concept, especially those early on their creative paths, tend to adopt the new concept and incorporate it into their creative work.

VIRGINIA WOOLF'S CREATIVE BREAKTHROUGH

In Chapter 8 I described Virginia Woolf's statement in "The Mark on the Wall" of a guiding conception for a new literature of reflections, paired with the guiding principle of "leaving the description of reality more and more out" of stories. As quoted there, brilliant and exciting as this was, it was also frustrating to her because it was so abstract—"these generalisations are very worthless," she wrote at the time.

Regardless of her immediate feeling of frustration, her conceptualization unleashed a period of creative ferment for Woolf as she explored how to realize it. She wrote a series of short stories trying out different approaches; she also experimented stylistically in her diary. The creative breakthrough came two and a half years later in December 1919–January 1920, writing the story "An Unwritten Novel." This breakthrough enabled her to recast her guiding conception in a way that provided constructive guidance.

Woolf wrote a series of five stories after "The Mark on the Wall" that can be seen as explorations of her guiding conception. The stories become freer, more playful, and leave more of reality "out" as she progresses, until finally she had a creative breakthrough realization.

"Kew Gardens," the first of the stories, is the most structured, thus more closely aligned with traditional narrative.[2] However, it also has elements that create some distance from this tradition. The story is set by a flower bed in Kew Gardens on a Sunday afternoon. By setting the story in just one spot at one time, Virginia voids the standard narrative structure that involves actions and movements from one place and time to the next; this makes it easier to leave connective description out of the story. Further, the descriptions that are given are highly subjective, focused on the flowers and immediate surroundings.

"Kew Gardens" begins with a description of the flowering plants, with colors playing a large part—red, blue, yellow, and gold; a drop of water is described, as the flowers' shadows sway over it altering its coloring. As a further device to emphasize subjectivity and the fixed location, a snail has a prominent role: it moves very slowly, spending much of the story contemplating how to navigate a fallen leaf, as colors reflect off of it. Against this setting the story features a series of couples who stroll by. They are drawn from different phases of the life span and different social classes. As each couple passes by we hear snippets of their conversation and catch glimpses of their thoughts—reflections of their lives. For example, a middle-aged married couple caught up in memories of earlier visits to the gardens stroll by, and a young couple excited for their blossoming relationship and life ahead, about to enjoy their first tea at Kew Gardens. Thus reflections are featured, but in a fairly regimented way—note the careful setup of a series of disconnected couples—and without much depth of penetration into the lives of the people strolling by. The guiding conception in "The Mark on the Wall" lies behind the story but is realized only in a limited way.

"The Evening Party" is the second story in the series.[3] From the start the story challenges our conventional sense of reality and perspective, as we see the earth "rising in a mound against the sky" and "clouds look down upon Atlantic waves." This challenges the Victorian world with its traditions and fixed perspective and thus fits with Woolf's guiding principle. Shortly the protagonists enter a house where there is a party, and the narrator gazes into a looking glass illuminated by candles and finds that his face has "dissolved," reflection breaking down objectivity. In some ways this links Woolf's guiding conception with her guiding principle, opening the door to this way of developing the pair. At this point the story shifts to a sequence of conversation snippets, with little surrounding description and little actual plot. The conversations certainly show us reflections in the form of a stream of opinions; however, the overall effect is somewhat disjointed. We hear many literary figures discussed, including Shakespeare; childhood memories are recounted, and the adult conventional world is held up for its narrowness. At the end of the story the narrator and his partner head outside onto the moor, away from the party and its stuffy, conventional adult world, seeking liberation from the stifling objectivity. Overall, this story is especially strong in the way it showcases Woolf's desire to oppose objectivity and the Victorian worldview.

"Solid Objects," the third story in the sequence, is the story of a young man with a promising career whose life shifts when, while sitting on the beach with an acquaintance, he discovers an "almost opaque" green piece of glass that has been smoothed by the sea.[4] Just before this occurs, as he is sticking his hand deep into the sand, "his eyes lost their intensity, or rather the background of thought and experience which gives an inscrutable depth to the eyes of grown people ... leaving only the clear transparent surface, expressing nothing but wonder, which the eyes of young children display." Thus there is a break from the adult world of reflections showing depth of experience and self, back to the innocence of childhood; however, we see Woolf still struggling with how to convey this—in particular, she conveys this directly in the narrative, rather than more indirectly (befitting reflections).

The young man becomes obsessed with collecting found objects— pieces of broken china, iron, and so on—and the story juxtaposes this childlike world of wonder and discovery against the conventional adult world that cannot understand his behavior and ultimately rejects him. The juxtaposition is sharply drawn, as in "The Mark on the Wall," in this case through the central character and the large chasm that opens up between him and the adult world. The green piece of glass and other found objects also call to mind the conception of reflections in "The Mark on the Wall," for they are ideal vessels for reflections of feelings and memories, like Rorschach inkblots.

In the fourth story in the series, "Sympathy," the narrator reads in the newspaper of the death of Humphrey Hammond, husband of her friend

Celia. This sparks a chain of thoughts—of Humphrey's last visit, how he looks now lying dead, and then of Celia, imagining her as a widow, imagining taking a walk in the hills with her.[5] The narrator realizes that although she can see the outward signs of widowhood, she will never fully understand the inner meaning: "The outward sign I see and shall see for ever; but at the meaning of it I shall only guess." The drapings of widowhood are a device Woolf hits upon here to highlight the gaps between external reality, reflections, and the inner self.

At this point the story shifts. The narrator returns to her present situation and finds that the presence of death "has changed everything!—as, in an eclipse of the sun, the colours go out, and the trees look thin as paper and livid while the shadow passes." She compares the changed experience to being on an express train rapidly passing by images, including a man working in a field and lovers lying in the grass, then imagines her friends also departing, "stepping off the rim of the world." Her stream of thought then returns to young Humphrey and his sudden death. The narrative in this second part of the story flows freely, moving swiftly—symbolized by the express train—in this altered reality. Thus there is a break from conventional reality both in the content but also in the fast-moving style that leaves details of description aside. This is a key creative step, as we shall see next. At the very end of the story the narrator discovers that Humphrey is in fact not dead. This reversal serves to highlight that the entire story is a fictional tale, a loosely constructed train of thought sparked by a phantom death. Though Woolf herself pointed to the next story as her breakthrough, the second part of this story foreshadows that breakthrough.

It was in writing the fifth story, "An Unwritten Novel," completed in January 1920, that Virginia made her creative breakthrough.[6] A narrator sitting on a train is drawn by the unhappy expression of a woman sitting opposite. The narrator comments: "Life's what you see in people's eyes"—note the link both with "The Mark on the Wall" and "Solid Objects," the eyes as the windows into the self and its experiences. As the train travels on, the other travelers in the car depart and the woman and the narrator converse, the woman mentioning her sister-in-law with a "bitterness" of tone. The narrator feels a bond of some kind with the woman, symbolized by the way the woman rubs a spot on her window in what the narrator interprets as possibly a gesture of guilt, and the narrator responds in kind. The woman falls silent, while the narrator, drawn to imagine her life, invents a name for her, Minnie Marsh, and for her sister-in-law, Hilda, and spins a tale of Minnie's life as she imagines it.

From this point the narrative flows freely, gliding along from one imagined scene to the next. Hilda greets Minnie as she arrives at her house, and thinks, "Poor Minnie, more of a grasshopper than ever—old cloak she had last year. Well, well, with two children these days one can't do more." Minnie is taken upstairs, then Hilda descends the stairs and Minnie is left alone. She takes out "a meagre nightgown" and "furred felt slippers" and contemplates her fate: "And then the sniff, the sigh, the sitting by the window. Three o'clock on a December afternoon; the rain drizzling." We see Minnie first from Hilda's perspective, then are given a sense of her own mood, which in turn is reflected in the rainy December afternoon. Thus in the span of a few sentences there are three different perspectives or "reflections" of Minnie.

The narrator invents a crime for Minnie to fit the way she seemed to be attempting to rub out guilt by rubbing the window on the train: "I have my choice of crimes," she comments, then is off again with new scenes imagining Minnie's life. A second passenger enters the car, and the narrator incorporates him into the story as a friend of the family, James Moggridge. After pausing to describe him, the narrative moves on to him attending a family dinner, and the narrator's gaze rests momentarily on his eyes—"They see something: black, white, dismal"—Minnie: "Marsh's sister—not a bit like Marsh; wretched, elderly female... [ellipses in original] You should feed your hens."[7] This passage highlights one of the key innovations, which is that we are shown characters thinking about other characters—reflections within the story itself.

At places, the narrator steps back, pausing to reflect upon the freedom she is taking in inventing a fictitious life for Minnie, while at the same time considering her options. Eyes and the human face figure as central, again hearkening back to the original guiding conception in

"The Mark on the Wall." In one passage the narrator reflects: "Have I read you right? But the human face ... holds more, withholds more. Now, eyes open, she looks out; and in the human eye ... there's a break—a division—so that when you've grasped the stem the butterfly's off.... The eyes of others our prisons; their thoughts our cages."[8]

Because the story is presented as a fictional tale invented on the fly, the narrator feels little pressure to provide much background, fitting Woolf's guiding principle of leaving descriptions of "objective reality" out. This seems to be key in creating the loose-knit structure, showing a central character and her life depicted in a series of vignettes. The sense of playfulness and quickness is matched by the setting, a train ride: moving, occasionally stopping, with passengers exiting and new ones entering, random figures not personally known to the narrator. Although Woolf would go on to employ this form to write about far more personal topics, including her brother Thoby and her mother and father, its first incarnation here may have been sparked or at least made more natural by the informality of the setting, including the anonymity of the passengers she imagines.

"An Unwritten Novel" triggered Woolf to recast her guiding conception and prescribe an additional guiding principle for her writing. Shortly after writing the story, on January 26, 1920, the day after her thirty-eighth birthday, Virginia wrote an entry in her diary describing her new conception. "This afternoon," she wrote, "[I] arrived at some idea of a new form for a new novel." She described her idea, referring to "The Mark on the Wall," "Kew Gardens," and "An Unwritten Novel":

> Suppose one thing should open out of another— as in An Unwritten Novel— only not for 10 pages but 200 or so— doesn't that give the looseness & lightness I want: doesnt that get closer & yet keep form & speed, & enclose everything, everything? My doubt is how far it will ⟨include⟩ enclose the human heart— Am I sufficiently mistress of my dialogue to net it there? For I figure that the approach will be entirely different this time: no scaffolding; scarcely a brick to be seen; all crepuscular, but the heart, the passion, humour, everything as bright as fire in the mist. Then I'll find room for so much— a gaiety— an inconsequence— a light spirited

stepping at my sweet will. Whether I'm sufficiently mistress of things—
thats the doubt; but conceive mark on the wall, K. G. ["Kew Gardens"] &
unwritten novel taking hands & dancing in unity.[9]

Just as with the earlier passage in "The Mark on the Wall," this passage mixes together a guiding conception and guiding principles. Also,
being a diary entry meant mainly for Woolf herself, it is elliptical, and
we must flush it out to extract all of its guidance.

Understandably, Woolf focuses on the new elements, not the old.
In this regard the final sentence is important: "conceive mark on the
wall, K.G. & unwritten novel taking hands & dancing in unity." Her new
conception borrows from all three stories. Reflections are not directly
mentioned, but this is a key element from "The Mark on the Wall" and
implicitly the approach she will take. However, whereas the conception
of reflections in that story was abstract, she has discovered a new way to
represent reflections, embedded *inside* the story, especially reflections
of the central character seen through other characters' thoughts.

From "Kew Gardens" what is borrowed is the structure of a story as a
series of vignettes. "Suppose one thing should open out of another," the
phrase that opens the diary entry, conceives of a novel constructed this
way, as a series of scenes. But here again Woolf's approach has evolved.
In "Kew Gardens" each vignette is about a different set of characters,
and they are completely separate, so that each stands alone and is in
no way connected with the others. This limits the cohesion and richness of depicting human life, which we know, reaching all the way back
to Woolf's comment in Italy about wanting to depict a human life ("the
mind[']s passage through the world") as a "whole made of shivering fragments," is one of her aims. In "Kew Gardens" the fixed location links the
different scenes together, but the overall effect is somewhat stilted and
cumbersome. In contrast, Woolf's conception now is to follow a character through a series of scenes. Her aim is to manifest a character this
way, just as she does with Minnie in "An Unwritten Novel." I believe
this desire to show a full human life is part of what she means when
she writes of her desire to "enclose the human heart." This approach
links back to Woolf's guiding conception in "The Mark on the Wall"

with its notion of an "almost infinite number" of reflections. Thus to her conception of reflections in "The Mark on the Wall" and her initial expression of it in "Kew Gardens" she now adds the innovation of following a single character as is done in "An Unwritten Novel."

This brings us to the critical new element that Woolf was greatly excited about that she had discovered writing "An Unwritten Novel": a style that has a "looseness & lightness" of tone, "speed," "humour," and a sense of freedom that is clearly evident in that short story, "a gaiety—an inconsequence—a light spirited stepping at my sweet will." I take this statement of a literary style as a guiding principle: it provides a standard for what the writing should attain. We can imagine her using it as a check: if a passage did not seem to have this lightness of tone, she would have gone back and reworked it.

Woolf's first guiding principle of leaving descriptions of reality out, acting against the rigid, masculine Victorian world, continues to be central for her. "No scaffolding; scarcely a brick to be seen" is exactly this principle, here restated more lyrically but also with a more certain, confident tone because now she sees more clearly how to adhere to it. She follows this statement of what will be left out with a positive statement: it will be "all crepuscular, but the heart, the passion, humour, everything as bright as fire in the mist." This is very much a guiding conception, what she will aim for. With no description all will be twilight, but against this misty backdrop she will show human life and the inner world "as bright as fire" via reflections. We can imagine this conception would help her generate ideas for what needs to be included in a narrative and particular scenes to attain this result of showing a human life "bright as fire in the mist." However, this also has some of the elements of a guiding principle, since again it provides a standard for what the mood and result should be like. Not surprisingly, in the real world of creativity it is not always as easy to separate guiding conceptions from guiding principles, although I believe making a clear theoretical distinction is valuable.

Woolf has thus enriched her original guiding conception, adding several elements: a series of scenes, the idea of creating reflections inside stories via characters' thoughts about other characters, and the conception of depicting human life with all its richness of feeling and significance set brilliantly against a crepuscular backdrop. Together with this she has a pair of guiding principles: her original principle of leaving description of reality out, and the style of writing, one of lightness and speed, gaiety and freedom. All the different elements fit together, "dancing in unity."

Woolf is excited to have hit upon this new conception with its different elements and clearly imagines great potential for it. Not that she does not have her doubts. She hopes to "enclose" the human heart, which for her certainly includes the inner self and its rich subjective life, but worries whether she has the necessary skill. In particular, since there will be little descriptive connective tissue, she will need to rely on dialogue to convey this rich inner life: "Am I sufficiently mistress of my dialogue to net it there?" But overall there is optimism.

In a letter to Ethel Smyth ten years later, Virginia commented on this period of her literary development. "I shall never forget the day I wrote the *Mark on the Wall*—all in a flash, as if flying, after being kept stone-breaking [writing *Night and Day*] for months. The *Unwritten Novel* was the great discovery however. That—again in one second—showed me how I could embody all my deposit of experience in a shape that fitted it."[10]

Although Woolf pointed to these stories as critical, we should also not overlook the important stylistic innovations in her diary and its impact on her creative writing. Writing for herself, composing on the fly, it was relatively easy and natural to experiment. The stylistic breakthrough to a looser, freer style she achieved in "An Unwritten Novel" is foreshadowed in the diary. Writing about her diary in an entry in it dated April 20, 1919, about eight months before "An Unwritten Novel," she writes that her diary "loosens the ligaments." She speculates about what it might become or what might become of it:

> I might in the course of time learn what it is that one can make of this loose, drifting material of life; finding another use for it than the use I put it to, so much more consciously & scrupulously, in fiction. What sort of diary should I like mine to be? Something loose knit, & yet not slovenly,

so elastic that it will embrace any thing, solemn, slight, or beautiful that comes into my mind.[11]

The resonance with her January 1920 diary entry is unmistakable.

Woolf's creative development followed a more complex pattern than the core two-step model. She developed a guiding conception and explored it in a series of stories, very much in line with the basic model. But rather than leading directly to creative outcomes that she viewed as successful, this experimentation led instead to a discovery that enabled her to evolve her conception, adding to it. Whereas the two-step model emphasizes a "top-down" flow from a guiding conception to the generating of project seed ideas, in her process we see also a "bottom-up" flow in which a creative discovery in turn triggers a modification of her higher-level guiding conception. The diary connection also represents this kind of flow: casual writing helping spark a higher-level realization. It makes sense that both flows occur and are important for creativity. Modeling this reverse flow requires being able to describe when and in what way the reverse flow occurs. Doing this requires adding more elements to the model and describing the conceptual impacts of creative outcomes on guidance structures.

Three months after writing her diary entry in January 1920, Woolf began work on *Jacob's Room*, the first in her series of brilliant modernist novels. *Jacob's Room* follows Jacob, who is based on her brother Thoby, from young childhood into adulthood. Each chapter is a difference scene and time in Jacob's life, and the chapters are loosely linked just as Woolf envisioned in her diary entry. Jacob is at the center but speaks only rarely—a strong, silent presence. We see him primarily in terms of how the other characters see him, again just the way she has envisioned: reflections building up a character study. The tone is light, ironic, with a sense of whimsy at times, a sense of freedom in the narration, very much like "An Unwritten Novel" and fitting her conception in her diary entry.

After *Jacob's Room* Woolf went on to write the stories that coalesced into *Mrs. Dalloway*, and then her masterpiece *To the Lighthouse*. *To the Lighthouse* centers on reflections; in particular, the mother Mrs. Ramsay is the central figure, and much of the book details other characters' thoughts and views of her, and hers of them. The book memorializes Virginia's memory of her mother and father, artfully, through imagining Mrs. Ramsay's own thoughts and feelings and, simultaneously, others' thoughts and feelings about her.[12]

Interestingly *To the Lighthouse* also goes beyond reflections to build an even richer character study of Mrs. Ramsay. She has "a wedge-shaped core of darkness, something invisible to others."[13] Thus her character is a composite of reflections and the exact opposite, a part that is thick (wedge-shaped) and thus not surface-based like reflections are, dark not light, and invisible to others, escaping their gaze. Although a step further, the original guiding conception of reflections set up this creative step, which thus can be seen as also emanating from that conception. This additional creative step also fits the thesis of this book, even while extending beyond the core two-step model. It is based on two higher-level conceptual elements paired in opposition—reflections and the precise opposite of reflections—realizing this pairing in the fictional work.[14] Thus it shows yet another path by which higher-level conceptual thinking can spark creativity.

VLSI BREAKTHROUGH: LYNN CONWAY

Lynn Conway also went through an extended path of creative development leading up to her important contributions to the development of VLSI design methodology. As described in Chapter 12, Conway formed a set of linked guiding principles dating back to her years working at IBM. One focused on the importance of simple, standardized notation and communication protocols. A second emphasized the importance of ease of communication and interconnection across design levels. A third meta-level principle was that the design process should itself be designed.

In 1976 Conway joined the joint Caltech-PARC project team that had been formed to develop a "design philosophy" for designing integrated circuits more efficiently and better.[15] A key to the team's approach was set forth in an article Ivan Sutherland and Carver Mead published in *Scientific American*. Sutherland and Mead called for a shift away from the traditional focus on processor speed and efficient logic execution to a focus on minimizing communication distances and carefully designing spatial layouts or topology, arguing these factors would come to the fore for large-scale circuits.[16]

Initially Conway focused on learning about chip design and programming and building protoypes. As she gained familiarity with the technology, she realized that rather than getting ever more complicated, it would be fruitful to focus on simplifying design protocols:

> Instead of visualizing an ever more complex future into which all current and evolving developments were projected, why not begin by simplifying, simplifying, simplifying? ...
>
> ... My key idea was to sidestep tons of accumulated vestigial practices in system architecture, logic design, circuit design and circuit layout, and replace them with a coherent but minimalist set of methods sufficient to do any digital design.[17]

Conway's guiding principle of simplicity in communication protocols is at the heart of the insight. Conway has written that she believed that if the rules were simple enough, many programmers could learn them and embrace the emerging new technology of systems-level circuit design—a belief that turned out to be prescient and fully justified. Conway's guiding principle of focusing on the design process itself would seem also to lie behind this insight, for it is very much about the "design of the design proces."

Conway's insight triggered a shift in the guiding conception for the project:

> With this theory in mind, I convinced Mead we should set a far more ambitious goal for the work. We should move to create a simplified methodology for designing whole systems in silicon, not just circuits—and aim it specifically at computer architects and system designers.[18]

The initial guiding conception, focused on circuit design, layout, and topology, was replaced by a different although related conception, focused on innovating around the design methodology itself, simplifying as much as possible, and shifting to a higher-level focus on whole systems. Thus in part the guiding conception shifted to a higher level of abstraction, which is an interesting pattern of development, evolving to what Conway herself describes as a more ambitious conception.

Over the next year the team pursued this revised guiding conception. Conway recalled: "We sketched cell topologies as stick diagrams, using blue, red and green pencils to indicate cell wiring." The link to Conway's guiding principle emphasizing simple notation is evident in the color scheme and simplified diagram notation. Further, the approach was meant to facilitate design bridging levels, from individual cells to whole systems, and thus was aligned with her second guiding principle.[19]

While this step was important, it left still to be determined the issue of spacing or tolerance levels in the actual physical design layouts. In the semiconductor industry at that time there were complex layout design rules that were specific to each type of circuit and fabrication process, reflecting specific tolerances. And the rules were lengthy: Conway mentions forty-page articles specifying design layout guidelines for specific processes. Thus the state of the art was exactly opposite to her guiding principles of standardized rules and simple notations, and this opposition would have been a red flag for her. We can think of these complexities as additional aspects that needed to be worked out and hopefully simplified and integrated into the emerging design methodology, akin to step 2 of the two-step model presented in Chapter 14. Guiding principles come to the fore in this situation, helping to identify the key elements needed to make a project come together successfully.

In this case the insight came from an earlier contribution by Mead. He had developed a "covering" set of simplified rules for his students. His experience and knowledge enabled him to do this effectively, but the rules were still tied to specific circuits and particular fabrication processes, which were constantly changing as the technology evolved.[20]

Conway was not satisfied. She writes that she asked herself the question, "What is the simplest possible set of layout design rules?"[21] It is clear from Conway's account that her guiding principles of simplicity of notation and ease of communication pushed her ever further in search of ways to simplify the design methodology, in much the way Steve Jobs's guiding principle of simplicity pushed him and his team to continue iterating on designs.

Ultimately, Conway found an answer to her question, based on computing the maximum among all tolerance constraints, this giving the minimal feasible tolerance for a given set of constraints.

> The resulting, minimalist covering rules were crude and non-optimal, but they fit onto a single page—that in itself, a breakthrough. I also noticed something else: The minimalist-rules generated layouts having a timeless quality. They remained unchanged, even as the process scaled down.
>
> Suddenly it beamed down to me: MOS design rules should not be framed as sets of lengths but as sets of ratios of lengths. Such dimensionless rules could then be scaled to any process as multiples of a basic length unit in microns, a unit I called **Lambda** (λ).[22]

The resulting designs would last even as the technology kept improving, with absolute scales dropping but ratios remaining more constant, making the whole design process more scalable and efficient.[23] Again Conway's approach was on target: By the end of 1977 the VLSI revolution was underway, and Conway and Mead had written the first three chapters of their highly influential text *Introduction to VLSI Systems*.[24]

It is noteworthy that Conway employed her guiding principles in a highly creative manner. Her use of the phrase "it beamed down to me" is classic language individuals use to describe a creative breakthrough, and her guiding principles were surely an essential backdrop to making this creative insight about simplification of design rules, for she kept pushing to simplify further.

Overall, the story of Conway's role in the VLSI design revolution fits the two-step creativity model, although with more steps. An initial guiding conception that the team developed evolved, at least in part driven by her insight. Then she innovated further to develop even simpler scalable, minimalist covering rules. Her guiding principles were central throughout this process based on her own account and the evidence of how key ideas align with them.

The stories of Woolf and Conway illustrate the richness and diversity of creative paths. In fitting in broad terms with the creative model I have described, they show the promise of this model and the guidance approach to creativity. Their greater complexity also shows that much more work remains to be done to describe real-world, inherently more complex creative processes.

CHAPTER 16

MODELING RICHER
CREATIVE PROCESSES

The model in this book captures important features of the creative process and provides an approach for modeling creativity in large-scale contexts. To describe richer, more complex real-world creative processes such as those described in the last chapter, however, it will need to be developed further.

In this chapter I describe five ways in which the model can be extended and developed further. First I discuss modeling more complex contexts, in particular contexts with more than two layers and nodes representing sets of elements. Next I discuss modeling richer guiding conceptions, key to so much creativity as shown by examples such as Virginia Woolf. After this I discuss modeling larger seeds and projects. The model with simple two-element seeds and three-element project designs is clearly just a starting point. I have done some computer modeling extending seed and project size and discuss that here, outlining potential approaches for addressing this extension. The end of the chapter links to the examples of the last chapter and discusses richer, multistep processes: first the project revision process, and then longer, more complex developmental processes, including evolving guiding conceptions.

I discuss modeling approaches for each of these steps but do not present a full-scale model development. That will require more detail than can be presented here—in my judgment it is better to keep this book focused on the main point, which is that in large-scale contexts, guidance is essential for creativity. Each step outlined here is important in its own right, but even more, collectively they hold the promise of delivering a model rich enough to describe complex and realistic creative processes.

To capture the rich complexity of real creativity in a model is, ultimately, an aspiration: we must strive to approach this level of description as best we can. Holding this aspiration in mind, it is better to start simple, which I have tried to do, then add complexity. The discussion in this chapter is meant to point the way forward, with the hope that this will spur additional work to help us build ever-better-structured, more realistic, more informative models of creativity.

CONTEXTS WITH MORE LEVELS AND MORE COMPLEX STRUCTURE

Contexts of creativity in the real world are more complex than the analytic model and simulated contexts I have presented and analyzed in this book. It is useful to discuss how the model can be extended to model more complex contexts, while still preserving its essential features.

A main simplification I have employed has been a focus on contexts with just two levels, top and bottom. This is the shortest possible hierarchy and has been very useful for model development and exposition. However, actual creativity contexts have more than two levels. Both the Hans Krebs and Clifford Possum contexts presented in Part I in Figures 4 and 5 illustrate this: each of these diagrams, itself a great simplification of the actual context, has seven levels. Standard descriptions of conceptual organization also include more than two levels. Psychologists who study human conceptual organization generally argue that for most categories there is a *basic* concept level that is most widely understood, has many feature associations, and is widely used in discourse.[1] In *The Big Book of Concepts* Gregory Murphy focuses on three levels: *superordinate*, which are general concepts; *basic*; and *subordinate*, more specific.[2] Three levels is a natural extension of the model and would enable connection with some of the psychological literature. However, it is clear there are more than three levels for many knowledge contexts. For example, Murphy discusses dogs, and an example of the three-level hierarchy for his discussion is *animal-dog-poodle*. However Figure 1 demonstrates that there are more than these three levels: there are three types of poodles, so that the hierarchy extends down another level, and there are seven levels up from "dog" in the taxonomy of living creatures, the domesticated dog being a subspecies.[3]

Extending the model of context to more levels is feasible and in some ways reasonably direct. There are two main issues: extending the context model itself, and extending the definitions and modeling of the creativity elements, especially guiding conceptions, seeds, and projects. Formally, constructing a context with more than two levels means adding middle levels, elements that have both parents and children. Once this is done, levels may not be so clear-cut as in simple top-bottom contexts. Thus, an element may be at level 2 on one path down from a top-level element, but at level 3 or 4 on a different path. If one peruses the Krebs and Possum contexts, one sees many examples of this. This pattern is common in lattices and arises because elements can have multiple parents. However, the model does not depend on any given element being assigned one specific level, and so this issue does not pose a major challenge.

The creativity model components can all be defined for contexts with more levels. Guiding conceptions and principles, since they possess a degree of generality and breadth, will be formed out of elements in the upper to middle levels of these contexts. Guiding conceptions especially will not generally be formed out of top elements, as these are too broad for effective guidance, but rather elements slightly lower in the hierarchy. Hans Krebs's guiding conception was formed out of elements at level four in his context as depicted in Figure 12, thus in the middle of the context in terms of abstraction. Likewise, as shown in Figure 13,

Clifford Possum's guiding conception was also formed out of elements in the middle of his context or at least not elements at the very top or bottom. Guiding principles are if anything more general and thus would be formed out of elements located at higher levels—although recall I have not attempted to place guiding principles and their constituent elements at specific context locations.[4]

Projects will be formed out of elements in lower levels. Seeds and core project designs, my focus in this book, will typically not involve bottom elements but rather elements somewhat higher, with project elements being added and often becoming more specific as the project is developed. Indeed, the extended vertical range enables a clearer demarcation between seed ideas and project design elements, both slightly higher in the context, and the elements used in the projects themselves, many of which are located at or near the bottom of the context. For example, as illustrated in the discussion of Lynn Conway's approach to VLSI design, a circuit design will specify types of circuit elements and their overall pattern of arrangement, but will not specify exact details such as model and make of components and their precise locations, whereas the actual physical circuit will be specified down to this level of detail.

Extending the model to contexts with more levels will enable exploration of a number of interesting issues. For example, which levels are best for defining guiding conceptions, enabling them to most effectively guide creative search? The answer will likely depend on context structure, and this relationship between context structure and the nature and level of abstraction of effective guiding conceptions is both of theoretical interest and also has practical implications.

A second model extension is modeling sets of elements. This is important for many creativity contexts. For example, a creative field is populated by the creative contributions that have been made in the field. Such a contribution is typically composed of a set of elements that have been joined together to create the contribution, just as projects in the model consist of three elements. Each element included in a project may be a singleton or may be a set in its own right, so that the context builds on itself. Thus in a more thoroughgoing representation of a creativity context, some elements are singletons and others are sets that contain other context elements.

Hypergraphs are generalizations of standard networks that allow sets of elements to be connected together, rather than just pairs. For example, a family might be a set consisting of parents and children. This provides one approach to modeling structurally richer contexts.[5]

Developing richer forms of representation of context also may involve a wider variety of kinds of linkages. The field of knowledge representation provides a variety of formalisms for describing more complex kinds of relationships, such as causality, part-whole relationships, and metaphor.[6] These approaches add a layer of complexity, and I have not pursued them in this book. But bringing these more semantically oriented approaches into the modeling framework holds the promise of representing contexts more richly, which may aid describing and predicting different parts of the creative process. For example, the intuition lying behind a person's formation of a guiding conception, which I have taken as given, may be able to be unpacked into a series of cognitive steps and structures.

Ultimately empirical data is required to build careful models of specific contexts, from which general patterns can be recognized, enabling more abstract modeling. Greater complexity promises greater range of empirical application and fit with empirical data, but also poses many challenges in terms of data gathering and analysis. The empirical contexts I have presented and draw upon for Krebs, Possum, Woolf, and others in this book were themselves the product of much study and gathering together and analysis of materials, including biographical materials. I also have experience mapping the conceptual hierarchy of an entire field: in prior work my colleague Arthur Campbell and I worked with several students to map the concept hierarchy of all concepts taught in first-year core graduate microeconomics courses, developing a map containing around 1,400 concepts arranged in a multilevel hierarchy.[7] This project, like the contexts described in this book, was highly empirical and data intensive, and it remains to be seen what sort of general approaches and models can be developed, perhaps drawing on recent advances in large-scale neural network learning models.

If daunting, the prospect of developing richer, structurally more complex descriptions of real-world creativity contexts is also exciting. The field of creativity is hardly even at the beginning of this kind of effort. The framework in this book clarifies why this kind of richer description and modeling, together with and based on rich data from case studies, is so important for describing the creative process.

RICHER GUIDING CONCEPTIONS

In the formal model I have focused on the simplest form of guiding conceptions, two higher-level elements. This fits certain cases—for example Hans Krebs's guiding conception can be described at least approximately this way. But most real-world guiding conceptions are more complex than this. Given how important guiding conceptions are for the creative process, developing the ability to model more complex guiding conceptions is clearly essential for enabling the model to fit a wider range of empirical cases. Greater complexity means more elements and also more structure in terms of how the elements jointly define seed pools.

Most directly, guiding conceptions can be composed out of more than two elements. As an example, a simple guiding conception for a story might be "flying dogs," while a more complex one might be "dogs flying in outer space," so that an additional element is added. Typically a more complex guiding conception will be more refined and focused as in this case. I have explored adding elements in this way in simulations. In fact I have explored a few different kinds of three-element guiding conceptions. The most direct extension of the model is the case in which all three guiding conception elements act positively via children, so that seeds are composed of triplets of children, one from each guiding conception element. I have also explored cases in which one of the guiding conception elements acts to restrict possible seeds; for example, the guiding conception "fast flying dogs" will rule out seeds for which the motion is slow and will draw attention to seeds in which the motion is explicitly fast, like a race.

Based on the exploration I have done, extending the model to these cases is reasonably straightforward. In general there can be more seeds and seeds can be larger than two elements. For example, when seeds are defined as combinations of children, each from a different guiding conception element, and guiding conceptions are composed of three elements that all act positively, seeds will increase to three elements. Further, the number of seeds in a seed pool will increase more rapidly as the number of children of top elements increases. For example, if each guiding conception element has 2 children, then the number of seeds in a pool is at most 4 for two-element guiding conceptions and at most 8 for three-element guiding conceptions, a modest difference, whereas if each top element has 10 children, these maximum pool values rise to 100 and 1,000, a far larger difference. This makes efficiency in evaluation of seeds even more important. Increases in seed size and seed pool size increase the computational burden of modeling.

Structural complexity is both important and more challenging to model. What I mean by structural complexity is that a guiding conception functions as a whole—an integrated meaning complex—to generate project seed ideas. Virginia Woolf's conception of reflections has this kind of structural wholeness: the main term "reflections" links to the self and perception of self by others, and this set of elements, jointly, is what defines the main meaning of the guiding conception, the self as seen in the reflections of others' views of self. There is also the concept of an "almost infinite" number of reflections, which adds richness and links to the idea of manifesting a whole life through a series of reflections. All of these elements work together to generate seed ideas for stories—for example, a setting like a party in which we hear a series of conversations during which characters comment about other characters, or the setting of "An Unwritten Novel" in which the narrator speculates about the life of a fellow passenger on a train.

To model these kinds of conceptually richer guiding conceptions and the way they function to generate seeds requires extending the model of guiding conceptions in two ways. First, guiding conceptions must be modeled as sets of elements that have a meaning defined by the set as a whole. Although some of the guiding conceptions in this book do function this way, I have not really addressed this issue formally.

The second extension, building on the first, is key: to define what these kinds of guiding conceptions, for which meaning is defined holistically, can lead to creatively. This requires defining the seed pools they generate. In the base model that is the focus of analysis in this book, a guiding conception consists of two higher-level elements; each has children, and pairs of these children, one from each guiding conception element, define the seeds generated by this guiding conception. Thus the seed pool generated by the guiding conception is a set, and it consists of sets, in that each pair of children can be thought of as a set of two bottom elements. Framed this way, the generalization to guiding conceptions for which meaning is defined holistically follows: A guiding conception defines a seed pool that is a set consisting of sets, that is, in which each seed is a set of elements.

In this more general formulation a seed is not necessarily composed out of children of individual guiding conception elements. Rather a seed is a set that is functionally linked to the guiding conception as a unit, so that the two sets are linked. This link may, for example, be based on the seed possessing an attribute (as a set as a whole, distinct from its component elements and their attributes) that links to the same or a related attribute associated with the guiding conception. For example, in a visual domain a seed consisting of alternating black and white lines possesses the attribute "striped," and we can imagine this linking with an artistic guiding conception that includes the idea of generating compositions with stripes. Likewise, for VLSI design a design conception might have certain features in terms of function and overall layout, and circuit elements that, as a group, match these features would be potential seeds.

This way of modeling guiding conceptions and seeds links to the discussion in the preceding section about sets and hypergraphs. Frameworks from semantic networks and other knowledge representation formalisms including commonsense reasoning may also be valuable in developing this kind of model. For example, elements might be divided into categories, the way words divide into categories including nouns, verbs, adjectives, and adverbs; then a guiding conception might be defined as a "sentence" that links a set of elements in a meaningful way.[8]

Notwithstanding the increases in complexity of the extended model I have outlined, it is noteworthy that the overall model structure will remain intact, suitably extended: guiding conceptions generate seeds, and guiding principles help evaluate seeds and identify additional elements to turn promising seeds into full projects. It will be of great interest to explore a range of properties of the creativity model developed in this book in this extended model. First it will be interesting to explore seed pool sizes and the variability in seed pool sizes over different guiding conceptions, including the relationship of seed pool size to the nature and complexity of guiding conceptions. It will likewise be interesting to explore project coverage and the relative number of "rare" projects covered by just a few guiding conceptions in this extended model in which there are more kinds of guiding conceptions. It is an open question whether the complementarity between guiding conceptions and guiding principles discussed in Chapter 13—that smaller seed pools are associated with greater distances to additional project elements— will continue to hold true in models with more richly defined guiding conceptions.

Extending the way guiding conceptions are modeled will certainly be helpful in aligning with empirical case studies. Ideally, for any given individual or team, both their context and their guiding conception and guiding principle will be modeled in sufficient richness to match empirical data, including especially being able to describe their guiding conception and how it generates seed project ideas.[9]

LARGER SEEDS AND PROJECTS

The model of seeds and projects used in this book has been made as simple as possible. It assumes that a seed consists of just two elements, the minimum necessary for a new creative link, and a project (really project design) consists of just three elements: the seed plus one additional element. Also, the model does not include later stages of project development, so implicitly once a three-element project is created, it maps directly into a creative outcome.

Reality of course is far more complex. Both seeds and especially projects, even core project designs, frequently consist of more elements.

Further, project work involves revisions, indeed iterative revisions, in order to complete a project. I discuss the issue of revisions in the next section; here I focus on the first issue, extending the model to allow for larger seeds and projects.

Extending the model to larger seeds and project designs increases model complexity, specifically combinatorially. Consider seeds as an example. If there are mN bottom elements, there are at most $mN(mN - 1)/2$ seeds defined as pairs of bottom elements, which scales with $N^2/2$. For seeds defined as triplets, the number scales with $N^3/6$. As overall scale measured by N increases the difference grows: if for example $N = 1,000$ the number of seed triplets is on the order of 330 times greater than the number of seed pairs! This greatly increases computational complexity.

One approach to extend the model while avoiding a "combinatorial explosion" is defining seeds and projects as clusters of elements. Consider seeds first. Even if the essence of a creative project seed is a creative connection, that connection might not be thought of as being between two isolated elements, but rather between two clusters of elements. In this approach each cluster consists of elements that are near one another in the existing context, meaning either directly linked or a short distance away from one another. But—critically for the creativity of the seed—the clusters themselves can be and likely are some distance apart, meaning that the minimum path between any pair of elements i and j for which i belongs to cluster 1 and j belongs to cluster 2 is not too small, for example at least 3 steps. I have used computer modeling on simulated networks similar to the ones presented in this book to determine the full set of valid seeds of this kind in a given network. For example, consider a seed that has 5 elements total, in 2 clusters. There are two possible patterns: 3 elements in one cluster and 2 in the other, or 1 element in one cluster and 4 in the other. In evaluating closeness of elements in a cluster, the approach I have used is to look at the minimum distance from an element to the other elements in the same cluster. Thus for example a cluster of 4 elements might have a star pattern where one element is central and the others are all linked directly to it but not to each other; or alternatively a cluster of 4 might have a linear pattern in which one element links to a second, which in turn links to a third, which in turn links to a fourth.[10] Calculations show that the number of valid seeds with 5 elements and 2 clusters in simulated contexts with 100 top elements and 200 bottom elements is around 16 million.[11] This is large, but not unmanageable computationally.

How might project designs and ultimately projects be developed from such seeds? There are two main patterns of development. One is to add elements to each existing cluster. In this pattern the core idea for the project remains the idea embodied in the seed, connecting the two clusters, with additional elements added to flush out the conception. The other pattern, more in keeping with the model in this book, is to add a third cluster of elements, thus adding a further creative connection. A guiding principle will help identify this cluster—perhaps one key element, or perhaps a cluster that has a jointly attributed meaning. Guiding principles will also be important in evaluating seeds and projects, in this case operating on linked clusters.

Creative projects can of course grow far beyond the seeds that initiate them. For example, a novel, a painting, an automobile, or any large-scale design may ultimately include thousands of elements. Again a basic distinction is building up clusters, by adding adjacent or nearby elements, versus adding new clusters. Extending the framework to model this process seems possible, but many choices about how elements are added must be modeled. Some additions may come about through trial and error—this will work better for adding elements to existing clusters, for which options are more limited. For adding new clusters, guiding principles, and possibly continuing to draw on a guiding conception, are likely to be more important. In general, many decisions must be made; thus if anything, guidance becomes even more important as complexity increases.

In the cluster model of seeds and projects, additional issues arise. A given guiding principle may be more effective in identifying elements for one cluster than another, and it is possible that there is one guiding principle that makes judgments about the project as a whole, thus integrating over clusters, while other guiding principles function more on individual clusters. Clusters must fit together successfully. Hence while an individual or team may focus on one cluster at a time, they must always be thinking about how the elements brought into one cluster will impact the way all the clusters fit together. The process of developing a feature-length film, for example as has been described at Pixar, might be an example of this kind of process: Ed Catmull comments that a film contains "literally tens of thousands of ideas" ranging over the dialogue, visual sets and camera locations, characters, and soundtrack, producing ultimately a very complex product with thousands of interlocking elements, growing out of what is oftentimes a relatively simple project seed.[12]

Considering modeling seeds and projects with clusters also raises the issue of extended local search. I have focused on a model in which potential seeds lie directly in a guiding conception search pool. But the search for a candidate seed or for additional elements to develop a seed further can extend beyond the seed pool to neighboring elements. This is especially relevant for the cluster model: A seed cluster might begin from one or two elements that are in the original seed pool, but additional elements may be added to the cluster as the project grows that lie one or two steps outside the original pool. Here search extends via paths to what we can label an "outer" pool consisting of elements close to seed pool elements. This outer pool will typically be larger than the original seed pool, thus offering many options for seeds and project development. Expanding search in this way is quite natural. For example, once a writer has explored the original seed pool associated with their guiding conception, it is natural that story ideas that are linked with this pool, but just one or two steps away, will come to mind via associational thinking.

In terms of the network context model, there a variety of paths to outer pool elements. A seed pool element can link to a second parent element (not the guiding conception parent) and this parent can in turn link to a bottom element that is not part of the original seed pool. Or, in a slightly longer path the second parent can link to another higher-level element that in turn links to a new bottom element—here the new element is more of a "cousin" to the initial element. A third possibility is that a guiding conception element links to another higher-level element that in turn links to possible bottom elements. All of these paths are relatively short. Longer paths are possible but will involve more wide-ranging exploration and may be less likely. The goal in terms of modeling is to describe the set of possible paths that may help an individual develop a promising seed project. It will also be interesting to explore empirically how such paths are utilized in the creative development of seeds and projects.

THE REVISON PROCESS

The formal model in this book includes just a single step to move from a project seed to the final project. In reality building up a project is an iterative process, a cycle of exploration, evaluation, and revision.

This larger, more realistic process might be modeled in the following way. Beginning from a seed, a new element is added, just as in the base model of this book. Then the proposed project is evaluated. If it is assessed as not sufficiently well aligned with the guiding principle, a search is made either to replace one of the project elements (or more than one in some cases) or add a new element. In turn, this triggers a new assessment, and again if the project is found not to be sufficiently well aligned with the guiding principle, this again triggers exploration to replace or add elements. Note that in some cases the same element or cluster that was replaced or had elements added or dropped in the previous round is again identified as the "problem" and is again replaced or has elements added or dropped, while in other cases a different element or cluster is identified as the current problem. This cycle continues until either a successful project is developed or the decision is made to abandon the project. At some point after repeated failures, or because of new information, the decision may be made to shift to a different guiding conception, in most cases evolved from the current one.[13]

Although the details are different than the simpler model delineated in this book, the overall process is similar. As with the simpler model, the distance to new elements is important and relates to the creativity needed in the revision process.

Revisions are hugely important for the creative process. In the overall cycle of creativity, projects take up the bulk of time and energy, and most of this time and energy is spent on revisions, trying out different possibilities and making changes in order to produce the best final result. The example of Hans Krebs's work on the urea project described in Chapter 14 illustrates this. Revisions also can be hugely creative. For example, Picasso added arguably the most creative proto-cubist elements in his great early modernist painting *Les Demoiselles d'Avignon* as revisions to the original plan—see my book *The Nature of Creative Development*, Chapter 12, for more.[14] Thus extending the model to incorporate project revisions and the role of guidance in revisions is important.

LONGER, MORE COMPLEX DEVELOPMENTAL PROCESSES

The examples of creative journeys in the preceding chapter highlight that creative paths can be long and involve multiple phases. I have discussed some aspects of longer creative paths in that chapter and the chapter preceding it. Here I discuss additional issues and patterns of development over longer time periods.

A common pattern of creative development and the pattern Virginia Woolf followed is guiding conception evolution. Indeed I believe evolution of guiding conceptions is integral in many if not most longer creative paths.

The model in this book essentially describes a single creative cycle, from guiding conception to seed and then, assisted by a guiding principle, to project, leading to project outcome. To describe creative paths more fully requires describing what happens at the conclusion of this cycle, and how a new cycle emerges. Empirically there are of course many different patterns. But a basic distinction is between maintaining a guiding conception largely as it has been—although possibly using it to explore differently based on what one has learned—versus significantly altering it or even abandoning it in favor of a new guiding conception. Maintaining a guiding conception tends to be associated with continuity, whereas altering it or shifting to a new guiding conception is associated with change.

Even in periods of relative stability when a guiding conception remains more fixed, there will be ongoing creative development. Individuals and teams learn from each project they engage in and its result, which, together with their guiding principles, helps them refine their understanding of which seeds have greatest potential and how best to turn seeds into full projects. They also have ongoing experiences and are often actively learning, growing their context, which can open up new elements to serve as potential seeds and also provide more options for developing seeds into successful full projects.

Eventually even this relative stability gives way to change. Empirically the most common change is evolution of a guiding conception. This is more common than simply abandoning a guiding conception in favor of a completely different one. Individuals have invested much time and creative effort in their guiding conception, and have at least in the beginning pursued it believing in its creative potential; they will not abandon it readily. But their thoughts and beliefs change over time in ways that naturally lead them eventually to revise and refine it. Change is natural, even inevitable. As noted above, individuals are continually learning as they pursue creative projects, both through working on the projects as well as from the project outcomes, including both their own assessments and feedback they receive from others. Also events happen around them, in their fields and larger cultures, altering their context. Further, after some time they will have tried the most promising seeds their guiding conception covers—its seed pool will begin to seem dried up. All of these factors point toward the inevitablity of change, to individuals reconceptualizing and reorienting their creative work.

Guiding conception evolution often involves refining a conception, by adding new elements that extend and enrich it and sharpen its focus. Virginia Woolf wrote a short story that illuminated how she could enrich and refine her original guiding conception, a development that opened the way to her great modernist period. Lynn Conway's guiding conception expanded in terms of its scope and ambition. Sometimes the change in a guiding conception is more of a shift in focus, so that an individual pivots their direction while still maintaining a link with their original conception.[15]

Guiding conceptions also contribute to their own evolution through helping to guide individuals' learning processes. It is natural that an individual will seek to learn new elements that they perceive as fitting in some way with their guiding conception, since these elements may serve as seeds for projects. More broadly, their guiding conception orients them toward being open to certain kinds of experiences that fit with their conception. Both activities help build their context. This can trigger new seed ideas and can also contribute to the subsequent evolution of their guiding conception. Thus the overall process is iterative and can generate rich creative dynamics.[16]

Modeling the evolution of guiding conceptions has two parts. One, which is simpler, is describing a new evolved conception as it relates to the original conception. This can be done by identifying the new elements that are added, any elements dropped, and shifts in larger set-based attributes. The other, deeper level is modeling why and through what pathway the change occurs. This is challenging because the thought processes involved can be complex and multifaceted, and traditionally are not described even by individuals who give quite rich accounts of their creative journeys. There are different possible pathways that can lead to an evolved conception. One is a project outcome triggering awareness of a new element to add to the existing conception, as happened for Virginia Woolf. A second pathway is encountering a new element, perhaps at random, and recognizing how it or something related to it links with one's conception, triggering a change. This fits with Einstein's evolution: he (quite possibly) saw a man on a ladder and recognized that there is an equivalence in terms of physical effects between a gravitational field and uniform acceleration in open space. A third pathway is reflecting over a series of projects pursued under a stable guiding conception and having an insight—for example making a generalization, which in turn triggers a change in an existing conception.

All of these paths can in principle be brought into the model framework. But I write "in principle" because it is clear much work remains to be done to formalize these ideas, and the full model description, and implications, must be worked out. It is also clear that the formation of an initial guiding conception involves related kinds of pathways. Thus developing a modeling approach for these kinds of pathways of thought and response can significantly strengthen the model.

CHAPTER 17

THE CREATIVE DEVELOPMENT OF FIELDS

Creativity arises out of the interaction of individuals with their contexts. That is the grounding premise of this book and the perspective from which I have described the creative process. I have argued further that contexts are large scale and rich, providing many opportunities and avenues to creativity, if individuals can find their way using guidance. My analysis has focused on single individuals, both to present my framework of analysis and to show the value of modeling individuals' contexts and creative paths in detail. In this chapter I discuss how the framework can be expanded to model multiple individuals working in a creative field.[1]

Many questions arise when we extend the framework to multiple individuals in a field. How do we describe the contexts of multiple individuals in a common model? When we describe the contexts of multiple individuals, how do we calibrate how different they are from one another? How do we assess differences across individuals in their guiding conceptions and principles? To what extent and how do differences in individuals' guiding conceptions and principles translate into differences in their creative ideas and outcomes? I discuss these questions in this chapter. I also present two examples of creative fields, Indigenous Australian contemporary artists and VLSI technology.

OVERLAPPING CONTEXTS

Individuals who enter and work in a field around the same time will almost inevitably share some parts of their contexts in common. They will all be aware of current trends and puzzles and recent contributions that have garnered attention in the field. They also are likely to share common knowledge of many of the "basics" of their field and its history.

To evaluate this overlap requires modeling individuals' contexts in a common framework. Fortunately, the network approach I have presented in this book works well for this. The overall context will encompass each individual's context, which will be a subset of the whole. The degree of overlap between two or more individuals can be assessed in terms of how much their individual contexts overlap. We expect more overlap for higher-level broader concepts and well-known elements, and less for more idiosyncratic and specific elements. Field structure will also play a role in degree of overlap. Highly centralized fields in which a few higher-level hub elements have many links will most likely have higher degrees of overlap, as compared with less centralized fields in which links are more uniformly distributed. A "hot topic" may generate a good deal of overlap among individuals who enter the field around the same time. The broader cultural setting may also play a role in context overlap, especially in fields like some of the arts, the social sciences, and areas of business and technology in which broader cultural elements are integral to the creative process. While exploring this issue fully is beyond the scope of this book, the two empirical examples illustrate many of these points.

Two further issues arise once we develop a means to assess context overlap. One is the relationship between degree of overlap and the pace of creative activity and innovation in a field. Clearly less overlap has the advantage of being more readily able to spawn a greater variety of different paths to creativity. However, if some particular topic area is especially promising and is recognized as such, this may contribute to considerable overlap and may also be correlated with a high degree of creative forward movement in the field. A second issue is whether there may be "too much" or "too little" overlap, perhaps due to economic and social forces, in terms of generating creativity and innovation in a field. This would have implications for teaching and managing individuals, especially recent entrants into a field, and for public policy.

INDIVIDUALITY REMAINS

Regardless of the fact that there will be overlap among individual contexts, it remains a fascinating truth that each individual in a creative field follows a unique creative path. In most cases individuals also produce distinctive, even unique creative outcomes. This is not always the case, of course. Individuals sometimes find their way to the same outcome, as in simultaneous discovery in the sciences. This fits with the formal model in this book, in which there are multiple paths starting from different seeds to the same project outcome. Further, beyond identical outcomes there are often correlations among the creative outcomes produced by different individuals working in a field at the same time—for example, common themes. This is not surprising, given that individuals are working in overlapping contexts. But at the end of the day it is the case that diversity and individuality remain.

I came to understand this point when I began interviewing individuals for my first book, *The Nature of Creative Development*. In each of three fields (English and American literature, neuroscience, mathematics), I selected a year and interviewed the majority of individuals who had received their doctorate from one of the top-ranked programs in the field in that year. It was fascinating to see how despite considerable commonality in graduate education, every individual pursued their own unique creative path and produced an original dissertation. It was then that I understood that to more fully understand creativity and innovation—and the human life course—we must develop a framework rich enough to enable us to grasp the differences among individuals even while the framework itself is common to all.

CONTEXT AND DIFFERENCE

Consider a collection of individuals who have entered a field and been learning about it for some time, but are yet to take their most important creative steps—a cohort of aspiring creators. Examples are Hans Krebs around the time he was working in Warburg's lab together with other young biochemists and chemists of that time; Virginia Woolf around the time she sat down to write "The Mark on the Wall" together with other aspiring writers of the time such as her friend Katherine Mansfield; and Clifford Possum at Papunya in the early to mid-1970s with the other Indigenous painters such as Kaapa, his brothers Tim Leura and Billy Stockman, and many others. This is a key time for individuals in their creative journeys, when they form guiding conceptions that are central in guiding their creative activity and may lead them to highly valuable creative outcomes, as was the case for Krebs, Woolf, and Possum.

Among such a collection of individuals there are likely to be significant overlaps in their contexts. They all will have learned both the basics and the classics of their field and something about its history. Contemporaries of Hans Krebs would have received similar basic training in chemistry as he received, although not identical; hence their contexts would share some elements and network substructures in common with his, such as generally accepted principles of chemical reactions of the time and standard examples illustrating them. Katherine Mansfield, T. S. Eliot, and other contemporaries of Virginia Woolf did not read exactly what she read, and she of course read very widely, but they read many authors she read, especially well-known, iconic sources like Shakespeare and nineteenth-century authors.[2] As mentioned above, if there are recent contributions to a field that have sparked excitement, many if not most of the individuals entering the field are likely to learn about them. Some will be especially inspired by a particular contribution, and it will become a central topic of learning for them, so that they will learn a good deal about it and contributions that are being made building on it. Individuals who share an interest in a particular current topic will share network substructures about this topic in common, especially if they learn about these recent contributions from similar sources. Individuals in a cohort will also share broader cultural experiences in common. Woolf and her contemporaries had the shared experience of living through World War I and were all aware of the many changes occurring in early twentieth-century life. Jack Dorsey and his contemporaries in the world of computer programming and technology would all have been aware of the rise of the Internet and a host of related social and technological changes during the mid to late 1990s and turn of the twenty-first century.

But—although there are similarities—there will also be significant context differences among individuals in a field cohort. As we have seen with the examples in this book, a person's local environment and family are an important part of their creative context, and these typically differ. Virginia Woolf's case is a notable example I have discussed: her mother and father were on her own account central to her life, and their deaths when she was young, depriving her of key reflections of self, were linked to her guiding conception and then depicted through transmutation in *To the Lighthouse*. Her contemporaries shared many general social and cultural factors in common with her, but not these specifics. Neither Mansfield nor Eliot had a father with anything like the close tie and impact on their literary development that Woolf had. Mansfield grew up in a colonial "frontier" setting in New Zealand, very different than Woolf's upbringing. Gender is another fundamental distinguishing factor: the difference in gender between Eliot and both Woolf and Mansfield is linked to many differences in attitudes and beliefs. As another example, Jack Dorsey's environment growing up in St. Louis was an important part of his context, clearly something most programmers and tech workers would not have shared and an important factor in his guiding conception.

There will also be differences in what individuals learn about their fields. In many fields there are rival schools of thought, and they teach their students different things and different orientations, meaning there are differences in both higher-level principles and theories as well as detailed teaching points. Although Woolf and Eliot did share much literature knowledge in common, each focused on different topics—for example, Eliot on philosophy and religion including Eastern religions, and Woolf loving the Elizabethans like Hakluyt and focusing on Victorian and modern novels.[3]

In economics, for decades in the United States there was a rivalry between the "freshwater" school of thought—associated with the University of Chicago as well as other universities around the Great Lakes—and the rival "saltwater" school of thought associated with Harvard and UC Berkeley, among others. These schools of thought taught different material including different higher-level paradigms and principles. As discussed in earlier chapters, Arthur Campbell and I and several research assistants collected and analyzed required reading lists for core microeconomics courses from eight top-ranked graduate economics programs in the United States (one full year of coursework), including the University of Chicago, Harvard, and others. We coded the readings for concepts, organized in a hierarchy, identifying more than 1,400 concepts in total across the universe of eight programs. We then computed correlations in concepts taught across the programs, at each of three levels of hierarchy. Our findings show clear differences among the schools, and interestingly they cluster into two groups.[4] The overlap between pairs of programs in covered concepts ranges from around 90 percent to a low of just 50 percent. The implication is that students in different programs are exposed to different concepts in required readings, and while it is true that students learn more than what they are exposed to in class readings, these differences will generate differences in their contexts. Beyond this, there will be differences in their peer groups, which will also generate differences in their contexts.

As presented throughout this book, context can be represented as a network of interconnected elements. It follows that even if two or more individuals share a set of elements in common, they may have different patterns of interconnections among these elements, and this makes their contexts different. Differences in interconnection arise from three main sources. One is learning patterns: even if individuals learn the same set of elements, the interconnections among these elements may be different due to differences in how they are taught or presented. The second source of difference is simple associations: we naturally associate elements we learn at the same time or place, so when and where we encounter elements influences our connection pattern. The third source is the active organization of context: individuals do not simply learn elements and interrelationships passively but instead actively think and restructure their contexts through reflecting upon and integrating their experiences and learning. Every individual has their own chain of thinking and will reorganize what they learn and experience in their own way. This does not necessarily lead to greater differences between individuals' contexts, as they may recognize common linkages that in fact they were not all taught; but it can, especially if it leads an individual to connect a more widely shared part of their context with a more distinctive part.

Related to this third source of difference is a more general point: the dynamic nature of context. As we encounter elements we make connections, learn, reflect, integrate, and reshape our context. This mental shaping and reshaping leads in turn to further learning and experience, further expanding and reconfiguring our context. We might want to learn more about a particular topic, might be drawn to a puzzle or paradox the way Albert Einstein was, or develop a collaboration with someone new who brings their own perspective and knowledge. Thus context is inherently dynamic and builds upon itself through an iterative cycle of learning, synthesizing, and exploring: it is continually evolving. I have not focused on these dynamics in this book because they are complex and deserve their own treatment. They are central for understanding how individuals end up developing distinctive contexts even if initially their contexts might have been more similar to those of other people in their field. They are also central for understanding creative and life paths.

DISTINCTIVE GUIDING CONCEPTIONS

The framework and examples in this book make the argument that forming a guiding conception is a key step for generating successful creative outcomes. When we expand our analysis to multiple individuals in a field, two questions arise: How different are their guiding conceptions, and how important are these differences for differences in their creative outcomes?

When someone forms a guiding conception, it is based on two factors: their context, which provides the raw material, and their intuition, which enables them to form a conception that they believe holds promise. Intuition is critical, as we have seen over and over again in the examples, enabling individuals to home in on elements and facets of context that have creative potential. But it is also true that context shapes intuition. Virginia Woolf's intuition that reflections could form the basis for literature had roots in her own life experiences and was defined also in opposition to Victorian literature and the Victorian worldview. We are far from understanding how intuition works on such an abstract conceptual level. We can say that in many cases certain elements are highly salient for an individual, drawing their interest and focus. Also, the structure of context is important, meaning not just single elements but interconnections among elements, as well as larger complexes that reveal significance and opportunity. Hans Krebs did not just learn of the Warburg methods, he spent a year and a half in the Warburg lab learning the methods in detail before forming his guiding conception linking these methods with the field of intermediary metabolism. The direct experience seems to have been essential for him, and it seems doubtful—and did not apparently happen—that someone else just learning about the methods from afar would have recognized the link with intermediary metabolism with the same clarity and recognition of genuine possibilities. It follows that even if two individuals' contexts overlap in significant ways, they will still end up forming different guiding conceptions if certain parts of their contexts are more salient for one than the other, triggering particular intuition. At the same time, individuals whose contexts are largely different but overlap in a few key areas might end up forming similar guiding conceptions if they both recognize creative potential in these overlapping areas.

In most cases individuals in a creative field, even when they have entered the field at around the same time, end up forming distinctive guiding conceptions. The main exception is likely to be when there is a current hot topic area in the field that draws the attention of many individuals entering the field. Even in this case there are often nuances of difference. A number of the neuroscientists I interviewed for my first book were interested in axon pathfinding and the development of neural circuitry, hot topics at the time. Nonetheless the guiding conceptions they formed, in terms of project areas they envisioned working on, differed. On reason this tends to occur is that a guiding conception typically links two or more concepts or topics together and thus may link a hot topic with a second, more idiosyncratic topic or mode of analysis. Thus one individual focused on individual axon paths and their remarkable turning properties (turning to reach a target), while another took a more systems-level view and was interested in how the system as a whole gets "wired up."[5]

Even if individuals' guiding conceptions overlap, they will typically ultimately produce different creative products. This may happen due to randomness and variation in their local environments leading them to focus on different seed ideas. Or it may come about because they have different guiding principles and thus end up evaluating seeds differently, so that even if they think of or encounter similar seeds, they nonetheless end up pursuing different projects. Even if two individuals pursue similar seeds, they still may complete them differently, again due to differences in their guiding principles or the opportunities available in their local environments. Of course multiple discoveries of the same phenomenon do occur, and not necessarily due to individuals or teams having very similar guiding conceptions—for as we have seen in the model, there can be multiple pathways to the same project.[6]

MODELING MULTIPLE INDIVIDUALS: CONTEXT, GUIDANCE, OUTCOMES

The model of creativity in large-scale contexts presented in this book can be extended to model multiple individuals engaged in creative work in a field. I discuss some important issues and outline one way to develop this kind of model here, but provide just a sketch—there is much work to be done.

A key part of extending the model to multiple individuals is delineating the context of each individual in a way that shows both how individuals' different contexts overlap and how they differ.

One approach to doing this is to define a "universal" context that will contain each individual's context as a subcontext and thus specify each individual's context within this universal context.[7] This requires modeling the universal context, which may be quite challenging. The reverse approach may in fact be more practical: construct the context of each individual and then define the union of these as the universal context that embeds all of them. The first approach makes sense for abstract modeling, whereas the second will have advantages for empirical modeling but might miss some elements.

Regardless of which approach is employed, an important issue is the structure of the overall field context. A basic distinction is between fields in which, at the time being modeled, there is a clear center in terms of dominant higher-level topics, paradigms, and approaches, as compared with fields in which there is less of a clear center. In terms of the kind of model described in earlier chapters, the case of a clear center can be modeled as a network having a power law degree distribution for higher-level elements, just as I have done in the simulations and for the analytic bounding result in Chapter 10. A field with a less clearly defined center may look more like a random network. Clustering is likely to be important in all fields.

Consider a field in which there is a clear center. Some higher-level concepts will be hubs and will have many links with many lower-level elements as well as other higher-level elements. Individuals in the field will have many if not all of the hub elements in their context. In addition, each individual will know many of the lower elements linked to these hub elements, although not necessarily all or even most, depending on how large the field is and how many such lower elements there are. There are likely to be some lower elements linked to hubs that are especially-well-known examples, and these will be part of the contexts of most individuals; but other lower elements linked to hubs may be known by just a few individuals. Overall there will be considerable overlap among individuals' contexts in terms of central regions of the field, especially for higher-level elements. We expect much less overlap for the more peripheral regions of the field.

In this kind of field environment, one form of guiding conception that I believe is common is linking a hub element with a more peripheral element. For example, an individual might form a guiding conception imagining applying a well-known theory to a novel application or, in the arts or engineering, an established technique to a new kind of material. In a field in which each individual forms this kind of guiding conception, there will be overlap across guiding conceptions but also differences given the diversity of ways to combine a hub element with other more peripheral elements. We expect different individuals to make different ultimate contributions, but their contributions may also share some features in common given one or a few common hubs. It is interesting both theoretically and empirically to evaluate the degree of distinctiveness and overlap in contributions and how this impacts field dynamics. The application to VLSI in the next section fits this model quite well and illustrates the powerful creativity this kind of hub-periphery interaction can unleash.

Now consider a field in which there is not such a clearly defined center. In this case there may be multiple "centers" vying for dominance, as for example how in earlier times the "freshwater" and "saltwater" schools of thought vied for dominance in economics. Or the field may be quite diffuse with no real center, with many different approaches being pursued.

A field with multiple centers can be modeled as a cluster network in which each cluster is a center. Individuals whose contexts all center on the same cluster will clearly share much of their contexts in common, while individuals in different clusters will share less. If the most successful creative contributions require linking elements from different clusters, which makes sense since these kinds of connections can be quite creative, it is natural to wonder through which kinds of creative paths individuals will be able to make these kinds of connections. Forming a guiding conception that involves at least one element outside one's home cluster may be one approach—this will naturally lead to seeds composed of elements from different clusters. Alternatively there may be longer, more indirect pathways, in which case guiding principles, applied creatively, may be crucial in helping to identify key intercluster links, similar to the issue of long paths to the key third element to complete a project described in Chapter 13.

In a diffuse field we expect to see the least amount of overlap among individuals' contexts. These field environments may resemble random networks. One modeling approach simply assigns higher- and lower-level elements to individuals at random to generate individual contexts. Correlation can also be built into the model so that subsets of individuals are more likely to share some elements in common. Given a set of "golden projects" in the field, we can then ask, for each such random assignment, what if any are the feasible paths to discover these projects. This model is relatively close to the random network model presented in this book. Empirically it should be possible given sufficient data to determine for each individual whether they have the capability, based on their individual context, to form a guiding conception that can lead to a golden seed and thence to a golden project. More broadly, empirical work may also help identify how well this kind of model explains observed patterns of learning and creativity.

Beyond the issue of centrality of some top elements, there are other factors that are important for field development. Overall scale of a field is likely to be central to how individuals go about creative engagement, as I have argued throughout this book, and also likely to be an important factor in broad field dynamics. A major theme of this book is that guidance is especially important in large-scale contexts. Hence we expect it to be especially important for individuals to form guiding conceptions in larger fields, with successful guiding conceptions being those that harness intuition to define promising seed pools to explore. The number of levels and the density of linkages in a field is also important—we expect more of both of these in more developed fields.

There is clearly an opportunity to better understand the development of creative fields through exploring the kind of modeling and empirical analysis discussed in this chapter and this book. The two empirical case studies presented next depict creative fields burgeoning and help us appreciate how fascinating creative field development is as a subject for study.

VLSI DESIGN UNLEASHED

The outpouring of VLSI design innovation that followed Conway and Mead's development of their simplified design methodology is a great example of how an innovation disseminated and incorporated into the thinking of individuals in a field helps spawn a wave of further innovations. In this case the dissemination happened through courses taught at universities. Students and early career professors introduced to the design methodology developed creative ways to apply it, with their process often based on envisioning how to apply it to topics they were already interested in. This is reminiscent of Hans Krebs learning the manometric tissue slice method and envisioning using it to study intermediary metabolism. However, whereas that method was not so widely known at the time and was adopted only gradually, the Mead-Conway method was disseminated rapidly through teaching.

Lynn Conway spearheaded the process of spreading the design methods she and Carver Mead had developed, with help from many other people. In her "MPC Adventures" lecture delivered at the Second Caltech Conference on VLSI, Conway discussed how the Mead-Conway design approach was disseminated and effectively scaled up to become available to many individuals. "The sort of question that really interests me," she stated at the start of her lecture, was "How can we best organize to create, validate, and culturally integrate new design methods in new technologies?"[8] In her view, in a field of technology such as VLSI, when new design methods are introduced, "large-scale exploratory application of the methods by many designers is required in order to test and validate the methods."[9] Only when this has been done will the typical user feel comfortable shifting to these new methods. In this passage we can identify her guiding conception over these years: to develop a method for doing this systematically rather than the way it has usually happened, which she describes as "ad hoc, undirected," and inherently slow. "I believe we can discover powerful alternatives" to this ad hoc slow process, she writes, "methods ... to direct this evolutionary process," enabling "rapid directed creation, validation, and cultural integration of the ... methods."[10] It was this she set out to do with help from many colleagues.

Conway first taught the design methods in a course at MIT in 1978. Half the course was lecture, and during the other half students developed design projects, a format Mead had previously used at Caltech. Conway realized as the course entered the project phase that "things were working out very well, and that some amazing projects would result," and "cast about for a way to get them implemented." In her view that was the only way to learn if the course really worked and, if so, to have "demonstrable evidence that it had."[11] Making chips involves many steps—converting the design into a patterning format, making masks, processing wafers, dicing wafers into chips, and mounting and wiring chips into packages—and the process is expensive. Following an approach that had been first tried at Caltech, Conway arranged to have all the student projects merged into a single job, which greatly saved on costs, and was able through her PARC group to find a company to do the work. Ultimately the projects were implemented and returned to students six weeks after the end of the course.[12]

Growing out of her experience at MIT, Conway looked to expand. She and Mead and a few others "began to train instructors from a number of universities in the methods of teaching VLSI design."[13] Conway prepared an *Instructor's Guide* based on her MIT course, and there was also *A Guide to LSI Implementation* that had been written by two UC Berkeley researchers.[14] In the 1979–80 school year the course was launched at around a dozen universities. Perhaps the biggest challenge was implementation, especially with rapid turnaround.[15] PARC received, made, and distributed eighty-two projects back to their home universities—all within a month. Overall, this first wave of expansion proved successful. In the following year, the time at which Conway gave her lecture, VLSI design courses were offered, in her estimation, at around eighty universities.[16] Thus in the space of just two years the Mead-Conway VLSI design methodology became widely disseminated across US universities.

The student projects were not just academic exercises—a number of projects were important innovations. Two examples of technologic innovations that came out of VLSI design courses and were spurred by the Mead-Conway design approach are the development of a graphics chip by Jim Clark and colleagues at Stanford, and the development of Reduced Instruction Set Computers (RISC) at Berkeley and Stanford. Clark's innovation was the springboard for his founding of Silicon Graphics a few years later, and RISC was widely adopted and is used today in smartphones and many other devices.

Clark's innovation was a device he called a "Geometry Engine." He had been introduced to graphics computers while earning his doctorate in computer science at the University of Utah and also worked briefly at the New York Institute of Technology's Computer Graphics Lab. Thus he already had both knowledge and interest in computer graphics, especially hardware development.[17] He attended an intensive short course taught by Mead and Conway and others, was in his own words "super inspired," and was able to envision that he could use the Mead-Conway design approach to pursue his interest in graphics, thus wedding the methodology to his own particular interest.[18] Clark describes the origins of his project in a paper published in 1982.[19]

> In July of 1979, Carver Mead of Caltech and Lynn Conway and several other people from the LSI Systems Area at the Xerox Palo Alto Research Center presented an intensive, three day course on designing nMOS circuits to some of the faculty and staff of Stanford. In search of a project, the author recalled … the Clipping-Divider, designed and built by Ivan Sutherland (Sproull and Sutherland 1968).[20]

The Clipping Divider was a device that would "clip" objects to fit in a window display on a computer screen; it executed a simple graphical procedure. Clark built on this, adding additional features, described in his article, including manipulating objects in a series of planes for three-dimensional representation.[21]

> Key to the design has been the use of design techniques advocated by *Introduction to VLSI Systems* (Mead and Conway 1980). Since this book was the author's first exposure to nMOS circuit design, it has had a significant influence on the methodology used in arriving at the architecture.[22]

Thus the Mead and Conway course provided exposure to the new design paradigm, and Clark, interested in adapting it to graphics, made the creative link to the earlier Clipping Divider device, which triggered his own project. We don't know from his account whether or when Clark formed a guiding conception along the lines of thinking that he would like to apply these new design techniques to graphics, but some process of thinking led him to recall the Clipping Divider, and it would seem natural that it involved thinking about graphics as a potential application. The output of Clark's project was a graphics system with a "very high degree of parallelism" that achieved high performance. And it led to his founding of Silicon Graphics.[23]

The development of RISC was also triggered by the Mead-Conway design approach. RISC was developed in different variants at Berkeley and Stanford, and at each location the Mead-Conway design approach played a pivotal role.

A series of articles written by Berkeley computer scientists show their path to RISC. In February 1980, David Patterson and Carlo Séquin published "Design Considerations for Single-Chip Computers of the Future," which mentions the Conway and Mead text in passing, but has not integrated its basic simplicity of design approach; this article stays quite broad, raising a host of considerations for VLSI chip design.[24] The article shows that Patterson and his colleagues were already thinking about simplified design; over the ensuing months their thinking evolved and became more focused, and, based on the timing, exposure to the Mead-Conway approach was a central factor. An article published in October 1980 mentions RISC and notes that a project was underway at Berkeley to develop such a machine.[25] This project is described in more detail in two later articles. The second of these states that the project has been pursued in the context of "a new graduate curriculum of the Electrical Engineering and Computer Science Department at the University of California, in which students propose and evaluate architectural concepts, learn Mead-Conway design methods, form teams to build the system, and then test their design."[26] Further, the introduction of the first article states that "the chips were designed using ... the simple and scalable Mead-Conway design rules (fabrication lambda = 2 microns)." The discussion later in the paper refers to the use of the "simplified Mead-Conway design rules" to reduce design layout time.[27] The articles describe a process very much in line with Conway's description of how the VLSI design approach spread across universities, and suggest that familiarity with the Mead-Conway design principles was central in helping the Berkeley group envision a practical way forward to explore, design, and build RISC chips. As with Clark, we don't know exactly how thinking progressed along this line of development, but one plausible model is that an initial guiding conception in improved chip design efficiency was then combined with the Mead-Conway design tools, which may have provided the critical missing piece to enable the project to move forward. Alternatively the Mead-Conway approach may been influential in forming the initial guiding conception, thus earlier in the process, and also helped shape project development.

At Stanford John Hennessy and colleagues developed a related device called MIPS (Microprocessor without Interlocked Pipeline Stages). In their article "MIPS: A VLSI Processor Architecture" they list three principle elements: data path components, which take up most of the chip; control; and software. The description of the chip design specifically defines feature size in terms of "λ," the parameter introduced by Conway.[28] More details about the link with the Conway and Mead approach are provided in an article by Hennessy about the control program called SLIM (Stanford Language for Implementing Microcode) developed prior to the full MIPS.[29] Presenting at the Second Caltech Conference on VLSI, at which Conway gave the talk that I have quoted from, Hennessy writes:

> VLSI chip design has rapidly become an area of great importance and interest. Mead and Conway have proposed a design methodology for VLSI systems that has been widely employed. Their design methodology proposes a chip organization using: finite state control implemented with a PLA [Programmable Logic Array], functional units controlled by the PLA, and a set of data paths.[30]

Situating his work in this context, Hennessy states that at present "few tools exist to assist the user in designing and debugging the microcoded [finite state] control." His paper was meant to help fill this gap: "This paper describes a language for synthesizing the control units of a chip from a high level language description."[31] After describing SLIM, he presents an example of a traffic light control system drawn directly from the Mead and Conway text.[32] His project's link with the Conway and Mead design methodology is evident, and the fact that he presented his work at the Caltech conference shows that he was part of the world of VLSI design they helped create.

In her discussions of how the VLSI design methodology was disseminated through courses, Conway lists dozens of projects developed by students and faculty. While few of these had the impact of the ones I have discussed, it is a testament to how broad the influence was.[33] Students and other interested individuals learned the approach, integrated it into their overall creative context, and were able to generate creative links, forming guiding conceptions they were able to develop into innovative projects. The field was changed and moved forward as a result of the Mead-Conway design methodology innovation.

INDIGENOUS AUSTRALIAN CONTEMPORARY ART

The Indigenous Australian contemporary art movement has brought Indigenous art to the forefront of world art. The movement draws upon traditional Indigenous culture, but has grown beyond its cultural roots through innovations in technique and modes of expression. It has also brought the Indigenous artists a great deal of attention and interaction with the wider world. My discussion here has two aims. First, I place my description of Clifford Possum's creative path in the larger context of the art movement as it began at Papunya in central Australia in the early 1970s, to help explain why he and not someone else developed the idea of painting "maps of the country," and to situate his innovation within the larger movement. Second, I discuss the expansion of the movement beyond Papunya, describing a series of artists and their stylistic innovations and calling attention to the fact that much of the innovation and expansion has been due to women becoming involved in what had been a male activity.

The Indigenous Australian contemporary art movement is less a case of a specific innovation unleashing many subsequent innovations, as happened with VLSI design, but rather a case in which many individuals have participated and made creative contributions. It is true that Papunya is recognized as the birthplace of the movement (although it has roots extending farther back—for example to Albert Namatjira), but the movement has spawned a range of creative styles and forms of contributions over the ensuing decades. Thousands of Indigenous artists have participated in the movement over the past fifty years. *The Oxford Companion to Aboriginal Art and Culture* states that at the time of the book's publication in 2000, there were approximately ten thousand Indigenous artists throughout Australia, including visual as well as other kinds of artists such as performers.[34] Unfortunately we don't have detailed biographical information for most of these individuals on a par with the information available for Clifford Possum and a handful of others. To understand the creative development of a field in a truly satisfactory way, we must trace the creative path of each participant, and here, as in most cases, we are far from being able to achieve this.[35]

These artists share elements of their contexts in common. Indigenous Australian peoples share a belief in the Dreaming. However, there are significant regional and tribal differences in how the Dreaming is described. Further, this part of context is in fact quite individualized. As I have discussed in regard to Clifford Possum, every individual has custodianship over specific Dreamings associated with specific sites located in their traditional lands, many linked to their lineage but others linked to other events such as conception and birth. Hence, even within a single people, every individual's context is, in terms of the Dreaming, distinct in its details.

Other important context domains for many Indigenous artists are, as for Clifford Possum: social connections, especially family; art, including cultural traditions, techniques, and materials; and the broader world, especially non-Indigenous Australia. Again details differ. Different individuals are trained in different artistic traditions—the discussion of Utopia women artists below is a good example, showing how traditional design motifs can be adapted in many different ways. The wider context varies depending on geography and the modalities of interaction a given individual experiences and explores; it may include formal schooling, city life, market transactions, and, as for Possum, who worked on cattle stations, working in white establishments. Differences in context and upbringing are reflected in art. Tracey Moffatt's art described below illustrates this, as her art, based in a mixed racial and more densely populated setting, is radically different from the art of the Papunya and Utopia artists.

The Indigenous Australian contemporary art movement is generally agreed to have begun at Papunya in central Australia in 1971–72. Geoffrey Bardon, a white Australian, was hired as a teacher at the Aboriginal children's school and began teaching art to the students. He writes that he noticed the children making sand diagrams with stylized motifs out of school, and that he encouraged them in school to paint these designs.[36] As he recounts it, the adult men, seeing the children painting and the available art supplies, took painting up themselves. Here we see how a novel element—in this case art supplies—introduced into context can trigger a response.[37] It is noteworthy that visual representation was already an important part of the culture, and the men were steeped in drawing sand diagrams and body painting. Further, as Vivien Johnson notes, a few, including Clifford Possum, his cousin Kaapa, and his brother Tim Leura, were very experienced artists, which may have made them more interested, confident, and able more effectively to form guiding conceptions to pursue with this new medium of painting.[38] Another important factor was that most of the men worked minimally and were not actively engaged in their work, often being disparaged by the white people in Papunya, so that they had the time and energy to engage in painting and could take it up as a major activity.

An event that catalyzed the movement was the painting of murals on the school building's outside walls, including the famous *Honey Ant Mural*. Bardon calls this mural a "public affirmation of Aboriginal identity at Papunya." The "Aboriginal men," he wrote, "saw themselves in their own image ... and upon a European building. Truly, something strange and marvelous had begun."[39] We can interpret this event as producing a change in the men's mental representation, and hence their context: the mural gave them a stronger sense of identity around painting as a legitimate way to express their culture, opening up this avenue for meaningful cultural expression.

Art at Papunya evolved rapidly in the first year of the painting movement. Initially the men made simple sketches and paintings with relatively few elements. As they gained experience their paintings became richer and innovations emerged. Two forces were at work. One was toward using traditional design motifs. Bardon pushed the men to paint this way and not to include any Western-style images. As the movement coalesced around him in the space he helped provide, the "great painting room," artists including Possum and his cousin Kaapa, who had been depicting ritual figures, shifted to using strictly traditional motifs.[40] Thus a guiding principle articulated by Bardon became a central tenet of the movement.

The other force was toward innovation. The most recognizable innovation was the development of intense, extensive dotting as a background, a technique that became one of the hallmarks of the Indigenous art movement. Dotting was used in traditional ceremonial designs such as body paint, but relatively sparsely and often closely allied with a design element such as a circle or line. The painters expanded the use of dots so that they became a unifying element. Some developed subtle, refined dotting techniques, giving their paintings a rich aesthetic. Johnny Warangkula is the most likely original innovator of the dotting technique. Warangkula's principle Dreaming was the Water Dreaming, and this is likely to have been important in his development of the dotting technique. His early painting *Water Dreaming with Lightning*—dated May–June 1971 and thus very early, even before the painting of the *Honey Ant Mural*—shows lightning line patterns with background dotting over the entire painting surface depicting rain and hail. Thus the association of rain with dotting, a traditional link, may have enabled him to take the step of filling the painting with dots.[41] In terms of the framework of this book, his guiding conception (which we do not know much about) would have centered on depicting the Water Dreaming using traditional design elements, and in the course of pursing this he found that, in depicting rain and hail with dots, dotting over the entire background gave a desirable effect. A series of paintings he executed over the next year developed this technique. The dotting becomes extremely fine, sometimes with different patterns on different parts of a painting, and the dots come to represent not just rain but also bush tucker and in a sense the land itself in its variegated terrain and vegetation—which is how this technique was viewed by other artists who took it up.[42]

For the innovation did spread. Bardon notes that the artists, sitting adjacent to one another in the "Great Painting Room," could not help but notice and be influenced by what others around them were doing. The dotting technique, whether invented just by Warangkula or in combination with a few others, spread throughout the group. By 1972 it was standard and spread with the art movement itself to other places.

It was against this backdrop at Papunya—several dozen painters each painting their own Dreamings, and an adherence to strict design motif principles with the dotting technique—that Clifford Possum developed his innovation of "maps of the country." This innovation scaled up the complexity of painting and shifted the main focus from depicting a single Dreaming to depicting instead Dreamings associated with a site and its surrounding area. As I have discussed in Chapter 8, this not only was an artistic innovation but also made a political statement, staking a claim to the land in a way that paintings of single Dreamings did not.

Given that there were many painters at Papunya, it is natural to ask why Clifford Possum took this step and not someone else. In terms of the framework of this book, his context and linkages had several unique features that may have helped him develop his distinctive guiding conception. First, Possum was a highly accomplished artist. Tim Leura said he couldn't "beat him," and even Geoffrey Bardon, who was not as close to Possum as to some of the other men, clearly respected his skill. His skill made him more ambitious in what he imagined possible, bringing the complex conception he had in mind in range. Second, he had considerable contact with non-Indigenous people, more than most of the other painters. This would have made the nascent political struggle to reclaim land more salient to him, so that he would have been drawn to a guiding conception through which he could, through his art, contribute his voice to the cause. Additionally, his adoptive father One Pound Jimmy had served as a guide to tourists, and this would have contributed to making Possum more cognizant of white visitors and the making of maps to guide them. His "maps" would be a counterpoint to these Western maps, staking a claim to the land through deep cultural lore. We do not have enough information to know through what process Possum arrived at his ambitious guiding conception, but it is a reasonable hypothesis that these factors in combination led to it.

Possum's brothers Billy Stockman and Tim Leura were the two most similar to him, also having considerable experience with white people and connected with One Pound Jimmy. Stockman's paintings of 1971 and early 1972 are simpler and also show little dotting, thus less of the background landscape important for shifting to a more geographic focus.[43] Tim Leura, Bardon's closest friend and also very close to Possum, developed a subtle dotting style together with highly articulated and subtle designs and figures. Thus, without knowing the details, it seems that he formed a different guiding conception.[44] The contrast between Possum's art and Leura's illustrates how two individuals with contexts that share much in common can nonetheless form very different guiding conceptions leading to different creative outcomes. This makes sense, for in a rich context there are many possible directions to pursue—a central argument of this book—so that not only is the guiding conception an individual forms hugely important for their creative path, but also there are many guiding conception possibilities.[45]

In the decades after the emergence of the Indigenous Australian desert art movement at Papunya, it spread to many other communities, in the central desert and beyond.[46] It truly became a continent-wide movement, extending to the eastern and southern cities where it became a more urban art, and also to the west.

A key step in the further development of this movement has been the involvement of women, bringing their own Dreamings and cultural and artistic knowledge and sensibilities.[47] In fact the most famous center of art to emerge after Papunya was Utopia in the 1980s and 1990s, which was a women-led movement. The women's art movement at Utopia emerged in two steps. Batik, a method of producing textiles with colored designs, was introduced to the women in the later 1970s through a government-sponsored program. Prior to this time the women would have engaged in traditional body painting and drawn sand diagrams. The batik program both gave them a creative outlet and enabled them to earn money, and they felt a sense of pride in their work.[48] Ten years later painting on canvas was introduced to the women, unleashing a torrent of creativity.

The Utopia women, like the Papunya men, paint their Dreamings. But their painting style is different. Rather than the sense of a high aerial view of a Dreaming and journey over the land, there is a sense of being close to the land, sometimes showing what is underneath the surface. Jennifer Isaacs describes the painting as "close and particular" and writes that in the traditional Indigenous culture, "The Earth itself, the land and its plants, is a woman."[49] As compared with the earlier Papunya art, the Utopia art has an abstraction of design that reflects both the women's many plant-based dreamings, such as yam tubers extending out, as well as female body-painting practices.

Emily Kame Kngwarreye is the most famous of the Utopia women painters. She took up painting in the late 1980s in her late seventies, and is estimated to have produced three thousand paintings in the next eight years up until her death, a truly prodigious output.[50] Asked what she painted, Kame responded:

> Awelye (my Dreaming), arlatyeye (pencil yam), arkerrthe (mountain devil lizard), ntange (grass seed), tingu (Dreamtime pup), ankerre (emu), intekwe (favourite food of emus, a small plant), atnwerle (green bean), and kame (yam seed). That's what I paint, whole lot.[51]

In the middle years of her painting, Kame seems to have developed a more focused guiding conception. One critic has written that she strove to "incorporate a feeling of the wholeness of experience" of the land, its cycles, and immersion in it.[52] She strove to depict the cycle of creation of her landscape, thus its Dreaming, in terms of the seasons and life-giving events, showing how life responds, making her depictions at close range sometimes even under the ground. Paintings fitting this include

Kame (1991), the yam plant flowering and seeding, in rich yellow and green tones; *Kame-Summer Awelye I* (1991) showing the yam plant in summer, with "hot summer" colors—oranges, yellows, and reds; *Kame-Summer Awelye II* (1992); *Summer Yams* (1992), again with red hues; and *Spring Yam Flowers* (1992). The series culminated in her masterpiece *Desert Storm* of 1992. As Terry Smith describes, the painting shows a storm and its aftermath in the desert: water running down in rich blue tones, collecting in aquifers that run through the center of the painting, and then, when one rotates the painting 45 degrees counterclockwise, one sees the flowering yam rising up. Thus the painting shows the landscape in the midst of storm and its response afterward.[53] Thus Kame's guiding conception was different from Clifford Possum's, and this painting is quite different from anything Possum or other Papunya painters had done, both in style and also in the way it represents the Dreaming and the land.

The Indigenous contemporary art movement has also become urban, and artists have explored the tension, power dynamics, and complexity of the interactions between Indigenous people, viewed as black in Australia, and white culture and society. Tracey Moffatt is a well-known filmmaker and photographer who has explored these issues in a series of works. Her film *Nice Coloured Girls* of 1987 shows Indigenous Australian women taking advantage of a white man in an urban nightlife setting, leading him on and eventually robbing him and escaping, thus inverting the standard white man–black woman power dynamic, but in an ironic way that also shows its grip. Interspersed through the film is a second narrative, voiceover readings from journals kept by white males from the time of first encounter of the Europeans with the Indigenous people of the continent in the late eighteenth century. One describes his encounters with an Indigenous woman whom he alternately views as "shy" and a "wanton strumpet," and a later voiceover describes how such a woman at the end evades the white men's clutches (maneuvering her canoe away), just as the three Indigenous women do in the urban story.[54] Moffatt's film *Night Cries* depicts a younger woman identified as Indigenous caring for her elderly white mother. The film manifests a huge range of emotions, shows how fraught the relationship is, and sets this against vivid images of the Austalian landscape that evoke Albert Namatjira's and Georgia O'Keeffe's paintings.[55] Thus Moffatt uses a postmodern sensibility to manifest and probe the constant power dynamics at work between Indigenous and non-Indigenous people and culture.

There are other important facets of the Indigenous Australian contemporary art movement that I have not focused on here but that deserve mention. It has brought great recognition to some, such as Clifford Possum who met the Queen and Tracey Moffatt who represented Australia in the Venice Biennale in 2017.[56] It has been part of the political struggle of the Indigenous peoples of Australia for land rights and social equality, a struggle both Possum and Moffatt would view their work as contributing to.

Indigenous Australian contemporary art is not only a cultural statement of the Dreaming: It is also an economic commodity bought and sold in the market. The art has clearly provided economic opportunity, from the time of Clifford Possum and the early Papunya artists, who gained much income from their art, to more recent artists who identify themselves professionally as artists and earn a living through their art. The Papunya Arts Council was formed as an organization led by Indigenous people to market their art, the first organization of its kind in Australia, and this was surely empowering. But for many artists it has been a tenuous existence, and there has been much exploitation. Many stories circulate of Indigenous artists selling art to charlatan dealers for very small amounts of money; some of the older artists did not understand the notion of their work being sold from one person to another for profit without them, the artist, receiving any benefit. Further, there have been issues with forgeries; Clifford Possum's work was one of the targets of forgeries, and Johnson states that the media coverage and court case "took a heavy toll" on his health.[57]

Understanding how these economic, social, and political factors impact the artists in their creativity is an important topic but also beyond the scope of this book. Many, especially more recent and urban artists, have formed guiding conceptions that reflect and are in dialogue with the political and social issues around them. Thus incorporating these issues into representations of their contexts would be essential to understand their guiding conceptions and creative expressions, and would also illuminate how the framework in this book is best adapted to focus on these factors.

HUMAN CULTURE UNFOLDING

Human culture advances through the multitude of creative contributions and innovations contributed by innumerable individuals, organizations, and groups. The whole process is staggering in its complexity, and we have hardly even begun to model it in a serious way.

It has not been my purpose in this book to take on this challenge directly. Rather, my purpose is to contribute toward modeling individual contexts and creative processes better, emphasizing the large-scale, rich nature of context and the importance of this for creativity. Once this is underway it is possible to extend, as I have described in this chapter, to describe how a field comprising individuals with overlapping contexts develops. In turn this can lead even further, to exploring creative interactions among fields and cultures that drive human cultures forward.

Like with so many aspects of creativity and innovation, there is a tendency to oversimplify creative fields. When we look back over the history of a field, we tend to see each creative step as "obvious" and less challenging than it was in reality. We also tend to overlook the large numbers of creative steps that were taken during a given time period, many of which might not be as well known but were in fact key stepping stones that influenced other individuals on their creative paths. By building up fields and cultural dynamics more systematically from individual creative paths, including contextual overlaps and influences across individuals and fields, we can gain a more accurate, richer sense for how fields develop and broader cultural innovation dynamics, and perhaps develop better ability to predict future paths of innovation. Further, this approach will contribute toward a greater appreciation of the role each individual and team has in the larger creative process—not just the stars and celebrities but all individuals, each in their own way. See the Conclusion for more.

CHAPTER 18

SUPPORTING CREATIVITY

The framework in this book can help individuals and organizations unleash greater creativity. While I have discussed this throughout the book as I introduced different elements of the framework, in this chapter I focus on it.

As wonderful as it is to feel creative and generate positive creative outcomes, it is by no means automatic or easy to attain the creative heights one aspires to. Many people struggle to be creative and wish they could be more creative, and many organizations would like to tap into and unleash greater creativity. The conventional view of creativity as a mystery that cannot be explained is not helpful. It provides no guidance as to how to go about being creative. If anything it leaves people feeling helpless, waiting for the lightning bolt of creativity to strike, wondering why it doesn't, and sometimes leading them to decide they cannot be creative and not even try.

The framework in this book can help people learn how to engage in creative endeavors through providing structure and a sense of what the process entails. The framework breaks the creative process down into steps, each of which can be worked on individually. This is a powerful way to help individuals and teams enhance their creative engagement, for they can identify which steps they need to improve on and focus on those in a conscious, reflective way. Applying the framework can help identify reasons for failure, gaps in the creative process, and promising new directions. The framework is also a powerful tool for managers to use to better understand the creative process and structure feedback.

The framework also provides a natural platform for designing creativity exercises that help individuals experience and reflect upon the creative process in a learning environment. These can include individual as well as group exercises, presentations, and discussions. Indeed an entire curriculum can be built around the framework.[1]

In this chapter I outline some of the exercises and approaches I have developed that employ the framework to structure education about the creative process and support creative engagement. I draw upon my experience teaching creativity and innovation at Yale and in workshops.

Essentially I present a creativity inventory. It includes questions for reflecting upon and evaluating one's creative process, as well as exercises to orient engagement and help produce positive creative outcomes. This takes us again through the main elements and core creative process I have described in previous chapters, but this time from the point of view of assisting individuals in their creative engagement.

There are many facets to creativity and a variety of approaches that can help individuals learn to be creative. The framework in this book works best coupled with complementary approaches, including addressing psychological blockages, helping individuals access their unconscious and emotionally playful sides, and providing a supportive social environment. In my class I incorporate all of these different approaches and find that different students respond most strongly to different approaches.

I organize this chapter in terms of the basic building blocks of the creative process described through the book: context; forming productive guiding conceptions and guiding principles; the core creative process of generating high-potential-value seeds that are developed into high-value creative projects; iterating to form updated, evolved guiding conceptions, and reflecting on one's creative path; and the nature and development of creative fields. Last, I discuss how the framework can help structure the management of creativity.

CONTEXT

The contexts in which we pursue creativity are large and rich. This poses challenges for creativity, but also provides opportunities. Because creativity is not customarily thought of as happening in large-scale contexts the way I describe it in this book, most individuals and managers do not make the connection between the rich, large-scale nature of context and the nature of creative engagement. The failure to make this connection has several consequences.

First, there is a tendency to focus too narrowly too quickly, which can lead to missed opportunities and failure to make wider creative connections. Sometimes this narrowing of focus is dictated by career concerns, even by an advisor or manager. Hans Krebs's case is illustrative. If he had focused solely on extending the ongoing work in Warburg's lab, he would not have made the creative connection between the manometric tissue slice methods he was learning and the emerging field of intermediary metabolism. Interestingly, Warburg actively discouraged Krebs from pursuing this connection, a good example of a manager not promoting the creativity of those under his guidance. Krebs was able to leave Warburg's lab within a few years, and this gave him the opportunity to pursue the connection he had recognized as a guiding conception. That was fortuitous, but it is not always possible, and managers will do better to encourage those they manage to consider the wider context, extending beyond the boundaries of their current work environment.

Second, there may be a failure to appreciate the richness of context. This can contribute to a narrow focus and lead to a failure to recognize potential creative connections that span widely over a person's context. We have seen examples in this book of individuals who made wide-spanning connections—not only Krebs, but also Steve Jobs finding inspiration for design from objects he encountered, and Albert Einstein reading David Hume's *Treatise of Human Nature* and connecting its ideas with the paradox he was struggling to resolve. There are many famous examples of this kind, showing that some individuals do this very well, exploiting the broader cultural context: for example, Picasso visited an African art exhibit and saw traditional tribal masks, which seems to have helped push him in his first steps toward cubism in his pioneering painting *Les Demoiselles d'Avignon*.[2] Many individuals may not do this so naturally, however, and may miss creative opportunities.

One approach to help individuals appreciate the richness and scope of their context and recognize wider opportunities is to ask them to perform an inventory of their context. Mapping their context, not necessarily completely systematically but sufficiently well so as to be able to see that there are many different parts to it and innumerable elements, can help them begin thinking about wider creative connections that can spawn productive guiding conceptions. I believe individuals entering a field and learning about it often do tend to think more broadly about what they are learning. Virginia Woolf, for example, clearly had an encyclopedic knowledge of English (and not just English!) literature and undoubtedly would run over this in her mind, just as she describes in "The Mark on the Wall"—thinking about Shakespeare and other authors, seeing patterns, connections, and, ultimately, opportunity. However, many individuals may be too narrow in thinking about what they have learned. There may be a tendency not to integrate and not to consider the wider span, including ideas and works they may have heard about but do not know well. Woolf surely was broad: she integrated her literary acumen with broader cultural currents she had been exposed to as part of the Bloomsbury circle and through experiencing the great social and cultural shifts of the first years of the twentieth century, and also—perhaps more unconsciously—with her personal experiences of loss and challenging relationship with her father.

Mapping context visually can be helpful in terms of perceiving the breadth of context. I have done this for both Clifford Possum's and Hans Krebs's contexts in Figures 4 and 5. As I have discovered developing these visualizations, in the course of developing a visual mapping one perceives connections and patterns of connections that one was not aware of previously. While in my case I have used this to gain greater understanding about someone else's creative development, when someone maps their own context, they can gain insights about their own development and potential interconnections. In my experience individuals enjoy mapping out their context once they engage with the task. But there is work involved to produce these visual maps, and that can produce resistance. Mentors and managers can help by providing encouragement and space for individuals and teams to engage in this activity. Providing a checklist in terms of areas and life stages to think through can be helpful. The end result—a person's or team's visual map of their context, manifesting its breadth and richness—can be both surprising and empowering. Individuals working in larger organizations can also work to map out the context of the organization, which will bridge multiple parts of the organization and reveal rich interconnections.

Overall, thinking about context can be helpful for creative engagement in several ways. It can help us appreciate the richness and breadth of our context, perceive creative opportunities we may have missed, and identify areas we would like to explore and learn more about, "gaps" in our context we believe it would be productive to explore and possibly exploit.

GUIDING CONCEPTIONS AND GUIDING PRINCIPLES

The key lesson of this book is that in large-scale contexts, guidance is essential to achieve successful creative outcomes. I have described two kinds of constructs that provide guidance, guiding conceptions and guiding principles. The examples in this book show that some individuals develop these forms of guidance intuitively. But others struggle, as I have found in helping individuals learn about creativity and unlock their own creative potential.

In my creativity class I have students engage in a guiding conception exercise, in which they formulate a guiding conception of their own. My instructions for this exercise are shown in Figure 21. Note that I encourage students to think freely and imaginatively. I emphasize that they should not worry about what is possible, which can be overly confining and shut down creativity, but rather should "dream big" and focus

Imagine and describe a guiding conception for yourself, following our discussion in class and examples we have discussed. This might be, for example, a creative theme or imaginative conception you would like to develop creatively, topics you would like to find ways to combine, or a creative challenge or aspiration. Remember to think in broad terms but also to provide some creative details, like Virginia Woolf did. Remember the best guiding conceptions are original, your interest and conception–Jack Dorsey wasn't thinking about social media when he developed his. The best conceptions have both some details and originality, so they are novel and provide some guidance. Be imaginative, don't be constrained by what is "possible" or what you know at this moment–think beyond that, to what would be great if you could find a way to develop it.

Finally, think about the origins of your conception: What sparked it, when and why, and are there ways you have been learning about it and pursuing it, on your own or as part of a job or with others?

FIGURE 21. GUIDING CONCEPTION ASSIGNMENT

on imagining what they would love to create, leaving constraints aside. This is one of the key benefits of guiding conceptions: rather than trying to find the perfect creative idea immediately, it is often advantageous to put less pressure on oneself and initially focus on imagining what one hopes to create more abstractly without worrying about details. Thinking more generally can help one leverage one's intuition about the kind of creative outcome/product one hopes to produce—for intuition, as so many of the examples in this book have demonstrated, often functions on this higher, more abstract level. As part of the exercise I also ask students to reflect on how their guiding conception has developed, its antecedents and personal history. This helps them think about creativity as not just an isolated moment of creative thinking but a path unfolding over time; it also helps them build a sense of their own creative identity. Before this assignment I present examples of guiding conceptions, including several I have discussed in this book such as Virginia Woolf's vision of a literature based on reflections and Jack Dorsey's conception of a mobile platform that would make it possible to provide friends with status updates in real time.

I have found that students respond to this exercise creatively. They produce guiding conceptions, sometimes surprising themselves in the process by recognizing creative passions and areas to develop that they have perhaps not recognized so consciously previously. Thinking at the more abstract level so deliberately for creative guidance is new to many of them, and the ones who embrace it find it liberating. Others struggle with the assignment; in these cases I usually ask them to try again, because they especially need to work on this phase of the creative process. Of course this is a class assignment, and most of the guiding conceptions do not embody the kind of field- or cultural-level creativity of the guiding conception examples in this book. But they illustrate the approach and how it can forge a path forward. Many students pursue their guiding conception in their class project, which provides further insight about how guiding conceptions relate to downstream creative projects.

There are two main difficulties individuals seem to have with the guiding conception exercise. Some individuals form guiding conceptions that are very narrow; they articulate a very tightly defined creative project, rather than a broader conception. This may be due to anxiety and low confidence, or limited experience. When a student does this, when possible I ask them to redo the exercise and try to become broader, more ambitious, freer in their thinking. The second difficulty is feeling unable to formulate a guiding conception at all. This is related to the general problem that some individuals don't think they can be creative. I prefer not to let this stand but to push a student to try. My approach with these students is to open up a dialogue with them. I ask them to think about their interests, important work and personal experiences, and recent presentations or readings that sparked their interest. With encouragement, and some guidance, usually they are able to take the step of formulating a guiding conception and at least feel a sense of satisfaction in having been able to take this step.

A companion exercise asks individuals to articulate guiding principles they believe are important and want their creative work to adhere to. Again it is best to present examples first, such as design principles or the principle of relativity Albert Einstein was so deeply committed to. If anything this exercise is easier for most individuals, since guiding principles are more familiar as a construct. One issue is to help individuals recognize which guiding principles they are most deeply committed to, as opposed to parroting principles that are popular in their industry or field but may actually resonate less with them.

As noted, in parallel with the exercises I also educate about guidance and its role in creative practice. Examples of highly successful creatives who have used guidance helps people appreciate the value of guidance, which motivates them to work on developing their own and help others to do so. I also outline how guiding conceptions function to help generate creativity—not in as much detail as I have done in this book, but in enough detail to help individuals grasp how guiding conceptions and principles fit in the larger creative process. The standard view of creativity as the province of "genius" and something that happens in a flash has to be overturned in order for individuals to be able to work on developing their own creative process and support others. Teaching the framework together with examples and exercises helps achieve this.

CORE CREATIVE PROCESS

In a classroom or workshop setting, once guiding conceptions and principles have been introduced individuals can be unleashed on creative projects. In my class I have students engage in both shorter-term (one week) and longer-term projects. I ask them to generate project ideas rooted in guiding conceptions and then go from there. My students are amazing at these creative activities, and I think even surprise themselves with the creativity that emerges. There is no better way to learn about creativity and how to manage it than to engage in creative activities. It is also better for the projects to be "low stakes," like a class assignment or exercise, as then individuals are freer to try a new approach.

A common mistake novices make is to commit to an early project idea too quickly. This can shut down promising alternatives that would emerge later in the process and can restrict revisions that may be critical for attaining a strong creative outcome. The model of this book can help individuals address this issue in two ways. First, focusing on how guiding conceptions are associated with seed pools that can spawn many initial project ideas can help individuals appreciate that they can have not just one but many project ideas and select the most promising to pursue. I believe the image of a "seed pool" can be helpful in this regard, suggesting a rich pool of potential ideas. It is also helpful for individuals to understand the importance of forming a high-potential guiding conception, which is the conduit to a great project. This approach emphasizes that creativity unfolds in multiple steps: the lesson is to focus more on guiding conception development and not just on specific project ideas.

Second, the model emphasizes using guiding principles to find critical "missing pieces" to revise and complete projects, and this can help individuals embrace the need for revisions and execute successful revisions. Novices often do not appreciate how much scope there is to revise an incipient project. In my class at Yale I devote a class session and exercises to the revision process, providing many examples of experienced creators—for example, Steve Jobs and authors such as Hemingway, Morrison, and Faulkner—who have stated in strong terms how crucial the revision process is. The examples are motivating, but even with them novices often remain quite timid in the revisions they are willing to consider: they are too willing to accept a project as "good enough" and not willing to try harder to improve it. Having a clear guiding principle that they are committed to can help individuals engage more fully in the revision process, the way Steve Jobs brought his guiding principle of simplicity to bear on Apple projects. A guiding principle, strongly and clearly stated, is hard to "get around" and will make flaws more glaringly apparent. This can be critical in helping individuals realize the need for changes. Further, a guiding principle is motivating of change: individuals want their projects to live up to the high standards their guiding principles set.

Individuals will benefit from engaging repeatedly in the core creative cycle of using their guiding conceptions to spawn seed ideas and then using their guiding principles to develop seed ideas into full projects. As they do this repeatedly, they begin to appreciate in a deeper way that creativity truly is a process and that this core cycle is central to creative engagement.

REFLECTION

Another facet of supporting individuals in their creative endeavors is helping them reflect on their creative engagement. This is yet another aspect of the creative process that many individuals and organizations overlook. There is often a desire to forget about past creative efforts, especially if they are not viewed as having been successful. Yet in reality we can learn a great deal from reflecting on our creative engagements and especially our failures. It is important to emphasize this and mentor individuals to recognize the importance of slowing down to reflect on their creative past, as a way to improve in the future.

Reflection can focus on short-term as well as long-term creative engagement. Reflection on relatively short-term recent engagements can help pinpoint sources of project failures and successes. Sometimes failure is simply a random outcome, and one should just try again with the same process, just as in the model of this book some seeds spawned by a guiding conception, even one that is based on sound intuition, do not spawn successful projects, while others do. Other times, however, failure is due to a more systemic failure of process. Examples of this include not forming a sufficiently creative, well-defined guiding conception; making the classic novice mistake of pursuing an initial project idea rather than exploring multiple potential seeds; and not being strict enough in conforming with a guiding principle and pushing hard to revise a project repeatedly. Reflection on recent project processes and outcomes can help identify these kinds of issues. A great way to help individuals and teams engage with this kind of reflection is to offer them questions as prompts:

- Looking back, did you have a sound, sufficiently creative and well-defined guiding conception?
- Did you jump to pursue an early project idea, even if perhaps you were aware it might have flaws, rather than generating multiple project ideas?
- Did you work hard enough to revise and improve your project? Did you conform strictly enough to your guiding principles and live up to their high standards?

Considering these questions can help an individual or team become aware of failings in their process, which they may not have recognized, and this awareness can in turn be a key step toward correcting the deficiency.

Project postmortems have become a standard of best practice in many organizations.[3] This is an excellent practice to follow. However, it is important to recognize that, although a project focus clearly can be useful, it can also be helpful to conduct a postmortem more broadly on a set of recent projects. This is especially valuable for identifying larger failures of process. A single guiding conception may have spawned several projects, and examining the results of these projects collectively may make it readily apparent that the guiding conception was flawed in some way, or that opportunities to form even more creative guiding conceptions—for example spanning organizational boundaries—have been missed. Likewise, issues with applying guiding principles may be more apparent when a set of projects are evaluated jointly. A standard I would suggest is engaging in postmortems regularly both on single projects and sets of projects.

Reflection on longer-term creative journeys is also valuable and not done as regularly as it should be. It is probably most natural to engage in this kind of reflection at certain junctures, including at the conclusion of a large project or a series of projects that have been pursued under the guidance of a common guiding conception, or when one has hit a rough patch creatively and is feeling either at sea or frustrated.

There are several different ways reflection on longer-term creative development can be beneficial. Oftentimes as we embark on a creative journey, we do not realize we will travel as far as we ultimately do. Reflection on our creative journey helps us appreciate how much we've grown and learned.[4] Conversely, reflection may also reveal ways we are unnecessarily limiting ourselves. For example, an artist may take years to recognize that they have stayed with a certain approach longer than necessary.[5]

Reflecting on our journey in comparison with our field and how it has changed can also be illuminating. We may have stayed too close to some paradigm that is no longer as central to our field. Or we may have wandered very far from our field's core activity and must either accept this or shift our focus back. Steve Jobs left Apple, and then arguably was a better manager, with more insight about Apple's vision, clearly linked with his own guiding principles, on his return in the late 1990s. Returning, having had some different experiences, may have helped him gain a larger perspective. This may have helped him recognize that Apple was not holding true to its guiding principles, at least as he understood them; it also may have helped him recognize emerging trends. He thus could help Apple surge forward with the iPod, linking music with computers, and then with the iPhone.

Reflection on one's creative journey can also help trigger shifts in direction. For example, reflection may contribute toward the evolution of a person's guiding conception, which can be quite important for moving forward on their creative journey. Although Virginia Woolf did not explicitly mention reflection on her own journey, it seems clear that "The Mark on the Wall" was a kind of reflection on her own journey and wanting to identify a new direction forward.

Thus reflection can contribute to improving creative engagement and outcomes in multiple ways. It can be supported with structured reflection exercises like postmortems or more personal inventories on creative trajectories. It can also be encouraged by having more experienced creative individuals model it for less experienced individuals. Teaching my students about Virginia Woolf and Albert Einstein—their long, rich, creative journeys and the kinds of reflection they engaged in—helps the students appreciate the value of this kind of thought process.

MANAGEMENT OF CREATIVITY

A manager who has internalized the lessons of this book and applies them can be more effective in managing creativity. Management has not been the focus of this book, and it is not my purpose here to discuss the management of creativity in the kind of depth it deserves. It is a large field of study with many different approaches and much active work, as evidenced by the recent Edward Elgar *Handbook of Research on Creativity and Innovation*, which contains discussions of different facets of this field as well as creativity more generally.[6] It is, however, useful to outline some of the ways that the framework in this book may help managers manage the creative process.

There are two important components to supporting management of creativity. One is to educate managers about the creative process. In terms of the framework of this book, this means educating managers about the different elements: context, especially its scope and richness; the role of guiding conceptions and guiding principles; the core two-step model—not in technical terms, but as a conceptual framework; and discussion of longer creative journeys and creative fields. Case studies are a very useful device for this, just as I have used in this book. Having managers engage in some of the exercises discussed in earlier sections of this chapter, such as articulating a guiding conception and guiding principles, is a way for them to engage with the concepts. Also, having them reflect on their own experiences in their industry or field and how their experiences connect with the framework is valuable. The aim is to help managers develop a more systematic, structured framework for thinking about and managing the creative process.

Once managers have grasped the framework, the second key component is helping them introduce the framework to those they manage and help these individuals work on improving their creative engagement. Exercises like those described in earlier sections in this chapter can be a good way to introduce these ideas. Retreats and workshops provide a forum for this—providing the opportunity to explore creativity in a way that is linked to work activities but also freer—not tied to specific ongoing projects with deadlines. This can help individuals engage creatively and come to recognize their own creativity.

Best practice combines direct learning, experience applying the framework, and reflection. Here is an example outline of how this might be done.

Session 1: An organization might begin by holding a retreat or workshop in which individuals first reflect on their creative journeys thus far, and then are introduced to the framework as a way to structure their creative engagement. Participants are asked to formulate a guiding conception of their own, and then given time before the next session to explore their guiding conception and generate seed project ideas.

Session 2: Participants present seed ideas and garner feedback from the group. Then they explore using their guiding principles to evaluate seeds and select a seed to pursue. They are given time before the next session to develop their seed as far as they can as an incipient project.

Session 3: Participants present their projects or at least more complete project outlines for discussion. This is followed by time for reflection on the activity, a kind of postmortem. This should include comparing creative engagement in this workshop activity to other work activities and projects, as a way to learn about how to improve creative engagement more broadly at work.

This cycle can be repeated, and over time the cycle of creative engagement will be instilled, both at the level of learning but also on the level of active engagement. This kind of holistic approach, encouraging interconnections among direct learning, engagement, and reflection, is powerful. It will serve to enrich the organization's culture around creative practice.

The role of guidance in the creative process is naturally aligned with management. Managers think of themselves as providing guidance for their organization. But they may not have recognized the importance of guidance for creative activities. Helping them recognize the important role of guidance for creativity empowers them. This provides them a way to help others gain a greater appreciation for guidance in creativity—for example communicating guiding principles clearly and forcefully as Steve Jobs did at Apple. They can also hold discussions with teams and individuals about their guiding conceptions, helping them develop conceptions with greater creative potential and align their conceptions with organizational values and objectives.

Thus the framework in this book can empower managers, while also enabling them to empower those they work with. One important challenge is that creativity takes time, and many creative journeys are quite long, as shown by many of the case studies in this book. In direct contrast, in many organizations there is much time pressure and demand for short-term creative results. The better managers understand the creative process, the better they can navigate and negotiate between these competing demands in the service of helping individuals be more creative. Individuals will surely feel better about their work when they feel they are supported in their creativity. Supporting individuals in their creative engagement, and providing time for them to be creative, can in turn boost innovation at the organization level.

Overall, the framework in this book is aligned with management and I believe can enhance creative practice in organizations. In many ways it fits with existing best practices, such as postmortems, but it also adds to these, bringing new elements and structure. It is my hope organizations will learn to use it creatively and well.

CONCLUSION: THE PATH FORWARD

While the main purpose of this book is to present a new approach for modeling creativity in large-scale contexts, it has a second purpose as well. I remain committed to the vision I set forth in the epilogue of my first book: *to develop a rigorous modeling framework able to depict each individual's rich, distinctive conceptual world and life path, while also having sufficient structure and scope to be able to include all individuals in a common framework.* I have taken some steps toward realizing that vision—but much more remains to be done.

In this book I have provided a framework for modeling the context in which individuals create. My approach models contexts as networks and captures the key feature of hierarchy with vertical links that link broader and more abstract concepts with more specific elements. The contexts in which individuals create are large scale, as I have emphasized. They are also rich in structure. This richness is partly objective but also subjective, as each individual has their own network of associations and distinct pattern of connections, even with respect to elements shared in common with others. In comparison with this rich structure, the network models in this book are quite rudimentary. Thus one key path ahead is to develop better models of context that capture more of the structural richness, subjectivity, and detail of the contexts in which individuals live, develop, and create. I have discussed some approaches to modeling richer contexts in Chapter 16, but there is still a long way to go.

I have argued and shown with examples throughout this book that the vertical structure of context provides the basis for guidance. Guidance structures—guiding conceptions and principles—provide conceptual focus and clarity for individuals as they dive down into the thicket of details and possibilities. My focus in this book is how guidance operates to develop creative projects. More broadly, guidance also functions to guide individuals as they explore and learn, traveling creative paths and building up their contexts. This is a lifelong process, dynamic, building on itself, with periods of continuity and periods of change, as discussed in earlier chapters. In turn, this dynamic process links to the issue of the richness and individuality of contexts. For it is through this dynamic lifelong process that over time individuals develop highly individualized contexts different from all others, even those in their same cohort and field. Thus a second key path ahead is to extend the model to incorporate this dynamic process.

Of course there are many approaches that are relevant for modeling individual life paths and conceptual worlds, including neuroscience, cognitive and developmental psychology, and biography. Ideally these different approaches should complement one another and both inform and be informed by the kind of modeling approach I envision. How does the kind of modeling I envision fit in this larger landscape?

First, modeling should as much as possible be linked with empirical evidence. I have oriented my modeling approach in that direction in this book, but the connection needs to be—and I am convinced can be—made tighter. This requires both more empirical data and building context structures that align as closely as possible with the empirical data. As an example, we have a good deal of information about Virginia Woolf's context and activities, and the challenge is to represent this formally as a context and describe how her context developed over time.

Second, modeling can be used, perhaps in combination with other approaches, to investigate many questions about life paths, creativity, and the development of creative fields. A dynamic model can be used to explore how life paths unfold and how context and its structure influence these paths—a truly fascinating topic. A dynamic model can also be used to explore how individuals shape their contexts through the choices they make and projects they undertake. A model depicting multiple individuals, with overlapping contexts, can be used to explore how creative fields develop through the joint activity of many individuals.

The model I envision is large scale and rich in structure. Fortunately with the large-scale computing power available today, it is feasible to construct this kind of model. Thus I am convinced that with focus, effort, and creativity, much progress can be made.

I am convinced also that, beyond the specific aims I have outlined, richer models of individual life paths, including life activities, life events, conceptual learning, and creativity, will enrich our understanding of the human condition. We will develop a deeper appreciation for the richness of a human life path when we can see its complexity and development visualized before us. We will also appreciate the diversity of life paths and experiences, and how this diversity contributes to the richness and creativity of human society. There is much to be done and much understanding still to come!

ACKNOWLEDGMENTS

Many people helped me develop my ideas and write this book, and I am grateful for their support, advice, and insights. My brother David inspired me to develop the formal model that is at the heart of this book. This is the second time in my life that his example has helped me pursue developing my ideas (the first was in college), and I am grateful to him for providing inspiration at these critical junctures. His inspiration stands out amid the many facets of our not always simple relationship. My sister Susan and her husband, Randy, read an early draft of this book and provided many helpful suggestions that helped me clarify how to organize the book and simplify the exposition. My friend Terry was, as always, a thoughtful reader and listener. She has helped me pursue the development of my ideas over these many years, and I am very grateful for her friendship and support. My wife, Leslie, and my daughters, Sara and Ariel, heard much about the book along its journey to completion. They shared many valuable comments and were always on my side.

Many colleagues provided useful comments about my project, helping me clarify my thinking and focus. Liane Gabora has been a valuable colleague for a number of years. Her quick mind, store of knowledge, insights, and appreciation of my intellectual agenda have been of great value to me. Glenn Dutcher and Cortney Rodet share my interest in creativity and how it intersects with economic thinking and modeling, and provided many valuable comments, including both during and after my virtual seminar at Ohio University in the winter of 2022. Petra Moser also shares my interest in creativity and its intersection with economic modeling, and I always benefit from her perspective. Benno Torgler has been a wonderful colleague to get to know and a wonderful host at Queensland University in Brisbane where I presented some early versions of these ideas in December 2019. We have spoken often and freely about creativity and related issues, and he has provided many valuable insights and references. I have also presented earlier versions of these ideas at the Southern Oregon University Creativity Conference, which is always so enjoyable and informative. Michael Barzelay has been supportive, invited me for a wonderful visit at the London School of Economics and Political Science, and has shared with me a number of useful references to related books and papers. Although I have not spoken with Matthew Rabin specifically about the model in this book, I have always valued our conversations as we share a common interest in building bridges linking economics more deeply with the other behavioral and social sciences. Likewise I have not discussed this book directly with Craig Alexander, but I have always appreciated the bond we share and our shared interest in human culture and its development. Colleagues present and former here at the Yale School of Management have also been supportive and provided valuable comments. Olav Sorenson saw me present a precursor to the model in this book, and his support and comments were helpful as I developed my ideas further. Jidong Zhou read an outline of an earlier model, and his reactions helped me appreciate the need to focus on a more structured model of creativity. Ed Kaplan doesn't study creativity himself, but I always benefit from our conversations. Other colleagues including Stan Garstka (who has especially encouraged my art), Will Goetzmann, Peter Schott, Arthur Campbell (now at Monash), and Kyle Jensen have been supportive each in their own way. A number of former colleagues provided encouragement and support during the earlier stages of my creativity journey, including the two Joels—Joel Demski and Joel Podolny—Dave Baron, Sharon Oster, and Sigal Barsade.

Producing this book has involved collaboration with many individuals, and I am grateful for their contributions. Cathy Cornish did wonderful work on the figures for this book. She was professional, creative, and a pleasure to work with. Steve Dionne did an admirable job on the tables and also was a pleasure to work with. This is my second book with Stanford University Press, and I am very grateful for the relationships I have forged and the opportunity to publish my work with such an outstanding press. My acquisitions editor Steve Catalano was enthusiastic from the very first email exchange we had when I submitted my proposal, and I am grateful for his strong support. Steve helped move the project along efficiently and helped it stay "on mission," as he put it. Kate Wahl served as my editor in the final stages of manuscript development, and I am grateful to her for stepping in to fill this role among her many obligations. This is the second time I have worked with Kate, and she is simply stellar. I thank her for her amazing editorial acumen that has made this book better in many ways, as well as her organization and efficiency in moving my manuscript along. Thank you also to editorial assistant Cindy Lim for staying with this project and helping it move forward through the many stages to publication. Thank you also to Richard Narramore who joined the project for its final phase and helped see it through to publication. The reviewers of my initial proposal and full manuscript at SUP provided many extremely helpful comments and suggestions. I have incorporated many of these, and, even beyond this, the reviewers' perspectives have helped shape the book. Finally, the production team at the press led by Chris Peterson has done an amazing job producing this book just as they did for my first book; I thank them for their excellent work. Thanks also to the team at Newgen led by Charlie Clark and the copy editor Kristine Hunt for their excellent work on this project. For their marketing efforts on behalf of the book I thank the SUP marketing team and the Yale SOM Media Relations team.

APPENDIX

In this Appendix to Chapter 10 I outline the bounding argument to compute the lower bound on the number of valid seeds in a network, the lower bound on the number of valid projects, and, from these, the lower bound on the number of seeds that must be investigated in order to cover one-half the lower bound number of projects. The discussion here builds on the discussion in the main text, and I do not duplicate parts of the argument presented there.

Recall the network: there are two layers, top and bottom; the number of top elements is N and the number of bottom elements is mN; N is assumed to be large and m is fixed. There are l top elements that have high degree, ranked so that the first has highest degree; the degree of element i in this set is approximately (up to integer constraint) $\theta_i mN$ where θ_i is a fraction. The remaining top elements each have degree no greater than k, where k is fixed or grows sufficiently slowly with N. All bottom elements have number of parents no greater than h, where h is fixed or grows sufficiently slowly with N. Define $\bar{\theta}$ to be the fraction of bottom elements that have links to at least one of the high-degree top elements. $\bar{\theta}$ is assumed to be bounded by a number smaller than 1.0.

Visualize the bottom elements as arrayed along a line from 1 to mN—see Figure 15 in the main text (p. 168). The bottom elements that are linked to high-degree top elements are placed on the left-hand side of the line and the remainder are placed on the right-hand side, with $\bar{\theta}mN$ the division point (as noted in Chapter 10, if this value is not an integer, place the boundary at the smallest integer above it). Define region I to be the line segment to the left of this boundary and region II to be the segment to the right. In terms of computing a lower bound on the number of valid seeds, which then extends to a lower bound on the minimum number of valid projects, the worst case is when there is just a single high-degree top element that has links to every bottom element in region I (this is noted originally in Chapter 10 and in particular footnote 16 of that chapter). The reason this is the worst case is that none of the pairs of bottom elements in which both elements lie in region I is a valid seed. In contrast, when there is more than one high-degree top element with links into this region, then some of the pairs of bottom elements in this region may be valid. Thus, assuming all other aspects of the network are the same, the assumption of a single high-degree top element will yield the smallest lower bound. Note in justification of this that I do not use in the argument any restriction on the number of top elements with links into region II, so that the exact number of top elements not of high degree is irrelevant to the argument—all that is relevant is that N is large whereas l is fixed and small compared with N.

For convenience, let $I \times I$ denote the set of valid seed pairs for which both members come from region I—as just stated, assume a single high-degree element, therefore this set is empty. Let $I \times II$ denote the set of valid seed pairs for which one member comes from region I and the other from region II. Finally, let $II \times II$ denote the set of valid seed pairs for which both members come from region II. I compute bounds on the number of elements (valid seed pairs) in each of these last two sets.

Consider the set $I \times II$. Elements in II do not have the high-degree top element as parent by construction. However, elements in I may have parents other than the high-degree top element that in turn have children in II. Each such I element has at most $h-1$ other parents, and each of these has at most $k-1$ other children. Thus, considered from the viewpoint of linking each element in I to valid partners in II, the number of elements in this set is at least as large as:

$$V_{I \times II} = mN\bar{\theta}\left[mN(1-\bar{\theta}) - (h-1)(k-1)\right]$$

Note that for large N and fixed h and k values, as long as $\bar{\theta}$ is bounded away from 1, this value will be large and scales with N^2. Now consider pairing each element in II with valid partners in I, the opposite approach. Each element in II has h parents and each of these has $k-1$ other children. In the worst case scenario for this calculation, all of these children reside in I. Thus, under that worst case, as a lower bound, the number of elements in this set is at least as large:

$$V_{II \times I} = mN(1-\bar{\theta})\left[mN\bar{\theta} - h(k-1)\right]$$

Note again that for fixed h and k and $\bar{\theta}$ bounded away from 1, this is also on order N^2. The overall lower bound for the minimum number of valid pairs for $I \times II$ is the greater of these two bounds since it must be larger than both. ($V_{I \times II}$ is greater when $\bar{\theta} > \frac{h}{2h-1}$.) For calculations I compute both and use the larger. Note also that if $\bar{\theta} = 0$, meaning there is no top element with more children than k, then region I is null and the calculation for $I \times II$ is not relevant.

Now consider the set $II \times II$. Each element in II has at most h parents, and each of these has at most $k-1$ other children (the high-degree top element cannot be one of these parents). In the worst case scenario for this calculation, all of these children also lie in II. Thus the number of valid partners is at least as large as $mN(1-\bar{\theta}) - h(k-1)$. Thus the number of elements in this set is at least as large as:

$$V_{II \times II} = \frac{1}{2}mN(1-\bar{\theta})\left[mN(1-\bar{\theta}) - h(k-1)\right]$$

where note the division by 2 because each valid pair is counted twice. As above, for h and k fixed, $\bar{\theta}$ bounded away from 1, and N large, this quantity scales with N^2. If there are no high-degree top elements, as in a random network, this expression simplifies to $(1/2)mN[mN - h(k-1)]$.

The overall bound for the minimum number of valid seeds is $V_{II \times II}$ plus the maximum of $V_{I \times II}$ and $V_{II \times I}$. Table 4 in the main text shows this value for two representative networks, the first of which corresponds with the large-scale random simulated networks, the second of which has a large hub.

Now consider the lower bound on the number of valid projects. I compute this starting from the bound on the number of valid seeds, since this is the smallest number of pairs that can be expanded into a triplet for a full project. I then compute, for each of $V_{I \times II}$, $V_{II \times I}$, and $V_{II \times II}$, the minimum number of valid projects each set can be expanded into.

Given that there is assumed to be a single high-degree element that links to all elements in I, the only valid project sets are $I \times II \times II$ and $II \times II \times II$.

Consider the set $I \times II \times II$. The set can be computed two ways, as the minimum $I \times II$ set crossed with II, and alternatively as the minimum $II \times II$ set crossed with I. Consider the first approach. Each seed in $I \times II$ has one element in I and one element in II. Elements in I have at most $h - 1$ parents that have children in II, each of which can have at most $k - 1$ other children. Elements in II have at most h parents that have children in II, each of which can have at most $k - 1$ other children. Thus for each valid seed pair in $I \times II$, the number of valid third element partners from II is at least as large as $mN(1 - \bar{\theta}) - (h - 1)(k - 1) - h(k - 1)$. Viewed this way, and recognizing that each triplet is counted two ways (its two elements in II can have either order, one being in the initial $I \times II$ and the other added, or vice versa), the number of elements in this set computed using this approach is at least as large as:

$$V_{I \times II \times II} = \frac{1}{2} Max[V_{I \times II}, V_{II \times I}] \left[mN(1 - \bar{\theta}) - (h - 1)(k - 1) - h(k - 1) \right]$$

Using the second approach starts from the minimum number of valid seed pairs in $II \times II$, $V_{II \times II}$. Each element in such a pair has at most h parents, and each of these has at most $k - 1$ other children, which in the worst case for this calculation all reside in region I. Thus the number of elements in the set computed this way is at least as large as:

$$V_{II \times II \times I} = V_{II \times II}\left[mN\bar{\theta} - 2h(k-1)\right]$$

The minimum number of projects for projects that join one I element with two II elements is then the maximum of $V_{I \times II \times II}$ and $V_{II \times II \times I}$.

New consider the set $II \times II \times II$. Start with the minimum number of valid pairs $V_{II \times II}$. For each such pair, each element has at most h parents, each of which has at most $k-1$ other children, which in the worst case for this calculation all reside in region II. Thus the number of elements in this set is at least as large as:

$$\frac{1}{3}V_{II \times II}\left[mN(1 - \bar{\theta} - 2h(k-1)\right]$$

Note the division by 3 because each triplet shows up in three different orders (note that, denoting the triplet (a, b, c), the double counting of (a, b) and (b, a) has already been addressed so there is just effectively one of these; the three possible orderings are then (a, b) with c, (a, c) with b, or (b, c) with a).

The minimum bound on the total number of valid projects is then $V_{II \times II \times II}$ plus the maximum of $V_{I \times II \times II}$ and $V_{II \times II \times I}$. This minimum bound is also given in Table 4 in the main text for the representative networks for which it has been calculated.

One final note is that for these calculations, h and k fixed is not really required to show that the minimum bounds on the number of valid seeds and projects is large for networks with large N. Looking at the formulas, what is required is that the product hk grows slower than linearly in N. For example, if h grows at N^{α_h} and k grows at N^{α_k} what is required is that the product grows slower than linearly, hence $\alpha_h + \alpha_k$ is a fixed value smaller than 1—for example, each is below square-root level.

NOTES

INTRODUCTION

1. See Alex Fornito, Andrew Zalesky, and Edward Bullmore, *Fundamentals of Brain Network Analysis*, 2016, Academic Press, for an edited volume discussing the brain and its analysis as a network.

2. See Liane Gabora, "Honing Theory: A Complex Systems Framework for Creativity," 2017, *Nonlinear Dynamics, Psychology, and Life Sciences*, Vol. 21, No. 1, pp. 35–88; Liane Gabora and Diederik Aerts, "A Model of the Emergence and Evolution of Integrated Worldviews," 2010, *Journal of Mathematical Psychology*, Vol. 53, No. 5, pp. 434–51; Jonathan S. Feinstein, *The Nature of Creative Development*, 2006, Stanford University Press, especially Chapter 2. For templates see my discussion in Chapter 3, and for creative vision my discussion in Chapter 9.

3. See Henri Poincaré, *Science and Method*, trans. F. Maitland, 1952 (originally published 1924 in French), Dover, especially pp. 52–53; Graham Wallas, *The Art of Thought*, 1926, Harcourt, Brace and Company. Wallas's description actually involved more detail than is typically discussed: see Eugene Sadler-Smith, "Wallas' Four-Stage Model of the Creative Process: More than Meets the Eye?," 2015, *Creativity Research Journal*, Vol. 27, No. 4, pp. 342–52.

4. R. Keith Sawyer, *Explaining Creativity: The Science of Human Innovation*, 2006, Oxford University Press; James C. Kaufman and Robert J. Sternberg, *The Cambridge Handbook of Creativity*, 2019, Cambridge University Press.

5. Mihaly Csikszentmihalyi, *The Systems Model of Creativity: The Collected Works of Mihaly Csikszentmihalyi*, 2014, Springer, especially Chapter 4, "Society, Culture, and Person: A Systems View of Creativity"; Pierre Bourdieu, *Distinction: A Social Critique of the Judgement of Taste*, 1984, Harvard University Press.

6. Subrata Dasgupta, *A Cognitive Historical Approach to Creativity*, 2019, Routledge.

7. Robert J. Sternberg, "A Propulsion Model of Types of Creative Contributions," 1999, *Review of General Psychology*, Vol. 3, pp. 83–100; Robert J. Sternberg, James C. Kaufman, and Jean E. Pretz, "The Propulsion Model of Creative Contributions Applied to the Arts and Letters," 2001, *Journal of Creative Behavior*, Vol. 35, pp. 75–101.

8. Ben Depoorter, Peter Menell, and David Schwartz, *Research Handbook on the Economics of Intellectual Property Law*, 2019, Edward Elgar, for intellectual property; Joel Mokyr, *The Gifts of Athena*, 2002, Princeton University Press; Petra Moser, "How Do Patent Laws Influence Innovation? Evidence from Nineteenth-Century World Fairs," 2005, *American Economic Review*, Volume 95, No. 4, pp. 1214–36.

9. Kenneth J. Arrow, "Economic Welfare and the Allocation of Resources for Invention," 1962, in *The Rate and Direction of Inventive Activity*, ed. R. Nelson, Princeton University Press, pp. 609–26.

10. Adam Jaffe, Manuel Trajtenberg, and Rebecca Henderson, "Geographic Localization of Knowledge Spillovers as Evidenced by Patent Citations," 1993, *Quarterly Journal of Economics*, Vol. 108, No. 3, pp. 577–98.

11. A good example is Zvi Griliches, "The Search for R&D Spillovers," 1992, *Scandinavian Journal of Economics*, Vol. 94, Supplement, pp. S29–47.

12. Matthew O. Jackson, *Social and Economic Networks*, 2010, Princeton University Press. Daron Acemoglu, Ufuk Akcigit, and William R. Kerr, "Innovation Network," 2016, *Proceedings of the National Academy of Sciences*, Vol. 113, No. 41, pp. 11483–8 do have a network orientation but quite different: they discuss innovation in terms of network links between industries that are based on input-output flows and hence production based.

13. Gabora, "Honing Theory: A Complex Systems Framework for Creativity"; Gabora and Aerts, "A Model of the Emergence and Evolution of Integrated Worldviews."

14. Steven M. Smith, Thomas B. Ward, and Ronald A. Finke, *The Creative Cognition Approach*, 1995, MIT Press.

15. Thomas B. Ward and Yuliya Kolomyts, "Creative Cognition," 2019, Chapter 9 in *The Cambridge Handbook of Creativity*, ed. J. Kaufman and R. Sternberg, Cambridge University Press. See also Victoria S. Scotney, Jasmine Schwartz, Nicole Carbert, Adam Saab, and Liane Gabora, "The Form of a

'Half-Baked' Creative Idea: Empirical Explorations into the Structure of Ill-Defined Mental Representations," 2020, *Acta Psychologica*, Vol. 203, 102981.

16. Max Wertheimer, *Productive Thinking*, 1945, Harper and Brothers.

17. Robert W. Weisberg, *Creativity: Beyond the Myth of Genius*, 1993, W. H. Freeman; and Robert W. Weisberg, *Creativity: Understanding Innovation in Problem Solving, Science, Invention, and the Arts*, 2006, John Wiley & Sons.

18. Gilles Fauconnier and Mark Turner, *The Way We Think: Conceptual Blending and the Mind's Hidden Complexities*, 2002, Basic Books.

19. Dedre Gentner, "Structure-Mapping: A Theoretical Framework for Analogy," 1983, *Cognitive Science*, Vol. 7, pp. 155–70; Adam Green, "Creativity, within Reason: Semantic Distance and Dynamic State Creativity in Relational Thinking and Reasoning," 2016, *Current Directions in Psychological Science*, Vol. 25, No. 1, pp. 28–35, links to cognitive neuroscience.

20. Howard E. Gruber, "Darwin's 'Tree of Nature' and Other Images of Wide Scope," 1978, in *On Aesthetics in Science*, ed. Judith Wechsler, MIT Press, pp. 121–40.

21. Mark A. Runco, *Problem Finding, Problem Solving, and Creativity*, 1994, Ablex.

22. Robert E. Evenson and Yoav Kislev, "A Stochastic Model of Applied Research," 1976, *Journal of Political Economy*, Vol. 84, No. 2, pp. 265–81; Samuel S. Kortum, "Research, Patenting, and Technological Change," 1997, *Econometrica*, Vol. 65, No. 6, pp. 1389–419.

23. Donald Campbell, "Blind Variation and Selective Retentions in Creative Thought as in Other Knowledge Processes," 1960, *Psychological Review*, Vol. 67, No. 6, pp. 380–400; Dean K. Simonton, "Scientific Creativity as Constrained Stochastic Behavior: The Integration of Product, Person, and Process Perspectives," 2003, *Psychological Bulletin*, Vol. 129, No. 4, pp. 475–94. Random combinations also figure in Poincaré's discussion in *Science and Method*.

24. Martin L. Weitzman, "Recombinant Growth," 1998, *Quarterly Journal of Economics*, Vol. 113, No. 2, pp. 331–60.

25. Jonathan S. Feinstein, "Optimal Learning Patterns for Creativity Generation in a Field," 2011, *American Economic Review, Papers & Proceedings*, Vol. 101, No. 3, pp. 227–32.

26. Cortney S. Rodet, "The Wellspring of Creativity? Using Divergent-Thinking Tasks to Understand Creative Characteristics," 2021, *Managerial and Decision Economics*, Vol. 42, No. 6, pp. 1435–53; E. Glenn Dutcher and Cortney S. Rodet, "Learning by Doing What? Learning and Knowledge Transfer in the Creative Domain," 2021, working paper, Ohio University.

27. Krishna Dasaratha, "Innovation and Strategic Network Formation," 2021, working paper; Ufuk Akcigit, Santiago Caicedo, Ernest Miguelez,

Stefanie Stantcheva, and Valerio Sterzi, "Dancing with the Stars: Innovation through Interactions," 2018, NBER Working Paper 24466; Michela Giorcelli and Petra Moser, "Copyrights and Creativity: Evidence from Italian Opera in the Napoleonic Age," 2020, *Journal of Political Economy*, Vol. 128, No. 11, pp. 4163–210.

28. John S. Mill, *On Liberty*, 1978 (originally published 1859), Hackett; Friedrich A. Hayek, *The Constitution of Liberty*, 1960, University of Chicago Press.

29. See as one noteworthy contribution in this tradition Israel M. Kirzner, *Discovery and the Capitalist Process*, 1985, University of Chicago Press.

30. Nick Bloom, Charles I. Jones, John Van Reenen, and Michael Webb, "Are Ideas Getting Harder to Find?," 2020, *American Economic Review*, Vol. 110, No. 4, pp. 1104–44.

31. R. Keith Sawyer, "The Cognitive Neuroscience of Creativity: A Critical Review," 2011, *Creativity Research Journal*, Vol. 23, No. 2, pp. 137–54; Anna Abraham, *The Neuroscience of Creativity*, 2018, Cambridge University Press. Adam Green provides a review focusing on links with analogical reasoning in his article "Creativity, within Reason."

32. Suzanne Nalbantian and Paul Matthews, *Secrets of the Mind: What Neuroscience, the Arts, and Our Minds Reveal*, 2020, Oxford University Press.

33. David D. Preiss, Diego Cosmelli, and James C. Kaufman, *Creativity and the Wandering Mind*, 2020, Academic Press.

34. For example, International Conference on Computational Creativity (ICCC), *Proceedings of the Eleventh International Conference on Computational Creativity*, 2020, ed. F. Amílcar Cardoso, Penousal Machado, Tony Veale and João Miguel Cunha, Association for Computational Creativity.

35. This same view echoes in some critiques of the field—for example, Joanna Zylinksa, *AI Art: Machine Visions and Warped Dreams*, 2020, Open Humanities Press.

36. On perceived need, Subrata Dasgupta, *Technology and Creativity*, 1996, Oxford University Press; on using what is at hand, Navi Radjou, Jaideep Prabhu, and Simone Ahuja, *Jugaad Innovation: Think Frugal, Be Flexible, Generate Breakthrough Growth*, 2012, Jossey-Bass; and as a byproduct of activity, Ainissa Ramirez, *The Alchemy of Us*, 2020, MIT Press.

37. Thomas S. Kuhn, *The Structure of Scientific Revolutions*, 1962, University of Chicago Press.

38. David L. Hull, *Science as a Process*, 1988, University of Chicago Press.

39. Howard E. Gruber, *Darwin on Man: A Psychological Study of Scientific Creativity*, 1974, E. P. Dutton; Doris B. Wallace and Howard E. Gruber, *Creative People at Work*, 1989, Oxford University Press; John L. Lowes, *The*

Road to Xanadu: A Study in the Ways of the Imagination, 1927, Houghton Mifflin.

40. Frederic L. Holmes, *Investigative Pathways: Patterns and Stages in the Careers of Experimental Scientists*, 2004, Yale University Press.

CHAPTER 1

1. The importance of the material, physical elments in a field has been stressed for example by Peter Galison in *Image and Logic: A Material Culture of Microphysics*, 1997, University of Chicago Press.

2. Many of Wordsworth's poems have the natural world as an important focus; a wonderful example is "Lines Composed a Few Miles above Tintern Abbey, On Revisiting the Banks of the Wye during a Tour. July 13, 1798," first published in *Lyrical Ballads, with a Few Other Poems* by William Wordsworth and Samuel Taylor Coleridge, 1798, J. & A. Arch. For Dillard, see Annie Dillard, *Pilgrim at Tinker Creek*, 1974, Harper's Magazine Press.

3. This is a theme of Richard Ellmann's biography of James Joyce, *James Joyce*, 1982 (first published 1959), Oxford University Press. I discuss transmutation further in Chapter 9 in relation to the formation of guiding conceptions.

4. See my paper "The Creative Development of Fields: Learning, Creativity, Paths, Implications," 2017, *Journal of the Knowledge Economy*, Vol. 8, 23–62, for a model of field dynamics.

CHAPTER 2

1. Peter Berger and Thomas Luckmann, *The Social Construction of Reality*, 1966, Doubleday.

2. For an overview see Stanley Wasserman and Katherine Faust, *Social Network Analysis*, 2012, Cambridge University Press. Also see the cites I provide in Chapter 4 linked to the specific kinds of network contexts I model mathematically.

3. See https://tomgruber.org/writing/definition-of-ontology, retrieved February 18, 2022.

4. The GO specifically "describes our knowledge of the biological domain with respect to three aspects": molecular functions, cellular components, and biological processes. See geneontology.org, specifically the section "Gene Ontology Overview," retrieved February 18, 2022.

5. I had the opportunity to visit CYC headquarters and attend a workshop and interrogate the CYC system for myself in 2008. My materials from that are *Cyc 101* workshop manual, October 20–22, 2008. During my time at the CYC headquarters I was able to interrogate the system and learn quite a

bit through discussion with programmers about its structure and how it has been developed. For commonsense reasoning see also Nils Nilsson, *Artificial Intelligence: A New Synthesis*, 1998, Morgan Kaufmann, in particular Chapter 18, "Representing Commonsense Knowledge," and Erik T. Mueller, *Commonsense Reasoning: An Event Calculus Based Approach*, 2014, Morgan Kaufmann.

6. For a review of such approaches in the field of engineering design see Ji Han, Serhad Sarica, Feng Shi, and Jianxi Luo, "Semantic Networks for Engineering Design: A Survey," 2021, *International Conference on Engineering Design, ICED 21*, DOI: 10.1017/pds.2021.523. For a good discussion of one such system see Feng Shi, Liuqing Chen, Ji Han, and Peter Childs, "A Data-Driven Text Mining and Semantic Network Analysis for Design Information Retrieval," 2017, *Journal of Mechanical Design*, Vol. 139, No. 11: 111402. For patents see Serhad Sarica, Jianxi Luo, and Kristin Wood, "TechNet: Technology Semantic Network Based on Patent Data," 2020, *Expert Systems with Applications*, Vol. 142, No. 15: 112995.

7. See Joseph Novak, *Learning, Creating, and Using Knowledge: Concept Maps as Facilitative Tools in Schools and Corporations*, 1998, Lawrence Erlbaum. Dasgupta's discussion in *A Cognitive Historical Approach to Creativity* also fits with this orientation.

8. For ontology visualization see Nassira Achich, Bassem Bouaziz, Alsayed Algergawy, and Faiez Gargouri, "Ontology Visualization: An Overview," presented at *International Conference on Intelligent Systems Design and Applications, 2017, ISDA*, published in *Advances in Intelligent Systems and Computing*, 2018, Vol. 736, pp. 880–91. In my approach the knowledge representation is visual from the start. But oftentimes a preexisting knowledge is developed into a graph, either by hand or using software such as OWL (Web Ontology Language). An example of a paper outlining how to develop a graph representation of an ontology is Miguel Ángel Rodríguez-García and Robert Hoehndorf, "Inferring Ontology Graph Structures Using OWL Reasoning," 2018, *BMC Bioinformatics*, Vol. 19, Article No. 7.

9. This kind of approach is associated with semantic analysis; see John Sowa, *Knowledge Representation: Logical, Philosophical, and Computational Foundations*, 2000, Brooks/Cole, and *Principles of Semantic Networks*, 1991, ed. John Sowa, Morgan Kaufmann. See also Hermann Helbig, *Knowledge Representation and the Semantics of Natural Language*, 2006, Springer. The approach is also central to a number of other computer science approaches and languages such as KL-ONE and its descendents.

10. Logical reasoning can be important in creativity for assessments of proposed ideas and creative projects. In my model these kinds of assessments are linked to guiding principles discussed in Chapters 11–13. The well-known

article by Randall Davis, Howard Shrobe, and Peter Szolovits, "What Is a Knowledge Representation?," 1993, *AI Magazine*, Vol. 14, No. 1, pp. 17–33, is a good example outlining the need for both and for balance.

11. See John Sowa, *Knowledge Representation*; Michael K. Bergman, "Hierarchies in Knowledge Representation," AI3:: Adaptive Information Blog, November 14, 2017.

12. See George A. Miller, Richard Beckwith, Christiane Fellbaum, Derek Gross, and Katherine Miller, "Introduction to WordNet: An On-line Lexical Database," 1993, https://wordnetcode.princeton.edu/5papers.pdf, Retrieved February 20, 2022.

13. This is based on my own exploration of the *CYC* program during my visit to CYC headquarters, and the introduction to *CYC* given during the workshop.

14. Arthur Campbell, Jonathan Feinstein, Soonwok Hong, Sharon Qian, and Trevor Williams, "Diversity, Knowledge Clusters, and Job Placement: Graduate Economics Teaching of Core Microeconomics," 2017, *Journal of Economic Education*, Vol. 48, No. 3, pp. 146–66.

15. See Michael Ashburner, et al., "Gene Ontology: Tool for the Unification of Biology," 2000, *Nature Genetics*, Vol. 25, pp. 25–29. See geneontology.org for current information about the project.

16. The classic reference is the work of David Hubel and Torsten Wiesel. See for example their paper, "Receptive Fields, Binocular Interaction and Functional Architecture in the Cat's Visual Cortex," 1962 *Journal of Physiology*, Vol. 160, pp. 106–54.

17. See P. Taylor, J. Hobbs, J. Burroni, H. T. Siegelmann, "The Global Landscape of Cognition: Hierarchical Aggregation as an Organizational Principle of Human Cortical Networks and Functions," 2015, *Scientific Reports*, Vol. 5, No. 1, pp. 1–18.

18. For a relatively recent example developing a hybird model linking hierarchies and networks see Bahareh Sarrafzadeh, Adam Roegiest, and Edward Lank, "Hierarchical Knowledge Graphs: A Novel Information Representation for Exploratory Search Tasks," 2020, *ACM Transactions on Information Systems*, Vol. 4. I think more can and will be done in this area.

19. Sowa presents attribute links as labeled to keep them clearly distinct from hierarchy parent links, in his graphical semantic network approach—see his discussions in *Knowledge Representation*.

20. "Ode on a Grecian Urn," first published 1819.

21. Some lateral links occur between elements that share a common parent element they link to: for example, the San Francisco Giants and Los Angeles Dodgers are both baseball teams. It might seem that in these cases the lateral link is not needed. But for the purposes of creative exploration, these lateral

links can come to mind more rapidly and be more salient than indirect links via common parents—the natural link between the Giants and Dodgers may mean that a train of thought naturally goes from one to the other. Hence these lateral links should be included in the description of context from the viewpoint of describing creative process.

22. Marvin Minsky, "A Framework for Representing Knowledge," 1975, in *The Psychology of Computer Vision*, ed. Patrick Winston, McGraw-Hill. Frames are also part of the KL-ONE model and often are used within a hierarchy structure—see Richard Fikes and Tom Kehler, "The Role of Frame-Based Representation in Reasoning," 1985, *Communications of the ACM*, Vol. 28, No. 9, pp. 904–20; see also Robert MacGregor, "The Evolving Technology of Classification-Based Knowledge Representation Systems," 1991, Chapter 13 in John Sowa, ed., *Principles of Semantic Networks* for an overview and link to semantic networks.

23. For frames see Charles Fillmore and Beryl Atkins, "Toward a Frame-Based Lexicon: The Semantics of RISK and Its Neighbors," 1992, in *Frames, Fields and Contrasts: New Essays in Semantic and Lexical Organization*, ed. A. Lehrer and E. F. Kittay, Lawrence Erlbaum Associates, pp. 75–102. Sowa's semantic network formalism also emphasizes depiction of functional relationships. To the extent functional analysis has to do with diagnosing why a given set of elements does not fit together well to conform with the functional requirements, this approach fits most closely with my discussion of guiding principles and the assessment and completion of projects in Chapters 11–13.

CHAPTER 3

1. *The Essays of Virginia Woolf*, Volume Two, 1912–1918, 1987, ed. Andrew McNeillie, Harcourt Brace Jovanovich, p. 56. Woolf did not keep a journal during the year she was twenty, so we don't have a direct record. Her reading notes for this time are also limited.

2. *A Passionate Apprentice: The Early Journals, 1897–1909*, 1990, ed. Mitchell A. Leaska, Harcourt Brace Jovanovich. The 1897 journal is most detailed in the first half of the year and peters out after the death of her half-sister Stella in July, though Woolf continues to record what she is reading after that point, but possibly less completely. Page 95 for the reference to devouring books.

3. She describes this in her early journals. It is no wonder she associated English literature with her father and her early life.

4. "It was the Elizabethan prose writers I loved first & most wildly, stirred by Hakluyt, which father lugged home for me—... I became enraptured." *The Diary of Virginia Woolf*, Volume Three, 1925–1930, 1980, ed. Anne Olivier Bell, Harcourt Brace, December 8, 1929, p. 271. Her reference is to Richard Hakluyt,

Hakluyt's Collection of the Early Voyages, Travels and Discoveries of the English Nation, Made by Sea or Overland to the Remote and Farthest Distant Quarters at Anytime within the Compass of these 1600 Yeares, A new edition, with additions, 1809–12, R. H. Evans (original publication in the period 1589–1600).

5. *Passionate Apprentice*, pp. 181–84, 231–34, 240–42, 245. *Reading Notebooks* XXVIII, XXXIV. The Woolfs' library—discussed further below—includes more than one hundred entries for ancient Greek authors, many multivolume works.

6. *Passionate Apprentice*, pp. 80, 87, 79, 256, 269. As examples of more general history, her 1897 journal lists, among other works, Macaulay's *History of England* (5 volumes), and Froude's *History of England* (a full 12 volumes). She also read histories of ancient Greece and Rome, Europe, and the United States, though not as widely. For example she mentions Arnold's *History of Rome*, Bury's *History of Greece to the Death of Alexander the Great*, and Carlyle's *French Revolution*. As she matured Woolf read somewhat more widely in nonfiction. Her husband, Leonard Woolf, had strong interests in public affairs, economics, and politics, and this surely enhanced her awareness of these domains. But the center of her nonfiction reading in the time period I am focusing on was history and especially biographical materials.

7. *The Essays of Virginia Woolf*, Volume One, 1904–1912, 1986, ed. Andrew McNeillie, Harcourt Brace Jovanovich, pp. 22, 67, and *Essays*, Volume Two, pp. 140–43, 83.

8. If we take her as having read perhaps a few hundreds of books prior to 1897, probably a significant underestimate, there are then a total of 20.5 years from 1897 through mid-1917. If we reduce this to 18 years of reading to account for illness and other factors, we may estimate she read 1,800 books over the period 1897–1917, and thus would have read more than 2,000 books by mid-1917. Of course this is just a guess based on the available information, but it is hard to believe she read fewer than 1,000 books.

9. *The Library of Leonard and Virginia Woolf*, 2003, compiled and edited by Julia King and Laila Miletic-Vejzovic, Washington State University Press. The library is currently housed at Washington State University. The figure of 2,000 is based on author calculations. Multiple entries of the exact same title are not counted more than once; undated entries are not counted; and a single entry is counted once, even when it refers to multiple volumes, which is common. A few hundred of these books are political and economic tracts most likely of greater interest to Leonard Woolf. Some of the books were purchased later.

10. "A Sketch of the Past," in Virginia Woolf, *Moments of Being*, ed. Jean Schulkind, 1985, Harcourt Brace, pp. 80, 64, 83. She describes another "first" memory of being on her mother's lap, very aware of her mother's dress with "flowers . . . purple and red and blue."

11. "A Sketch of the Past," pp. 108, 116. *Passionate Apprentice*, p. 214. The note is published as "Impressions of Sir Leslie Stephen" in *Essays, Volume One*, pp. 127-30, and was also published in the volume dedicated to Sir Leslie.

12. *Moments of Being*, "A Sketch of the Past," p. 138.

13. *Moments of Being*, "A Sketch of the Past," p. 69 and before. In "A Sketch of the Past" Woolf describes being sexually harrasssed by Gerald. Woolf also mentions sexual repression in a letter to Ethel Smythe. See the account in Hermione Lee, *Virginia Woolf*, 1996, Vintage, pp. 123-24. Woolf also had a mentally impaired half-sister Laura and half-sister Stella who died in 1897.

14. She formed more of these relationships beginning around 1917 and after—see Chapter 15 for more.

15. To give one example, in her 1906 journal during a two-week stay at Giggleswick in the north of England, she has many descriptions of the landscape, such as: "The great melancholy moors, sweeping all round us, like some tragic audience, or chorus, mutely attendant, grew black, & veiled with mist. Rain came down, & the country seemed well pleased at this change of mood. Storm & rough weather suit it better than bland & innocent skies. But words! words! You will find nothing to match the picture." *Passionate Apprentice*, p. 305.

16. *Passionate Apprentice*, pp. 320, 322, 328, 250, 333. Even with her focus on the ancient remains, she still attends to the countryside: "Greece is always in a state of ferment & effervescence .... There is no rest; but a perpetual curve and flow" Other countries she visited—Spain, Italy, Turkey—also become subject of many descriptions.

17. As youths she and her siblings were avid bug collectors, especially and most famously engaging in night hunting of moths.

18. See David Lewis, "Observations on Route Finding and Spatial Orientation among the Aboriginal Peoples of the Western Desert Region of Central Australia," June 1976, *Oceania*, Vol. 46, No. 4, pp. 249-82. The geography is based on the map on pp. 42-43 in Vivien Johnson, *Clifford Possum Tjapaltjarri*, 2003, Art Gallery of South Australia. She also shows a map Possum himself drew on p. 40.

19. See Lewis, "Observations on Route Finding," especially pp. 252–54.

20. For one example of Johnson's reference to Possum's encyclopedic knowledge see *Clifford Possum*, p. 82. Some of the sites named in Figure 4 are sites Possum was not custodian of, including Warlugulong, site of a famous mythologic fire that figures prominently in many of his paintings, although his mother was connected with this site. Also, individuals would be custodians of some sites, and in other cases managers of a site, meaning watchers as the custodians performed important functions such as rites.

21. Johnson, *Clifford Possum*, pp. 28, 35, 45–48. Vivien Johnson, *Lives of the Papunya Tula Artists*, 2008, IAD Press, p. 33.

22. A short biography of Billy Stockman is Janusz Kreczmanski and Margo Stanislawska-Birnberg, *"The Tjulkurra" Billy Stockman Tjapaltjarri*, 2002, J. B. Books. Johnson has entries on all three in *Lives of the Papunya Tula Artists*: pp. 17-19 (Kaapa), 28-31 (Stockman), and 44-46 (Leura).

23. See Richard Broome, *Aboriginal Australians: Black Response to White Dominance, 1788-1980*, 1982, Allen and Unwin, Australia.

24. Vivien Johnson discusses this in Chapter 1, "Beginnings," in *Clifford Possum*.

25. See Broome, *Aboriginal Australians*, Chapter 15.

26. *Land Rights News* is the central Australian Indigenous peoples' newspaper—the title speaks for itself about how important the land is for these communities. The importance of land/space is also evident in the striking difference between Indigenous accounts of historical events, which center on place, as compared with Western accounts that center on time. A good example of these differences is the story of Captain Cook's "discovery" of Australia, as discussed by Chris Healy, "Captain Cook: Between Black and White," 2000, section 4.2 in *The Oxford Companion to Aboriginal Art and Culture*, ed. Sylvia Kleinert and Margo Neale, Oxford University Press, pp. 92-96.

27. The Australian Human Rights Commission webpage "Questions and Answers about Aboriginal & Torres Strait Islander Peoples" lists important Australian land rights legislation in its Table 10.2. See https://humanrights.gov.au/our-work/questions-and-answers-about-aboriginal-torres-strait-islander-peoples#q8, retrieved October 2021. For a discussion of the struggle in relation to the Arrernte see Kleinert and Neale, *The Oxford Companion to Aboriginal Art and Culture*, pp. 49-52.

28. Johnson discusses the connection of Possum's art with the struggle for land rights in *Clifford Possum*, pp. 80, 82.

29. Song was also integral to the art. In her section "Song as an Indigenous Art" in Kleinert and Neale, *The Oxford Companion to Aboriginal Art and Culture*, pp. 328-35, Linda Barwick describes how music and song were interwoven with other art forms and specifically states in the subsection "Song and Visual Representation," "There are many reported instances of Western Desert painters singing as they execute Dreaming designs in acrylic paintings" (p. 332). See also Geoffrey Bardon and James Bardon, *Papunya: A Place Made After the Story*, 2006, Lund Humphries, pp. 12, 16-17.

30. Johnson, *Clifford Possum*, Chapter 2, "Start from Carving." One carving, "Cheeky Snake," is shown on p. 51 and gives a sense of how realistic Possum's carvings are. For what he was earning from carving, p. 49.

31. Johnson, *Clifford Possum*, p. 42 and footnote 4 on p. 212. Namatjira's style was carried on by descendents, both familial and artistic, as shown in the figure.

32. Johnson has documented this in her revisionist history *Once Upon a Time in Papunya*, 2010, NewSouth, Chapter 1, "The School of Kaapa." Geoffrey Bardon also viewed Kaapa as the leader of the art movement in its early days—in Bardon and Bardon, *Papunya: A Place Made After the Story*, he states, "It was around his classic artistry the painting movement of Papunya in 1971 was built" (p. 86). I discuss the early history in more detail in Chapter 17.

33. Another factor was that some of the early paintings included secret-sacred elements. As it became clear that the paintings would be viewed by a wider audience, the painters felt uncomfortable sharing this information, and also received pressure from other tribesmen not to share it. Thus these elements dropped out of the paintings.

34. See Bardon and Bardon, *Papunya: A Place Made After the Story*, pp. 13–18.

35. Johnny Warangkula was a key early innovator of the dot technique—see his early paintings of Water Dreamings shown in Bardon and Bardon, *Papunya: A Place Made After the Story*, pp. 160–61. See Chapter 17 for more about Warangkula and his development of the dot technique.

36. Frederic Holmes, *Hans Krebs: The Formation of a Scientific Life, 1900–1933*, Volume 1, 1991, Oxford University Press. Holmes interviewed Krebs in the 1970s, and the transcripts of these interviews are housed in the Yale Library. Hans Krebs, *Reflections*, 1981, Oxford University Press.

37. Holmes does discuss these broader issues as part of his overall biography, and the interested reader is referred to his discussion. These broader issues, such as economic and political turbulence, may have exerted influence indirectly—for example, on Krebs's attitude toward work and his career. I note that, although not directly entering into this knowledge context, economic considerations were also important, as they factored into his training apprenticeships, hence what he was exposed to, and ultimately, his having the ability to form his own lab.

38. General concepts includes "nature of life" discussed below. It also includes under arts and literature Goethe's *Faust*, which Krebs read in college and which, as his biographer Holmes states, held a lifelong importance for him—see Holmes, *Hans Krebs*, pp. 69–70. The figure does not include a segment for places, though they could also be shown, including where Krebs grew up and traveled, and locations and institutions where he trained.

39. Holmes, *Hans Krebs*, Chapter 3.

40. Under intermediary metabolism I depict important reactions that had been worked out by the late 1920s, Knoop's β-oxidation theory and the lactic acid cycle, that we are certain Krebs knew about. Other elements, such as the Wieland-Knoop-Thannhauser scheme, may not have been as well known to him and are not shown, but he may have known of

them, and in that sense the figure is conservative in what it shows of his knowledge.

41. See Holmes, *Hans Krebs*, pp. 76–77. The quote is from Franz Knoop, *Lebenserscheinungen und Chemie: öffentliche Antrittsrede*, 1921, Speyer and Kaerner, pp. 10–11.

42. Holmes, *Hans Krebs*, p. 96. Krebs stated this view I believe during his interview with Holmes. During his student years Krebs presented in a student discussion group an interpretation of work on the vitalist, nonmechanistic view of life, and Holmes notes that this may have contributed to shaping his own viewpoint.

43. Holmes, *Hans Krebs*, pp. 92–93, 101, 109–110, 118, 122.

44. Holmes, *Hans Krebs*, p. 93.

45. Holmes, *Hans Krebs*, pp. 103–9, 113–19, 121–22. The syphilis gold sol and cerebrospinal fluid project was under the direction of Doctor Annelise Wittgenstein. The first paper Krebs reviewed, which made him realize the problem of what did and did not cross the blood-brain barrier was not well understood, was by Lina Stern and R. Gautier, and the paper that drew his attention to the Donnan Equilibrium was by Lehmann and Meesmann. This paper hypothesized, based on the equation, that anions (negatively charged compounds) might cross the barrier more readily than cations, and Krebs pursued this idea by injecting dyes of positive and negative charge into spinal fluid. Krebs told Holmes he studied Leonor Michaelis's text *The Hydrogen Ion Concentration: Its Meaning for Biology and the Methods for Measuring It* around this time and found it stimulating; Holmes, *Hans Krebs*, pp. 88–89; he also read Michaelis's *The Physical Chemistry of Cells and Tissues*.

46. Under general activities, piano is listed as well as hiking. Krebs was an avid hiker and seems to have often chosen to vacation in the mountains; see Holmes, *Hans Krebs*, Chapter 2, and pp. 99, 109, 153.

47. Holmes, *Hans Krebs*, pp. 81–83, 121–24, 127. In the final year of his training, as noted above, Krebs enrolled in an extended course that covered methods of inorganic chemistry, quantitative analysis, organic chemistry, and physical chemistry. In another research project that he undertook with a friend, focused on the agglutination of red blood cells, Krebs gained experience with electrodialysis, electrolytes, and the quantitative measurement of pH.

48. Krebs obtained this position via his friend Bruno Mendel.

49. Holmes, *Hans Krebs*, pp. 131–38, 154. The Warburg apparatus immersed the system in a constant temperature bath, allowed for six reactions to be conducted simultaneously, and had a system for continual shaking of the reaction vessels. Warburg also asked Krebs to write a review paper outlining the manometric and tissue slice methods, which surely helped solidify his grasp of them.

As an indication of how innovative and influential Warburg's methods were, a U.S. text on manometric techniques I consulted from the 1940s devotes its first chapter to "The Warburg Constant Volume Respirometer," and the following three chapters also are based on Warburg's setup and modes of analysis: *Manometric Techniques and Tissue Metabolism*, W. W. Umbreit, R. H. Burris, and J. F. Stauffer, 1949, Burgess.

50. Holmes, *Hans Krebs*, pp. 163–78. Warburg had previously studied other animals, but believed to be more convincing he needed to extend his investigations to human tissue, and this was the genesis of Krebs's project. Specifically, Warburg had found that the rate of glycolysis through which lactic acid is produced is higher in cancer cells than in normal tissue. For his project Krebs interfaced with a surgery department and obtained human cancer tissue that had been surgically removed from patients, making tissue slices.

CHAPTER 4

1. Another issue in empirical applications is determing the level on which a particular element resides. Textbooks are an example where the levels are often quite clear; but in other less formal descriptions, this may be less clear and the determination of level is a matter of judgment.

2. Note that contexts with additional vertical links are akin to lattices—actually semi-lattices, as the bottom layer is expanding and does not contract back to a single element at the very bottom of the network.

3. Lateral links between bottom elements may have a personal resonance. A person may link two books that are not typically viewed as related, because they read one just after the other, and so tend to think of one when thinking of the other.

4. In models with more than two levels, the definitions above continue to apply, suitably extended.

5. Another issue that modeling can be used to address is the diversity and distribution of creative paths and outcomes generated by a cohort of individuals embedded in identical or similar contexts, a topic I discuss in Chapter 17.

6. For each top element considered separately, the number of bottom elements it is linked to is governed by the binomial distribution. For all top elements jointly it is a multinomial distribution that takes into account the joint dependence among them—when a bottom element connects to one top element, it cannot connect to any others.

7. Edgar Gilbert, "Random Graphs," 1959, *The Annals of Mathematical Statistics*, Vol. 30, No. 4, pp. 1141–44.

8. See the review by Mark Newman, "The Structure and Function of Complex Networks," 2003, *SIAM Review*, Vol. 45, No. 2, pp. 167–256.

This phenomenon is sometimes described as a heavy right-tailed degree distribution—see my discussion in the next paragraph and the next section. Newman discusses this on pp. 185–86.

9. See Newman, "The Structure and Function of Complex Networks." An early discussion of academic citation data is Derek J. de Solla Price, "Networks of Scientific Papers: The Pattern of Bibliographic References Indicates the Nature of the Scientific Research Front," 1965, *Science*, Vol. 149, pp. 510-15. For a further discussion see Gerald Silverberg and Bart Verspagen, "The Size Distribution of Innovations Revisited: An Application of Extreme Value Statistics to Citation and Value Measures of Patent Significance," 2007, *Journal of Econometrics*, Vol. 139, No. 2, pp. 318–39, and Dietmar Harhoff, Frederic Scherer and Katrin Vopel, "Exploring the Tail of Patented Invention Value Distributions," 2003, in O. Granstrand, ed., *Economics, Law and Intellectual Property*, Springer, pp. 251–81. If we think of an individual's context being built up at least in part by starting from a paper and then reading all the papers it cites, this will result in a context exhibiting this phenomenon since the starting paper will have many links.

10. Alex Fornito, Andrew Zalesky, and Edward Bullmore, *Fundamentals of Brain Network Analysis*, 2016, Academic Press, Chapter 4, "Node Degree and Strength," especially Figure 4.3 and the discussion around it. I do not focus on the very top attenuation, partly because my networks, although large scale from the viewpoint of standard creativity analysis, are far smaller than brain networks, so that the highest degree nodes do not have extremely high degrees. As a reviewer pointed out, it is important to recognize that the brain as network exhibiting this phenomenon that a few nodes have a large number of links does not conclusively show that the concept networks individuals form instantiated in their brains also exhibit this phenomenon—but it is suggestive.

11. For an early paper on the power law and implication of scale-free networks see Albert-László Barabási and Réka Albert, "Emergence of Scaling in Random Networks," 1999, *Science*, Vol. 286, pp. 509–12.

12. See Anna Broido and Aaron Clauset, "Scale-Free Networks Are Rare," 2019, *Nature Communications*, 10, Article 1017. They assess the evidence for nearly 1,000 networks drawn from the Colorado Index of Complex Networks, and note that many can be described just as well or better by a log-normal distribution or other probability distributions for which the right-hand tail is relatively "heavy."

13. See Newman, "The Structure and Function of Complex Networks," especially pp. 183–85. There are different ways to define clustering and evaluate it in networks, and they do not all agree; see Scott Emmons, Stephen Kobourov, Mike Gallant, and Katy Börner, "Analysis of Network Clustering Algorithms and Cluster Quality Metrics at Scale," 2016, *PLoS ONE*, Id=10.1371.

14. The parameter p defines the probability that a given bottom and top pair is linked. I set the parameter p equal to $\frac{1}{(N-1)}$. Given p, the computer generates a (pseudo)random number from the interval $[0, 1]$ with a uniform distribution; the link is created if the random number is less than or equal to p. More generally, this type of model can be specified as $p = \frac{c}{N}$. For discussion see Albert-László Barabási, *Network Science*, online at: networksciencebook.com, retrieved December 20, 2021; and Alan Frieze and Michał Karoński, *Introduction to Random Graphs*, online book at math.cmu.edu/~af1p/BOOK.pdf, retrieved December 20, 2021. An alternative that is sometimes used is $p = c\log N/N$; but for the finite size networks I work with, these two approaches are essentially equivalent (given N and a desired p, the two can be made equivalent with appropriately chosen different values of c).

15. I specify the parameter r to be the probability a given top element links to any other top element. r is set approximately to $\frac{1}{2(N-1)}$. In fact $1/(N-1)$ is multiplied by a term slightly larger than 1/2. Call this factor x. The exact expression to make the expected number of links equal to 1 is the (positive) solution to the quadratic equation: $(-1/(N-1)^2)x^2 + 2x - 1 = 0$. For $N = 100$ this implies x approximately equal to 0.502.

16. See See Broido and Clauset, "Scale-Free Networks Are Rare," for a discussion and evidence for k around 2.

17. I assign 5 elements a weight of 6, 8 elements a weight of 5, 8 elements a weight of 4, 12 elements a weight of 3, and 20 elements a weight of 2.

18. I divide the unit length $[0, 1]$ into 100 intervals; each top element is associated with an interval, and the length of its interval is equal to its likelihood of being selected, with lengths proportional to weights. For each bottom element the computer generates a pseudorandom number from the uniform $[0, 1]$ distribution, and the bottom element is linked with the top element associated with the interval in which the random number lies. It does not matter how intervals are assigned. For convenience, I simply number the top elements and assign weights and intervals in sequence from smallest weight to largest.

19. The procedure is slightly more complicated. For each bottom element I remove from the list of top elements the element it has been connected to in step 1, then sum the weights of the remaining top elements, defining a new normalization factor, and divide each weight by this factor to define new normalized weights. For each remaining top element, I then draw a random number from the unit interval (uniform distribution) and if its value is less than or equal to the element's new normalized weight, the link is established, and otherwise not.

20. For each top element, call it A, I sum the weights of the remaining top elements, then divide each such remaining element by this sum, forming new normalized weights. Then for each top element except A I draw a random number over [0, 1] uniform distribution, and this element links with A if the random number is less than or equal to its normalized weight divided by two. If this element is already linked with A, a second link is not made (but note that its weight is still included in forming the normalized weights). Note that this approach is only approximate. If elements i and j have different base weights, then their renormalized weights are different and the probability i links to j is in general different than the probability j links to i. Solving for a set of correction factors such that each element has a given expected number of horizontal links is somewhat complex because these factors are jointly determined, and I do not pursue this.

21. I assign 2 elements a weight of 40; 4 elements to each of weights 30, 25, and 20; 8 elements to weights 18 and 16; 12 to weights 14 and 12; 14 to weights 10 and 8; 17 to weight 7; 18 to weight 6; 30 to weight 5; 50 to weight 4; and 100 elements to weight 3.

22. My approach follows the approach described by Girvan and Newman for generating cluster networks—see Michelle Girvan and Mark Newman, "Community Structure in Social and Biological Networks," 2002, *Proceedings of the National Academy of Sciences*, Vol. 99, No. 12, pp. 7821–26. This approach has also been adapted for use in networks that exhibit both clustering and power law degree distributions, though I do not combine the two features here; see Andrea Lancichinetti, Santo Fortunato, and Filippo Radicchi, "Benchmark Graphs for Testing Community Detection Algorithms," 2008, *Physical Review E*, Vol. 78, Id 046110.

23. Girvan and Newman, "Community Structure in Social and Biological Networks."

24. Given *ncluster* top elements in a cluster (10 for the small-scale networks and 100 for the large-scale), for a given bottom element, the probability of a link to each top element other than its first parent is $p = q * \frac{1}{ncluster-1}$ if the top element is in the same cluster and $p = (1 - q) * \frac{1}{9*ncluster}$ if not.

25. There are often multiple paths at the shortest distance between a pair of elements. Not all pairs of elements are connected in a network: some top elements are isolates, and occasionally there is a small separate component in a network. But the vast majority of pairs are connected: for the random and cluster models typically around 99 percent of elements are connected; for the power law models there are more pairs not connected, on the order of a few percent of bottom pairs and 10 percent to 20 percent of top-bottom pairs.

CHAPTER 5

1. A widely accepted view. It is described by Henri Poincaré in *Science and Method*, trans. F. Maitland, 1952 (originally published 1924 in French), Dover; and more explicitly by Sarnoff A. Mednick, "The Associative Basis of the Creative Process," 1962, *Psychological Review*, Vol. 69, No. 3, pp. 220–32.

2. Mednick makes this point in his original article, "The Associative Basis of the Creative Process."

3. John Locke, *An Essay concerning Human Understanding*, 1975, ed. with a foreword by Peter Nidditch, Oxford University Press (originally published 1689).

4. Of course ideas may also arise through conversations with other people. See Ufuk Akcigit, Santiago Caicedo, Ernest Miguelez, Stefanie Stantcheva, and Valerio Sterzi, "Dancing with the Stars: Innovation through Interactions," 2018, NBER Working Paper 24466, for a model in which ideas emerge either through one's own thinking or through discussion with others.

5. Creative fusions can be made out of elements that share a common parent; an example is forming a new dog hybrid. But here the creativity is more in the execution and actually creating the hybrid. Thus the creativity is more about the process, and this involves different kinds of elements—for example, biology lab techniques—that in fact may represent a more distant creative connection.

6. A full-scale analysis of how initial project seeds grow into large-scale outcomes is of great interest, and I believe can be developed using the framework I present, but I do not attempt it in this book. It is also worth noting that in general larger-scale projects may be organized in subsets with particular elements linked together in clusters, the way a painting or a circuit has different subparts. I discuss this further in Chapter 16.

7. Note that this is less than the combinatoric value of 18 choose 3; that is because elements that share a common parent cannot be included together in a project.

CHAPTER 6

1. Another example is Alexander Fleming's discovery of the effect of penicillin on bacteria in 1928. While the actual discovery was serendipitous, due to mold spores entering his lab through an open window while he was on summer holiday with his family and landing on an uncovered Petri dish that had *Staphylococcus* bacteria on it, he had worked for years on related topics. His interest was sparked initially by observing many soldiers dying of infections during World War I. He had also previously discovered that lysozyme present in nasopharyngeal mucus on a Petri dish inhibited growth of some bacteria. Thus he had the mindset that enabled him to grasp the significance of the phenomenon he observed. See Siang Yong Tan and Yvonne Tatsumura,

"Alexander Fleming (1881–1955): Discoverer of Penicillin," 2015, *Singapore Medical Journal*, Vol. 56, No. 7, pp. 366–67. For a biography see Gwyn Macfarlane, *Alexander Fleming: The Man and the Myth*, 1984, Harvard University Press. For a different perspective, focusing on Fleming's proclivity to play and create mosaic patterns see Robert and Michèle Root-Bernstein, *Sparks of Genius: The Thirteen Thinking Tools of the World's Most Creative People*, 1999, Houghton Mifflin, pp 246–48.

CHAPTER 8

1. The quotations in this paragraph and the preceding one are from Frederic Holmes, *Hans Krebs: The Formation of a Scientific Life 1900–1933*, Volume 1, 1991, Oxford University Press, pp. 178–79. See also Jonathan S. Feinstein, *The Nature of Creative Development*, 2006, Stanford University Press, pp. 167–70.

2. The second project Krebs worked on in Warburg's lab involved the lactic acid cycle in muscle tissue and thus does fit with this link; although his experience working on this project may have helped Krebs recognize the potential to apply the techniques to other problems, Krebs nowhere stated that he was specifically drawn to this question.

3. See Geoffrey Bardon and James Bardon, *Papunya: A Place Made After the Story*, 2006, Lund Humphries, "The Men and the Murals," pp. 12–19, including several photos of the murals taken at the time.

4. Geoffrey Bardon, *Papunya Tula: The Art of the Western Desert*, 1991, McPhee Gribble, p. 31.

5. See discussion in Vivien Johnson, *Clifford Possum Tjapaltjarri*, 2003, Art Gallery of South Australia, pp. 59–60. Bardon has a section in *Papunya: A Place Made After the Story* entitled "Paintings Influenced by European Conventions and Materials" the first page of which shows early Kaapa ceremonial boards including *Gulgardi*, see p. 135. Bardon also encouraged the men to paint with traditional colors and generally these were the color paints he supplied see pp. 25, 34.

6. Johnson, *Clifford Possum*, p. 79.

7. The quote also shows that Possum's guiding conception is rooted in his cultural traditions of telling the Dreaming stories. This reflects the overarching aspiration he had for his art, to transmit his cultural heritage to the younger generations. See Johnson, *Clifford Possum*, p. 16.

8. Johnson, *Clifford Possum*, pp. 80-81.

9. Johnson, *Clifford Possum*, p. 80.

10. Johnson, *Clifford Possum*, p. 163. In reference to the earlier 1984 exhibition *Painters of the Western Desert* in Adelaide, Craig Barry wrote, "By focusing on the representation of the sacred sites and Dreamtime jouneyings of their

totemic ancestors, there is a clearly stated reference to Aboriginal custodianship of particular territories and the primeval basis for these [land rights] claims. See Craig Barry, "Non-Violent Land Claims from the Centre," 1984, *Artlink*, Vol. 4. There were paintings by several artists in this exhibition, not just Possum, but his maps series had worked its influence.

11. Virginia Woolf, "The Mark on the Wall" in *The Complete Shorter Fiction of Virginia Woolf*, 1985, ed. Susan Dick, Harcourt Brace and Company, pp. 83–89. These quotes are from pp. 83–85.

12. Woolf, "The Mark on the Wall," p. 85.

13. Woolf, "The Mark on the Wall," pp. 85–86.

14. Reflection is used metaphorically in the passage; metaphor is one form of abstraction we often see in guiding conceptions.

15. One of the definitions the OED gives for "phantom" is "Not real; illusory," as in "The women suffered from phantom pain that no physician could ever find."

16. We might be tempted to add that the novelist will also somehow have to orchestrate them so that they coalesce into some kind of coherent story. But Woolf does not state this, and it is possible the novel of the future will not have coherence of this or any kind.

17. Woolf, "The Mark on the Wall," pp. 86–87.

18. Woolf, "The Mark on the Wall," pp. 87–88.

19. Heinz Kohut, *The Analysis of the Self,* 1971, International Universities Press, and *The Restoration of the Self*, 1977, International Universities Press.

20. Liane Gabora, "Honing Theory: A Complex Systems Framework for Creativity," 2017, *Nonlinear Dynamics, Psychology, and Life Sciences*, Vol. 21, No. 1, pp. 35–88.

21. "Phyllis and Rosamond," in *The Complete Shorter Fiction of Virginia Woolf*, pp. 17–29.

22. Virginia Woolf, *A Passionate Apprentice: The Early Journals, 1897–1909*, 1990, ed. Mitchell A. Leaska, Harcourt Brace Jovanovich, pp. 341–45.

23. Woolf, *A Passionate Apprentice*, pp. 392–93.

24. I draw mainly on two sources: David Sarno, "Twitter Creator Jack Dorsey Illuminates the Site's Founding Document. Part I," February 18, 2009, *Los Angeles Times*; and D. T. Max, "Two-Hit Wonder," October 14, 2013, *The New Yorker*. For more on the founding of Twitter and the personalities involved see Nick Bilton, *Hatching Twitter*, 2013, Penguin.

25. Sarno, "Twitter Creator Jack Dorsey."

26. Max, "Two-Hit Wonder."

27. Max, "Two-Hit Wonder." Dorsey also had a stint back home in St. Louis.

28. Sarno, "Twitter Creator Jack Dorsey."

29. Sarno, "Twitter Creator Jack Dorsey." Dorsey also attempted to implement his conception using a primitive mobile email device called the RIM 850, but it didn't catch on. See Chapter 14.

30. For Dorsey's father's role and his minimalist aesthetic see Max, "Two-Hit Wonder." For his speech impediment and his mother taking him around St. Louis see Bilton, *Hatching Twitter*, pp. 28–29.

CHAPTER 9

1. Indeed in many cases the two elements are not even a very short distance away from one another (distance being measured as shortest path length). When they are further apart it tends to make it more likely that any connection that is created between them will be viewed as highly creative, as for example in Mednick's discussion—see Chapter 5, note 1. Being further apart may also mean that they are less likely to be able to be linked successfully—this is where an individual's intuition is so important in envisioning a guiding conception that truly does have creative potential. Note that I allow for the possibility that the two guiding conception elements are linked already in the top level of the context network. Such a case is not very likely in the relatively sparse networks I consider; it is also less likely to lead to a highly creative outcome, but might if it leads to novel combinations of project elements—this will become clearer as the model is presented below and in following chapters. I also allow the two guiding conception elements to share children in common. One can argue that this makes any further connections between their children (or elements linked to their children) less creative. However, in rich networks with lattice structures, their children may reside in very different locations, so that connecting a new pair may be quite creative.

2. More complex exploration is possible. If none of the original seeds is successful, the individual may, for example, follow the links these child elements have to other bottom elements and try these elements in combinations. Network linkages are key for this kind of creative exploration and thinking, consistent with cognitive psychology and neuroscience approaches to creativity. See Chapter 16 for more.

3. I note that while in principle a single concept can defined a guiding conception, this seems uncommon. And conversely while in principle the number of elements used to define a guiding conception could be quite large, in my experience, at least based on individuals' descriptions of their guiding conceptions, the number of elements is usually not extremely large.

4. Douglas Hofstadter, *Fluid Concepts and Creative Analogies*, 1996, Basic Books.

5. President Kennedy stated this in an address to a joint session of the U.S. Congress on May 25, 1961; see https://www.jfklibrary.org/learn/about-jfk/historic-speeches/address-to-joint-session-of-congress-may-25-1961. As is well known U.S. astronaut Neil Armstrong was the first human to walk on the moon, on July 20, 1969.

6. See for example Nadia Drake, "Elon Musk: A Million Humans Could Live on Mars by the 2060s," September 27, 2016, *National Geographic,* https://www.nationalgeographic.com/science/article/elon-musk-spacex-exploring-mars-planets-space-science: retrieved January 14, 2022.

7. For a discussion see Jonathan S. Feinstein, *The Nature of Creative Development,* 2006, Stanford University Press, pp. 157–59, 303–15, 322–28.

8. See Feinstein, *The Nature of Creative Development,* pp. 103–6, 317–21, and 412–16. Darwin first mentions transmutation of species as a possible theoretical explanation for his observations in his "Red Notebook"—see Paul H. Barrett, Peter J. Gautrey, Sandra Herbert, David Kohn, and Sydney Smith, eds., *Charles Darwin's Notebooks 1836–1844: Geology, Transmutation of Species, Metaphysical Enquiries,* 1987, Cornell University Press, including the introductions to the Red Notebook and Notebooks *B* and *C.* My discussion in *NCD* draws on a number of Darwin's other writings as well, especially in discussing his observations as the *Beagle* sailed around South America: Nora Barlow, ed., *Charles Darwin and the Voyage of the Beagle,* 1945, Pilot Press; Charles Darwin, *Charles Darwin's Beagle Diary,* 1988, ed. Richard Darwin Keynes, Cambridge University Press; Richard Darwin Keynes, ed., *The Beagle Record,* 1979, Cambridge University Press; and Charles Darwin, *Voyage of the Beagle: Charles Darwin's Journal of Researches,* 1989, ed. Janet Browne and Michael Neve, Penguin Books. See also Howard Gruber's landmark study based on Darwin's journals, *Darwin on Man,* 1974, E. P. Dutton.

9. Israel M. Kirzner, *Perception, Opportunity, and Profit,* 1979, University of Chicago Press; see also his *Discovery and the Capitalist Process,* 1985, University of Chicago Press.

10. Thomas Kuhn, *The Structure of Scientific Revolutions,* 1962, University of Chicago Press, Chapter VI.

11. Howard Gruber, "Darwin's 'Tree of Nature' and Other Images of Wide Scope," 1978, in *On Aesthetics in Science,* ed. Judith Wechsler, MIT Press, pp. 121–42; Liane Gabora, "Honing theory: A Complex Systems Framework for Creativity," 2017, *Nonlinear Dynamics, Psychology, and Life Sciences,* Vol. 21, No. 1, pp. 35–88.

12. As noted in Chapter 2, Minsky introduced the notion of frames in "A Framework for Representing Knowledge," 1975, in *The Psychology of Computer Vision,* ed. Patrick Winston, McGraw-Hill. For scripts see Roger Schank and Robert Abelson, *Scripts, Plans, Goals, and Understanding,* 1977, Erlbaum.

13. Carolyn Lamb, Daniel Brown, and Charles Clarke, "A Taxonomy of Generative Poetry Techniques," 2017, *Journal of Mathematics and the Arts*, Vol. 11, No. 3, pp. 159–79.

14. See for example Jichen Wu, Maarten Lamers, and Wojtek Kowalczyk, "Being Creative: A Cross-Domain Mapping Network," 2020, *International Conference on Computational Creativity*, pp. 220–27.

15. Thomas Winters and Luc De Raedt have introduced the notion of template trees, thus building even more higher level structure, in "Discovering Textual Structures: Generative Grammar Induction Using Template Trees," 2020, in *International Conference on Computational Creativity*, pp. 177–80.

16. Donald Campbell, "Blind Variation and Selective Retentions in Creative Thought as in Other Knowledge Processes," 1960, *Psychological Review*, Vol. 67, No. 6, pp. 380–400; Dean Simonton, "Scientific Creativity as Constrained Stochastic Behavior: The Integration of Product, Person, and Process Perspectives," 2003, *Psychological Bulletin*, Vol. 129, No. 4, pp. 475–94.

17. In his article Simonton states quite directly that individuals have a large domain of elements they have learned and internalized, and then literally are trying all pairwise combinations until they hit upon one that is creative. See his section "Stochastic Explanation" and in particular point No. 4, p. 478. This is exactly the approach that is woefully inefficient and even infeasible in large-scale contexts—see the next chapter for more.

18. As discussed earlier in the Introduction. See for example Robert Evenson and Yoav Kislev, "A Stochastic Model of Applied Research," 1976, *Journal of Political Economy*, Vol. 84, No. 2, pp. 265–81; and Samuel Kortum, "Research, Patenting, and Technological Change," 1997, *Econometrica*, Vol. 65, No. 6, pp. 1389–419.

19. Martin Weitzman, "Recombinant Growth," 1998, *Quarterly Journal of Economics*, Vol. 113, No. 2, pp. 331–60.

20. Ahmed M. Abdulla and Bonnie Cramond, "The Creative Problem Finding Hierarchy: A Suggested Model for Understanding Problem Finding," 2018, *Creativity. Theories-Research-Applications*, Vol. 5, No. 2, pp. 197–229. This point was made earlier by Jacob Getzels, "Problem Finding: A Theoretical Note," 1979, *Cognitive Science*, Vol. 3, pp. 167–72.

21. This same distinction applies to the discussion of problem finding in Jacob Getzels and Mihaly Csikszentmihalyi's study, *The Creative Vision: A Longitudinal Study of Problem Finding in Art*, 1976, John Wiley & Sons. A few researchers, as noted by Abdulla and Cramond, have distinguished between two stages, problem discovery and a later stage of problem definition—and I would add, problem redefinition. See Abdulla and Cramond, "The Creative

Problem Finding Hierarchy," p. 204. Einstein seems to have viewed both as important: in his book *The Evolution of Physics* coauthored with Leopold Infeld they write, "The formulation of a problem is often more essential than its solution.... To raise new questions, new possibilities, to regard old problems from a new angle, requires creative imagination and marks real advance in science." See Albert Einstein and Leopold Infeld, *The Evolution of Physics*, 1938, Simon & Schuster, p. 95.

22. I retrieved this from https://manningtreearchive.com/tag/st-john-the-baptist/ on February 22, 2022, as part of a lengthy post about the creation and initial reception of the *David*, Joseph Sébastine, "A Florentine Ornament," dated August 17, 2021. However, as noted in this post, the quote is just attributed to Michelangelo and not certain. In his *Life of Michelangelo Buonarroti*, Ascanio Condivi states about Michelangelo that he was "endowed with a most powerful imagination," which led him to be dissatisfied with what he produced—"for it has not seemed to him that his hand realized the idea that he formed within." Thus he calls attention to Michelangelo's vision for a work that guided him. See *Michelangelo: Life, Letters, and Poetry*, 1987, selected and trans. George Bull, poems trans. George Bull and Peter Porter, Oxford University Press, Chapter 1, p. 71. In a letter written relatively late in life, Michelangelo wrote, in response to being exhorted to paint and not worry about other matters: "I reply that one paints with the head and not with the hands; and if he can't keep a clear head a man is lost." Thus he calls attention to the mental aspect of art. See Bull, *Michelangelo*, p. 112, letter No. 30, 1542.

23. Retrieved from https://www.masterclass.com/articles/jodie-fosters-tips-for-realizing-your-creative-vision-in-film#jodie-fosters-5-tips-for-realizing-your-creative-vision-in-film on February 22, 2022.

24. Ansel Adams, *Examples: The Making of 40 Photographs*, 1976, Little, Brown and Company, p. 5.

25. David Noton, *Waiting for the Light*, 2008, David & Charles, see especially pp. 12–16.

26. Dated October 18, 2013; retrieved from https://www.nyip.edu/photo-articles/photography-tutorials/finding-your-creative-vision February 22, 2022.

27. Retrived from renee-phillips.com/expressing-your-unique-vision-as-an-artist March 5, 2022. I have found many similar statements on websites about photography and other visual art forms.

28. Tom Wright, "The 101 Most Inspiring Vision Statement Examples For 2022!" retrieved from cascade.app on March 5, 2022. I have found many similar kinds of statements; for example, David Parrish writes on his website, "Vision describes where we are going—the 'promised land'," and "An organisation's Vision sets out its aspirations for the future. The Strategic Vision is the 'dream'

of the future, a picture painted in words, which is intended to inspire people by appealing to the heart as well as the head." This seems to mix guidance with a more emotional, inspirational role. Retrieved from davidparrish.com on March 5, 2022.

29. Retrieved from pfizer.com/about on March 5, 2022. It is noteworthy that other online sources state Pfizer's vision statement differently. For example, on the website mission-statement.com it is written that the "Pfizer vision statement is 'Innovate to bring therapies to patients that significantly improve their lives.' " Retrieved from mission-statement.com on March 5, 2022.

30. Retrieved from ibm.com on March 5, 2022.

CHAPTER 10

1. The two guiding conception elements are allowed to be directly connected. This might seem like a less creative pairing, but I do not rule it out, as an individual might believe there are further linkages to be made between these two high-level concepts. Also I do not rule out that they may share children in common, though this restriction may also be imposed. It is reasonable to think that if the two guiding conception elements already share children in common, a further connection between children will be less creative—but this may not always be the case, as children may be scattered widely in the context network. If a successful creative outcome is achieved, the context network will be updated and the guiding conception elements may then be viewed as linked, if they are not already, depending on how the outcome is viewed in terms of the new connections it establishes.

2. As in Part I, I assume no horizontal links between bottom elements.

3. When the model is extended to larger projects, it becomes even more important to search to find a high-potential-value seed first and then try to develop it into a full project, because the number of projects grows ever larger. Guidance becomes even more important when seeds are larger as well, since there will be more of them. See Chapter 16 for a further discussion.

4. If richer guiding conceptions are considered, the number of potential guiding conceptions will most likely be significantly larger.

5. For large-scale sparse network contexts, specifically random networks, it can be shown that the terms related to the issue of shared parents are small and can be neglected because most pairs of bottom elements do not share a common parent, leaving a relatively simple calculation. Consider a large-scale sparse random network with N top elements and m bottom elements for each top element. Linkages in this network are generated through a two-step process as for the random simulated networks introduced in Chapter 4. In step 1 each bottom element is assigned at random a top element as first parent. In step 2

a random network model is used in which each pair of top and bottom elements not linked in step 1 have a fixed probability of being linked, with this probability the same for all pairs and draws independent across pairs. When the probability of a link in step 2 is approximately $\frac{1}{N}$ so that on average bottom elements have one additional parent, it can be shown that the expected seed pool size for a guiding conception is approximately $4m^2$, validating the discussion in the main text preceding paragraph that neglects the issue of shared parents. Approximately here means to order $\frac{1}{N}$, and this result can be generalized so that the link probability is $\frac{g}{N}$ with g a small fixed value. Independence arguments are used, as well as the large-scale sparse nature of the network. See the online Appendix available at www.jonathanfeinstein.com for details of the calculation. For dense networks these arguments break down and the calculation is quite complex.

6. The computer finds the cut-off values for which this is true for each network separately, then computes average values within each of the three bins for the network. The overall average values in the figure shown next then average these ten values for each bin.

7. Random search is of course the standard search model in economics. But here guidance is layered first so that search is only random within the narrower confines of a given pool. See below in the main text for random search over the entire network. In fact as I discuss further below, the optimal sequence to try pairs is not strictly random for a full network with lattice structure.

8. Assuming that individuals can make an exact determination is strong since even a prototype project based on a seed pair may not reveal whether a full project developed from this seed will be golden. The assumption can be weakened: for example, more realistically individuals may gain a sense of the likelihood that a given seed pair can be developed into a golden project but not know for certain. I do not pursue this aspect of the model in order to stay focused on the main point about the efficiency of guidance. Further, this issue of exact determination is relevant regardless of whether the search over seeds is based on guidance or random; thus the comparison of these two approaches does not depend directly on this, although of course it may affect quantitative comparisons between them. As long as individuals' assessments are reasonably accurate, meaning that for a seed pair that can be developed into a golden project their assessment of this likelihood is relatively high whereas for other seed pairs their assessment is relatively low, the basic insights of the model should continue to hold true, although there may be more time and resources spent pursuing false leads.

9. For example, if there are 3 elements in the pool, the golden seed pair might be tried first, second, or third, and each of these positions is equally likely

and thus has one-third probability of occurring; thus the expected number of trials to discover it is $\frac{1}{3}1 + \frac{1}{3}2 + \frac{1}{3}3 = 2$, which is indeed $\frac{M(here\ 3)+1}{2}$.

10. Formally, the golden seed is equally likely to be located in each of the 100 slots from 1 to 100 in the sequence, and each of these positions has probability $\frac{1}{100}$.

11. Consider a hierarchy in which there are 4 top elements: A, B, C, and D. Each top element has 2 children: a_1 and a_2 under A and so forth. Valid seeds are based on pairs of children under different parents. There are 6 combinations of top elements: $A-B$, $A-C$, $A-D$, $B-C$, $B-D$, and $C-D$. There are 4 valid seeds under each, hence 24 valid seeds in total. There are 4 triple combinations of top elements: $A-B-C$, $A-B-D$, $A-C-D$, and $B-C-D$. There are 8 valid projects under each, hence 32 valid projects in total. One of these is the golden project; without loss of generality, assume it is project (a_2, c_2, d_2). Random search tries seed pairs in turn. Assume for example that seed (a_1, b_1) is tried first. If it is found not to have the potential to be developed into the golden project, then all 4 projects it participates in are ruled out: (a_1, b_1, c_1), (a_1, b_1, c_2), (a_1, b_1, d_1), and (a_1, b_1, d_2). This leaves 28 projects. As seeds are tried and ruled out, the list of active projects, that is the list of projects that have a nonzero chance of being the golden project, shortens. This also means that among the remaining seeds, some participate in more active projects than others. For example, consider two possible choices for the next seed to investigate in the example. Seed (a_1, b_2) still participates in 4 active projects. But seed (a_1, c_1) participates in just 3 because one of its projects, (a_1, b_1, c_1), has been ruled out. If we assume that all remaining projects are equally likely to be the golden project, this implies it is better to investigate (a_1, b_2) next. Interestingly, for hierarchies—and ONLY for hierarchies—the optimal search protocol is relatively simple. In this case it turns out it is best to pick a top element pair and investigate all seeds in its pool, and then if a golden seed is not found, move to another top element pair. The top element pair chosen at each step is based on which top element pair has seeds that participate in the most active projects. In the example if all (a_i, b_j) pairs were tried and ruled out, then it would be optimal next to try all pairs under a disjoint pair of top elements such as $C-D$. Thus for a hierarchy, random search proceeds by searching through a sequence of top element pair seed pools, and thus is equivalent to searching through a sequence of guiding conceptions. But the big difference is that there is no intuition guiding the selection of a particular top element pair under random search, so that in general many top element pairs will need to be tried in order to find a golden seed. Note further that for a large-scale network, the sequence of top element pairs chosen under random search will in fact be close to random at least through the first part of the search, because when one top element pair seed pool is searched,

it rules out relatively few projects in the full context and thus many remaining top element pairs will have seed pools in which all seeds continue to cover a full project list. In the random search protocol, these are all equivalent; hence the next pair is chosen at random from this set. It follows that one's first intuition for a guiding conception doesn't have to be correct: as long as one hits upon a guiding conception with valid intuition in a reasonable number of attempts, one will do better. Consider, for example, a symmetric hierarchy in which there are 100 top elements and each has 2 children. There are 4,950 pairs of top elements and hence this many guiding conceptions. A computation shows that, choosing top pairs in an optimal sequence, the number of top element pairs whose seed pools must be searched in order to have evaluated one-half of the total number of valid projects is more than 500 (author calculations). As long as intuition hits on a correct guiding conception sooner than this, it will be more efficient.

Now consider the general point that when searching seeds, it is always optimal to search next a seed for which the number of active projects is at least as large as for any other seed that has not yet been considered. The logic is straightforward. Suppose this is not the case. Then in the optimal search sequence at some point the next two seeds in the sequence are a and b—a is to be searched first and then b—and a has fewer active projects associated with it than b at this point (just before a is considered). In that case it is always better to swap their order and search b first. One, once both have been searched, for all remaining seeds the active projects associated with each will be the same. Two, if a and b share any projects in common, it does not matter which is searched first from the viewpoint of these common projects, because the elimination of a project is symmetric for all seeds linked to it. Thus it is better to search b first since it has more projects associated with it, any one of which might be the golden project. This is a contradiction of the assumption that a is searched first and therefore shows that optimally seeds are searched strictly in sequence in terms of their number of active projects.

12. The argument builds on the logic outlined in the text and note 11. Seeds are searched in order of the number of active projects associated with them. Conceptualize this as a graph. Given the optimal sequence that will be followed, array the seeds in order on the horizontal axis, the first seed to be considered at position 1, the second at position 2, and so forth. Each seed has associated a vertical bar of height equal to the fraction of the total number of projects that will be implicitly investigated when the seed is tried. So, for example, if there are 1,000 projects total and the first seed has 20 projects associated with it, its vertical bar has height .02. If the second seed will have 10 projects associated with it when it is searched, its vertical bar has height .01; note that any projects it has that overlap with seed 1 are not included since they have been ruled out

when the first seed was tried and found not to be a golden seed. The graph therefore establishes a probability distribution over projects. This distribution is nonincreasing with seed number since seeds are searched in order of number of active projects. In fact it must be decreasing somewhere, since once the first seed is searched, each project associated with it is ruled out for the other seeds that link to it—and those seeds cannot have had a larger number of projects to start or would have been searched first, and therefore now have a smaller number. The seed such that one-half of all projects have been considered is the median of this distribution. The expected number of seeds to search is the mean. For a decreasing distribution like this, it is the case that the mean is never to the left of the median. Proof of this: Suppose the mean is to the left of the median. This means that more than one-half of the distribution lies to the right of the mean. This part of the distribution has vertical heights that are no greater than the vertical heights to the left of the mean. Divide the probability distribution into two parts: on the left the mass at the mean and all to the left, and then all to the right, which must be at least one-half the total. Then in the worst case each side is one-half, and in this case the mean is the simple average of the average value for the seeds on the left side and the average value for the seeds on the right. But since the right-side seeds have smaller vertical bars, their average is further to the right of the mean (extends further out) than the average of the seeds on the left (including the mean) extends to the left of the mean. Hence the average of these two values must lie to the right of the mean, and the overall mean must be above its posited value. Hence this is a contradiction, and the mean cannot lie to the left of the median. Since the mean is either equal to or greater than the median, so too the expected search value is at least as large as the median value, i.e., the number of seeds such that one-half of all projects have been considered.

13. For this analysis it turns out that results are the same regardless of whether there are horizontal links between top elements (this is because guiding conception coverage and hence search pools are governed entirely by vertical links), so I do not include such links or discuss them.

14. Lateral links between bottom elements would affect the argument if bottom elements that are directly linked cannot form valid seeds or participate in a common project.

15. Note that bottom elements are not hubs, consistent with the general discussion in Chapter 4 and empirical examples I have given of creativity contexts.

16. Assuming a single hub does increase the number of nonhub top elements, but this number plays no role in the bounding argument. Thus given $\bar{\theta}$ replace the original network with a new network in which there is a single hub that

links to all elements in region I, and the remaining $l - 1$ top elements that were hubs now are similar to all the other nonhub top elements, in particular satisfy the restriction of no more than k children.

17. Since many bottom elements have multiple parents, and these parents in turn have multiple children, the actual number of projects associated with a given seed will generally be smaller than this.

18. Frederic Holmes discusses the projects Krebs was working on just before taking up the synthesis of urea in *Hans Krebs: The Formation of a Scientific Life, 1900–1933*, Volume 1, 1991, Oxford University Press, Chapter 8, pp. 240–46. See Chapter 14 for more details.

19. In her diary (*The Diary of Virginia Woolf*, Volume One, 1915–1919, 1977, ed. Anne Olivier Bell, Harcourt) over the time period August 1917 when she resumed it, through December 1919 when she began "An Unwritten Novel," there are no very direct mentions of ideas for stories. There are two places where she writes a comment that might be construed as her thinking about a story idea. On Tuesday, July 16, 1918, describing a visit with her mother-in-law, an outing with her children that her mother-in-law evidently took great delight in, she wrote: "But to give this effect I should need a chapter, & rather hope one of these days to take one" (p. 167). On Monday, November 4, 1918, she wrote: "I keep thinking of different ways to manage my scenes; conceiving endless possibilities; seeing life, as I walk about the streets, an immense opaque block of material to be conveyed by me into its equivalent of language" (p. 214). This latter isn't a story idea per se, but does show her thinking about her creative writing.

20. This approach relates to the field of computational creativity. However, the models in that field at least to this point place far less emphasis on intuition generating guiding conceptions, as discussed in Chapter 9.

21. "Modern Novels," *The Essays of Virginia Woolf*, Volume Three, 1919–1924, 1989, ed. Andrew McNeillie, pp. 30–37; it was first published in the *Times Literary Supplement* in April 1919. See also Hermione Lee, *Virginia Woolf*, 1996, Vintage, Chapters 21 and 23.

22. A good first step empirically is to examine data on the number of seeds an individual explicitly considered or actively pursued under a given guiding conception. Encouraging individuals to note ideas they consider, even fleetingly, would help make this measure more valid. Even so, once an individual discovers a promising seed and chooses to pursue it, they will not explore the remainder of their pool, thus truncating the data gathering process. As we have seen, under random search the size of the pool is approximately twice as large as the seeds explored.

23. The online Appendix outlines how to compute the distribution of the number of guiding conceptions that cover a given seed in a random network.

24. The sizes of the seed pools of these different guiding conceptions will in general be different. Of particular interest is the search pool size for the guiding conception that has the smallest search pool, for it will have the lowest expected number of trials to discover the seed pair.

25. For example, assume that one of the project elements has two parents, A_1 and A_2, and the other two elements each has one, B_1 and C_1; this is the next coverage up above each having just a single parent, in which case 3 guiding conceptions cover the project. In this case there are 5 guiding conceptions that cover the project: $A_1 - B_1$, $A_1 - C_1$, $A_2 - B_1$, $A_2 - C_1$, and $B_1 - C_1$. Thus it is not possible for 4 guiding conceptions to cover a project. Similar arguments apply to a series of integer values, including 6 and 10.

26. Consider the following example of a simple power law network with one hub and $N - 1$ other top elements, with N large. All bottom elements are the same, and the model follows the two-step simulation model used to generate the simulated networks. In step 1 there is a one-half probability the bottom element links to the hub; if it does not, then it links to one of the other top elements at random. Now consider step 2. If the bottom element links to the hub in step 1, it has probability $\frac{1}{N-1}$ of linking to each of the other top elements in step 2, so that the expected number of further links in this case is 1. It follows that in this case the probability the bottom element does not have any further connections, meaning it has just one parent the hub, is $(1 - \frac{1}{N-1})^{N-1}$, which can be computed using exponentiation and logarithmic approximations to be $\frac{1}{e}$ to order $1/N$. Alternatively, consider the case in which the bottom element links with one of the other top elements in step 1. In step 2 set up probabilities such that the expected number of links is again 1. Since there are now $N - 2$ other remaining top elements plus the hub, this reworks probabilities such that the probability of linking to the hub in step 2 is $\frac{N-1}{2N-3}$ or 1/2 in the limit of large N, and the probability of linking with each of the other remaining top elements is $\frac{1}{2N-3}$ or $\frac{1}{2N}$ in the limit of large N. It can then be computed again using exponentiation and logarithmic approximations that the probability the bottom element in this case does not link to either the hub or any other top element is $\frac{1}{\sqrt{e}}$ to order $1/N$. Overall $\frac{3}{4}$ of bottom elements link to the hub. These elements have probability $\frac{2}{3e}$ of having just one parent in the limit of large N (to order $1/N$). Elements that do not link to the hub have probability $\frac{2}{\sqrt{e}}$ of having just one parent. It follows that elements not linked to the hub are more likely to have just one parent. Therefore projects for which all three elements are not linked to the hub are more likely to be covered by just three guiding conceptions than projects with elements linked to the hub. Further, since the hub has many

children, guiding conceptions that include the hub will have larger seed pools than guiding conceptions without the hub. Thus projects with low coverage will on average be covered by guiding conceptions with smaller seed pools.

CHAPTER 11

1. Ideals provide not only guidance but also motivation. A person may strive for years to attain an ideal, or to come ever closer to it. William Faulkner remarked about writing: "All of us have failed to match our dream of perfection." "If I could write all my work again, I'm convinced I could do it better. This is the healthiest condition for an artist. That's why he keeps working, trying again: he believes each time that this time he will do it, bring it off." Cited at https://www.goodreads.com/author/quotes/3535.William_Faulkner?page=2, retrieved January 27, 2022; see also Ta-Nehisi Coates, "The 'Ode on a Grecian Urn' Is Worth Any Number of Old Ladies," *The Atlantic*, July 3, 2012. However, while I recognize the importance of motivation in creativity, in the model of this book, which centers on context and cognitive processes, I focus on guiding principles in terms of their role in guidance.

2. The philosopher George Santayana argues that beauty is not an inherent quality of an object but rather a subjective sensibility that the perceiver imputes to it—see George Santayana, *The Sense of Beauty*, 1955, Dover. The representation of a guiding principle may be quite rich. Individuals gain experience applying such principles repeatedly, and may develop a rich, subtle interpretation of them, including some experiential knowledge that may be largely unconsciously applied.

3. See Walter Isaacson, "The Real Leadership Lessons of Steve Jobs," *Harvard Business Review*, April 2012, in particular the section "Simplicity."

4. Even this may not be sufficient: Steve Jobs's employees did not always agree with his assessments—see the discussion slightly further on in the main text and the reference in note 5.

5. See Walter Isaacson, "How Steve Jobs' Love of Simplicity Fueled a Design Revolution," September 2012, *Smithsonian Magazine*, especially the discussion of the design of the Macintosh. The movie *The Last Portrait*, 2017, based on the book *A Giacometti Portait* by James Lord, 1980, Farrar Straus Giroux, illustrates this process of revision taken to an extreme by Alberto Giacometti. Giacometti paints in Lord's portrait, then erases it, not satisfied with it, and begins again—over and over. Finally, frustrated and about to travel home, Lord steals away with a completed (or partially completed) version before Giacometti can erase it, while the artist is distracted.

6. John Rawls, *A Theory of Justice*, 1971, Harvard University Press. For health policy see Norman Daniels, *Just Health Care*, 1985, Cambridge University

Press. Rawls's theory in relation to the environment raises some complexities, especially as his theory is human centered and seems to support resource exploitation. But there have been attempts to develop an environmental ethic based on it. For a recent contribution see John Töns, *John Rawls and Environmental Justice; Implementing a Sustainable and Socially Just Future*, 2022, Routledge; for a discussion of some of the issues see Andrew Greene, Rawls's Theory of Justice; A Necessary Extension to Environmentalism, 2011, master's thesis, University of Central Florida.

7. See Barbara Rose, ed., *Art as Art: The Selected Writings of Ad Reinhardt*, 1975, University of California Press, especially the essays "Abstract Art Refuses," pp. 50–51, and "Art-as-Art," pp. 53–56, as well as the Introduction, pp. xi–xvii.

8. Of course a guiding principle would have been first stated by some individual or group, or perhaps developed gradually, but most individuals employing a guiding principle have adopted it.

9. Heuristics figure prominently in the well-known work on decision making by Amos Tversky and Daniel Kahneman, "Judgment under Uncertainty: Heuristics and Biases," 1974, *Science*, Vol. 185, No. 4157, pp. 1124–31; and Daniel Kahneman, Paul Slovic, Amos Tversky, eds., *Judgment under Uncertainty: Heuristics and Biases*, 1982, Cambridge University Press. Margaret Boden discusses heuristics in *The Creative Mind: Myths and Mechanisms*, 2004, Routledge—see especially her discussion in Chapter 8, "Computer-Scientists." See also Gerd Gigerenzer, Ralph Hertwig, and Thorsten Pachur, *Heuristics: The Foundations of Adaptive Behavior*, 2011, Oxford University Press.

10. Donald Schön, *The Reflective Practitioner*, 1983, Basic Books. Robert Weisberg has written a pair of interesting books that focus on creative problem solving: *Creativity: Beyond the Myth of Genius*, 1993, W. H. Freeman, and *Creativity: Understanding Innovation in Problem Solving, Science, Invention, and the Arts*, 2006, John Wiley and Sons. See also the conceptual blending literature that gives insights on problem solving, e.g., Gilles Fauconnier and Mark Turner, *The Way We Think: Conceptual Blending and the Mind's Hidden Complexities*, 2002, Basic Books.

11. Gerald Holton, *Thematic Origins of Scientific Thought*, 1988, Harvard University Press; quote is on p. 17.

12. Holton, *Thematic Origins*, p. 33. Isaac Newton, *The Principia*, 1982, trans. I. Bernard Cohen and Anne Whitman, University of California Press, pp. 794–95.

CHAPTER 12

1. Vivien Johnson, *Clifford Possum Tjapaltjarri*, 2003, Art Gallery of South Australia, pp. 86–93.

2. Johnson, *Clifford Possum*, p. 227.

3. Johnson, *Clifford Possum*, p. 228.

4. Frederic Holmes, *Hans Krebs: The Formation of a Scientific Life, 1900–1933*, Volume 1, 1991, Oxford University Press, pp. 266, 272.

5. Holmes, *Hans Krebs*, p. 247.

6. Interaction Design Foundation, "Design Principles," http://interaction-design.org/literature/topics/design-principles.

7. Interaction Design Foundation, "Design Principles." As a related rule, classically, the golden ratio specifices a specific ration of width to height that is widely viewed as aesthetically appealing. The ratio is $\frac{1+\sqrt{5}}{2}$ or approximately 1.618.

8. William Lidwell, Kritina Holden, and Jill Butler, *Universal Principles of Design*, 2010, Rockport.

9. Edward Tufte, *The Visual Display of Quantitative Information*, 1983, Graphics Press.

10. Tufte, *Visual Display*, p. 13.

11. Tufte, *Visual Display*, p. 77.

12. Walter Isaacson, "How Steve Jobs' Love of Simplicity Fueled a Design Revolution," September 2012, *Smithsonian Magazine*.

13. See D. T. Max, "Two-Hit Wonder," October 14, 2013, *The New Yorker*; the article attributes to him the phrase, "constraint inspires creativity."

14. Lynn Conway, "ACS Logical Design Conventions: A Guide for the Novice," November 29, 1967, retrieved from https://ai.eecs.umich.edu/people/conway/conway.html.

15. Lynn Conway, "The Computer Design Process: A Proposed Plan for ACS," August 6, 1968, pp. 1–2; retrieved from https://ai.eecs.umich.edu/people/conway/conway.html.

16. Conway, "The Computer Design Process," especially Figure 1 and thereafter.

17. Lynn Conway, "IBM-ACS: Reminiscences and Lessons Learned from a 1960's Supercomputer Project," in *Dependable and Historic Computing: Essays Dedicated to Brian Randell on the Occasion of his 75th Birthday*, 2011, ed. Cliff B. Jones and John L. Lloyd, Springer-Verlag, p. 194.

18. Conway, "IBM-ACS," p. 194.

19. Conway, "IBM-ACS," p. 195.

20. Conway, "IBM-ACS," pp. 196–97.

21. Lynn Conway, "Reminiscences of the VLSI Revolution: How a Series of Failures Triggered a Paradigm Shift in Digital Design," Fall 2012, *IEEE Solid-State Circuits Magazine*, Vol. 4, No. 4, pp. 8–31. See also Conway's website: https://ai.eecs.umich.edu/people/conway/conway.html.

22. Albert Einstein, "Autobiographical Notes," 1949, in *Albert Einstein: Philosopher-Scientist,* ed. and trans. Paul Arthur Schilpp, Tudor Publishing Company, copyright the Library of Living Philosophers, p. 53.

23. Einstein, "Autobiographical Notes," p. 53.

24. The memo was written most likely also at age sixteen: see *The Collected Papers of Albert Einstein,* Volume 1: *The Early Years, 1879-1902,* 1987, trans. Anna Beck, Princeton University Press, pp. 4-6. Gerald Holton also mentions that Einstein's close friend Michele Besso stated that at this time Einstein was thinking about the concept of the ether—see Gerald Holton, *Thematic Origins of Scientific Thought,* 1988, Harvard University Press, Chapter 6, "On the Origins of the Special Theory of Relativity," p. 213.

25. In a letter to Mileva Marić dated 1899, he states that the notion of the ether describes a "medium of whose motion one can speak without being able, I believe, to associate a physical meaning with this statement. I think that the electric forces can be directly defined only for empty space." He seems to have continued to have some interest in experiments to detect the ether, but over time his attention shifted away from this topic. See *The Collected Papers of Albert Einstein,* Vol. 1, pp. 130-31.

26. Albert Einstein, "Fundamental Ideas and Methods of the Theory of Relativity, Presented in Their Development," in *The Collected Papers of Albert Einstein,* Volume 7: *The Berlin Years: Writings, 1918-21,* 2002, English translation of selected texts by Alfred Engel, Princeton University Press, p. 135.

27. Arthur Miller, *Albert Einstein's Special Theory of Relativity: Emergence (1905) and Early Interpretation (1905-1911),* 1998, Springer-Verlag, pp. 135-55. The special relativity paper Einstein published in 1905 begins with the induction problem, probably reflecting how well known it was and its importance as an example highlighting the importance of the principle of relativity.

28. Reproduced from: Albert Einstein, "How I Created the Theory of Relativity," 1982, trans. Yoshimasa A. Ono (translation of a lecture given in Kyoto on December 14, 1922), *Physics Today,* Volume 35, No. 8 p. 46, with the permission of AIP Publishing. The induction problem may have also played a role, for in his paper cited in footnote 26 above, Einstein wrote that the induction problem, "forced me to postulate the principle of (special) relativity."

29. Einstein credited his taking this revolutionary step with having been exposed to the ideas of Ernst Mach and especially David Hume, whose *Treatise of Human Nature* he said he "had studied avidly and with admiration shortly before discovering the theory of relativity." Albert Einstein letter to Moritz Schlick, December 14,1915, printed in *The Collected Papers of Albert Einstein,* Volume 8: *The Berlin Years: Correspondence, 1914-1918,* 1998, English translation of selected texts by Ann M. Hentschel, Princeton University Press, pp. 161-62. For more

on Hume's influence see Jonathan S. Feinstein, *The Nature of Creative Development*, 2006, Stanford University Press, Chapter 10, "Exploration of Creative Interests and Creativity Generation; Creative Expertise," pp. 303–15, 322–28. See also John Stachel, "'What Song the Syrens Sang': How Did Einstein Discover Special Relativity?" in *Einstein From 'B' to 'Z'*, 2002, ed. John Stachel, Birkhäuser, pp. 157–69. The connection has also been discussed by John Norton: see "How Hume and Mach Helped Einstein Find Special Relativity," 2010, in *Discourse on a New Method: Reinvigorating the Marriage of History and Philosophy of Science*, ed. M. Dickson and M. Domski, Open Court, pp. 359–86.

30. Einstein, "How I Created the Theory of Relativity," p. 47.

31. Norton provides a good overall account of Einstein's path: John D. Norton, "Einstein's Pathway to General Relativity," https://www.pitt.edu/~jdnorton/teaching/HPS_410/chapters/general_ relativity_ pathway/index.html, retrieved February 19, 2021. Norton makes reference to Einstein's earlier attempt, with restricted coordinate systems, in a paper coauthored with Marcel Grossmann, "Entwurf einer verallgemeinerten Relativitätstheorie und einer Theorie der Gravitation [Outline of a Generalized Theory of Relativity and of a Theory of Gravitation]," 1914, *Zeitschrift für Mathematik und Physik*, 62, pp. 225–61 (an earlier version was published in 1913).

32. Albert Einstein, *Relativity: The Special and the General Theory*, 1961, authorised trans. by Robert W. Lawson, Crown Publishers (first edition 1916 in German).

33. Einstein, *Relativity*, pp. 59–60.

34. Einstein, *Relativity*, pp. 97–99.

35. Olivier Darrigol provides a balanced account of Poincaré's views and how they relate to Einstein's theory in "The Genesis of the Theory of Relativity," 2005, *Séminaire Poincaré*, 1, pp. 1–22. See also Holton, *Thematic Origins of Scientific Thought*, Chapter 6, "On the Origins of the Special Theory of Relativity," especially pp. 197, 202–6; Shaul Katzir, "Poincaré's Relativistic Physics: Its Origins and Nature," 2005, *Physics in Perspective*, Vol. 7, pp. 268–92; "Relativity Priority Dispute," https://en.wikipedia.org/wiki/Relativity_priority_dispute#cite _note-mborn-30, retrieved April 21, 2022, for an overview of different viewpoints.

CHAPTER 13

1. The main reason to specify guiding principles in the context would be because they have links to related high-level concepts, often connected principles, as well as exemplars. In a richer, more iterative model, these links may come into play as an individual modifies their principle or uses exemplars to help evaluate projects. For example, if one of an artist's guiding principles is "balance," and in their subjective context balance is (or becomes) linked with

another principle such as "harmony," this may influence their evaluations. But I eschew such richer evaluation processes and dynamics here.

2. I thank my brother David for calling my attention to this example.

3. He is reported to have said this during his Herbert Spencer lecture at Oxford on June 10, 1933. See Albert Einstein, Alice Calaprice, and Freeman Dyson, *The Ultimate Quotable Einstein*, 2010, Princeton University Press, pp. 384–85.

4. For example, an important topic of study is the analysis of shortest paths between nodes. Sometimes analysis extends to shortest distances from a node to a subset of other nodes, an approach I follow below, or between two subsets.

5. I note that the hypergraph framework, in which links are defined between sets of elements, may be useful to model guiding principles, but I do not pursue that approach. For hypergraphs see Claude Berge, *Hypergraphs: Combinatorics of Finite Sets*, 1989, North Holland; and for a recent discussion and application Sinan Aksoy, Cliff Joslyn, Carlos Ortiz Marrero, Brenda Praggastis, and Emilie Purvine, "Hypernetwork Science via High-Order Hypergraph Walks," 2020, *EPJ Data Science*, Vol. 9, Article 16. See Chapter 16 for more.

6. This may be a conscious recognition, or alternatively may be reactive and not fully recognized, even largely unconscious.

7. The assumption that each seed an individual generates lies in the domain of their guiding principle must be modified when modeling iterative project revision with guiding principles, since as a project is revised, it may shift away from the domain of the guiding conception, as new elements are substituted for old; I do not pursue this line of model development.

8. For larger, more complex seeds and projects, a guiding principle may focus evaluation on a subset of elements.

9. It may also be more difficult empirically to assess accuracy, whereas efficiency is more evident since it is linked to the number of attempts. For Hans Krebs, for example, we see in the laboratory records of his work on the urea project clear evidence of high efficiency in trying many things, whereas the degree of accuracy he brought to bear in evaluating alternatives and choosing not to pursue certain leads is more difficult to evaluate, since we do not know what he might have found had he pursued a lead he chose not to pursue.

10. An individual or team might have more than one guiding principle, as discussed at the start of this chapter, and in that case one principle might play a larger role in evaluation and another a larger role in identifying additional elements. It's also possible that there are a number of distinct guiding principles that might be able to identify the key additional element associated with a given seed. What is important is that the individual or team must have formulated at least one guiding principle that can help identify the missing element.

11. For example in Mednick's idea of remote associates cited previously in Chapter 5, note 1.

12. It should be noted that given a context structure with hierarchy links and horizontal links between top elements but not bottom elements, all paths must pass through top elements. But the paths may differ in terms of how many top versus bottom elements they pass through—the example below in the main text illustrates this. The model can be extended to allow for the fact that different types of paths—for example, differences in the number of top versus bottom elements along a path—may make the path more or less conducive to forging the creative link to the third element.

13. Note that the same seed may show up multiple times since it can be covered by more than one guiding conception. And a given project shows up at least three times and often more, since it can be reached from three different seeds.

14. See Walter Isaacson, "How Steve Jobs' Love of Simplicity Fueled a Design Revolution," September 2012, *Smithsonian Magazine*, pp. 3–4.

15. The functions are generally very similar at the smallest distance of 2 for which there are very few projects, and tend to all be very close to 1 by the greater distances. The biggest separation happens in the middle, which is where most third elements lie.

16. Strictly speaking this is not the only factor, as pairs of children of the two guiding conception elements that share a common parent are ruled out. But as noted in Chapter 10, for the sparse networks that are most relevant for creativity, this is relatively rare.

CHAPTER 14

1. The first project focused on the effect of methylene blue on respiration in human red blood cells and seems to have been prompted by recent research articles on the topic, but whereas those articles focused on the conversion of hemoglobin, Krebs focused on attempting to isolate the steps in the overall metabolic process where methylene blue had an effect, consistent with his guiding conception. The few attempts he made did not seem to carry a clear implication, however, and he dropped this project—thus we can think of it as a project seed that he evaluated as not sufficiently promising to pursue. The second project was stimulated by recent research showing that the compound iodoacetate blocks fermentation in yeast. Since fermentation is the first stage of yeast metabolism, this would seem to reduce overall yeast metabolic activity—or as it is called, respiration. Krebs decided to explore pushing this a step further, to see if adding a reagent that could replace the output of fermentation—alcohol— could restore full respiration in yeast. Krebs seems to have been interested in

whether if a reagent blocked the first stage, then by adding the purported product of the first stage, which in the case of yeast is alcohol, the second stage could then go forward. Here Krebs found promising results initially and pursued the project for about two weeks. Finding mixed results overall, he then abandoned this topic but continued with the idea of exploring the effects of iodoacetate. He now shifted to exploring its effects on metabolism in various kinds of animal tissue samples, his third project. He pursued this over some months, even continuing with it when he moved to Freiburg and publishing on the topic. Finally, the fourth project was on the metabolism of the choroid plexus. The choroid plexus is a brain structure that produces cerebrospinal fluid. Krebs explored its metabolic activity, thus again pursuing a project fitting with his overall conception. For more see Frederic Holmes, *Hans Krebs: The Formation of a Scientific Life, 1900-1933*, Volume 1, 1991, Oxford University Press, pp. 213–36.

2. Holmes, *Hans Krebs*, p. 253-54.

3. Holmes, *Hans Krebs* pp. 248-55. The method of detecting urea was based on using the enzyme urease. Biochemist Donald Van Slyke had developed a manometric method based on the use of urease, but in a somewhat more cumbersome way (at least for Krebs's purposes), and Krebs modified the method.

4. Holmes, *Hans Krebs*, p. 284.

5. Holmes, *Hans Krebs*, p. 256. See Hans Krebs, "The Discovery of the Ornithine Cycle of Urea Synthesis," 1973, *Biomedical Education*, Vol. 1, pp. 19–20.

6. If ammonia were an essential intermediary, then it would be able to produce urea as quickly and efficiently as any of the amino acids, so this was a way to investigate this question.

7. Holmes, *Hans Krebs*, pp. 256-66.

8. Holmes, *Hans Krebs*, pp. 267-71. They also developed an improved source of urease, the enzyme that they were using to detect urea. It is noteworthy that Krebs was concurrently pursuing a second project on carbohydrate metabolism, linked to his earlier project on iodoacetate.

9. Holmes, *Hans Krebs*, p. 272.

10. Holmes, *Hans Krebs*, pp. 277-78. He also tested methylamine to see if a non-amino-acid substance with nitrogen might also yield urea, which it did not. He also tested if the intermediary cyanate formed and was a route to urea production, a theory that had been put forth earlier in the literature, and found that it was not.

11. The urea molecule has two nitrogen atoms, and he was testing whether perhaps one would come from an amino acid (every amino acid has at least one nitrogen atom) and the other from an ammonia source.

12. Pursuing different paths, he also returned to exploring the impact of sugar and various compounds that were believed to have a role in aerobic metabolism in solution with an ammonia compound.

13. Holmes, *Hans Krebs*, pp. 284–86. Ornithine was expensive, which adds to the puzzle of why Krebs used it, but he may have had access through a colleague.

14. Holmes, *Hans Krebs*, pp. 287–99. He and his assistant also worked to regularize the experimental conditions both to ensure the finding was real and not an artifact and also to try to attain a rate of production of urea in the tissue slices that was comparable to the rate for a living organism. He also explored how amino acids react in kidney tissue to drop an amine group, a discovery that launched a parallel, related line of inquiry. In truth, during the winter of 1932 Krebs and his assistant were performing many experiments a day, but were not clear about answers.

15. Holmes, *Hans Krebs*, p. 324.

16. Holmes, *Hans Krebs*, pp. 301–2, 315, for the decisive experiment. The results were not so clear in all cases especially initially, because ornithine can also give rise to urea through a second noncatalytic pathway at high concentrations. Krebs also tested to see if ornithine donated a nitrogen to urea and found this in general not to be supported by the data, though again results were not always clear-cut.

17. Holmes, *Hans Krebs*, pp. 323–27.

18. Vivien Johnson, *Clifford Possum Tjapaltjarri*, 2003, Art Gallery of South Australia, p. 82.

19. Johnson, *Clifford Possum*, p. 82.

20. These comments are based on Vivien Johnson's summary of annotations by Peter Fannin, at the time the administrator of the Papunya Tula Artists organization. See Johnson, *Clifford Possum*, p. 83.

21. Johnson, *Clifford Possum*, pp. 87–88. Warlugulong is not Possum's Dreaming, and he stated that he was reluctant, but asked his mother and uncle, both of whom had a direct connection with the site, and they said he could paint it but apparently restricted what he was allowed to depict of the story.

22. For detailed discussions of the painting see Johnson, *Clifford Possum*, pp. 86–93 and 226–28.

23. Johnson, *Clifford Possum*, pp. 89–92.

24. Johnson, *Clifford Possum*, p. 92.

25. Johnson, *Clifford Possum*, pp. 93–115, 228–31, and 233–37. This interpretation is supported by the detailed notes on his other "map of the country" paintings made by individuals who were present when he painted them.

26. This episode is described by both David Sarno, "Twitter Creator Jack Dorsey Illuminates the Site's Founding Document. Part I," February 18, 2009,

Los Angeles Times, and D. T. Max, "Two-Hit Wonder," October 14, 2013, *The New Yorker*.

27. Text messaging was developed in the 1990s, but it did not catch on for some time. See https://en.wikipedia.org/wiki/SMS. The graph in the article indicates that text messaging was very limited in the United States prior to 2002.

28. Max, "Two-Hit Wonder."

29. Max states that Dorsey's mother told him "He was always a minimalist."

30. Sarno, "Twitter Creator Jack Dorsey."

31. My account draws on Mark Isaac, *Super Pumped: The Battle for Uber*, 2019, W. W. Norton. I have also learned from Steve T, "The History of Uber," April 12, 2018, https://biographics.org/the-history-of-uber/ retrieved on March 8, 2022. Interestingly, there was an earlier version of rideshare in the 1900s known as a "jitney"—this is discussed by Ben Labaschin, "A History of Ridesharing: From the Jitney to Uber," *Arity*, April 3, 2018.

32. Isaac, *Super Pumped*, pp. 43–44; Steve T, "The History of Uber." Isaac says the idea occurred when he was watching a movie; Steve T states he had the idea while holding his own iPhone in his hand.

33. Isaac, *Super Pumped*, pp. 20–22, 28–29; Steve T, "The History of Uber."

34. Isaac, *Super Pumped*, p. 49. Quote is from Steve T, "The History of Uber."

35. Isaac, *Super Pumped*, p. 84.

36. For details see Sunil Paul, "The Untold Story of Ridesharing—Part III: The Birth of Sidecar and Ridesharing," https://sunilpaul.medium.com/the-untold-story-of-ridesharing-part-iii-the-birth-of-sidecar-and-ridesharing-9f6e6c706d8d, retrieved March 9, 2022.

37. Billy Gallagher, "Founders John Zimmer & Logan Green Explain How Lyft Was Born Out Of Zimride," Sep. 9, 2013, https://techcrunch.com/2013/09/09/zimmer-green-from-zimride-to-lyft/, retrieved on March 9, 2022.

38. Isaac, *Super Pumped*, pp. 85–87. Other companies beyond these three also had the ridesharing idea but did not develop it as successfully as Lyft and Uber—for example, Carma, see https://en.wikipedia.org/wiki/Carma.

CHAPTER 15

1. Even for Einstein one could argue that the principle of relativity remained fixed; what changed was his understanding of its scope of application. Expanding its scope both fit with his desired guiding conception and also solidified his conception as to how to proceed to develop a general theory of relativity.

2. Virginia Woolf, *The Complete Shorter Fiction of Virginia Woolf*, 1985, ed. Susan Dick, Harcourt, Brace, and Company, pp. 90–95.

3. Woolf, *Complete Shorter Fiction*, pp. 96–101.

4. Woolf, *Complete Shorter Fiction*, pp. 102–7.

5. Woolf, *Complete Shorter Fiction*, pp. 108–11.

6. Woolf, *Complete Shorter Fiction*, pp. 112–21.

7. Woolf, *Complete Shorter Fiction*, pp. 114–15, 118–19.

8. Woolf, *Complete Shorter Fiction*, p. 117.

9. Virginia Woolf, *The Diary of Virginia Woolf*, Volume Two, 1920–1924, 1978, ed. Anne Olivier Bell, Harcourt Brace and Company, pp. 13–14, acknowledgment to the Society of Authors as the Literary Representative of the Estate of Virginia Woolf. Quentin Bell also quotes from this diary entry and the way Virginia lays out in it the writing project she would pursue over the years ahead. See Quentin Bell, *Virginia Woolf: A Biography, 1972*, Volume 2, Harcourt Brace and Company, pp. 72–73.

10. Virginia Woolf, *The Letters of Virginia Woolf*, Volume Four, 1929–1931, 1978, ed. Nigel Nicolson and Joanne Trautmann, Harcourt Brace Jovanovich, p. 231. The fact that Woolf views "An Unwritten Novel" as a kind of stand-alone "great discovery" fits with the general tendency we have, as I have described in the Introduction, to revere the pinnacle moments of creative breakthrough. But as I have noted in the text, the preceding story "Sympathy" foreshadows the breakthrough; thus the breakthrough may have developed more slowly and cumulatively.

11. Virginia Woolf, *The Diary of Virginia Woolf*, Volume One, 1915–1919, 1977, ed. Anne Olivier Bell, Harcourt Brace and Company, entry for April 20, 1919, p. 266, acknowledgment to the Society of Authors as the Literary Representative of the Estate of Virginia Woolf. Bell states in his biography that Woolf believed writing her diary contributed to improving her fiction writing; *Virginia Woolf: A Biography*, Vol. 2, pp. 44–45.

12. In "A Sketch of the Past" Woolf comments that both her mother and father obsessed her up until the time she wrote *To the Lighthouse*, revealing its cathartic value for her. "A Sketch of the Past," in Virginia Woolf, *Moments of Being*, 1985, ed. Jean Schulkind, Harcourt Brace and Company.

13. Virginia Woolf, *To the Lighthouse*, 1927, this edition 1989, Harcourt, Brace and Company, p. 62.

14. Of course it's possible Woolf thought of this wording without realizing the link with reflections. But it is such a precise opposition that this seems less likely. It is possible she thought of Mrs. Ramsay having a hidden part to her self that escapes the gaze of others, and then, hearkening back to the conception of reflections helped her present this part with this wording that is so precisely opposite. But of course having this conception in her mind so fully may have just intuitively led her to this wording; that still fits the model in this book.

15. Ivan Sutherland of Caltech wrote a letter to his brother Bert at Xerox PARC proposing this research collaboration to develop a "design philosphy."

I. Sutherland, "The Problem: How to Build Digital Electronic Circuits from Now to 1985," Letter to W. R. Sutherland proposing a Xerox-PARC/Caltech collaboration, January 26, 1976. Cited in Conway, "Reminiscences of the VLSI Revolution: How a Series of Failures Triggered a Paradigm Shift in Digital Design," Fall 2012, *IEEE Solid-State Circuits Magazine*, pp. 8–31, footnote 20, p. 31.

16. I. Sutherland and C. Mead, "Microelectronics and Computer Science," November, 1977, *Scientific American*, pp. 210–28.

17. Conway, "Reminiscences of the VLSI Revolution," p. 14.

18. Conway, "Reminiscences of the VLSI Revolution," p. 14.

19. Conway, "Reminiscences of the VLSI Revolution," pp. 14–15. The three-color diagrams also appear in Carver Mead and Lynn Conway, *Introduction to VLSI Systems*, 1980, Addison-Wesley.

20. Conway, "Reminiscences of the VLSI Revolution," p. 15. An important article showcasing Mead's expertise is C. A. Mead and B. Hoeneisen, "Fundamental Limitations in Microelectronics—I. MOS Technology," 1972, *Solid-State Electronics*, Vol. 15, pp. 819–29. See also the more general, influential discussion in Sutherland and Mead, "Microelectronics and Computer Science," *Scientific American*.

21. Conway, "Reminiscences of the VLSI Revolution," p. 15.

22. Conway, "Reminiscences of the VLSI Revolution," p. 15.

23. She writes that it "open[ed] the door to widely-sharable, time-durable MOS cell libraries." Conway, "Reminiscences of the VLSI Revolution," p. 15.

24. Mead and Conway, *Introduction to VLSI Systems*. The draft of these chapters is posted on the Lynn Conway online archives.

CHAPTER 16

1. Eleanor Rosch, Carolyn B. Mervis, Wayne D. Gray, David M. Johnson, and Penny Boyes-Braem, "Basic Objects in Natural Categories," 1976, *Cognitive Psychology*, Vol. 8, No. 3, pp. 382–439, is a foundational reference.

2. Gregory Murphy, *The Big Book of Concepts*, 2002, MIT Press. See in particular Chapter 7, "Taxonomic Organization and the Basic Level of Concepts."

3. See the cdn.cit1.illinois.edu/courses/ANSC207/week1/Domestication/web _data/file4.htm web posting. The web address is quite long & continues with #:͂text=The%20taxonomy%20of%20the%20dog,the%20animal20kingdom%2C% 20or%20Animalia. And then: &text=Dogs%20are%20further%20classified20in, as%20that%20of%20the%20wolf. For a discussion of levels from WordNet see Laura Hollink, Aysenur Bilgin, and Jacco van Ossenbruggen, "Predicting the Basic Level in a Hierarchy of Concepts," 2021, in *Metadata and Semantic Research*, ed. Emmanouel Garoufallou, María-Antonia Ovalle-Perandones, and

Andreas Vlachidis, Springer. They find as many as seven levels over three different examples.

4. For example, Albert Einstein's principle of relativity would be located below the broad category *physics*, under the branch for general laws of physics, much as Holton describes themes, thus in perhaps the third or fourth level of context depending on how fully the context is articulated.

5. For creativity context modeling, the approach must allow sets to be linked both to other sets and to singletons—as when a set of contributions are linked, whether because they were all created by the same person or team or one has directly influenced another. Further, as in the example given in the main text, a set can contain both singletons and other sets.

6. For example, John Sowa, *Knowledge Representation: Logical, Philosophical, and Computational Foundations*, 2000, Brooks/Cole, and *Principles of Semantic Networks*, 1991, ed. John Sowa, Morgan Kaufmann; see also Hermann Helbig, *Knowledge Representation and the Semantics of Natural Language*, 2006, Springer. Formal concept analysis is also identified with the work of Rudolf Wille— for example, Bernhard Ganter and Rudolf Wille, *Formal Concept Analysis*, 1999, Springer. Formal reasoning models and commonsense modeling may also be applied. See also my discussions in Chapters 2 and 9.

7. Arthur Campbell, Jonathan S. Feinstein, Soonwook Hong, Sharon Qian, and Trevor Williams, "Diversity, Knowledge Clusters, and Job Placement: Graduate Economics Teaching of Core Microeconomics," 2017, *Journal of Economic Education*, Vol. 48, No. 3, pp. 146–66.

8. I have discussed commonsense reasoning in Chapter 2. Two links are Doug Lenat's CYC project and also Nils Nilsson, *Artificial Intelligence: A New Synthesis*, 1998, Morgan Kaufmann, in particular Chapter 18, "Representing Commonsense Knowledge." It is worth remarking that this approach would also go beyond standard frames-based approaches, which tend to define potential seeds as individual elements in slots, rather than more holistically as in the example of a striped pattern.

9. Consider again as an example Virginia Woolf's guiding conception of reflections that sparked story ideas, such as "Kew Gardens." Although we don't know the conceptual pathway she followed to the core idea of this story, we can deduce some of the links. In the story conversations provide reflections of selves; it is interesting Woolf chooses not primarily a visual form of reflections, although those are also present, but an auditory form. This required making a conceptual step from reflections as customarily visually defined, but this would have been natural for her given that her conception is quite abstract. In terms of modeling, if context is sufficiently richly defined and Woolf's guiding conception is defined with its own web of meaning, then the model should be able

to capture this link from her guiding conception to auditory forms of reflection, and from this to overheard conversations. Also, the snail's perspective in "Kew Gardens" depicts the human world in a detached way that makes the human reflections stand out rather than being potentially submerged in an overly realistic plotline. This key element of the story does not necessarily follow just from Woolf's guiding conception, but also derives from her guiding principle of not including standard kinds of description: the snail's viewpoint provides a more detached perspective. This conceptual link should be able to be modeled if Woolf's context and guiding principle are sufficiently richly described. "Kew Gardens" is also quite linear, as noted in the previous chapter, which connects with the idea of an "almost infinite number" of reflections. To model all of these conceptual links clearly requires careful modeling of Woolf's context as well as the sets of elements representing her guiding conception and guiding principle, which in turn generate story ideas—sets of elements defining the main elements of a possible story.

10. For seeds with 5 elements and 2 clusters, there are 5 distinct kinds of patterns. This increases computational complexity. An approach I have used is to build seeds element by element, thus starting from two-element seeds determine all possible third elements that can be added, and store that set; then for each three-element seed determine all possible fourth elements, subject to clustering rules, and store, and make sure to winnow out all duplicates.

11. I have also explored guiding conception coverage where a guiding conception covers a seed if at least one element in each cluster is linked to a guiding conception parent element.

12. Ed Catmull and Amy Wallace describe some of the complexity and issues of fit in managing such large projects in their book *Creativity, Inc.: Overcoming the Unseen Forces That Stand in the Way of True Inspiration*, 2014, Random House. The quote is from Ed Catmull, "How Pixar Fosters Creative Collaboration," September 2008, *Harvard Business Review*, p. 4.

13. One aspect of the revision process that is not part of the simpler model is changing the way elements fit together. In the simpler model with just two-element seeds and three-element project designs, this issue doesn't really arise. For larger projects with many elements, this is an important part of how the project is built up, and a model must address it, related to the discussion in the preceding section.

14. My discussion in *The Nature of Creative Development*, 2006, Stanford University Press, draws on the two-volume work published by Musée Picasso, *Les Demoiselles d'Avignon*, 1988. Volume I in particular shows hundreds of sketches Picasso made while working on the painting, including more than a dozen of the composition as a whole.

15. As an example Shane Pickett, an Indigenous Australian artist, pivoted his conception from a more Western-style landscape sensibility to a more spiritual, abstract one. See Chapter 18, note 5, for more about Pickett and a key reference.

16. I am grateful to Glenn Dutcher for suggesting the "seed" of these ideas.

CHAPTER 17

1. I present a model of the development of creative fields in "The Creative Development of Fields: Learning, Creativity, Paths, Implications," 2017, *Journal of the Knowledge Economy*, Vol. 8, No. 1, pp. 23–62. The model of context and creative combinations is different than in this book and not as satisfactory. But the work develops a full representation of how a field progresses through individuals building on prior contributions. In particular, contributions are linear strings of elements. Individuals entering the field learn these prior strings, then take them apart and learn their constituent building blocks, which they then recombine to form new ideas. Complexity grows over time and the field expands and deepens.

2. Kathleen Jones discusses what Mansfield read in her biography *Katherine Mansfield: The Story-Teller*, 2010, Edinburgh University Press; Kindle Edition: 2012, The Book Mill. See, for example, Loc. 1036 and 1174 where Wilde, Meredith, Dickens, Tolstoy, Ibsen, and Shaw are mentioned. Further names are given by Gerri Kimber in *Katherine Mansfield—The Early Years*, 2016, Edinburgh University Press, including Paul Verlaine, Arthur Symons, and Edgar Alan Poe, pp. 112, 116, 173–74. Mansfield's reading included many nineteenth-century writers Woolf knew well; however, she did not read as widely. She was also influenced by the post-impressionist exhibition organized by Roger Fry—see *Katherine Mansfield: The Story-Teller*, Loc. 2171. Like Woolf, T. S. Eliot was widely read. He revered Dante, and he and Woolf would have shared deep knowledge not just of Shakespeare but of many English poets, playwrights, and novelists, as well as many other writers both ancient and modern. For some of Eliot's early reading see Lyndall Gordon, *Eliot's Early Years*, 1977, Oxford University Press; and for his nineteenth-century reading see David Ned Tobin, *The Presence of the Past: T.S. Eliot's Victorian Inheritance*, 1983, UMI Research Press.

3. For Eliot's reading in philosophy and religion, including during his doctoral work in philosophy at Harvard, see Gordon, *Eliot's Early Years*, pp. 43, 49–64. His preoccupation with spiritual development is evident in his poetry such as *The Waste Land*.

4. Arthur Campbell, Jonathan Feinstein, Soonwok Hong, Sharon Qian, and Trevor Williams, "Diversity, Knowledge Clusters, and Job Placement: Graduate

Economics Teaching of Core Microecoomics," 2017, *Journal of Economic Education*, Vol. 48, No. 3, pp. 146–66.

5. For a fuller discussion see Jonathan S. Feinstein, *The Nature of Creative Development*, 2006, Stanford University Press, pp. 237–44.

6. One of the neuroscientists I interviewed had this experience of simultaneous discovery. He had an insight linked to a guiding conception based on a recent publication that triggered a seed project idea, that as it happened also occurred to two other research groups at different universities. He and his group ended up publishing first in *Science* by just a few months, and the other groups published later but with somewhat more details. But the insight he had and publication still stood out for him as peak creative experiences during his time in graduate school. See Feinstein, *The Nature of Creative Development*, pp. 436–39.

7. I have followed this approach in Jonathan Feinstein, "Creative Development: Patterns of Learning," 2015, *IMCIC Conference Proceedings*, pp. 32–37.

8. Lynn Conway, "The MPC Adventures: Experiences with the Generation of VLSI Design and Implementation Methodologies," Transcribed from an Invited Lecture at the Second Caltech Conference on Very Large Scale Integration, January 19, 1981, Xerox PARC, p. 1.

9. Conway, "The MPC Adventures," p. 1.

10. Conway, "The MPC Adventures," p. 2.

11. Conway, "The MPC Adventures," pp. 3–4. The methods had been prototyped in the classroom previously at UC Berkeley, Carnegie-Mellon, and Washington University as well as Caltech.

12. Conway, "The MPC Adventures," p. 4. The development of a system to produce a suite of packaged chips is discussed in Lynn Conway, Alan Bell, and Martin E. Newell, "MPC79: A Large-Scale Demonstration of a New Way to Create Systems in Silicon," *Lambda*, Second Quarter, 1980, pp. 10–19.

13. Conway, "The MPC Adventures," p. 5.

14. Lynn Conway, *The MIT '78 VLSI System Design Course: A Guidebook for the Instructor of VLSI System Design*, 1979, Xerox PARC; R. Hon and C. Séquin, *A Guide to LSI Implementation*, 1978, Xerox PARC.

15. Conway and her PARC group pledged to instructors that if they ran the course, they would find a way to get designs sent to them implemented within a month after the end of their course—and this is just what they did. In these pre-Internet days, the ARPANET was used for electronic communication, and this is how the projects were transmitted. See Conway, "The MPC Adventures."

16. Conway, "The MPC Adventures," pp. 8–11.

17. Computer History Museum, "Oral History of Jim Clark," https://www.youtube.com/watch?v=phk0w1dGYic, retrieved November 17, 2021.

18. Clark mentions attending the course and being inspired in the "Oral History of Jim Clark," at approximately minute 35–36.

19. James H. Clark, "Structuring a VLSI System Architecture," 1980, *LAMBDA*, Second Quarter, pp. 25–30.

20. Clark, "Structuring a VLSI System Architecture," p. 27. The article cited is R. F. Sproull and I. E. Sutherland, "A Clipping Divider," 1968, in *Proceedings of the FJCC*, Thompson Books. Clark had interacted with Sutherland at the University of Utah.

21. Clark, "Structuring a VLSI System Architecture."

22. Clark, "Structuring a VLSI System Architecture." Clark states that he adapted many of the design structures as well as the timing methodology presented in Chapter 7, "System Timing," written by Charles Seitz.

23. Clark, "Structuring a VLSI System Architecture," p. 25.

24. David A. Patterson and Carlo H. Séquin, "Design Considerations for Single-Chip Computers of the Future," February 1980, *IEEE Transactions on Computers*, Vol. C-29, No. 2, pp. 108–16.

25. David A. Patterson and David R. Ditzel, "The Case for the Reduced Instruction Set Computer," October 1980, *ACM SIGARCH Computer Architecture News*, Vol. 8, No. 6, pp. 25–33. The Berkeley project is mentioned on p. 31.

26. John K. Foderaro, Korbin S. Van Dyke, and David A. Patterson, "Running RISCs," September/October 1982, *VLSI Design*. The quote is on p. 27. The article also thanks Lynn Conway and PARC in the Acknowledgments.

27. Daniel T. Fitzpatrick, John K. Foderaro, Manolis G. H. Katevenis, Howard A. Landman, David A. Patterson, James B. Peek, Zvi Peshkess, Carlo H. Séquin, Robert W. Sherburne, and Korbin S. Van Dyke, "A RISCy Approach to VLSI Design," January 1982, *ACM SIGARCH Computer Architecture News*, Vol. 10, Issue 1, pp. 28–32.

28. John Hennessy, Norman Jouppi, Forest Baskett, and John Gill, "MIPS: A VLSI Processor Architecture," 1981, in *VLSI Systems and Computations*, ed. H. T. Kung, Bob Sproull, and Guy Steele, Springer-Verlag Berlin, pp. 337–46; reference to Lambda is on p. 344.

29. John Hennessy, "SLIM: A Language for Microcode Description and Simulation in VLSI," January 1981, in *Proceedings of the Second Caltech Conference on VLSI*, ed. Charles Seitz, published by Caltech, pp. 253–67. The exact timing of development of SLIM versus MIPS is not spelled out, but the language implies SLIM was developed first. For my argument that is not the essential point. What is more relevant is that Hennessy seems to have, like the Berkeley team, pushed forward with implementing the idea of single chip simplified design having learned about the Mead-Conway methods. Clark is actually thanked for discussions about this in the MIPS paper, and in his oral history Clark says

that he mentioned the idea of building such a device on a single chip to Hennessy. We know Clark was influenced by Mead-Conway, so that may have been at least part of the path of influence.

30. Hennessy, "SLIM," p. 253.

31. Hennessy, "SLIM," p. 253.

32. Hennessy, "SLIM," pp. 257, 260, 265–66. The original example is in Mead and Conway, *Introduction to VLSI Systems*, Chapter 3, pp. 85–88.

33. For example, in her instructor manual based on her 1978 MIT course, *The MIT '78 VLSI System Design Course*, copyright 1979 Lynn Conway, Conway lists 25 projects, of which 19 were fabricated—see pp. 15–19.

34. Sylvia Kleinert and Margo Neale, eds., *The Oxford Companion to Aboriginal Art and Culture* 2000, Oxford University Press, p. 513. Considering just the Papunya art movement, Vivien Johnson includes approximately 270 artists in her book *Lives of the Papunya Tula Artists*, 2008, IAD Press, while Margo Birnberg and Janusz B. Kreczmanski, *Aboriginal Artists: Dictionary of Biographies; Western Desert, Central Desert, and Kimberly Region*, 2004, J. B. Publishing, lists more than 1,000 artists spanning a somewhat wider geographic range.

35. Not only is there limited biographical material, but there is no single history of the movement as a whole.

36. Geoffrey Bardon and James Bardon, *Papunya: A Place Made After the Story*, 2006, Lund Humphries "The Children Come First," pp. 3–11.

37. Bardon and Bardon, *Papunya*, p. 11. The idea of a creative response triggered by a new element resonates with my discussion of "creative responses" in Feinstein, *The Nature of Creative Development*, Chapter 9.

38. Vivien Johnson, *Once Upon a Time in Papunya*, 2010, New South, Chapter 1, "The School of Kaapa," especially pp. 11–26.

39. Bardon and Bardon *Papunya*, pp. 12, 16–17. Bardon wrote that the men would sit in front of the murals and sing, and that he realized later that making the murals was a "ceremony," "a convergence of dancing lines" between himself and the Indigenous men as ceremonial initiates, p. 13.

40. Bardon and Bardon, *Papunya*, pp. 17, 32. For Bardon's view of his influence on Kaapa, see Geoffrey Bardon, *Papunya Tula: Art of the Western Desert*, 1991, McPhee Gribble, p. 23. Bardon also restricted the paint colors he made available to what he viewed as traditional colors—see Bardon and Bardon, *Papunya*, p. 25.

41. Bardon and Bardon *Papunya*, p. 160.

42. Bardon thought Warangkula's series of Water Dreaming paintings were the finest of the early movement at Papunya. He shows several in Bardon and Bardon, *Papunya*, pp. 158–65.

43. Bardon shows several of Stockman's early paintings in Bardon and Bardon, *Papunya*, all of which are focused just on the Dreaming with little

background, including *Yam Dreaming* on p. 312 completed in May 1971, *Wild Potato Dreaming* on p. 313 completed in 1971, and *Budgerigar Dreaming* on p. 277 completed in December 1971. Later Stockman did use richer dotting backgrounds in some cases, for example, in *Woman's Bush Tucker Story*, shown on p. 373 and completed in May 1972.

44. Many of Leura's early paintings when he joined Bardon were ceremonial depictions, akin to Kaapa's early work. See, for example, the Honey Ant Dreaming paintings shown in Bardon and Bardon, *Papunya*, pp. 334–35. But at the same time he developed his subtle dotting and figure style—see *Wild Potato Spirit Dreaming [Version 3]* shown on p. 322, *Man's Yam Spirit Travelling Dreaming* shown on p. 323, and *Yam Spirit Dreaming [Version 5]* on p. 324, which Bardon states was at least up to that time "the most important of Tim Leura's works" (p. 324). The *Napperby Death Spirit Dreaming* done with Clifford Possum and completed in 1980 is generally viewed as his masterpiece; it is shown on p. 436.

45. Despite the differences from Possum, Stockman and Leura did paint an important precursor to Possum's *Warlugulong*, *Life at Yuwa*—although as discussed in Chapter 14, Possum had already begun experimenting with depicting multiple Dreamings. It is certainly possible that Possum discussed his conception with them and that they may have done this painting partly under the influence of his conception. Conversely, they may have contributed to his development of his conception, although that is not what he said, calling it his own idea.

46. See Artlandish, "The Story of Aboriginal Art," https://www.aboriginal-art-australia.com/aboriginal-art-library/the-story-of-aboriginal-art/ retrieved November 11, 2021.

47. Even at Papunya women became central—see Vivien Johnson, *Streets of Papunya: The Re-invention of Papunya Painting*, 2015, NewSouth.

48. See the short film "Women of Utopia," 1984, directed by Keith Gow, produced by Elizabeth Knight and Film Australia, National Film and Sound Archive: https://video.alexanderstreet.com/watch/women-of-utopia.

49. Jennifer Isaacs, "Anmatyerre Woman," in *Emily Kngwarreye Paintings*, with contributions by Jennifer Isaacs, Terry Smith, Judith Ryan, Donald Holt, and Janet Holt, 1998, Craftsman House. The quote is on p. 12. Isaacs refers in particular to Emily Kame—see my discussion that follows in the main text.

50. For a timeline of Kngwarreye's life see https://www.nma.gov.au/exhibitions/utopia/emily-kame-kngwarreye.

51. Emily Kame Kngwarreye, interview with Rodney Gooch, translated by Kathleen Petyarre, nd, https://www.nma.gov.au/exhibitions/utopia/emily-kame-kngwarreye, retrieved November 12, 2021. *Kame* means yam seed or flower.

52. See Emily Kame Kngwarreye, *Emily Kame Kngwarreye, Paintings from 1989–1995: Works from the Delmore Collection*, 1995, Parliament House, no page numbers. Cited by Terry Smith in his essay "Kngwarreye Woman Abstract Painter" in *Emily Kngwarreye Paintings*, p. 31. The critic is identified as D. Hart.

53. *Emily Kngwarreye Paintings*, pp. 31–32. *Desert Storm* is plate 34, pp. 100–101.

54. Caroline Vercoe, "Not so Nice Coloured Girls: A View of Tracey Moffatt's *Nice Coloured Girls*," 1997, *Pacific Studies*, Vol. 20, No. 4, pp. 151–59. Vercoe lists the sources for the voiceover readings from colonial-era journals in her footnote 2. See also Lisa French, "An Analysis of *Nice Coloured Girls*," 2000, *Australian Cinema*, Issue 5; and Janet Watson, "Fractured Realities, Fractured Truths in Tracey Moffatt's *Nice Coloured Girls* and *Night Cries: A Rural Tragedy*," 2008, *ART & LIES II*, Issue 9.

55. See Watson, "Fractured Realities." I have made my own attribution of the link to O'Keeffe, whom Moffatt has listed as an influence—for example, mentioned in Art Gallery of New South Wales, *Tracey Moffatt: Up In The Sky*, *Education Collection Notes*, p. 8, https://www.artgallery.nsw.gov.au/media/downloads/files/Tracey-Moffatt-collection-notes.pdf, retrieved November 15, 2021. There is much that is autobiographical in Moffatt's work. Her birth mother was Indigenous and her father white, and she was raised in a white family.

56. For Possum meeting the Queen, see Vivien Johnson, *Clifford Possum Tjapaltjarri*, 2003, Art Gallery of South Australia, pp. 169–71. For Moffatt representing Australia at the Biennale see Australia Council for the Arts, https://australiacouncil.gov.au/news/media-releases/tracey-moffatt-to-represent-australia-at-the-2017-venice-biennale/, retrieved November 13, 2021.

57. Johnson discusses Possum's economic vicissitudes in Chapter 6 of *Clifford Possum* and both economics and forgeries in Chapter 7. The quote is on p. 204. Much of her book *Once Upon a Time in Papunya* is devoted to chronicling the exploitation and also market success of the art; see notably Chapter 5, "The Midas Touch."

CHAPTER 18

1. Or the framework can be used in combination with other approaches—see the paragraph below in the main text. The synergies and interconnections between the framework in this book and other approaches mainly drawn from the field of psychology can be powerful and illuminating, both for teaching/mentoring and also for modeling the creative process.

2. See https://www.pablopicasso.net/african-period/; the exhibit was at the Musée d'Ethnographie du Trocadéro. See also Jonathan S. Feinstein, *The Nature of Creative Development*, 2006, Stanford University Press, p. 419.

3. Ed Catmull discusses the use of postmortems at Pixar in his article "How Pixar Fosters Collective Creativity," September 2008, *Harvard Business Review*.

4. This is discussed by Herminia Ibarra in her book *Working Identity: Unconventional Strategies for Reinventing Your Career*, 2003, Harvard Business School Press.

5. It took Indigenous Australian artist Shane Pickett many years to realize he could paint landscapes far more abstractly and in this way express his spiritual vision more powerfully. See the discussion of Pickett's creative path in Nick Tapper, ed., *Shane Pickett Meeyakba*, 2017, Mossenson Art Foundation in conjunction with the Pickett family. I think this pattern is common to many artists.

6. Jing Zhou and Elizabeth Rouse, eds., *Handbook of Research on Creativity and Innovation*, 2021, Edward Elgar.

INDEX